Digital SLR
Settings & Shortcuts
FOR
DUMMIES®

by Doug Sahlin

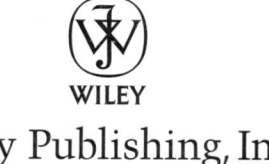

WILEY

Wiley Publishing, Inc.

Digital SLR Settings & Shortcuts For Dummies®

Published by
Wiley Publishing, Inc.
111 River Street
Hoboken, NJ 07030-5774

www.wiley.com

Copyright © 2011 by Wiley Publishing, Inc., Indianapolis, Indiana

Published by Wiley Publishing, Inc., Indianapolis, Indiana

Published simultaneously in Canada

For general information on our other products and services, please contact our Customer Care Department within the U.S. at 877-762-2974, outside the U.S. at 317-572-3993, or fax 317-572-4002.

For technical support, please visit www.wiley.com/techsupport.

Wiley also publishes its books in a variety of electronic formats. Some content that appears in print may not be available in electronic books.

Library of Congress Control Number: 2010941210

ISBN: 978-0-470-91763-3

Manufactured in the United States of America

10 9 8 7 6 5 4 3 2 1

WILEY

Dedication

This book is for the lovely and talented Roxanne, also known as "Nature Girl." Thank you for coming into my life. I love you, Sweetheart.

About the Author

Doug Sahlin is an author and photographer living in Venice, Florida. He is a professional photographer specializing in fine art photography. He also photographs weddings and events and writes books about computer applications like Adobe Acrobat and Adobe Photoshop. Doug's latest books have been about digital photography. In the past years he's written *Digital Photography Workbook For Dummies, Digital Portrait Photography For Dummies,* and *Canon EOS 7D For Dummies.* To find out more about Doug and see some of his work, visit www.dasdesigns.net.

Author's Acknowledgments

Photography is my passion, and I love to share information with other photographers. That's why I was so excited when Steve Hayes discussed the concept of this book with me. Thank you, Steve, for bringing this book to fruition. Many thanks to Nicole Sholly for doing a stellar job of coordinating everything with the editorial team at Wiley and for keeping me on my toes. Kudos to Mike Sullivan for making sure all the technical aspects of this book were correct. Thanks to literary agent extraordinaire Margot Hutchison for her part in this project.

Thanks to my friends and fellow authors for their support and inspiration. Hats off to my family for their continued support, especially Karen and Ted. Thanks to the furry kids, Niki and Micah, for being a constant source of amusement. And thanks to the lovely Roxanne for coming into my life and sharing my passion.

Publisher's Acknowledgments

We're proud of this book; please send us your comments at http://dummies.custhelp.com. For other comments, please contact our Customer Care Department within the U.S. at 877-762-2974, outside the U.S. at 317-572-3993, or fax 317-572-4002.

Some of the people who helped bring this book to market include the following:

Acquisitions and Editorial

Project Editor: Nicole Sholly

Executive Editor: Steven Hayes

Copy Editors: Laura K. Miller and Virginia Sanders

Technical Editor: Michael Sullivan

Editorial Manager: Kevin Kirschner

Editorial Assistant: Amanda Graham

Sr. Editorial Assistant: Cherie Case

Cartoons: Rich Tennant (www.the5thwave.com)

Composition Services

Project Coordinator: Katie Crocker

Layout and Graphics: Ana Carrillo, Erin Zeltner

Proofreaders: Lindsay Littrell, Mildred Rosenzweig

Indexer: Potomac Indexing, LLC

Publishing and Editorial for Technology Dummies

Richard Swadley, Vice President and Executive Group Publisher

Andy Cummings, Vice President and Publisher

Mary Bednarek, Executive Acquisitions Director

Mary C. Corder, Editorial Director

Publishing for Consumer Dummies

Diane Graves Steele, Vice President and Publisher

Composition Services

Debbie Stailey, Director of Composition Services

Table of Contents

Introduction

*M*any people graduate to a digital SLR and think it's the ticket for creating great photos. Well it is, but there's a bit of technique involved. Part of that is your creativity and the way you see the world around you. You translate the vision that is in your head into an image when you capture it with your digital SLR.

To fully master your digital SLR and create compelling photos, you have to venture forth into a brave new world that involves making decisions about settings that will enable you to capture the images you see in your mind's eye. This does not happen when you shoot in your camera's Automatic mode. When photographers have the urge to branch out, they turn to the manual for help. And then they get more confused. Which is where this book comes in. My goal in writing this book was to demystify taking photographs with a digital SLR.

About Digital SLR Settings & Shortcuts For Dummies

If you need to know how to photograph your children playing sports, there's a chapter for that. If you want to know how to photograph a racecar traveling 200 miles per hour, there's a chapter for that as well. In fact there are 100 chapters that show you which settings to use to take specific images.

Some of the things you can do with this book include learning to

- Determine which shooting mode to use for each picture-taking scenario.
- Photograph marathoners running, bicyclists racing, and horses galloping.
- Photograph artists at work, waterfalls, and pet birds.
- Photograph a newborn baby, animals in the wild, and city skylines.
- Overcome the challenges and pitfalls inherent to certain picture-taking scenarios. (I include a "Troubleshooting" section at the end of each chapter to help you overcome these challenges.)
- Master depth of field to control what's in focus.
- Make the histogram work for you.
- Calculate the 35mm equivalent of a focal length.

In addition, you'll learn many tips and tricks from a professional photographer who's been there, done that.

Foolish Assumptions

There are certain prerequisites for using this book effectively. First and foremost, you must have a digital SLR with at least one lens. Second you must have the desire to break free from the point and shoot mentality and stop using the automatic and scene modes. You must also have the desire to be a better photographer. Your digital SLR is a wonderful tool for expressing to others how you see the world. But it takes some thought and creativity to create a picture that makes people give it more than just a casual glance. If you have the desire to break free from the mode of point and shoot photography, read on.

Conventions Used in This Book

To help you navigate this book efficiently, I use a few style conventions:

- Terms that I want to emphasize are *italicized* (and defined).
- Web site URLs are shown in a special monofont typeface, `like this`.
- Numbered steps that you need to follow are set in **bold**.

What You Don't Have to Read

This book is designed to show you how to master specific picture taking scenarios. You don't have to read every chapter in this book, only the ones that pertain to the pictures you want to take. If you really want to cut to the chase, you don't have to read the introductory paragraph in each chapter.

What I Encourage You to Read

I do suggest that you read the "Setting the Camera" section of each chapter. This section shows you the logic behind the settings I suggest you use to take each type of picture. I also suggest that you read the steps in the "Taking the Picture" section as they contain important information and tidbits related to taking the photo. So if you're in a real hurry to learn how to take a picture of your wife twirling a baton while cooking tacos — kidding — or any picture scenario in this book, all you need to do is open the book to the chapter, dial the

Camera Settings into your camera, read through the steps, and take the picture. And please take lots of pictures. That's how you'll master the settings and steps and make them your own.

I also strongly suggest that you read the appendix: "Beyond Point and Shoot Photography." This appendix contains a lot of information about digital photography, including some very important information about the sensor in your camera model, and the difference it can have on the way a lens sees the scene in front of you. All digital camera sensors are not created equal.

If you don't have time to read the entire appendix, please read "Understanding focal lengths." This section takes about five minutes to read and demystifies what different focal lengths will do and how these focal lengths react on cameras with different size sensors.

How This Book Is Organized

Digital SLR Settings & Shortcuts For Dummies is split into six parts. You don't have to read it sequentially, and you don't even have to read all the chapters in any particular part. You can use the Table of Contents and the index to find the information you need and quickly get your answer. In this section, I briefly describe what you'll find in each part.

Part I: Action

This part of the book shows you how to photograph action. If you've wanted to photograph a marathon runner, a bike racer, or freeze a racecar dead in its tracks, you'll find out how to take those kinds of pictures in this part. You'll learn some creative techniques for portraying motion artistically as well.

Part II: Animals

If you want to create a portrait of your cat, take a picture of your dog catching a Frisbee, or photograph birds, I show you how to take these kinds of pictures and more in this part of the book. I also show you which settings and techniques to use to photograph animals in the wild, dangerous animal, and birds of prey.

Part III: Landscapes and Nature

If you live near a beautiful state park, or are going on vacation to a place like Yosemite, this is the section where I show you the settings you use to capture great pictures of the landscapes and nature you find there. In this section, I show you the settings to use to take pictures of waterfalls, sunsets, mountain ranges, rainbows, flowers, and much more.

Part IV: People

Whether you want to create a great portrait of your wife, or capture a candid shot of your child being himself, this is the part of the book where I show you how to take these types of pictures. You'll also find settings you use to photograph weddings, people at work, and so on.

Part V: Places

There are interesting things in the places you visit and the place where you live. In this part, I show you how to photograph these things. So if you have a beautiful church, historic buildings, or memorable skyline you want to photograph, check out the chapters in this part.

Part VI: Things

If you've had your share of photographing people and places, you may be interested in photographing things like buildings, lighthouses, cars, motorcycles, and so on. If so, the chapters in this section are right up your alley.

The Appendix: Beyond Point and Shoot Photography

The appendix introduces you to the wonderful world of digital SLR photography. It demystifies technical photography terms in non-technical lingo. It introduces you to the different shooting modes you'll use and discusses other items such as lens focal lengths, how an image is exposed, and much more.

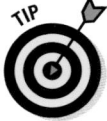

Read this appendix before you read any other part of the book, and you'll have a huge heads up on the information I discuss in each chapter.

Icons Used in This Book

What's a Dummies book without icons pointing you in the direction of really great information that's sure to help you along your way? In this section, I briefly describe each icon I use in this book.

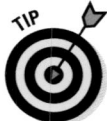

The Tip icon points out helpful information that is likely to make your job as a photographer easier.

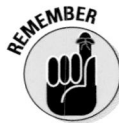

This is like a virtual piece of string. When you see this icon, it contains a fact that you should remember to help you perform the task at hand more efficiently.

This icon notes a pitfall that your friendly author has discovered so that you won't make the same wrong move.

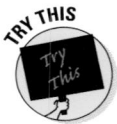

When you see this icon, you'll find an interesting technique to try that's associated with the photograph I show you how to create.

Where to Go from Here

Now that you've read the Introduction, you have a good idea of what's in this book. To learn the settings and steps involved in taking a specific photograph, jump to the Table of Contents or index. Find the chapter for the type of photograph you want to take, read that chapter, and take some photographs.

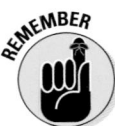

Refer to this book whenever you need settings to take a specific type of photo. But first I recommend you read the appendix, "Beyond Point and Shoot Photography." After you do, the individual chapters will be much easier to digest.

Use your camera often, take lots of pictures, and have a great time taking pictures of the people, places, and things that matter to you.

Part I
Action

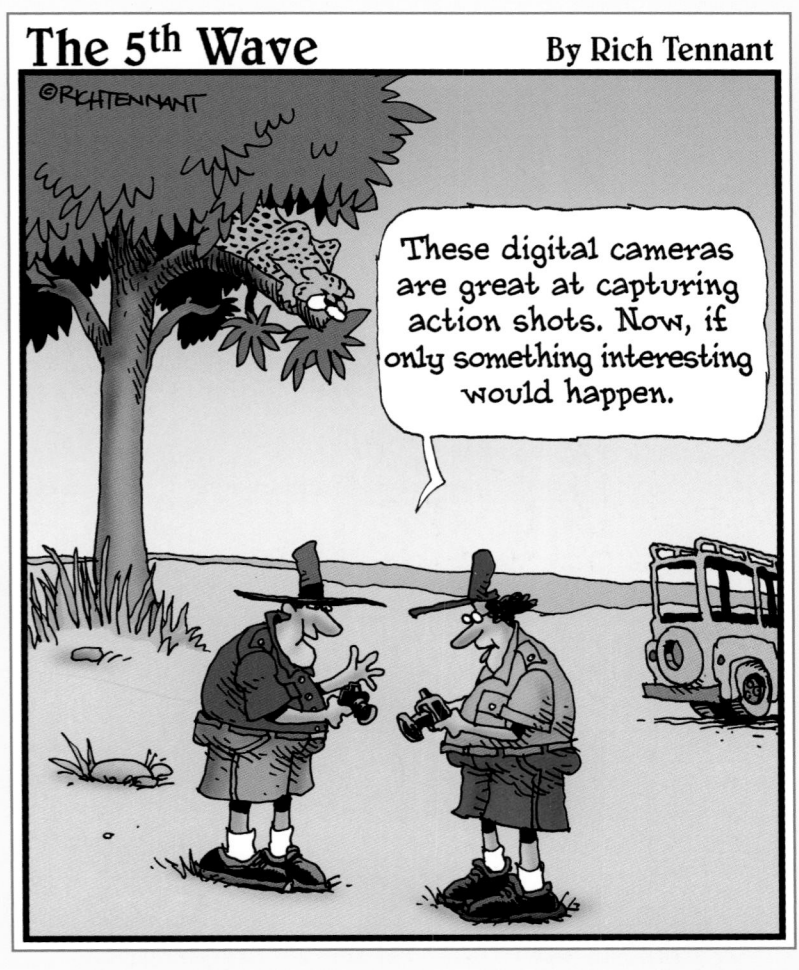

*1*f you like action such as a marathon runner racing toward the finish line, a horse and rider negotiating a steeplechase obstacle, or a race car gobbling up asphalt at top speed, but don't know how to capture the beauty of motion and speed with your digital camera, the chapters in this part will get you going in the right direction. In this part, I show you the settings to use to freeze action and to artistically depict the beauty of athletes and machinery in motion.

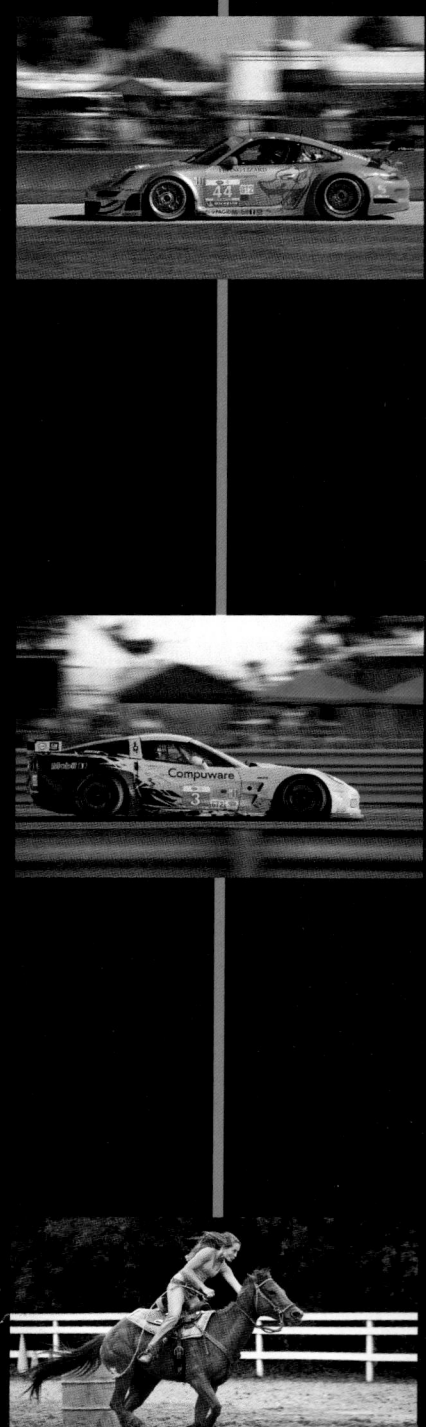

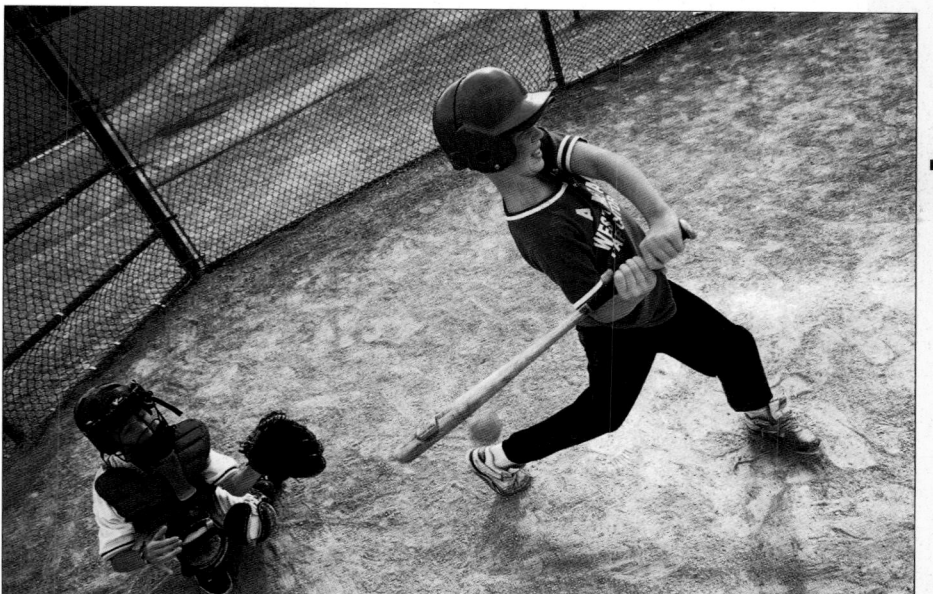

Corbis Digital Stock

Camera Settings

- **Metering Mode:** Evaluative
- **Drive Mode:** Single Shot or Continuous
- **Shooting Mode:** Shutter Priority
- **Shutter Speed:** 1/250 of a second
- **ISO Setting:** The lowest ISO setting for available light conditions
- **Focus Mode:** Continuous Auto-Focus
- **Auto-Focus Point:** Single auto-focus point
- **Focal Length:** 100mm or longer (35mm equivalent; see "Understanding focal lengths" in the appendix)
- **Image Stabilization:** On

If you're a soccer mom, you probably drive your kids to and from each soccer practice and match. Did you ever think of taking pictures of your children while they play? The resulting pictures can provide many wonderful memories in years to come. You just need to bring your camera to every practice and match. Your camera gear, your wonderful athlete, and the settings in this chapter provide the recipe for some wonderful images.

Setting the Camera

You may find creating great pictures of your children playing sports very rewarding. You can be the proud dad who shows all your coworkers what a great athlete and kid you're raising. You can use a Single Shot Drive mode for this type of photography or Continuous Drive mode to capture a series of images of your child scoring a goal. To stop action, shoot in Shutter Priority mode. The suggested shutter speed freezes the action. The focal length gets an up-close-and-personal image without requiring that you get up close and personal when taking it.

Taking the Picture

You have to be quick when you're photographing children playing sports. Unless you're really fit, they can give you a run for your money — especially if you're photographing football practice while your son is racing down the field toward the goal line.

1. **Enable the camera settings discussed earlier in this chapter.**

2. **Patiently wait until the kids begin playing.**

3. **When your child is ready to score a goal or do something exciting, zoom in on her, and then press the shutter button halfway to achieve focus.**

When you photograph with Continuous Auto-Focus mode enabled, the camera updates focus when your child moves, as long as you keep your finger pressed halfway on the shutter button. You may have difficulty composing an image when your child is in the heat of battle, but do your best. If your child is at a practice session, ask the coach whether you can get near the sidelines and photograph your child dribbling the soccer ball (see Figure 1-1).

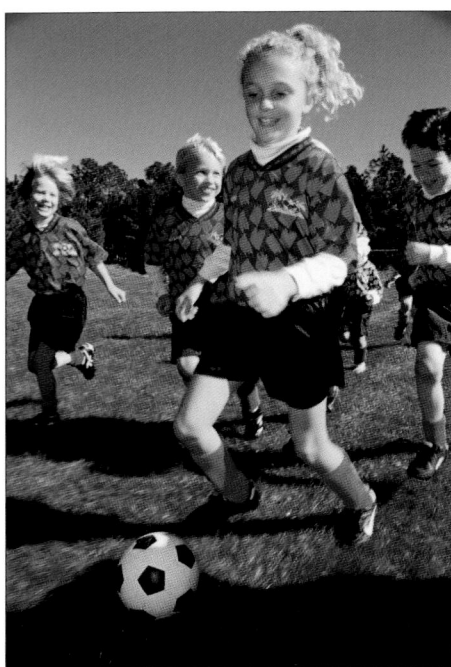

PureStock

Figure 1-1: Photograph your athlete from a unique vantage point.

4. **Press the shutter button fully to take the picture.**

If you photograph by using Continuous Drive mode, the camera continues taking pictures as long as you continue to hold your finger on the shutter button. The camera stops taking pictures when you release the shutter button.

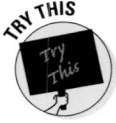

Tag along when your husband teaches your son how to bowl or play pool and then find an interesting vantage point. If your son is learning how to play pool, take a shot from overhead as your husband positions your son's hand over the pool cue. If your son is learning how to bowl, walk down the lane (when it is almost empty), and photograph your husband showing your son how to hold the ball. Just make sure your son doesn't send the ball down the alley while you're still there.

Troubleshooting

- ✏ **My child is not in focus.** Make sure the auto-focus point is your son when you press the shutter button halfway, and make sure the auto-focus point illuminates to signify that the camera has focused on your child.

- ✏ **The depth of field is too shallow.** You may have this problem when you photograph a sporting event in low-light conditions. To compensate for the low light, the camera chooses a larger aperture, which results in a shallow depth of field. In some instances, such as when you're photographing action (for example, your child running for a touchdown), you want to use a shallow depth of field. When you're photographing several children in action, you need a larger depth of field. To increase the depth of field, increase the ISO rating.

2 Runners

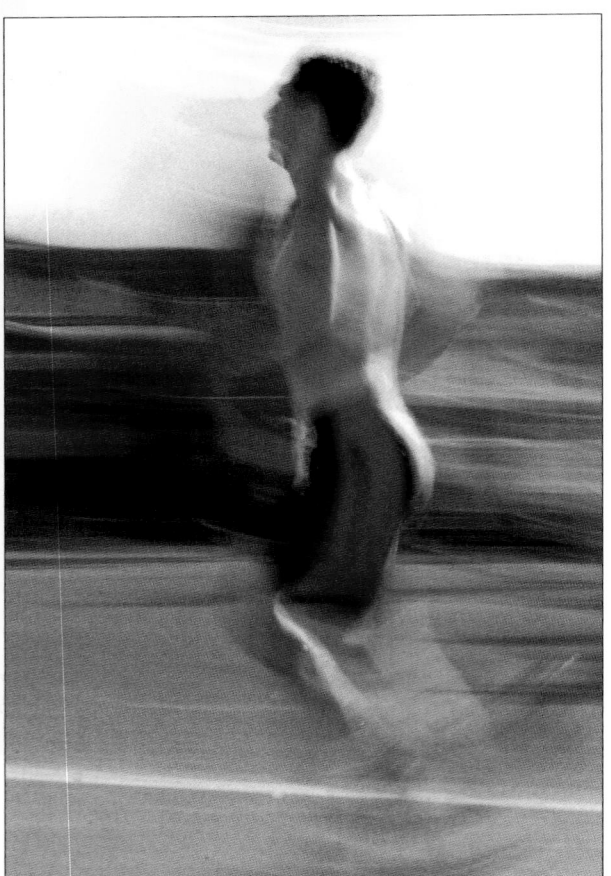

Athletes in motion personify beauty, grace under pressure, and power. If you've ever watched any type of a track and field event, or a marathon, you know that running isn't for wimps. You also know that capturing an artistic image of a runner involves more than just freezing the action of the runner.

When you photograph a solitary runner, you want to capture the beauty of the runner's fluid motion, which you can do by using the settings in this chapter.

Camera Settings

- ✓ **Metering Mode:** Evaluative
- ✓ **Drive Mode:** Single Shot
- ✓ **Shooting Mode:** Shutter Priority
- ✓ **Shutter Speed:** 1/15 of a second
- ✓ **ISO Setting:** 100
- ✓ **Focus Mode:** Continuous Auto-Focus
- ✓ **Auto-Focus Point:** Single auto-focus point
- ✓ **Focal Length:** Varies (see "Understanding focal lengths" in the appendix)
- ✓ **Image Stabilization:** On

Setting the Camera

For this type of photography, you shoot in Shutter Priority mode with a slow shutter speed. The low ISO setting gives you a noise-free image — as well as a small aperture, but depth of field is really not important with this type of photography. You're rendering an abstract image that shows the beauty of an athlete in motion. The runner's torso and head are recognizable, but his legs and arms are an artistic blur of motion. You use continuous auto-focus so that the camera updates focus continuously while you pan the camera with the runner. Your proximity to the runner determines your focal length. Image stabilization can help you correct for any up-and-down movement while you pan the camera with the runner.

Taking the Picture

When you photograph an athletic event, such as a track meet or a marathon, your vantage point is extremely important. If you photograph a track meet from the sideline, you need an unobstructed view of the runners. Photographing runners at a marathon also requires an unobstructed view, but you face different challenges at a marathon. You have to contend with city streets, buildings, and a lot of spectators. In either case, you need to arrive early to get a good spot from which to view and photograph the event. If you're photographing a marathon, you can move around a bit, first photographing all runners when they leave the starting line, and then positioning yourself where you can more easily photograph individual runners during the race.

1. **Choose a vantage point where the runners will be passing an innocuous background, such as a group of trees.**

   If you don't, the background may detract from the image.

2. **Enable the camera settings discussed earlier in this chapter.**

3. **When a runner you want to photograph comes into view, frame her in the viewfinder, zoom in, and compose the picture.**

   Leave some room in front of the runner to give the viewer the impression that the runner is going somewhere.

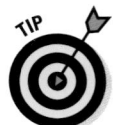

If you're photographing a marathon, capture a close-up picture of the runner's head and shoulders by using the settings in Chapter 68 when the runner nears the finish line. The runner's face will be etched in pain, and his hair will be matted with sweat, even on a cold day. You'll end up with a great shot that shows the pain and agony the runner goes through to complete a marathon.

4. **Press the shutter button half-way to achieve focus.**

5. **Pivot smoothly from the waist to pan the camera with the runner.**

6. **Press the shutter button fully to take the picture and follow through.**

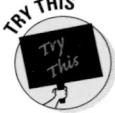

Create a story surrounding the event. Photograph the group when they leave the starting line, and then take several shots of your favorite runners by using the technique and settings in this chapter. Make sure you get a stop-action photo of your favorite runner crossing the finish line with her finishing time as part of the picture (see Figure 2-1). This of course requires a faster shutter speed to freeze the action of the runners as they cross the line. Use a shutter speed of 1/250 of a second or faster.

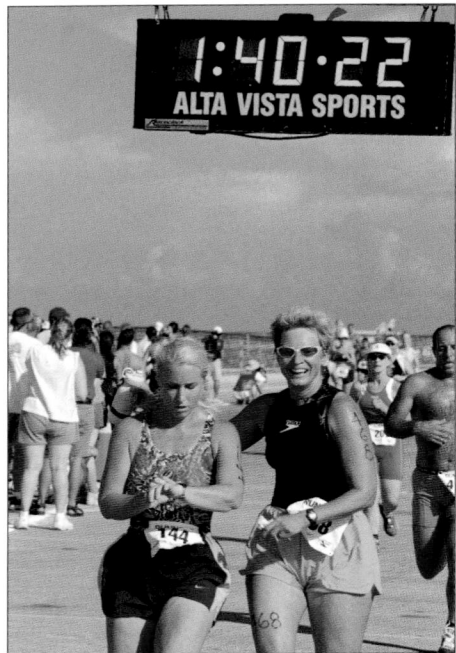

Figure 2-1: Tell the story of the event.

Troubleshooting

✔ **The runner's head appears to be bobbing up and down.** You don't hold the camera perfectly level while you pan. If you move the camera up or down while panning, the runner appears to be bouncing up and down. Image stabilization can also cure this problem if your camera or lens has this feature.

✔ **The runner is tilted.** You tilt your body while panning. Make sure you're perfectly upright while you pan with the runner.

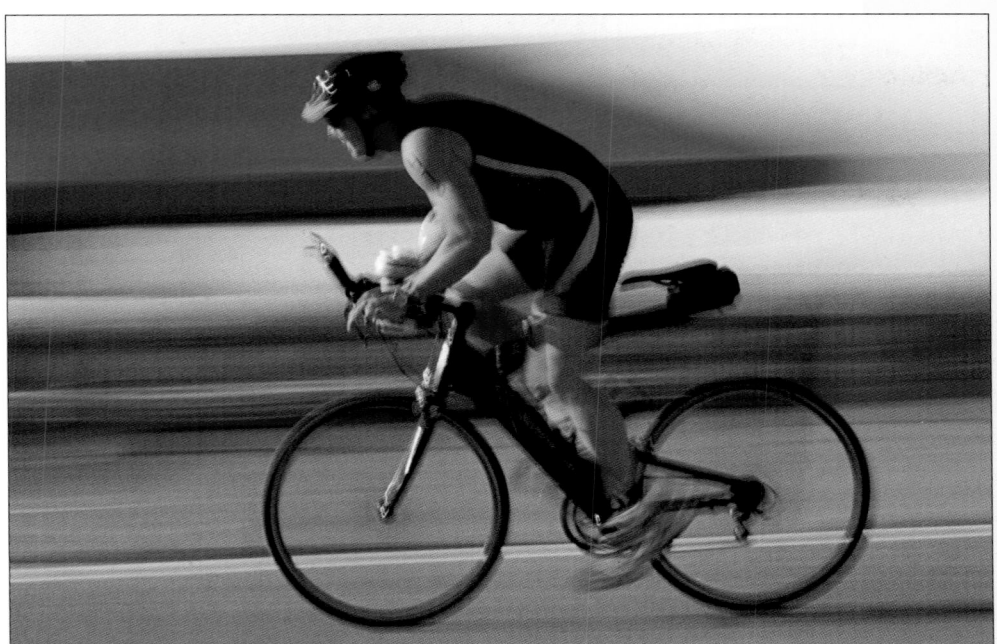

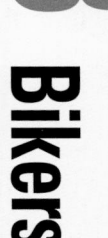

Camera Settings

- **Metering Mode:** Evaluative
- **Drive Mode:** Single Shot
- **Shooting Mode:** Shutter Priority
- **Shutter Speed:** 1/15 to 1/30 of a second
- **ISO Setting:** 100
- **Focus Mode:** Continuous Auto-Focus
- **Auto-Focus Point:** Single auto-focus point
- **Focal Length:** Varies (see "Understanding focal lengths" in the appendix)
- **Image Stabilization:** On

*1*f you enjoy events such as the Tour de France and have bike races or triathlons in your area, you can capture the thrills of a bike race digitally with you camera. Professional bike riders can attain tremendous speeds on their ultra-lite bikes. You can use the same techniques the pros use to capture compelling photos of bike racers, whatever the bikers' speed. When a biker is traveling perpendicular to you, pan the camera with the subject to capture the essence of motion. With amateur bikers, you use a fairly slow shutter speed, which creates a dreamy look that makes the rider look like he's going much faster than he is. You use the same technique with professional bike riders — albeit with a faster shutter speed.

Setting the Camera

For this type of photography, you shoot in Shutter Priority mode with a slow shutter speed, which gives you a slightly blurry picture that captures the essence of speed. The low ISO setting gives you a noise-free image, as well as a small aperture, but depth of field is really not important with this type of photography. The bike will be readily identifiable, but the wheels will be blurred and the detail will be soft because of the slow shutter speed. You use continuous auto-focus so that the camera updates focus continuously while you pan the camera. Image stabilization is helpful to correct for any up-and-down movement of the camera while you pan the camera to track the biker.

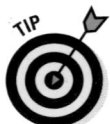

If you're photographing fast bike riders, use a shutter speed of 1/30 of a second. You'll still have a nice blurry background, but the bike rider will be in relatively sharp focus.

Taking the Picture

When you photograph an athletic event, your vantage point is extremely important. You need an unobstructed view of your subject. If you're photographing a triathlon, the bikers won't leave in a group, but you can get shots of them while they change from their swimming gear to biking gear. Then it's a matter of following these steps to get a great picture:

1. **Choose a vantage point where the bikers pass a non-descript background, such as a solid colored wall or dense shrubbery.**

   A busy background distracts the viewer's attention from your subject.

2. **Enable the camera settings discussed earlier in this chapter.**

   If you choose a focal length longer than 80mm, increase the shutter speed to 1/50 of a second.

3. **When a biker you want to photograph comes into view, frame her in the viewfinder, zoom in, and then compose the picture.**

   Leave some room in front of the biker so that your picture gives the viewer the impression that the rider is going somewhere.

4. **Press the shutter button halfway to achieve focus.**

5. **Pivot smoothly from the waist to pan the camera with your subject.**

6. **Press the shutter button fully to take the picture and follow through.**

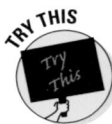

Every event — such as a triathlon that includes swimming, bicycling, and running portions — has a beginning, middle, and end. To document a whole triathlon, first photograph the athletes going through their pre-race rituals such as stretching and limbering up. Then photograph the start of the triathlon, when the group races from the start line and splashes into the water to begin the swimming portion of the event. Next take pictures of the bikes queued up for the riders (see Figure 3-1). Photograph the athletes as they don their biking gear and race off into the distance. Then photograph the transition when the athletes begin the running portion of the event. Finally, photograph the athletes as they race to the finish line, and then photograph them recuperating.

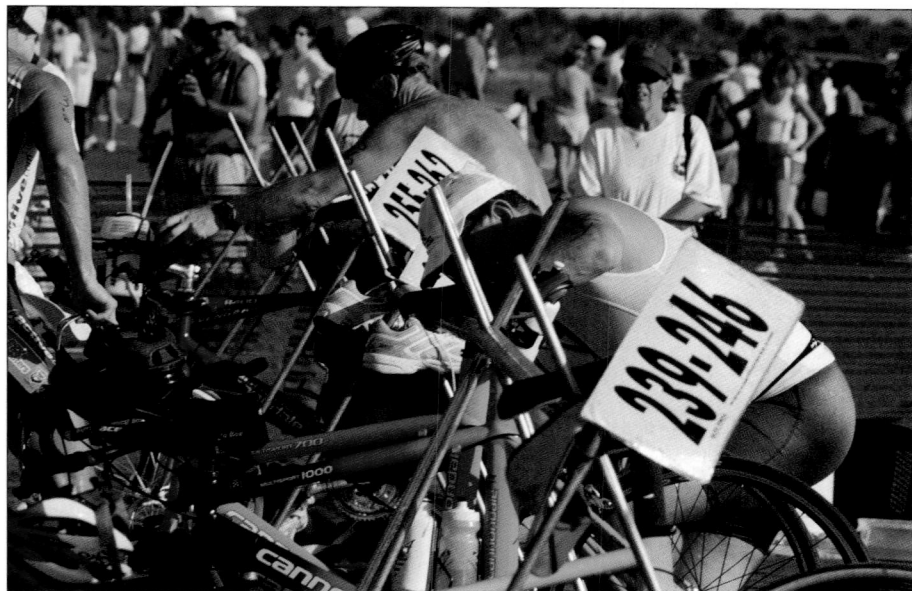

Figure 3-1: Tell the story of the event.

Troubleshooting

- **The biker is not in focus.** This problem happens when the camera doesn't achieve focus on your subject, and unfortunately, it's inevitable when you do a lot of panning. When your subject comes into view, make sure the auto-focus point is over your subject and that the point is illuminated, which indicates that the camera has focused on the right subject.

- **The picture isn't level.** Make sure the camera is level with the ground before you take the picture, and keep your body upright while you pan. If you tilt your body while panning, the camera is not level, hence the picture is not level.

- **The resulting image doesn't seem as sharp as it could be.** Make sure you follow through. If you stop panning when you press the shutter button, the image won't be really sharp because your subject is still moving and the camera isn't.

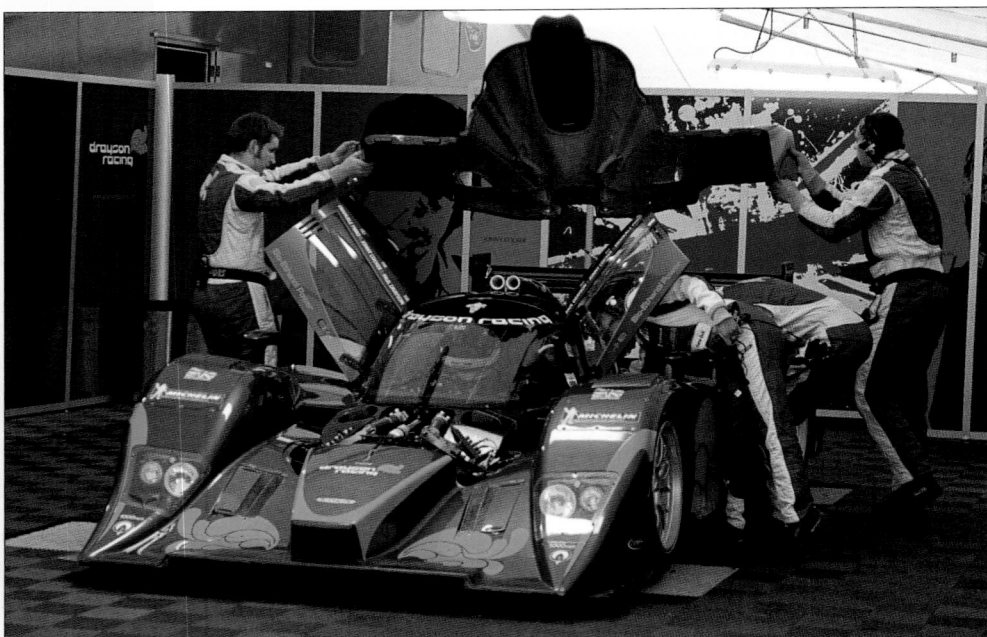

4 Sporting Events

*P*hotography is a wonderful pastime. You can use your camera to capture memories of the things that interest you. If you're a sports fan, you can photograph your favorite sport. You can photograph individual athletes (see Chapter 48), but sports have more to them than just the athletes. Whether your favorite sport is football or auto racing, each one has its own rituals. And every sport includes a supporting cast. When you photograph a sporting event, you photograph each chapter of the event, from the pregames festivities, to the opening kick off, to the winning touchdown. Your creative mind, a knowledge of the sport, and the settings in this chapter give you all the tools you need to tell a story. You begin at the beginning, before the athletes flex their muscles or the drivers start their engines.

Camera Settings

- ✔ **Metering Mode:** Evaluative
- ✔ **Drive Mode:** Single Shot or Continuous
- ✔ **Shooting Mode:** Shutter Priority or Aperture Priority
- ✔ **Shutter Speed:** 1/250 of a second or faster
- ✔ **Aperture:** Varies
- ✔ **ISO Setting:** The lowest possible ISO setting for the lighting conditions
- ✔ **Focus Mode:** Continuous Auto-Focus
- ✔ **Auto-Focus Point:** Single auto-focus point
- ✔ **Focal Length:** Varies (see "Understanding focal lengths" in the appendix)
- ✔ **Image Stabilization:** On

Setting the Camera

This chapter gives you a couple of different shooting scenarios. When you're photographing the pre-event festivities, you shoot in Aperture Priority mode. When your goal is to photograph an athlete preparing for the event, you want a shallow depth of field, therefore, you choose a large aperture (a small f/stop number). When you want to photograph the crowd, or a group of athletes practicing, you use a small aperture (a large f/stop number) to ensure a large depth of field. When your goal is to stop action, you shoot in Shutter Priority mode at a speed fast enough to freeze the action. For an athlete, you can freeze motion with a shutter speed as slow as 1/25 of a second. To stop a racecar dead in its tracks, you need a fast shutter speed of 1/2000 of a second (see Chapter 5). To capture the beauty of a speeding racecar with a motion blur, you pan the camera and shoot with a shutter speed of 1/125 of a second (see Chapter 6). The focal length you use varies depending on how close you can get to the action. If you're photographing a large crowd before the event, use a wide-angle focal length of 28 to 35mm. If you're photographing individual athletes, zoom in.

Taking the Picture

When you photograph a sporting event, you have to be in the moment. Before the event starts, you can capture interesting pictures of the crowd, the athletes performing their pre-event rituals, and the athletes warming up. When the event starts, you can capture the frenetic action. When the event is well and truly underway, keep alert for any interesting situations that may arise and, of course, any team player who scores. If you're photographing an automobile race, be sure to include pictures of pit stops and other associated activities. And you probably want a picture or two of the winning driver spraying the champagne.

1. **Arrive at the event early and take pictures of anything that interests you.**

   You have to change settings based on what you're photographing.

2. **Photograph the pre-event activities, such as the introduction of the players, the coach meeting with her team on the sidelines, or if you're attending a race, pictures of the drivers getting ready.**

   You can get creative with your composition when you photograph the pre-race events. Don't be afraid to turn the camera diagonally or venture to an interesting vantage point. Let your inner child run amuck and capture some unusual pictures.

3. **Photograph the start of the event.**

   The action can get a little crazy. Each team is trying to gain an advantage over the other. If you're photographing a race, drivers may battle fiercely to achieve the lead by the first corner. You never know what might happen. Stay alert for any possibility. Hold the camera and be ready to compose an image when you see something interesting about to happen. Be proactive: Have the camera to your eye a split second before the crucial moment.

4. **Photograph the middle of the event.**

The middle of any event is a great time for photographers. If you're photographing an event such as a basketball or football game, you can get some shots of substitutions. You can also photograph the fans to capture their reactions to a winning score and so on. If you're photographing an auto race (as shown in Figure 4-1), the cars are now a little battle weary, with tire marks, racer's tape, and other chinks in their armor.

5. **Photograph the end of the event.**

Be on your toes, especially if the score is close. In the final minutes or final laps, it's do or die. Athletes give their all to win the event, which gives you opportunities for some great pictures.

6. **Photograph the post-event activities.**

Take photographs of the winning team celebrating and capture the glum looks of the losers. Take photographs of any award ceremonies. Tell the complete story of the event.

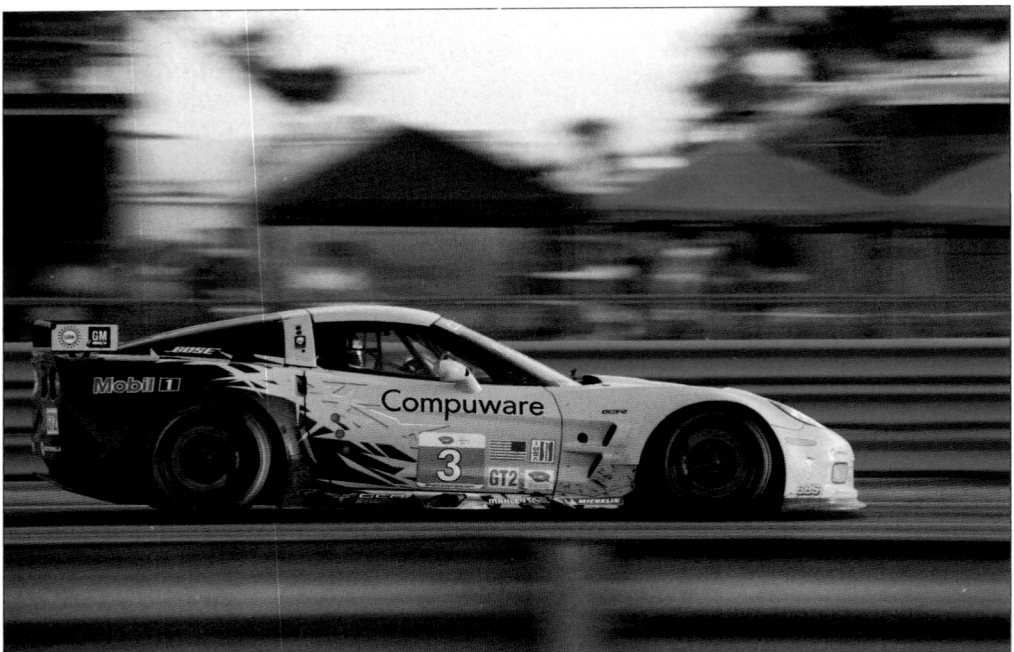

Figure 4-1: Photograph the middle of the event when the participants are a little battle weary.

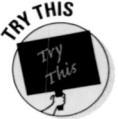

Photograph an athlete going through his pre-event ritual. Figure 4-2 shows champion driver Allan McNish with a mask of concentration at the drivers' meeting.

Troubleshooting

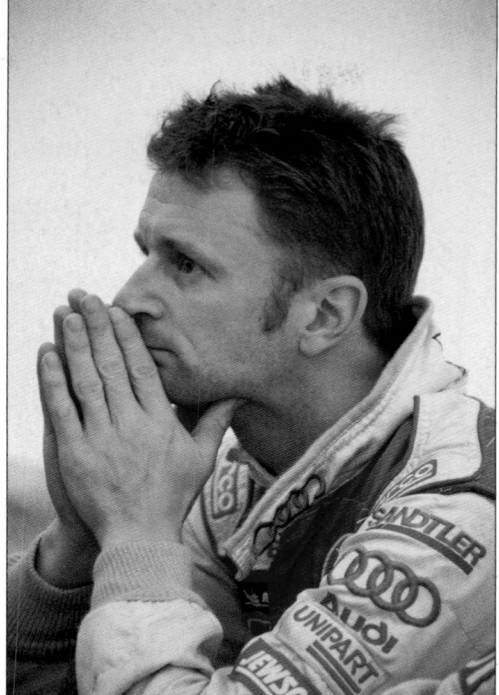

Figure 4-2: Photograph athletes performing their pre-event rituals.

- ✔ **I don't know which mode to use.** If you're photographing athletes in motion, use Shutter Priority mode to freeze motion. If you're photographing people and things before the event, use Aperture Priority mode to control depth of field.

- ✔ **The picture isn't level.** This problem often happens when you're photographing people in motion, especially when you're panning the camera. Make sure that you're standing straight and that you don't lean when you pan the camera. You may also want to use the grid that's built into many cameras as a guide.

- ✔ **I can't get close to the action.** When you photograph a spectator event, sometimes you just need to wait for someone to move. Of course, always try to get a good seat ahead of time. If the event doesn't include assigned seating, arrive early.

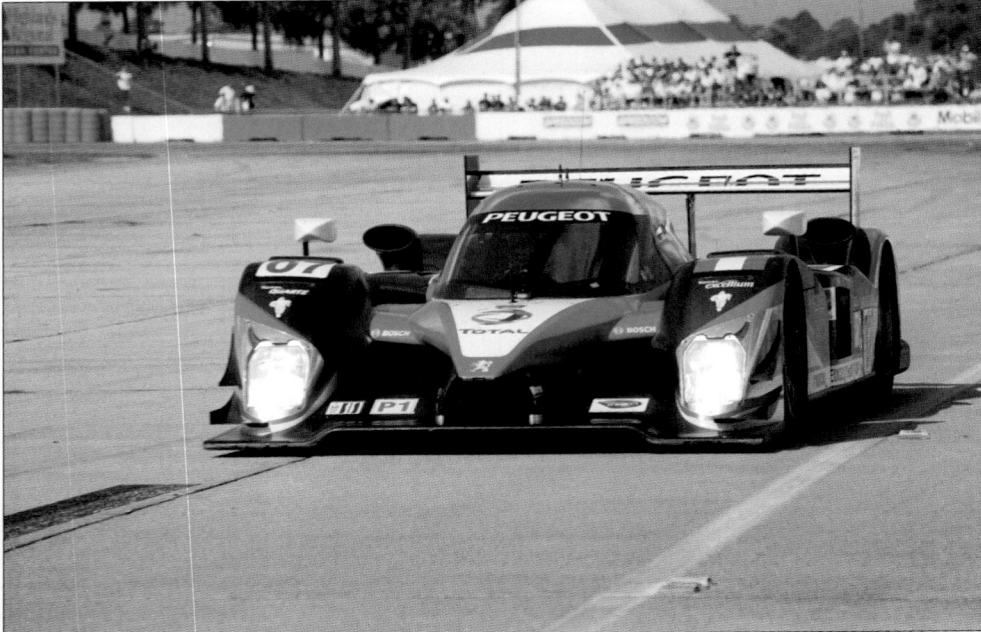

5 Race Car (Stop-Action)

*W*hen a racecar is coming almost straight at the vantage point from which you're photographing the race, your goal is to stop the motion of the car. Stop-action photography requires a fast shutter speed. The racecar, as well as any cars that are following closely, should be in sharp focus, and the background should be out of focus to draw the viewer's attention to the car. Having a long lens is helpful because it enables you to fill the frame with the car. A long focal length when you're shooting a group of cars can make the pursuing cars seem closer than they actually are.

To capture a good photo of a racecar requires some knowledge and a bit of planning. Get to know the series that you're photographing. If you're a NASCAR fan, watch some of their races on TV and get to know the lay of the land. When you watch a race on TV, you get an idea of what the course looks like and can often figure out the best vantage points to photograph the race from. If you just show up at the racetrack expecting to get good photos, you're sadly mistaken, especially if you're photographing a road race. Study a map of the track before you attend the event. If you can, get to the racetrack early so that you can watch practice for the event you're photographing and any support races. Armed with this knowledge and the following information, you can get some great pictures of racecars at speed.

Camera Settings

- **Metering Mode:** Evaluative
- **Drive Mode:** Single Shot
- **Shooting Mode:** Shutter Priority
- **Shutter Speed:** 1/2000 of a second
- **ISO Setting:** Choose an ISO that gives you an aperture setting of f/8.0 or smaller (meaning a larger f/stop number).
- **Focus Mode:** Manual Focus
- **Auto-Focus Point:** Single auto-focus point
- **Focal Length:** Varies from 100mm to 300mm (35mm equivalent; see "Understanding focal lengths" in the appendix)
- **Image Stabilization:** Not required

Setting the Camera

When your goal is to freeze action, use Shutter Priority mode. Shooting with a shutter speed of 1/2000 of a second freezes the motion of a fast racecar. You set the lens to manual focus because the camera can't lock focus on a car traveling at a high rate of speed. Focus on an object that will be in the same position as the car you want to photograph. If the track has expansion joints, for example, focus on one that's in the same position the car will be when you press the shutter button. Alternatively, you can focus on something on the side of the track, such as a guardrail or advertising banner that's in the same position as the car will be when you take the picture. The suggested focal length range covers situations where you can "safely" get close to the track (100mm), or you have to photograph from a distance (300mm). The ISO setting depends on the amount of available light. The focal length varies, depending on how close you can get to the action. If you're photographing a single car, choose a focal length that captures the entire car in the frame, and then zoom out so that you can see some of the track around the car. If you're photographing a group of cars, choose a focal length that captures all the cars in the frame, plus a little wiggle room.

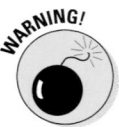

While you photograph the race, monitor your camera's f/stop. If the light gets brighter, decrease the ISO to maintain the desired f/stop. If it turns overcast or you're photographing a long race, increase the ISO setting to preserve the desired shutter speed when the racetrack gets darker.

Taking the Picture

To capture a crystal-clear photograph of a racecar traveling toward you at high speed, your focus has to be spot-on. Due to the speed the car is traveling, you have to anticipate where the car will be when the shutter opens, which means you'll have to press the shutter a fraction of a second before the car reaches the point at which you want to photograph it.

1. **Move to an unobstructed vantage point and enable the camera settings discussed earlier in this chapter.**

2. **Adjust the ISO setting until you have an f/stop of f/8.0 or smaller (meaning a larger f/stop number).**

   If you're shooting in overcast conditions, you may have to use a higher ISO setting.

3. **Manually focus on the part of the track where the car will be when you take the picture.**

4. **Zoom to the desired focal length.**

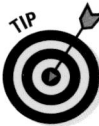

   Leave some room in front of the car to gives viewers the impression that the car's going somewhere.

5. **Press the shutter button fully just before the car reaches the point where you want to photograph it.**

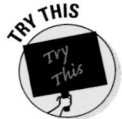

When you photograph one car that's closely following another, use a lens that has a focal length of 200mm or greater. This driving technique is known as *drafting* (in NASCAR speak) or *slipstreaming* (in sports-car and Formula 1 speak). The long lens makes those cars appear to be closer than they actually are. If you photograph a car that has its engine mounted in the rear or middle of the car body, the picture will show a heat haze, as well (see Figure 5-1).

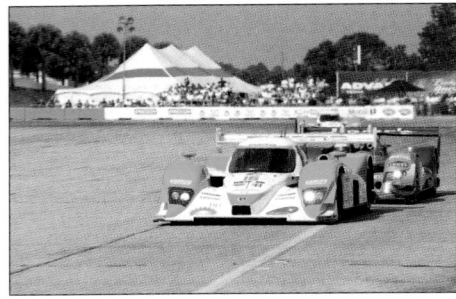

Figure 5-1: Photograph cars traveling in close company.

Troubleshooting

✓ **My image is blurry.** Choose a higher shutter speed and enable image stabilization if it's available on your lens or camera. Alternatively, you can mount the camera on a tripod. You can end up with blurry pictures if your arms get tired when you're photographing a long race, for example.

✓ **My image isn't level.** Make sure you're holding the camera level when you compose the shot. Most cameras give you the option of displaying a grid in the viewfinder. If you need assistance leveling the camera, enable this feature and align one of the grid lines with an object that should be horizontal in the resulting image, such as a guardrail.

✓ **The details on the car are not clear from front to back.** Choose a higher ISO speed to achieve a smaller aperture (larger f/stop number), which results in a greater depth of field.

✓ **The front of the car isn't in focus:** Make sure the shutter opens when the car is at the exact spot on which you focused. If the shutter opens when the car has moved beyond this spot, the front of the car will be out of focus and the part of the car that was on the place on which you focused will be in focus. Remember that you have to anticipate where the car will be and press the shutter button just before the car reaches that spot.

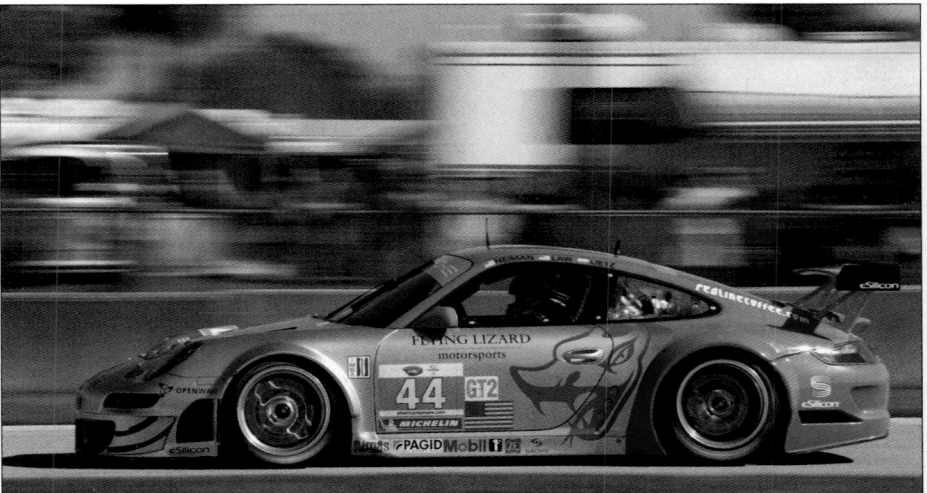

Camera Settings

- **Metering Mode:** Evaluative
- **Drive Mode:** Single Shot or Continuous
- **Shooting Mode:** Shutter Priority
- **Shutter Speed:** 1/125 of a second
- **ISO Setting:** Lowest ISO setting for available light conditions
- **Focus Mode:** Continuous Auto Focus
- **Auto-Focus Point:** Single auto-focus point in the center of the frame
- **Focal Length:** Varies (see "Understanding focal lengths" in the appendix)
- **Image Stabilization:** On

A car rocketing down a straightaway is a visual feast for any motor-racing fan. Racecars are sculpted works of art with colorful sponsor decals, exquisite graphics, and bold colors. Taking a picture of a parked racecar is fairly simple. But how do you capture the beauty of a racecar and the art of racing in one photograph when the car rushes past you at well over 100 mph?

The trick to capturing the details and speed of the car in a single shot is to use a relatively slow shutter speed and pan the camera. If you use a shutter speed fast enough to capture the fine details, you freeze all motion, and the car looks like it is parked on the track. If you use a slow shutter speed and don't pan the camera, you end up with a picture of the racetrack with a colorful blur in the center, which is the speeding racecar. In this chapter, I show you the settings that you need to use to photograph a racecar that's traveling at high speed and perpendicular to you.

Setting the Camera

The goal of this type of photography is to take a picture that shows every subtle detail of the car, yet blurs the background, which shows the car is traveling fast. If you shoot in Shutter Priority mode and use a shutter speed of 1/125 of a second while panning the camera, you get an image that shows the details of the car, yet renders the background an out-of-focus blur. Use a faster shutter speed, such as 1/160 of a second or faster, if you're using a lens that has a focal length greater than the 35mm equivalent of 200mm. Select an ISO setting that gives you an f/stop of 8.0 when you dial in the suggested shutter speed. Set your camera to auto-focus continually so that your camera updates focus while the car moves closer to you. Most modern cameras can track a rapidly moving object that's perpendicular to them.

If you want to take a series of pictures of the car while it rushes past, set the drive mode to Continuous to make the camera takes pictures as long as you hold your finger on the shutter button. The focal length varies, depending on how close you can get to the action. At many road courses (a race track that looks like a country road where the cars turn right and left as opposed to an oval track), you can get fairly close to the track, which can give you great results if you have a focal length that's the 35mm equivalent of 100mm. If you're photographing a race from a grandstand, you may have to use a focal length that's the 35mm equivalent of 200mm or longer. If your lens has the image stabilization feature, enable it. You'll be moving the camera horizontally (also known as *panning*) while taking the picture. Image stabilization counteracts any slight fluctuation in movement while you pan.

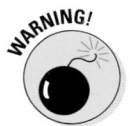

As you photograph the race, monitor the f/stop. If the light gets brighter, decrease the ISO to maintain the desired f/stop. If it turns overcast or you're photographing a long race, increase the ISO setting to preserve the desired shutter speed when it gets darker.

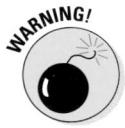

Don't use an ISO setting that causes the f/stop number to be greater than f/8.0. Even though panning with a fast moving object causes the background to be a blur, a larger f/stop number (meaning a smaller aperture) gives you a greater depth of field, and objects in the background may be sharp enough to be recognizable.

Taking the Picture

A motor race has an ebb and flow to it. You can get some great pictures during the opening laps, when drivers jockey for position, so be on your toes and ready to snap a picture if it looks like something exciting is about to happen. After a couple of laps, the action becomes somewhat predictable, when things calm down and drivers find their rhythm. After watching a race for several laps, you know where your favorite driver positions his or her car on a straightaway, and you know the point where he or she starts downshifting and braking for a corner. When the race settles down, analyze how your favorite drivers interact with the racetrack so that you can take more keepers.

1. **Move to an unobstructed vantage point and enable the camera settings discussed previously in this chapter.**

   If you're attending a race at which you're required to sit in a grandstand, order your tickets early and get as close to the action as you can. You can also ask the event organizer which seats are best for taking pictures.

2. **Stabilize the camera by positioning your legs shoulder-width apart, moving your feet so that they're angled slightly away from your body, and tucking your arms in gently by your side (see Figure 6-1).**

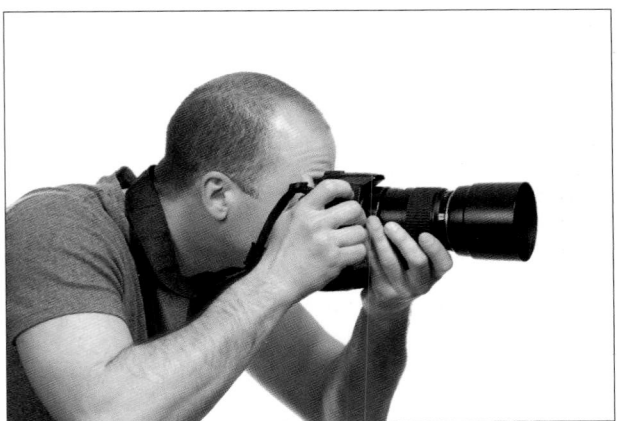

Figure 6-1: Stabilize the camera with your body position.

3. **Cradle the underside of the lens with your left hand and zoom in to the desired focal length.**

   Zoom in on the car until it fills the frame, and then back off a bit. Compose the photograph so that some room appears in front of the car and almost nothing appears behind it. This composition shows the viewer that the car's traveling somewhere.

4. **Pivot from the waist to the direction from which the car is coming and raise the camera to your eye.**

   When the car you want to photograph comes into view, pivot smoothly from the waist while you keep the car in the viewfinder and press the shutter button halfway to achieve focus. You want to match the relative speed of the car and keep the car in the same position within the frame. If you fail to do so, you end up with a blurry photo.

5. If your camera can't track the vehicle after you achieve focus, manually focus on the place where you plan to press the shutter button.

Look for a feature on the track, such as a line or a crack in the pavement, and manually focus on that spot. Alternatively, you can manually focus on a car that's several positions ahead of the car you want to photograph.

6. Press the shutter button fully and continue panning.

If you stop panning, when you take the picture, the resulting photo won't be sharp because the car is still moving quickly but your camera is still. Continue panning a second or so after you press the shutter button.

Panning takes a bit of practice. Get to the track early and try it out during the pre-race warm-up.

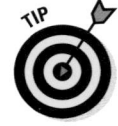
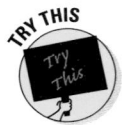

If you're photographing a race that takes place at night or an endurance race that starts in the morning and ends at night, photograph the cars when they brake for a corner after the light starts getting dim. You'll be rewarded with some great shots that show the brake rotors glowing red-hot as they dissipate the heat (see Figure 6-2).

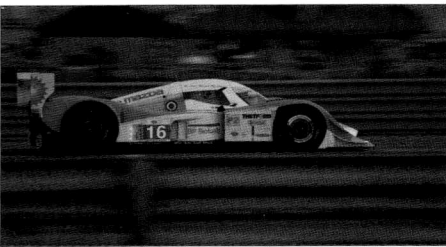

Figure 6-2: Photograph the race at dusk.

Troubleshooting

✓ **My image is blurry.** Pan smoothly. If you change the speed at which you pan when you press the shutter, the resulting image is blurry.

✓ **My image isn't level.** Don't sway your upper body while you pan. Your upper body must be perpendicular to the ground. If it's not, the car doesn't appear level in the resulting photograph.

✓ **The details on the car are not crystal clear.** This problem may occur late in the race when your arms get tired and you can't hold the camera steady, but it can also happen when you first start photographing. If you have this problem, try using the next highest shutter speed.

✓ **I'm having a hard time keeping the car in the frame.** Consider the position of the car on the track. If you're photographing the car on a straightaway, when that car is traveling at a constant speed, you pan at a constant speed. However, if the car is accelerating out of a corner or slowing down for a corner, you have to pan faster or slower to keep the movement of the car synchronized with the movement of the camera.

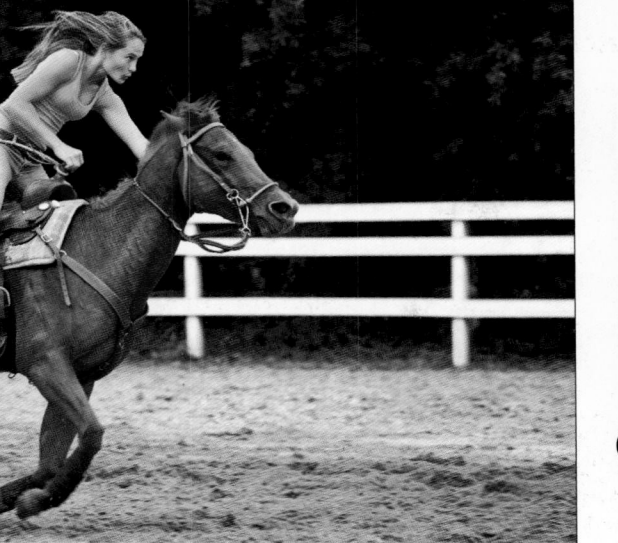

Camera Settings

- **Metering Mode:** Evaluative
- **Drive Mode:** Single Shot or Continuous
- **Shooting Mode:** Shutter Priority
- **Shutter Speed:** 1/250 to 1/1000 second
- **ISO Setting:** An ISO that gives you an f/stop setting of f/5.6 or smaller
- **Focus Mode:** Continuous Auto Focus
- **Auto-Focus Point:** Single auto-focus point
- **Focal Length:** 70mm to 150mm (35mm equivalent; see "Understanding focal lengths" in the appendix)
- **Image Stabilization:** On

The fluid motion of a horse and her rider are all the ingredients you need for an exciting picture. There are many forms of horse racing. When you photograph an event like steeplechase or barrel racing, you can hone in on the rider and her trusty steed as they negotiate the obstacles as shown here. If you photograph an event on a 5/8-mile course, you can photograph many racers at one time. This chapter focuses on events where a single rider and horse are racing against time. The rider is focused on making the horse do something that is not second nature to the animal. The pictures you capture show the interaction between the rider and her horse as she guides the animal around the obstacles.

Setting the Camera

When you photograph a horse race, you want to capture a slice of action, a frozen moment in time when horse and rider act in unison. To achieve this, you use Shutter Priority mode and a relatively fast shutter speed. If you're photographing a steeplechase or barrel race, you can use the slowest setting when the horse slows and navigates an obstacle. For other horse racing events, where the horse is going flat out, you need a faster shutter speed. If you want to capture a sequence of images as horse and rider negotiate obstacles, choose Continuous Drive mode. The ISO setting you choose will be dictated by the amount of light and the aperture the camera dials in. Because the horse and rider are your main subjects, you can get a good, crisp photo with an f/stop of f/5.6. Use Continuous Auto-Focus mode and the camera updates focus as the horse and rider move through the frame. Image stabilization is a plus because it ensures a sharp image if your arms get tired and your hand isn't as steady as it was at the start of the event. If you don't have image stabilization, and the light gets dim, you'll have to increase the ISO.

Taking the Picture

To create a compelling photo of a horse and rider at a horse race, your focus has to be spot on. You want to set up the shot before you take it. This involves a bit of thought and anticipation on your part. It's a good idea to watch a couple of racers negotiate the course before you take a picture.

1. **Move to an unobstructed vantage point and enable the camera settings discussed previously in this chapter.**

   Choose a vantage point where there's a lot of action, such as a place where the racers are jumping a hurdle or negotiating a barrel. (See Figure 7-1.)

2. **Adjust the ISO setting until you have an f/stop of f/5.6 or smaller (meaning a larger f/stop number).**

   If you're shooting in overcast conditions, or at a night race, you may have to use a very high ISO setting. This adds the risk of noise to the equation, but it's better than not getting the shot.

3. **Aim the camera at the horse and rider as they race toward the place where you're going to take the picture.**

   The camera updates focus as the team moves toward or away from you. If the horse and rider are parallel to you, you'll have to pan. (See Chapter 6 for more about panning.) The alternative is to prefocus on a horse and rider that negotiate the obstacle before the subjects you want to photograph get there.

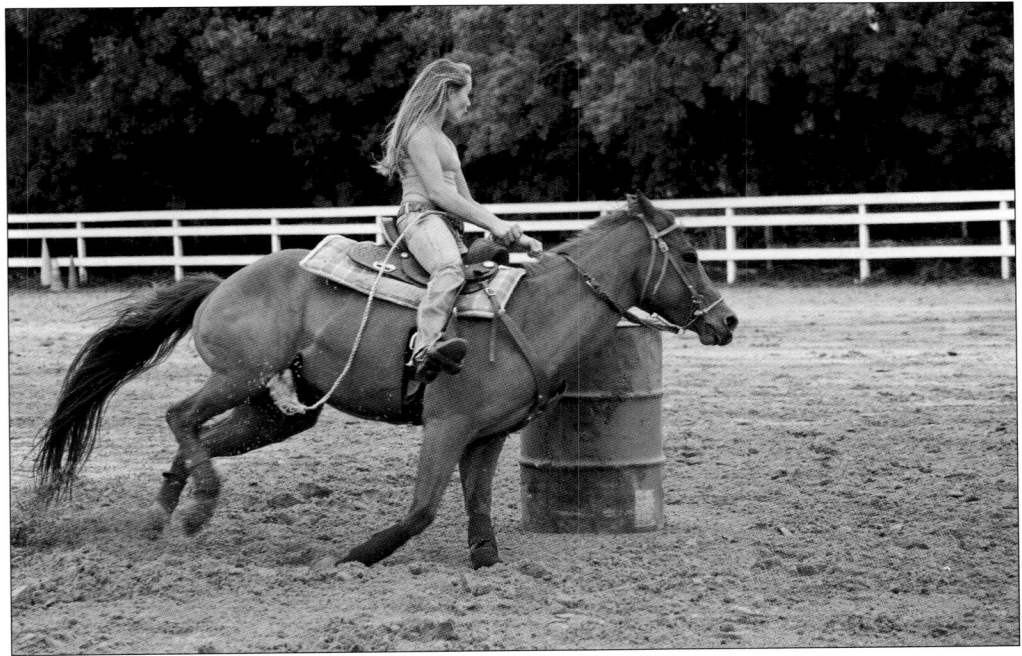

Figure 7-1: Photographing horse and jockey as they approach an obstacle.

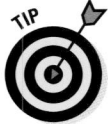

4. **Zoom to the desired focal length.**

   Leave some room in front of the racers to give viewers the impression that horse and rider are going somewhere.

5. **Press the shutter button halfway to achieve focus.**

6. **Press the shutter button fully to take the picture.**

   If you're photographing in Continuous Drive mode, release the shutter button to stop taking pictures. Review the images on your LCD monitor to make sure the image is properly exposed and that your subjects are in focus.

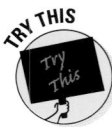

If you're photographing on an overcast afternoon, or at night, switch to a slow shutter speed of 1/6 or 1/15 of a second. Pan with the horse and rider to capture an artistic impression of speed, as shown in Figure 7-2.

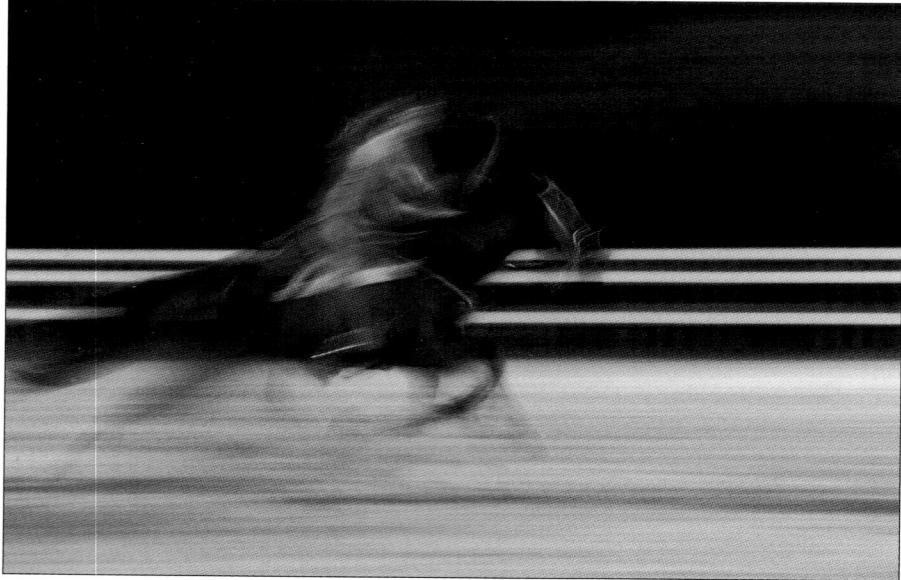

Figure 7-2: Use a slow shutter speed to capture an artistic impression of speed.

Troubleshooting

- ✓ **The largest f/stop number is blinking.** This happens when you switch to a slow shutter speed in bright light. There's too much light to properly expose the image. Switch to your lowest ISO setting. If this doesn't solve the problem, place a neutral density filter over the lens.

- ✓ **The horse and rider are not in focus.** Make sure the camera is in Continuous Auto-Focus mode. If it is, make sure the auto-focus point is over the horse and rider when you press the shutter button to achieve focus.

- ✓ **The horse is in focus, but the rider isn't.** This happens in low light conditions. The camera chooses a large aperture to accommodate for the low light, which gives you a limited depth of field. The first cure is to increase the ISO setting until you get an f/stop of f/5.6 or larger (smaller aperture). The other alternative is to position the single auto-focus point over the rider. Many cameras give you the option of moving a single auto-focus point to a different part of the viewfinder other than dead center.

Part II
Animals

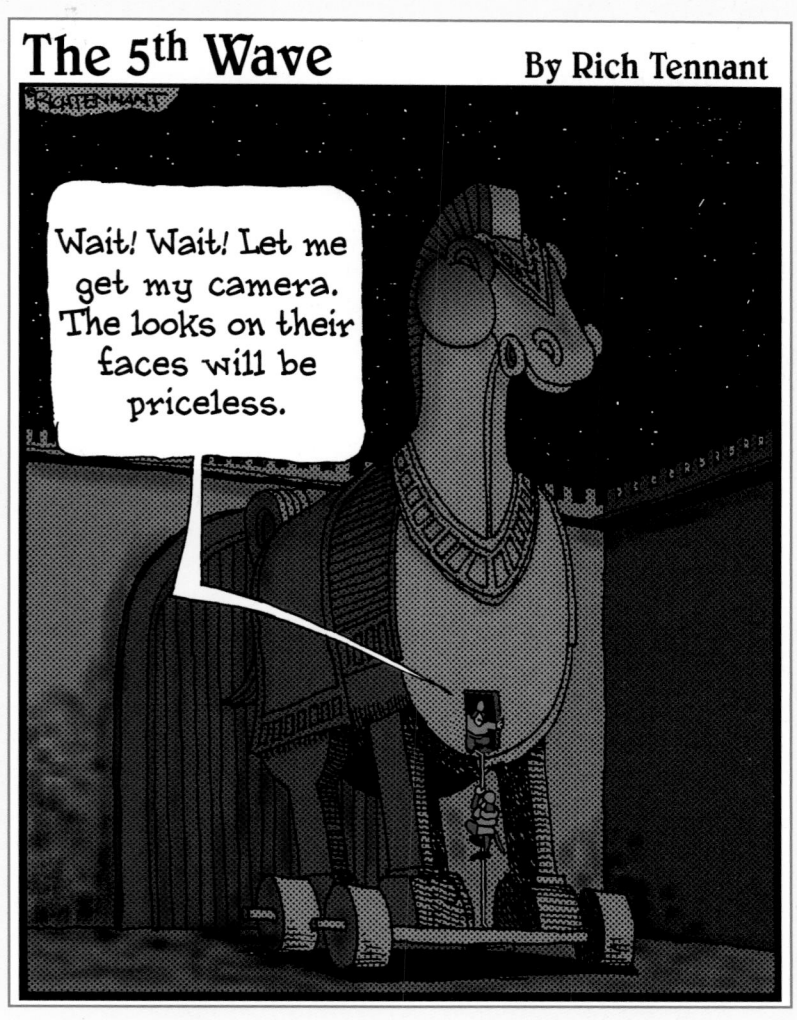

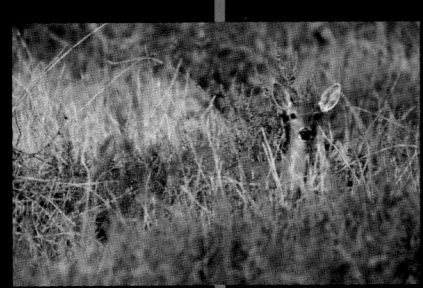

*Y*ou have a photogenic or playful pet. Or maybe you live near a wildlife management area that's teeming with wading birds and birds of prey. Or perhaps you live near a state park where wildlife such as deer, alligators, or bears live. You also have a digital SLR, but are wondering what settings to use to take pictures of animals. If that's your quandary, the chapters in this section were written for you.

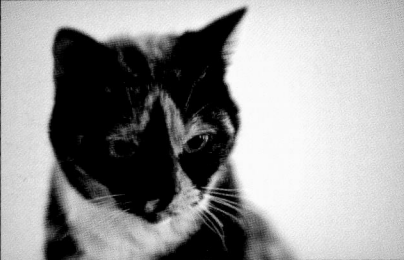

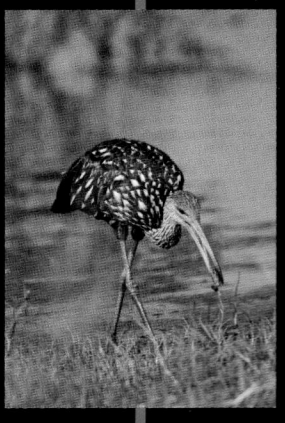

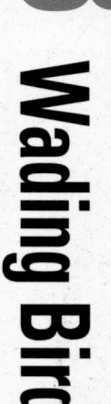

8

Wading Birds

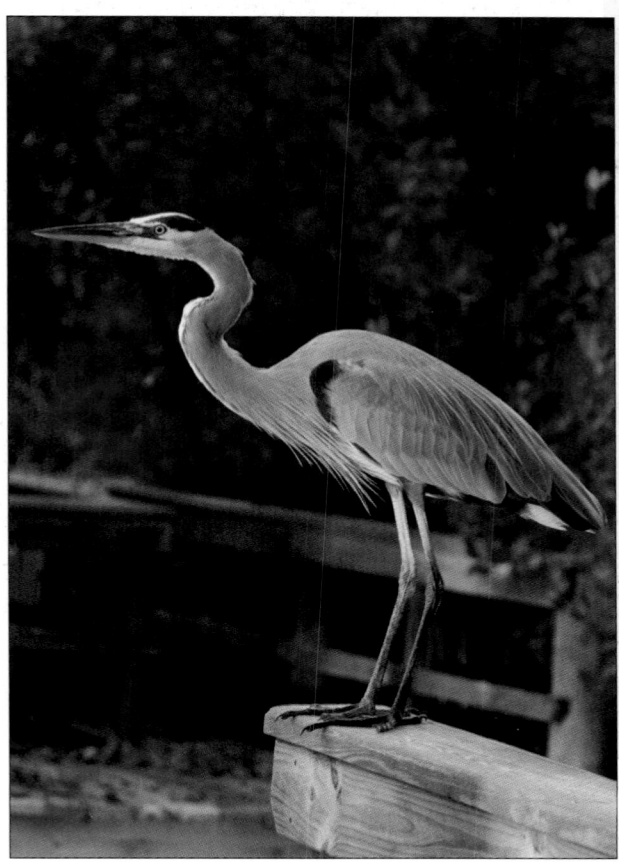

1 f you're fortunate enough to live near a state park with a river or lake, you have a wonderful opportunity to photograph wading birds. Egrets, herons, and sand hill cranes fly from place to place, but they hunt for food in shallow lakes and rivers. If the place in which you photograph is frequented by humans, the birds will not be frightened, and you'll be able to get fairly close to your subjects. However, if you're photographing wading birds in the wilderness, they'll be more wary of your presence and won't let you get as close, which means you'll need to photograph the birds with a long lens.

When you photograph birds, it's helpful to know their habits and their distinctive voices. Sand hill cranes make a distinct warbling sound as they fly, and herons squawk loudly when other birds approach them. It's imperative to know where your subjects hang out. You can find this information through research, networking with other photographers or birdwatchers, or just finding a great spot while you're out exploring the area near where you live.

Setting the Camera

Wading birds congregate near lakes and rivers when it's time to eat. You want to capture the bird and a little bit of his surrounding, which is why you use a large aperture (small f/stop number), and shoot in Aperture Priority mode. Your ISO setting varies depending on the ambient light. Use the lowest ISO setting possible that yields a shutter speed that enables you to handhold the camera at the desired focal length. Use a focal length of 100mm or longer. Birds are often wary of humans. In most instances, you won't be able to get close enough to frame the bird with a shorter focal length. Most birds stay put when feeding. Single shot Focus mode enables you to quickly establish focus using a minimum of battery power. Using a single auto-focus point allows you to focus precisely on your feathered friend. Image stabilization is always useful as it enables you to get a blur-free image.

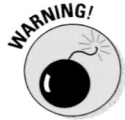

If you're photographing on a gloomy day or in a shaded area, you'll have to increase the ISO setting or mount the camera on a tripod. Don't use image stabilization if you mount the camera on a tripod — it may yield unexpected results.

Taking the Picture

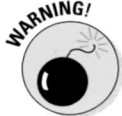

When you photograph wading birds in the wild, watch out for predators like alligators who often inhabit the same areas. If possible, travel with a friend who can keep an eye out for you while you photograph the birds.

When you find a spot with lots of wading birds, the previous settings and the following steps will get you some great photographs of birds.

1. **Enable the camera settings discussed earlier in this chapter.**

2. **Set up station at a place where you've seen wading birds in the past.**

   It's best to sit patiently and wait for the birds, especially if you're photographing in a place where the birds aren't used to humans. If you're photographing skittish birds, find a spot where you'll blend into the background.

   Choose a position with a background that contrasts nicely with the bird's colors. For example, green foliage provides a great background when photographing white birds.

   Birds are subject to attacks from predators, which makes them cautious. You'll have to be somewhat stealthy when you photograph birds. Don't make any sudden movements. When you find a photogenic bird, take one shot to get one in the bank and then move in closer to get your money shot.

3. **When a bird appears, zoom in and compose the picture.**

   Many wading birds have long necks. When a bird lowers his head, the neck forms an S-Curve that you can use as a compositional element in your picture. You can also use beaks and legs to compose your picture.

4. **Take the picture.**

   If you're photographing on a gloomy day or in a shaded area, you'll have to increase the ISO setting or mount the camera on a tripod. Don't use image stabilization if you mount the camera on a tripod — it may yield unexpected results.

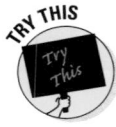

Photograph birds when they're feeding. (See Figure 8-1.) To freeze the action, you need a shutter speed of 1/250 of a second in conjunction with a large aperture to blur out the background. To achieve this when photographing in overcast conditions, increase the ISO setting until the shutter speed is fast enough to freeze the action.

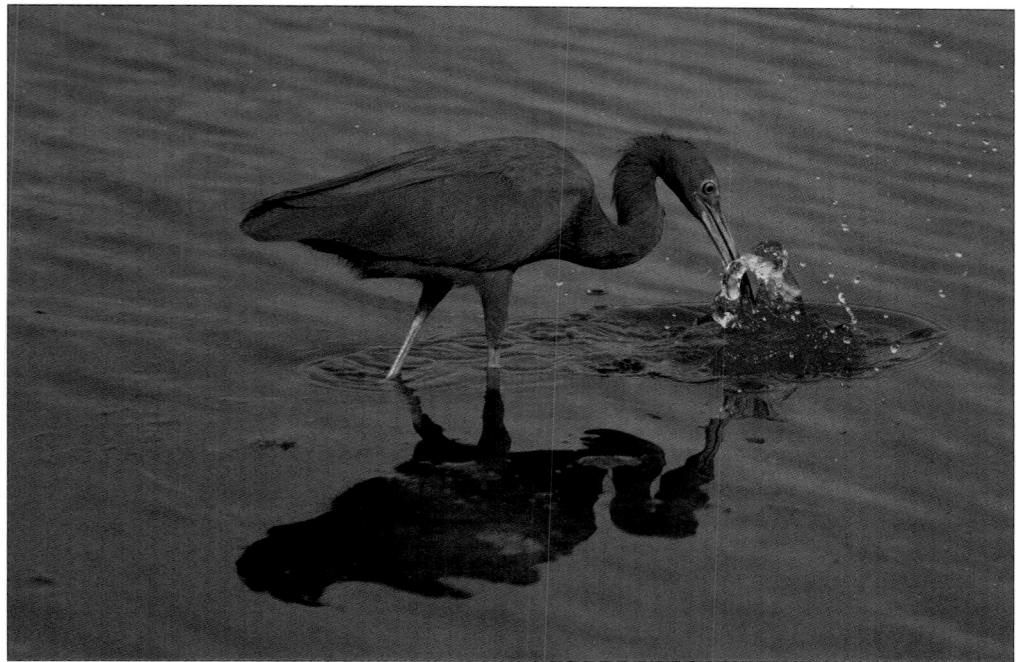

Figure 8-1: Photograph birds when they're feeding.

Troubleshooting

- **White birds are blown out.** If you photograph a white bird and notice that there are no details on certain parts of the bird, the camera has exposed for the entire scene while overexposing parts of the bird. The remedy for this problem is to use exposure compensation to decrease exposure by 1/3 or 2/3 a stop.

- **The bird's features are dark.** This can occur when you have a bright light source like the sun behind the birds. If you encounter this situation, use exposure compensation to increase the exposure. This, however, will blow out the background. Another alternative is to move to another position where the light is shining directly on your subject.

- **The bird is out of focus.** Make sure you place the single auto-focus point over the bird and press the shutter button halfway to achieve focus. With the shutter button still pressed halfway, move the camera to achieve the desired composition.

- **The bird blends in with the background.** This problem occurs when you photograph a dark bird against a dark background or a white bird against a light background. The easiest solution is to move to a slightly different spot to change the background.

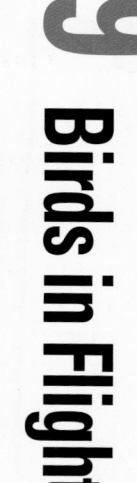

9

Birds in Flight

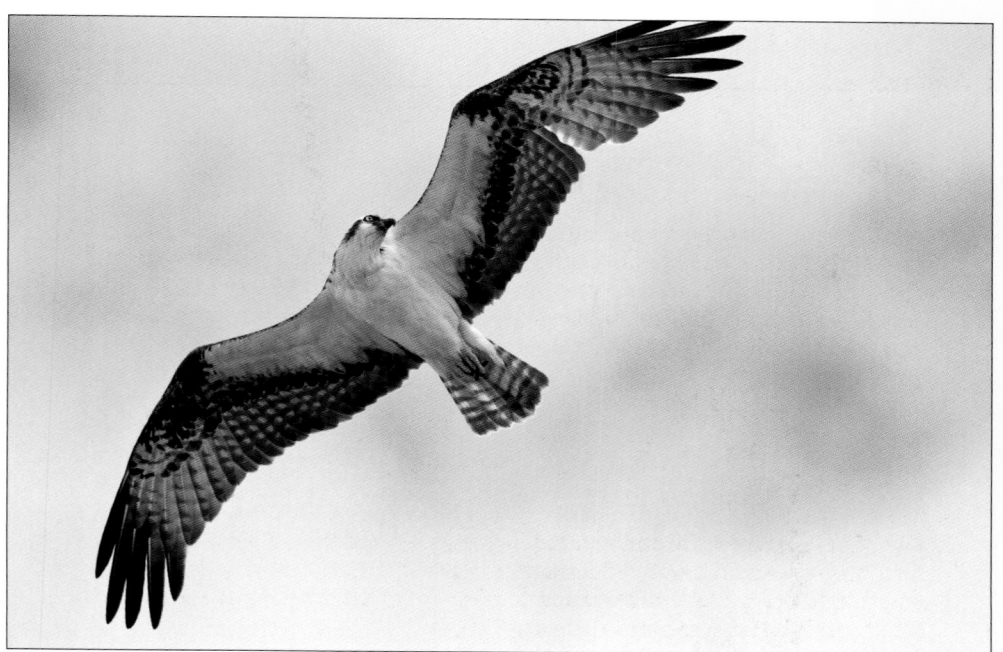

Photo courtesy of Roxanne Evans, www.dougplusrox.com.

Camera Settings

- ✔ **Metering Mode:** Evaluative
- ✔ **Drive Mode:** Continuous
- ✔ **Shooting Mode:** Shutter Priority
- ✔ **Shutter Speed:** 1/500 of a second
- ✔ **ISO Setting:** 100 or 200
- ✔ **Focus Mode:** Continuous Auto-Focus
- ✔ **Auto-Focus Point:** Single auto-focus point
- ✔ **Focal Length:** 100mm or greater (35mm equivalent; see "Understanding focal lengths" in the appendix)
- ✔ **Image Stabilization** (Optional): If available, use image stabilization if the lighting conditions yield a slow shutter speed.

*B*irds in flight are majestic creatures. You can get some great shots of birds roosting and feeding (see Chapters 8, 10, and 11), but you'll also want photos of birds when they take off or are in flight, as shown here.

When you see a bird in flight and you have your camera in hand, you have the opportunity to create a compelling photograph, suitable for framing. This type of photography requires you to freeze the motion of the bird and get close enough so that the bird is more than just a tiny speck in the frame.

Setting Your Camera

When you photograph a bird in flight, your goal is to stop the action. A shutter speed of 1/500 of a second is plenty fast enough to freeze a bird in flight. The suggested ISO setting should yield an f/stop of about f/4.0 in bright conditions, which is a large aperture that gives you a soft, out-of-focus background. You may need to increase to a higher ISO setting to achieve this f/stop if you're photographing in overcast conditions. You use Continuous Auto-Focus mode, which lets the camera update focus while the bird moves closer to or farther from you. Using Continuous Drive mode lets you capture a sequence of images, such as when the bird comes in for a landing at his nest. You can also capture a majestic series of images of the bird in flight.

The suggested focal length works when you can get fairly close to the bird. However, you may need a focal length of 200mm or greater if you're photographing an elusive bird, such as an eagle or an osprey.

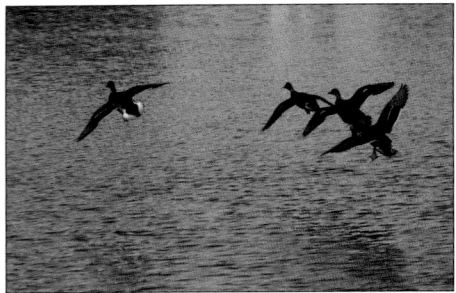

Figure 9-1: Taking a stop-action picture of a flock of birds.

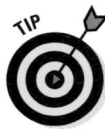 If you're photographing a flock of birds, switch to a higher ISO setting to get a smaller aperture (larger f/stop number), such as f/8 or f/11, which gives you a greater depth of field (see Figure 9-1).

Taking the Picture

When you capture a photo of a graceful bird or flock of birds in flight, you have a photo worth framing. You may find photographing flying birds in a metropolitan area a challenge because manmade structures may appear in the resulting image. However, with a keen eye and the settings suggested in this chapter, you can get some great pictures of birds in flight.

 Switch to Continuous Shooting mode to capture a series of photos while the bird flies past you, and then follow these steps:

1. **Select a suitable vantage point from which to photograph.**

    The ideal vantage point is one where the birds are flying in front of an innocuous background, such as trees or the sky. If you're photographing in an urban area, move around until you find a location that birds frequent and that has an unobtrusive background.

2. **Enable the camera settings discussed earlier in this chapter.**

3. **When a bird you want to photograph flies into view, line up the bird in your viewfinder and press the shutter button halfway to achieve focus.**

4. **Take the picture.**

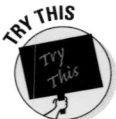

Switch to a slow shutter speed of about 1/50 of a second and pan the camera (see Chapter 5) to track the bird while it flies past you. The resulting photo renders the background as a soft, out-of-focus blur, yet the bird appears in sharp focus (see Figure 9-2).

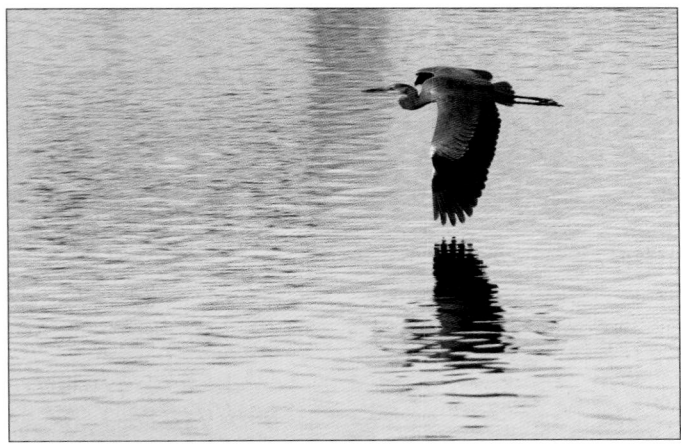

Figure 9-2: Pan with the bird to accentuate motion.

Troubleshooting

✓ **The bird is blurry.** Maybe you don't have a really steady hand. Switch to a slightly higher shutter speed and take a picture of the next bird that flies by.

✓ **Some of the birds in the flock are out of focus.** You may have this problem when you photograph a large flock of birds. Switch to a higher ISO setting to get a smaller aperture (larger f/stop number), which gives you a larger depth of field.

✓ **The bird isn't in sharp focus.** Your camera focused on the wrong part of the bird. When you photograph a single bird in flight, try to place the auto-focus point over the bird's head, and then press the shutter button halfway to achieve focus. The auto-focus spot illuminates to let you know you've achieved focus on the desired part of the bird. Then you can press the shutter button fully to take the picture.

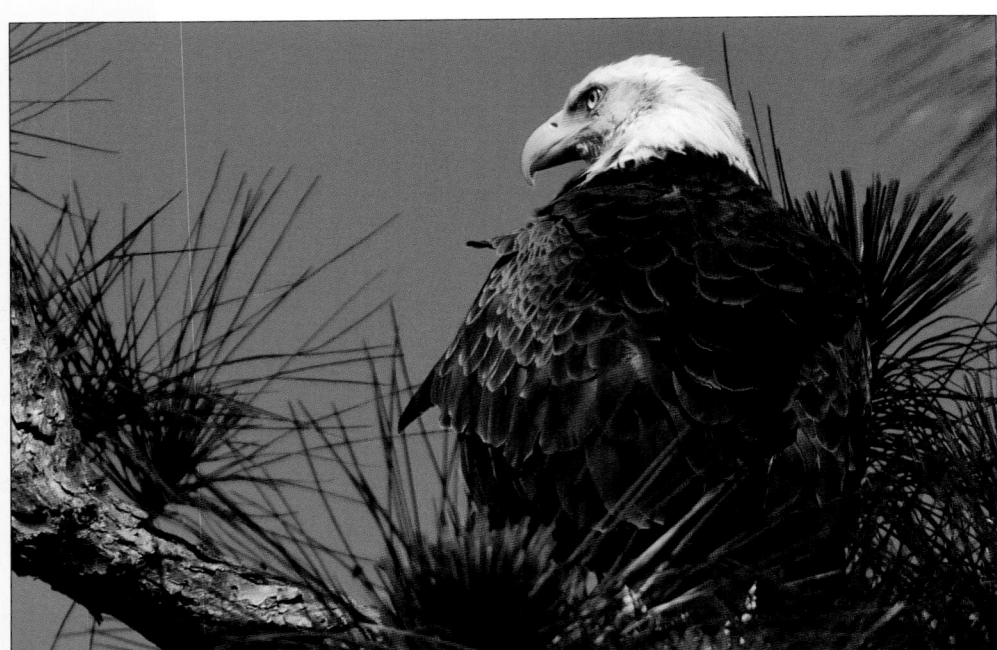

Courtesy of Roxanne Evans, www.dougplusrox.com.

*B*irds of prey are majestic birds, well equipped for hunting with razor-sharp talons and pointed beaks. They're also fantastic subjects for photographers.

If you live near the ocean, a lake, or a river, you may have a rich resource for this type of photography. But without the right equipment and settings, you'll have a tough time getting great pictures of majestic birds such as the American Bald Eagle.

Camera Settings

- ✔ **Metering Mode:** Evaluative
- ✔ **Drive Mode:** Continuous
- ✔ **Shooting Mode:** Aperture Priority
- ✔ **Aperture:** f/5.6 to f/8.0
- ✔ **ISO Setting:** 100 or 200
- ✔ **Focus Mode:** Single Shot
- ✔ **Auto-Focus Point:** Single auto-focus point
- ✔ **Focal Length:** 200mm or longer (35mm equivalent; see "Understanding focal lengths" in the appendix)
- ✔ **Image Stabilization:** Optional

Setting the Camera

Equipment is important when you're photographing birds of prey. The kit lens that comes with most cameras doesn't cut it. If you're serious about bird photography, you need a good lens with a long focal length to reach out to the bird's roost. A zoom lens that reaches out to 200mm or longer is the ideal solution. Shoot in Aperture Priority mode with a large aperture (a small f/stop number) to ensure that you have a shallow depth of field that draws your viewer's attention to the bird. A low ISO setting ensures that you get a crisp image with a minimum of digital noise. If you're shooting in low-light conditions, stabilize the camera with a tripod instead of increasing the ISO because a higher ISO setting will produce digital noise (noticeable in the shadow areas of the image).

Taking the Picture

Photographing birds of prey requires skill, persistence, and patience. You need to know something about the birds to photograph them properly. They survive by being canny, so it's rare you find them out in the open. They're secreted in nests in tall trees. If you know the sounds the bird makes, you stand a good chance of finding his nest and getting a shot.

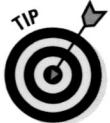

You have to become a hunter, just like the bird you want to photograph. Follow these steps to hone your "predatory" skills and get the shot you're after:

1. **Visit a location where you've previously seen the birds you want to photograph.**

   When birds of prey get ready to feed, they often perch in dead trees and survey the area for a suitable spot to catch dinner (see Figure 10-1).

   Large birds of prey, such as eagles and osprey, build large nests, which you can easily spot from the ground.

   If you know of a local Audubon group in your area, become active and ask the bird photographers where you can find the hot spots.

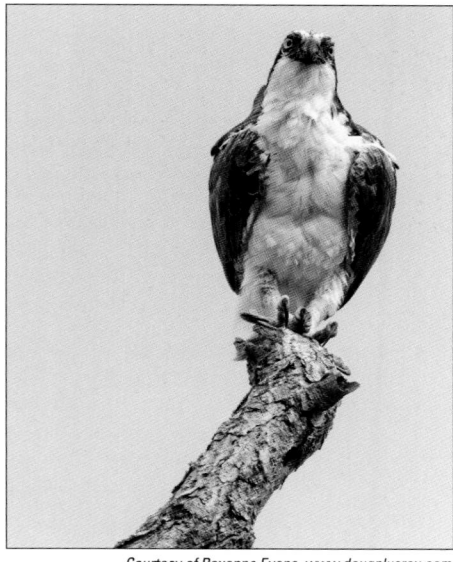

Courtesy of Roxanne Evans, www.dougplusrox.com.

Figure 10-1: Location is everything.

2. **Wait patiently until you see a bird that you want to photograph.**

   If you see a photographer whose camera has a long lens in a state park, tell her you're new to bird photography and ask her where to find the best places in the park to photograph.

3. **Zoom in on the bird and press the shutter button halfway to achieve focus.**

   If you're close enough, position the auto focus over the bird's eye that's closest to the camera, press the shutter button halfway to achieve focus, and then move the camera to achieve the desired composition. If the bird's eye is in focus, the entire bird appears to be in focus.

4. **Take the picture.**

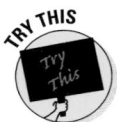

Even birds of prey can be comedians. If you've photographed a bird that doesn't fly away right after you take the picture, keep the viewfinder trained on him. After a while, he may wonder what you're up to and look at you with an expression worth capturing (see Figure 10-2).

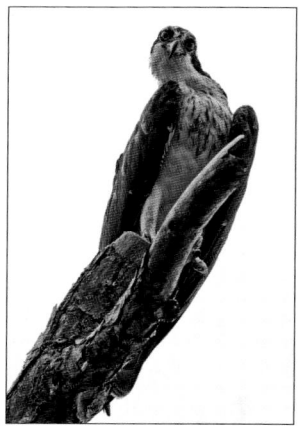

Courtesy of Roxanne Evans, www.dougplusrox.com.

Figure 10-2: A bird of prey with attitude.

Troubleshooting

✓ **The bird is blurry.** Make sure you're shooting at a shutter speed that's fast enough so that you can handhold the camera with the lens you're using. If you're shooting in low-light conditions, increase the ISO setting to get a faster shutter speed. Alternatively, put your camera on a tripod. If you put your camera on a tripod, disable image stabilization because you may get undesired results when image stabilization attempts to compensate for operator movement when there is none.

✓ **The bird isn't in focus.** Make sure you have the auto-focus point positioned over the bird — preferably over the eye nearest the camera — when you press the shutter button halfway to achieve focus. Also, make sure that the focus lamp illuminates before you move the camera to compose the image.

✓ **The camera doesn't achieve focus.** You may have this problem if the bird is surrounded by a lot of foliage or some twigs are between you and the bird. You can always move to a different location to get a better view of the bird. The better option is to quickly switch to manual focus and grab a picture of the bird while she's still there. Then, when you have one shot of the bird, you can move to a different position and try for another shot.

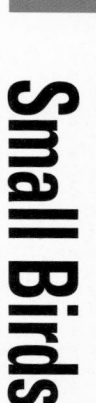

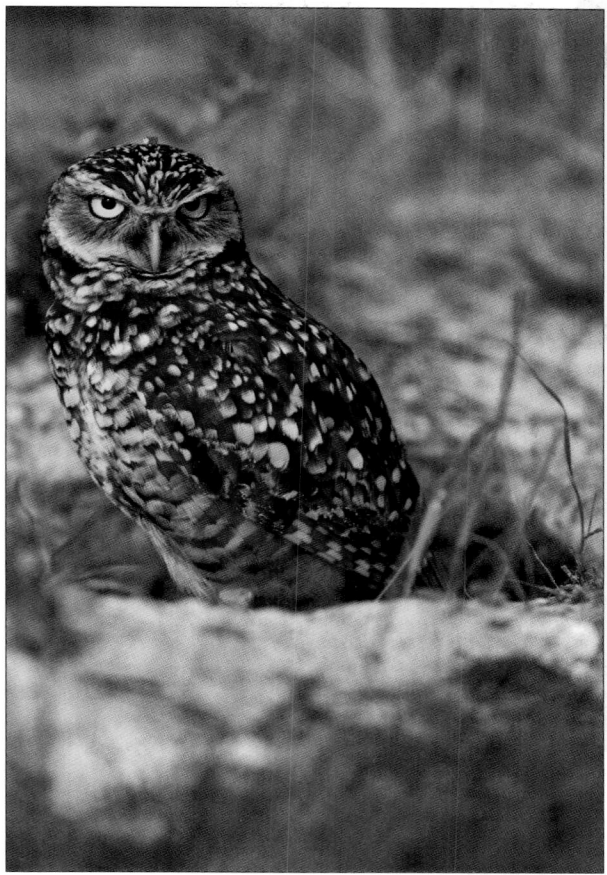

Camera Settings

- **Metering Mode:** Evaluative
- **Drive Mode:** Continuous
- **Shooting Mode:** Aperture Priority
- **Aperture:** f/4.0
- **ISO Setting:** 100 to 400
- **Focus Mode:** Continuous Auto-Focus
- **Auto-Focus Point:** Single auto-focus point
- **Focal Length:** 100mm or longer (35mm equivalent; see "Understanding focal lengths" in the appendix)
- **Image Stabilization:** On

*1*f you live in an area with a lot of small birds, you can capture interesting images of them with your digital SLR. You just need a bit of patience and some knowledge of the bird you want to photograph. If you have a bird feeder in your back yard, you can use it as an ideal place to photograph small birds. Or perhaps you live near an area where interesting species, such as burrowing owls, live. The equipment you use when you photograph a small bird depends on how close you can get to it. The bird feeder provides an ideal situation. If you spend a lot of time near the bird feeder, the birds begin to think you're part of the scenery and fly in for a meal while you're there. You can also place a feeder near a window and photograph the birds from inside your home.

Setting the Camera

You photograph a small bird in a way similar to shooting someone's portrait. You want your subject (the small bird) to be in focus, but you don't want the foreground or background in focus. Shoot this type of picture in Aperture Priority mode, using a large aperture (a small f/stop number). Use a single auto-focus point and, if possible, achieve focus on the bird's eye. The ISO setting range gives you the latitude of taking this type of picture in bright to overcast conditions. You use Continuous Auto-Focus mode because your subject will probably move after you achieve focus. Shooting in Continuous Drive mode allows you to take pictures as long as you hold your finger on the shutter button, so you can hedge your bets, hopefully getting a couple of interesting pictures when your subject comes into view.

Taking the Picture

When you find a great spot to photograph small birds, you just need to arrive at the right time and get your gear ready. Like any other type of outdoor photography, you get your best results if you don't photograph in the middle of the day when the light is very harsh. Also, arrive at the site when you know the birds will be feeding.

1. **Find a location where you can photograph the birds without being noticed.**

    If you have a bird feeder in your yard and are near it frequently, you may be able to get very close to the birds. If you're photographing birds in the wild, find a location that has an unobtrusive background (see Figure 11-1).

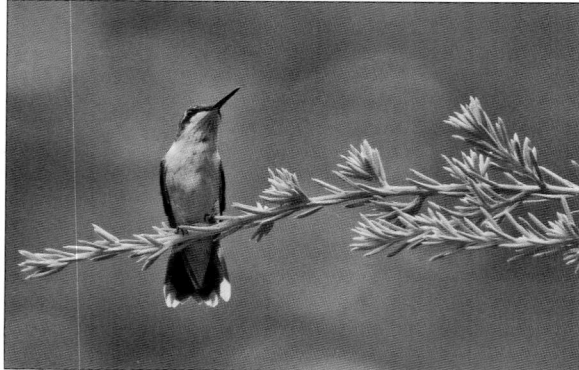

Image courtesy of Roxanne Evans, www.dougplusrox.com.

Figure 11-1: Find a suitable background.

2. **Enable the settings discussed earlier in this chapter.**

3. **When a bird comes into view, zoom in, and then press the shutter button halfway to achieve focus.**

   If possible, focus on the bird's eye.

4. **Press the shutter button fully to take the picture.**

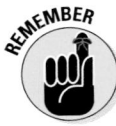

When you shoot in Continuous Drive mode, the camera keeps taking pictures as long as you keep your finger on the shutter button. This mode provides an excellent way to capture a series of pictures of a bird.

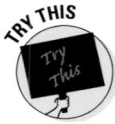

Visit a state park or area where small birds are protected. In Florida, scrub-jays are protected by law. They're actually quite tame and have been known to fly very close to humans, such as this scrub-jay who perched on the handlebar of my girlfriend's bike (see Figure 11-2). This bird has leg bands, which is how an individual bird is identified by organizations who track the activities of a protected species. This is an ideal way to get up-close pictures of birds in the wild.

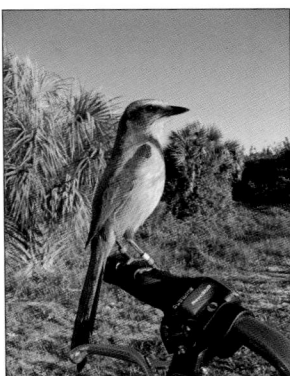

Figure 11-2: Photographing small birds that are tame.

Troubleshooting

- ✔ **The bird is blurry (#1).** The shutter speed you're using is too slow to hand-hold the camera with your focal length. Increase the ISO setting to get a shutter speed that's fast enough to take a blur-free picture when you hold the camera.

- ✔ **The bird is blurry (#2).** Your camera doesn't achieve focus on the bird. Make sure you position the auto-focus point over the bird (preferably over the eye closest to the camera), press the shutter button halfway and wait for the focus lamp to illuminate in the viewfinder. Then, you can move the camera to compose the picture.

- ✔ **The bird's wings are blurry.** You can have this problem when you photograph small birds, such as hummingbirds, when they're feeding. If they don't perch, they flap their wings to remain in one place. As long as the bird's body isn't blurry, you can actually end up with an interesting photo.

- ✔ **The bird is too small.** You can't get close to the bird and don't have a long focal length. If you're taking the picture with a camera that has a megapixel resolution greater than 12 megapixels, you can crop out some of the offending background in your image-editing application.

12 Pet Birds

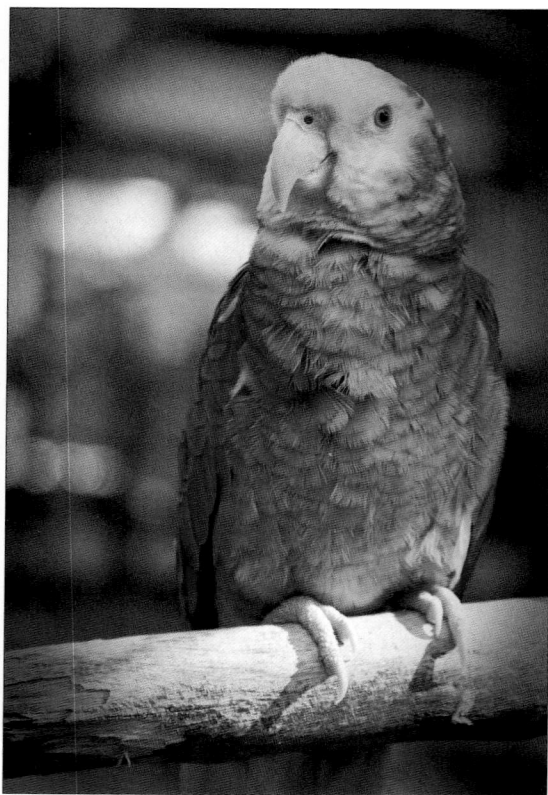

Some people are cat lovers, others love dogs, and some people prefer the comfort of fine-feathered friends. Some birds even have the one-up on dogs and cats; they can talk. If you're a bird lover, or you know a bird lover, you have a perfect subject for photography. Birds are colorful, and some are even well trained. However, some birds are also inquisitive, and they like shiny things such as camera strap snaps and the like. When you photograph a pet bird, have someone along who can keep the bird under control. The settings in this chapter and a good bird handler are all you need to capture great photos of a pet bird.

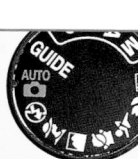

Camera Settings

- **Metering Mode:** Evaluative
- **Drive Mode:** Single Shot or Continuous
- **Shooting Mode:** Aperture Priority
- **Aperture:** f/3.5 or a smaller f/stop number
- **ISO Setting:** 100 to 200
- **Focus Mode:** Single Shot
- **Auto-Focus Point:** Single auto-focus point
- **Focal Length:** 80mm to 100mm (35mm equivalent; see "Understanding focal lengths" in the appendix)
- **Image Stabilization:** On

Setting the Camera

Even if you photograph a large bird by using the suggested focal length, you have to get fairly close to the critter. But you still want a shallow depth of field, which is why you take pictures of pet birds in Aperture Priority mode, using a large aperture. The ISO range is ideally suited for photography in bright conditions. You may have to increase the ISO if you photograph the bird in dim lighting. You have the option of using Single Shot or Continuous Drive mode. Use Continuous Drive mode to hedge your bets and take several pictures of your bird when he starts doing something interesting. Image stabilization always can help you ensure you get a blur-free shot, especially when your subject is small and you're zoomed in tight.

Taking the Picture

An enclosed patio is an ideal place to photograph a pet bird. If the patio is covered with a screen, you get diffuse light. If the patio has a ceiling through which no light can pass, photograph the bird when the morning or afternoon light passes through the screens. You'll get wonderfully warm light that's ideal for any type of photography.

1. **Find a spot that has a plain background.**

   A busy background creates a confusing message. A solid-colored wall that contrasts with the bird's colors is ideal. In lieu of that, you can photograph the bird with a natural background that contrasts well with the bird's colors.

2. **Have the bird's owner (or a friend, if you're the bird's owner) place the bird on a natural perch.**

   A twig or dead branch works ideally.

   If you're photographing a well-trained bird, you can easily get some great pictures. If you have someone to mind the bird while you mind the camera, you can also get some great pictures of an untrained bird.

3. **Enable the settings discussed earlier in this chapter.**

4. **Zoom in, position the auto-focus point over the bird's eye closest to the camera, and then press the shutter button halfway to achieve focus.**

5. **Compose the picture.**

   You can use the bird's features to draw viewers into the picture. A curved beak is an ideal compositional element (see Figure 12-1). You get a more interesting picture if you don't center the bird in the frame.

6. **Press the shutter button down fully to take the picture.**

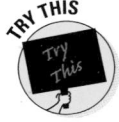

TRY THIS

Use a piece of dark-colored fabric as a background for a bird with light-colored feathers. The contrast makes the image pop (see Figure 12-2).

Troubleshooting

✔ **My bird is dark in the picture.** If a bright light source appears behind the bird, the camera attempts to compensate by making the image darker, which leaves your bird underexposed. Use exposure compensation to increase the exposure until the bird is perfectly exposed.

✔ **The colors don't look right.** Competing light sources — for example, natural light and interior lights — can fool your camera's white balance. You can correct this problem by manually setting the white balance or by turning off the artificial lighting.

✔ **The bird's beak is out of focus.** You always want the eyes to be in focus, which can cause the beak to appear blurry when you're photographing the bird from the front. Move to the side and take the photo.

✔ **The bird has a lot of dark areas.** An overhead light source can cast shadows under the bird's wing and beak. Have someone hold a white sheet of paper or a large shirt in front of the bird. Ask your assistant to angle the object to bounce light back at the bird. You can see the difference in your viewfinder.

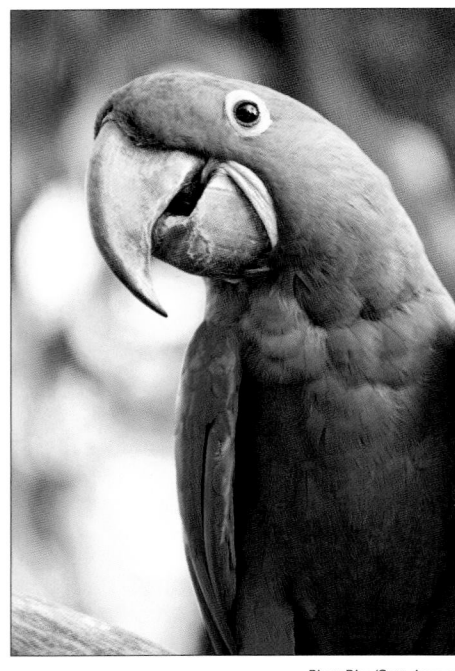

PhotoDisc/Getty Images

Figure 12-1: Use the bird's features to compose a compelling picture.

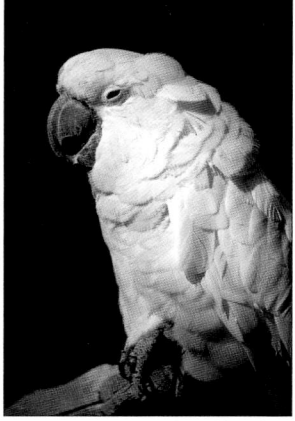

Corbis Digital Stock

Figure 12-2: Photograph a bird that has light-colored plumage on a dark background.

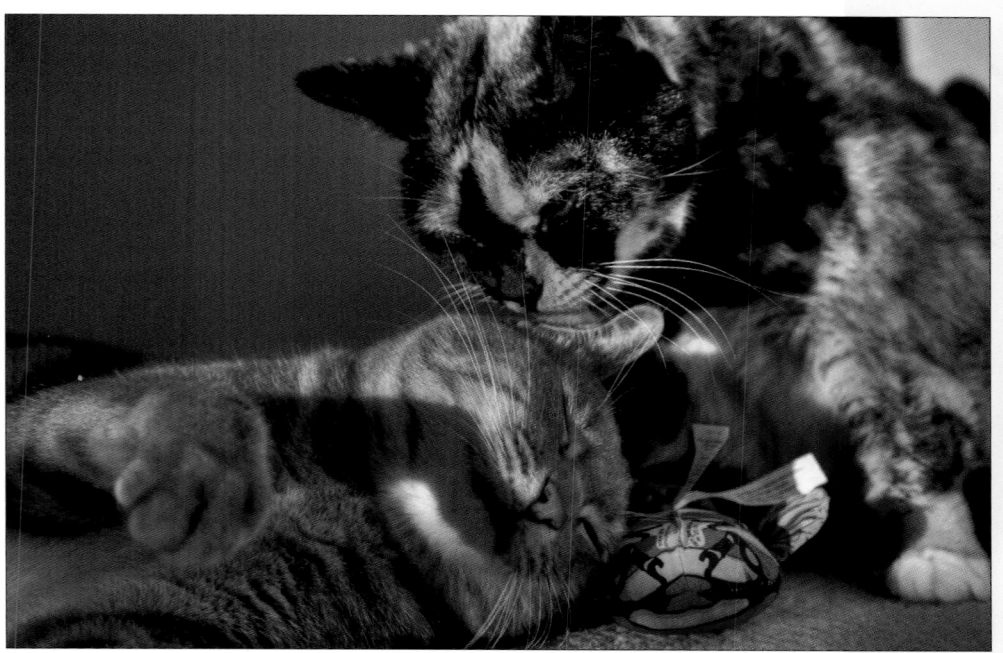

Photo courtesy of Roxanne Evans, www.dougplusrox.com

Camera Settings

- **Metering Mode:** Evaluative
- **Drive Mode:** Continuous
- **Shooting Mode:** Shutter Priority
- **Shutter Speed:** 1/125 of a second
- **ISO Setting:** 100 to 400
- **Focus Mode:** Continuous Auto-Focus
- **Auto-Focus Point:** Single auto-focus point
- **Focal Length:** 50mm to 150mm (35mm equivalent; see "Understanding focal lengths" in the appendix)
- **Image Stabilization:** On

Cats have minds of their own. They spend a large amount of their day sleeping, then they move to their favorite patch of sun for another nap, and then they look out the window for long periods of time contemplating the winged creatures outside.

What cats consider play is different than what dogs consider play. Most cats don't fetch, and they refuse to use the toys you buy them. For cats, an untended trashcan filled with crumpled Post-It notes is a treasure trove of toys. And sometimes cats play with other cats, totally ignoring their toys.

Setting the Camera

When you photograph your cat at play, you want to freeze action by using the Shutter Priority Shooting mode and a shutter speed of 1/125 of a second. The suggested ISO range lets you photograph your pet either in bright light or in shadow. If you dial in the shutter speed and the largest aperture (the smallest f/stop number) for the lens blinks when you press the shutter button halfway, you can't properly expose the image unless you select a higher ISO. If you're photographing in a room that's not well lit, you may have to increase your ISO setting to 800. Continuous Drive mode lets you capture a sequence of images for as long as you have the shutter button pressed, and Continuous Auto-Focus mode enables the camera to update focus while your pet moves. The suggested focal-length range lets you capture a picture of your pet and his surroundings, or zoom in for a tight shot of your pet pouncing on a bag of catnip.

Taking the Picture

If the cat you're photographing owns you — cats don't have owners, they adopt their humans — you need someone to engage the cat in play. You also need a lot of patience because your cat probably doesn't want to play when you want her to.

1. **Grab your cat's favorite toy and have your assistant start playing with the furry critter.**

   Don't rely on store-bought toys. Most cats refuse to touch them. However, you can dangle a piece of ribbon tied to the end of a stick in front of your cat to keep him amused for hours. Catnip works, too.

2. **Enable the camera settings discussed in the section "Camera Settings," earlier in this chapter.**

3. **Crouch down to the cat's level.**

   Your pictures look more natural if the cat is at eye level with the camera (see Figure 13-1).

4. **Find an interesting vantage point and zoom in.**

   Leave a little room around the cat in the frame. If you zoom in too tight and your cat moves, you end up with a picture of a cat minus a paw or tail.

5. **When your cat starts doing something interesting, press the shutter button halfway to achieve focus.**

   The camera updates focus while your cat moves.

6. **Press the shutter button fully.**

   The camera captures images as long as you keep the shutter button fully depressed.

7. **Release the shutter button when you're done taking the sequence of pictures.**

   You have a sequence of images that show your pet playing with his favorite toy.

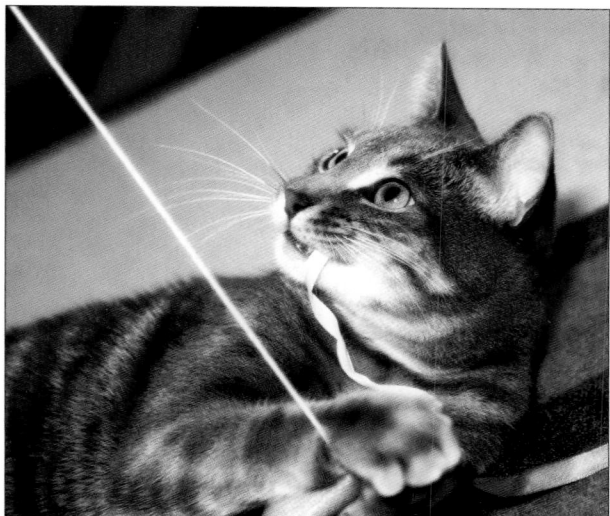

Photo courtesy of Roxanne Evans, www.dougplusrox.com

Figure 13-1: Photograph the cat at her level.

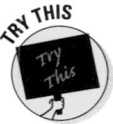

If you want to photograph young kittens who have claws, have someone dangle a string above your bedspread or above a piece of fabric draped over a table. Move to a position where you can capture a picture of them climbing the fabric to capture the alien string (see Figure 13-2).

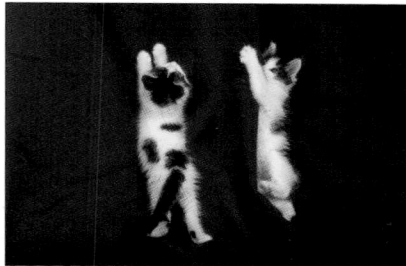

Corbis Digital Stock

Figure 13-2: Capture a picture of kittens climbing.

Troubleshooting

✓ **The entire cat isn't in focus.** This problem happens when you're shooting in dim conditions. Bump up the ISO until you have an aperture setting of f/7.1, which should keep the entire cat in focus. However, you may want to try a couple of shots in which the cat's head and paws are in focus and the rest of her body is out of focus. This is known as *selective focus*, which draws attention to a specific area of the image. In this case, it draws attention to the interaction between the cat and her toy.

✓ **The cat is blurred.** If your cat is running quickly when you take the picture, you may not be able to freeze the motion by using a shutter speed of 1/125 of a second. Try using the panning technique in Chapter 6, but use a shutter speed of about 1/30 of a second.

✓ **The cat is moving slowly.** If you have an older cat who doesn't play at warp speed, you can select a slower shutter speed of 1/60 of a second and still freeze the action.

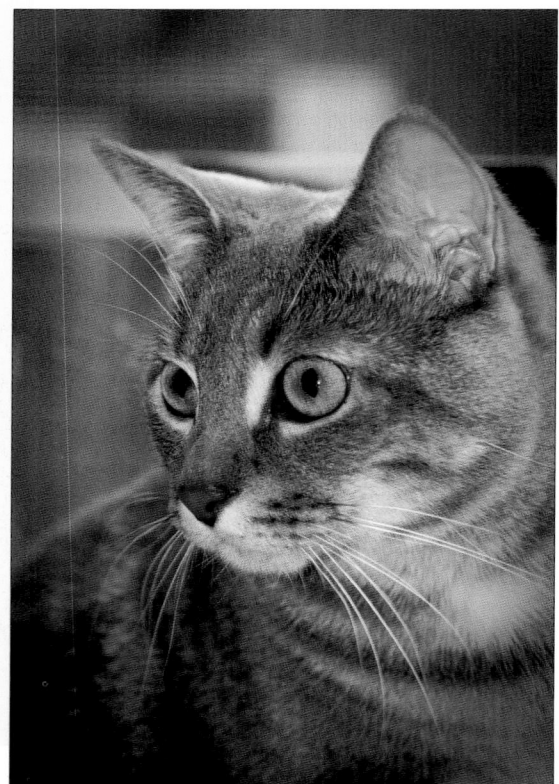

Photo courtesy of Roxanne Evans, www.dougplusrox.com.

14 Cat Portrait

Cats have three modes: the Zen Contemplative mode, Playful and Seriously Looped on Catnip mode, and Sound Asleep mode. To get a good cat portrait, you have to catch your pet in the Zen Contemplative mode.

Who knows what they're contemplating: maybe the next good hit of catnip or perhaps when a squirrel will wander in front of the window. This chapter shows you the settings to use when you want great portraits of your cat.

Camera Settings

- **Metering Mode:** Evaluative
- **Drive Mode:** Single Shot
- **Shooting Mode:** Aperture Priority
- **Aperture:** f/3.5 or a smaller f/stop number
- **ISO Setting:** The lowest ISO setting that enables you to achieve a shutter speed of 1/125 of a second or faster
- **Focus Mode:** Single Shot
- **Auto-Focus Point:** Single auto-focus point.
- **Focal Length:** 80mm to 100mm (35mm equivalent; see "Understanding focal lengths" in the appendix)
- **Image Stabilization** Optional

Setting the Camera

When you shoot an image in Aperture Priority mode with a large aperture (a small f/stop number), the background is a pleasant out-of-focus blur, which draws the viewer's attention to your lovely feline. A medium telephoto focal length lets you get close to your furry friend without spooking him and does a wonderful job of modeling his features. Shooting with the lowest possible ISO setting ensures a sharp image that contains minimal digital noise. Your cat may try to make friends with your lens, which is why a telephoto is handy — it puts a bit of distance between you and your subject. Use image stabilization if you're photographing your cat in low-light conditions and don't want to increase the ISO setting. If your cat's very active, you need a relatively fast shutter speed to freeze her motion.

Taking the Picture

The best way to take a picture of your cat is to know her routine. Cats are creatures of habit and do the same things at the same times of the day. Have your camera ready when your cat gets ready to meditate on the bird feeder in your yard. If something diverts the cat's attention, he'll move in a New York minute. You have to be quick when you're photographing a cat. Get your camera ready, and then follow these steps:

1. **When your cat strikes an interesting pose, position the auto-focus point over her eye and press the shutter button halfway to achieve focus.**

2. **Zoom in and compose the picture.**

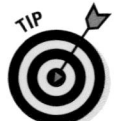

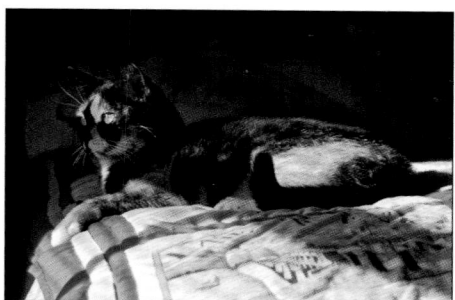

   Make sure your cat's eyes are a focal point in the image (see Figure 14-1). The eyes are the windows to the soul, and that saying also applies to your favorite feline.

   Don't compose the picture with your cat in the center of the frame. You create a more interesting shot if one of the cat's eyes is aligned on a power point, according to the Rule of Thirds.

Figure 14-1: The eyes are the windows to your cat's soul.

3. **Take the picture.**

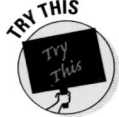

Photograph your cat several feet from a plain backdrop by using an 85mm focal length and your largest aperture (smallest f/stop number). If you use a fast lens that has a maximum aperture of f/2.8 or larger, you can capture a wonderful portrait of your cat with nothing to distract the viewer's eye (see Figure 14-2).

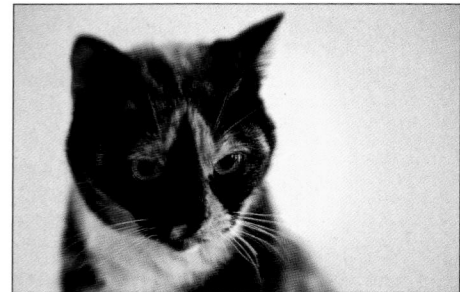

Photo courtesy of Roxanne Evans, www.dougplusrox.com.

Figure 14-2: Capture candid shots of your cat.

Troubleshooting

- **My cat gets too close to the camera.** Have a family member call your cat by name and take the picture when the cat moves away from you.

- **My cat moves too much.** Your cat may be ready for play. Refer to Chapter 13 and take some pictures of your cat playing. After your cat tires of playing, you can resume portrait photography.

- **The picture doesn't seem clear.** Make sure you focus on the cat's eye that's nearest the camera. When you take portraits of people or cats by using a large aperture, you have a very shallow depth of field. As long as the eye nearest the camera is in sharp focus, the animal appears to be in focus, and the background is a pleasant blur.

- **My cat is dark in the picture.** If your cat is backlit by strong window light, use exposure compensation to increase the exposure by 1 stop or more. You can use an auxiliary flash unit as fill flash, which helps fill in the shadows. Don't use auxiliary flash and exposure compensation at the same time. Using both simultaneously washes out the details in the image.

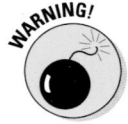

If you aim a flash directly at your cat, bright light may scare him and make him become wary of the camera. Direct flash also creates a photo that has the feline equivalent of red-eye, which is a ghastly white glow caused by the flash reflecting off the cat's retina. If you need to augment lighting with flash, bounce the flash off the ceiling or use a diffuser.

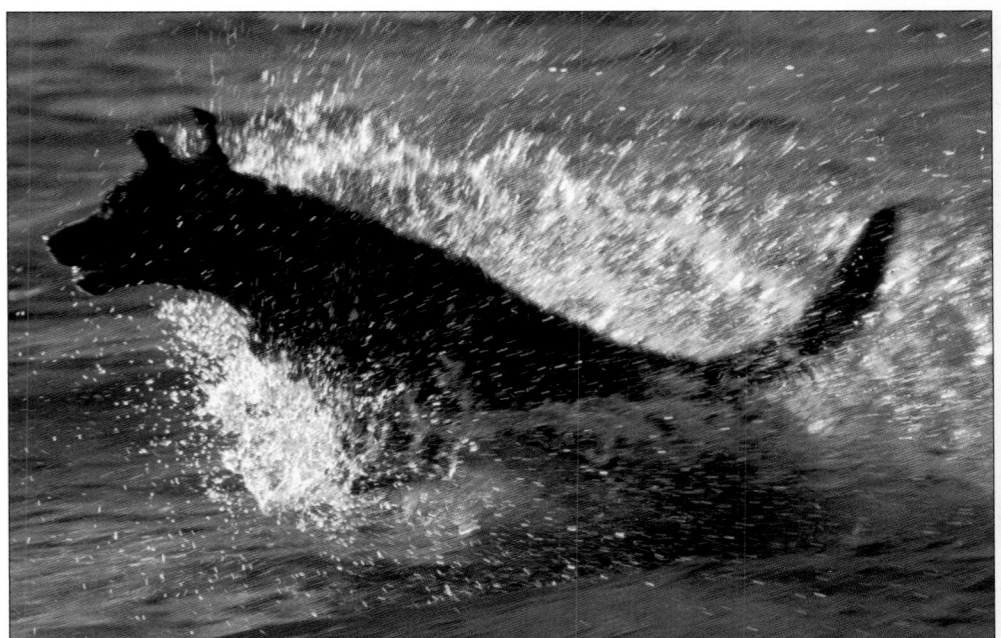

Corbis Digital Stock

Camera Settings

- ✓ **Metering Mode:** Evaluative
- ✓ **Drive Mode:** Continuous
- ✓ **Shooting Mode:** Shutter Priority
- ✓ **Shutter Speed:** 1/250 of a second
- ✓ **ISO Setting:** 100 to 400
- ✓ **Focus Mode:** Continuous Auto-Focus
- ✓ **Auto-Focus Point:** Single auto-focus point
- ✓ **Focal Length:** 50mm to 150mm (35mm equivalent; see "Understanding focal lengths" in the appendix)
- ✓ **Image Stabilization:** On

Dogs just wanna have fun. And that's what they do when their owners give them a chance. Dogs love to play with their toys, improvise with whatever they find, or just plain run 'til they're all tuckered out.

You can capture some wonderful images of your dog romping about, whether it's in your yard or by the ocean. To capture these kinds of images, you just need a playful pup and the settings in this chapter.

Setting the Camera

When you photograph your dog playing, you want to freeze the action, so you choose Shutter Priority mode and use a fairly fast shutter speed to shoot this type of image . The suggested ISO range is perfect for either bright, sunny days or cloudy days. If you're photographing your dog on a really dreary day, you have to up the ISO rating. If you're using a fairly modern camera, you may be able to increase the ISO up to 1000 and still have a relatively noise-free image. But heck, even if you do have a bit of noise, you can get a nice photograph of your pet hamming it up. The focal length you use depends on how close you are to your dog while he's playing. Image stabilization can always help you capture a blur-free image when you're photographing moving objects.

Taking the Picture

When you photograph your pet playing, you may want to have a family member or friend engage the dog. If you don't, the dog may think you're the playmate and your camera is something to investigate.

1. **Take your dog to a place where she likes to play.**

   A location with natural background such trees, a nicely landscaped yard, or the beach can give you a great-looking photo.

2. **Start playing with your pet or exercising her.**

   You can make this process a lot easier if you have someone along who can play with the dog while you set up the photo.

3. **Crouch down to the dog's level.**

   Your pictures look more natural if you're at the same level as your dog — unless you're photographing your dog jumping into the air to catch a ball or Frisbee that someone has thrown.

4. **When the dog starts playing, zoom in, and then press the shutter button halfway to achieve focus.**

   When your camera is set to Continuous Auto-Focus, the camera updates focus while your pet moves.

5. **When your dog starts doing something interesting, fully press the shutter button.**

   The camera takes pictures as long as you hold your finger on the shutter button.

6. **Release the shutter button when you're done taking the sequence of pictures.**

   If everything goes according to Hoyle, you have a nice sequence of pictures of your pet playing. Continue photographing until you get tired — or your pet does.

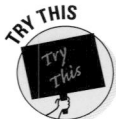

TRY THIS

Switch to a slow shutter speed of about 1/15 of a second. Pan the camera with the dog (see Chapter 6) to capture a picture that shows the frenetic motion of the dog's legs while he plays (see Figure 15-1).

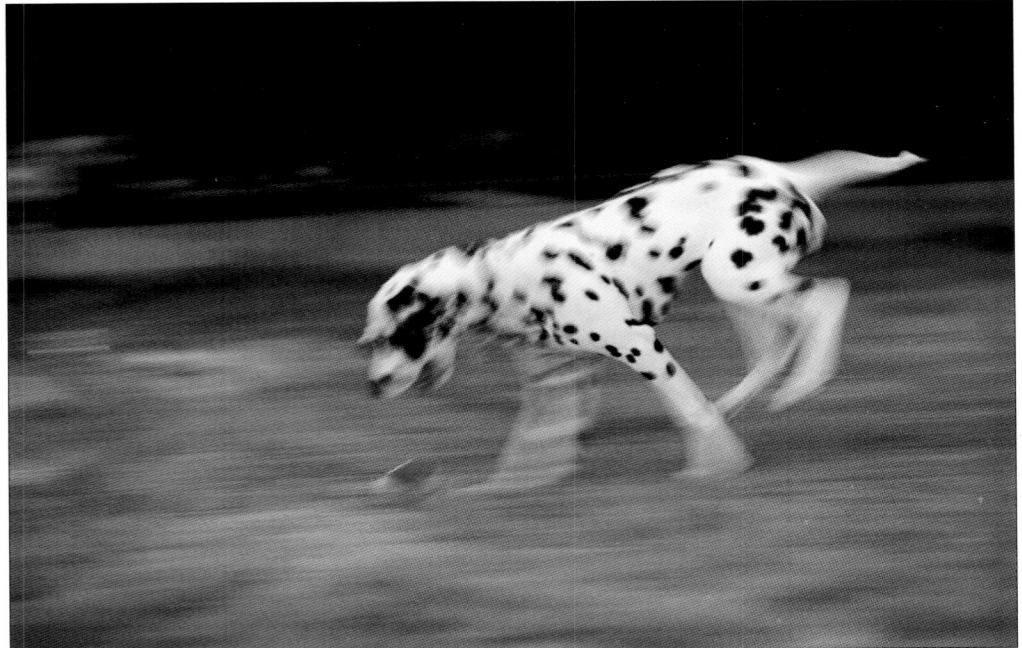

Corbis Digital Stock

Figure 15-1: Use a slow shutter speed to accentuate the feeling of motion.

Troubleshooting

- **The dog isn't completely in focus.** This problem can occur if you're photographing on a really dreary day. When you shoot in Shutter Priority mode, the camera chooses the aperture for a properly exposed image. On a dark day, the aperture may be large (small f/stop number), which means you get a very shallow depth of field, especially if you've zoomed to a focal length of 100mm or longer. Bump the ISO setting until you get an f/stop of f/7.1 or smaller.

- **Part of the dog is out of the picture.** This issue occurs when you're zoomed in tight and the dog moves closer to you. Always leave a bit of a fudge factor when you compose the picture. Also, when composing the picture, leave more room in front of the dog than behind her so that the photo gives viewers the idea that the dog is definitely going somewhere.

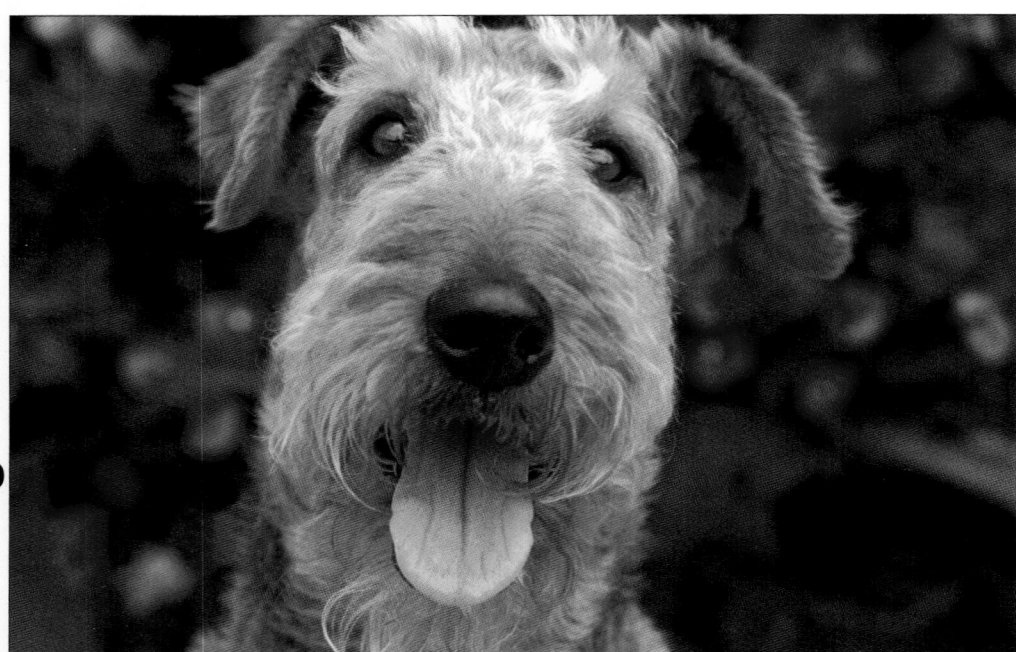

Corbis Digital Stock

*D*ogs have unique personalities and are wonderful subjects for portraits. When they look at you, they seem to be smiling.

If the dog you're photographing is trained, you or the dog's owner can get the dog in just the right position and possibly even get the dog to pose for his portrait. However, if you're photographing a playful pup, you may have your hands full. Instead of posing for you, the dog may run up to your camera to investigate with tail wagging, and then try to clean your lens with her tongue.

The settings in this chapter give you what you need to capture a nice photo of your dog. You or the dog's owner just need to keep the pet in check while you take pictures.

Camera Settings

- **Metering Mode:** Evaluative
- **Drive Mode:** Single Shot
- **Shooting Mode:** Aperture Priority
- **Aperture:** f/3.5 or a smaller f/stop number
- **ISO Setting:** 100 to 400
- **Focus Mode:** Single Shot
- **Auto-Focus Point:** Single auto-focus point
- **Focal Length:** 80mm to 100mm (35mm equivalent; see "Understanding focal lengths" in the appendix)
- **Image Stabilization:** On

Setting the Camera

When you capture a portrait of your dog, you want the pet to be the center of attention, which requires you to control the depth of field. Therefore, you take the picture in Aperture Priority mode and use the recommended f/stop to get a shallow depth of field. When you use a single auto-focus point, you can get your pet's eyes in sharp focus. The suggested ISO setting enables you to capture the portrait in bright light or cloudy conditions. If you're shooting the picture in very dim lighting, increase the ISO setting. The focal length of 80mm to 100mm gives you a natural-looking portrait of your pet. You may find image stabilization useful (if your camera or lens comes equipped with this feature) because image stabilization offsets any operator movement to ensure a blur-free image.

Taking the Picture

If you're photographing your pet outdoors, photograph him early in the morning or late in the afternoon, when you have golden light that doesn't cast harsh shadows. Overcast conditions are also great for photographing dogs because you get soft diffuse light that casts no shadows. Also, consider grooming the pet prior to the photo shoot.

1. **Find a suitable location to photograph the dog.**

   Find a location that has a plain background that contrasts well with the dog's colors. If you're photographing a pet that has dark fur, choose a light background. If you're photographing a pet that has light-colored hair, choose a dark background.

2. **Ask the pet to sit.**

   If you're not the dog's owner, make sure the owner is present when you take the pictures and ask her to get her pet to sit. You may have to bribe the dog with a treat.

3. **Get down to eye level with the dog.**

   You can get your most natural pictures if you get down to the dog's level. If you're photographing a short dog such as a Dachshund, put the dog on a table.

4. **Zoom in on the pet, position the auto-focus point over the pet's eye that's nearest the camera, and press the shutter button halfway to achieve focus.**

5. Compose the picture.

You get a better shot if the pet isn't symmetrical in the center of the frame. Have someone stand over one or your shoulders and call the pet's name. Another good pose is a three-quarter view of the pet. Tell the pet to stay and then call her name.

6. Take the picture.

Don't stop with just one picture. If the pet you're photographing is a ham, you can get a lot of wonderful photos. Eventually, the dog tires of being the subject of a pet paparazzo and goes somewhere for a rest. Follow the pet to get the opportunity to capture a wonderful candid photo (see Figure 16-1).

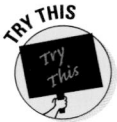

Photograph your dog when he's exploring his domain. Keep your camera ready, and call him when he's near an interesting place in your yard. Take several pictures when the dog turns his attention to you (see Figure 16-2).

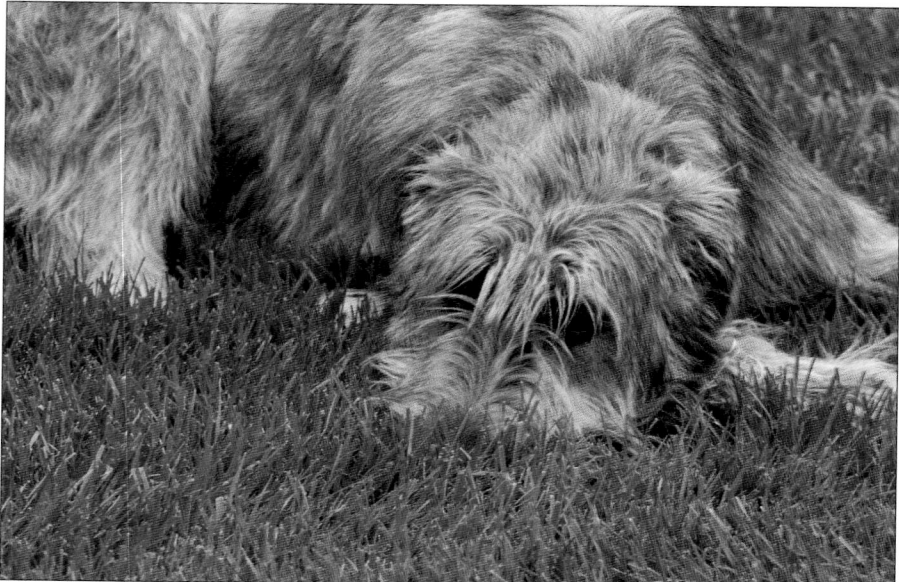

Figure 16-1: Capture a photo of your pet resting.

Troubleshooting

✔ **My dog gets too close to the camera.** Have a family member or friend lead the dog to an ideal position for your portrait, and then command the dog to sit. Ask the assistant to hold the dog while you set up the picture. Compose the picture, and then have the other person release the dog and move away. Call the dog's name and take the picture immediately.

✔ **The picture doesn't seem clear.** Make sure you focus on the eye that's nearest the camera. When you take pictures in Aperture Priority mode and use a large aperture, you have a very shallow depth of field. As long as the eye nearest the camera is in sharp focus, the entire pet appears to be in focus, and the background is a pleasant out-of-focus blur.

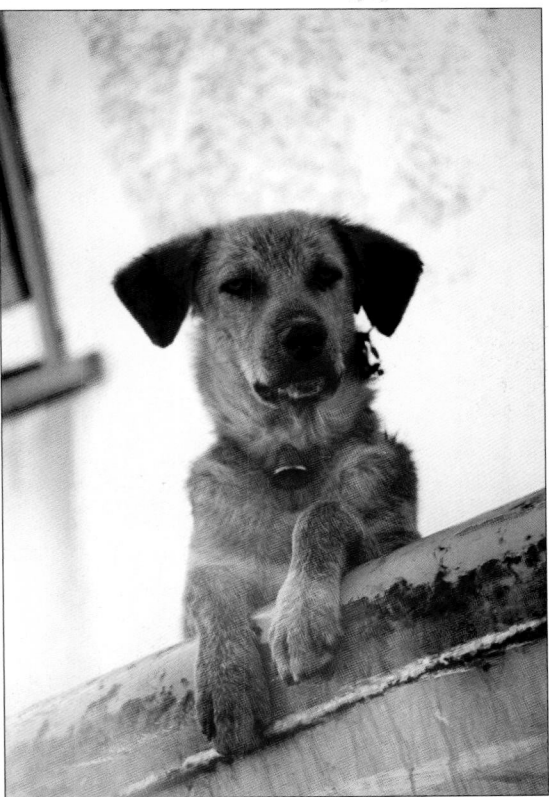

Corbis Digital Stock

Figure 16-2: Capture a candid picture of your dog.

✔ **I'm photographing a large dog and part of him is out of focus:** When you photograph a large dog, you need a slightly larger depth of field. Choose a smaller aperture with an f/stop of f/6.3 or f/7.1 to get the dog in focus from front to back.

✔ **My dog looks dark in the picture.** If your dog is backlit by strong window or sun light, use exposure compensation to increase the exposure by 1 stop or more. You can use an auxiliary flash unit as fill flash, which helps fill in the shadows. Don't use auxiliary flash and exposure compensation at the same time. Using both simultaneously washes out the details in the image. Flash causes the equivalent of red-eye if you don't diffuse the flash (see the appendix).

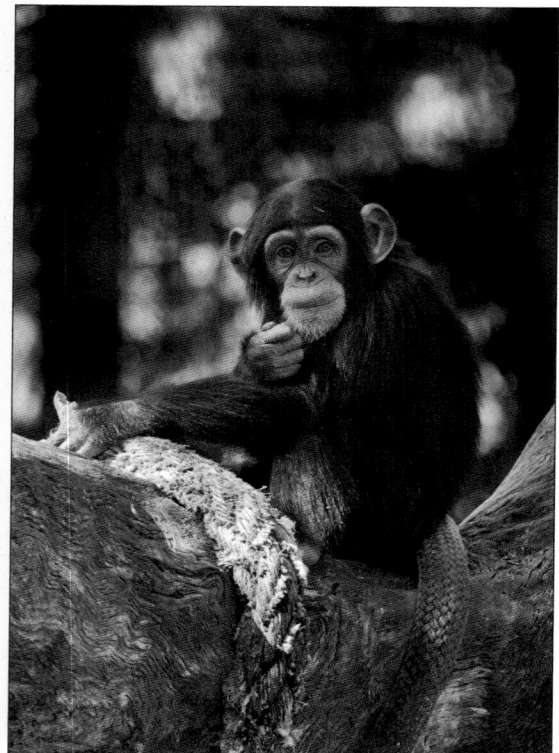

Someone told me it's all happening at the zoo. I do believe it. I do believe it's true. Zoos can be the subject of songs like Simon and Garfunkel's "At the Zoo," a place to visit on a Saturday afternoon, or a great place to photograph animals. With a bit of work and creativity, you can get some great shots of animals at a zoo, photos that look like you took them in the wild. I show you how to get great shots of zoo animals and also of animals at organizations that rescue abused animals, exotic cats, or retired circus animals.

Organizations that rescue exotic animals often provide tours during which you can photograph the animals. One such organization is Big Cat Rescue (`http://www.big`

Camera Settings

- **Metering Mode:** Evaluative
- **Drive Mode:** Continuous
- **Shooting Mode:** Aperture Priority
- **Aperture:** f/4.0 to f/7.1
- **ISO Setting:** 100 to 400
- **Focus Mode:** Continuous Auto-Focus
- **Auto-Focus Point:** Single auto-focus point
- **Focal Length:** 100mm to 200mm (35mm equivalent; see "Understanding focal lengths" in the appendix)
- **Image Stabilization:** On

`catrescue.org`) in Tampa, Florida. I had the pleasure of touring this facility while writing this book. They do a wonderful job of caring for exotic cats such as bobcats, tigers, and lions. They are well fed (500 lb of meat per day each for 120 animals) and cared for. If you have such a facility near where you live, it's a wonderful opportunity to photograph animals you may not see in a zoo. I've given credit to Big Cat Rescue for these photos even though I photographed them. I did this in the hope that you'll visit their Web site to see the wonderful work they are doing. (Find a similar organization near you by searching for **exotic cat rescue** online.)

Setting the Camera

Animals in a zoo are fairly sedentary, which makes Aperture Priority the ideal shooting mode because you don't need to stop action. The suggested aperture range does a nice job of blurring the foreground and the background, which draws the viewer's attention to your subject. If you choose a smaller aperture (a larger f/stop number), more of the background and foreground will be in apparent focus. The ISO setting range works well in direct sunlight, shade, or an overcast day. However, if it's very dark, use a higher ISO setting of 800.

Many zoo animals are fairly close to the spectators, but if you want to photograph an animal that's in a habitat designed to look like his native terrain, you may have to use a long lens to get the animal in the image without a huge amount of the background. Image stabilization is useful if your camera or lens has this feature, because even the slightest operator movement when using a long focal length will yield an image that is not tack sharp.

Taking the Picture

If you're visiting a popular zoo, make your visit on a day when the zoo isn't busy. Also, try to visit the zoo before or after they feed the animals because the animals will be a little more active then in anticipation of their meal. Usually, you can get this information by calling the zoo prior to your visit.

1. **When you find an animal you want to photograph, move around until you find a good vantage point.**

   You can get a photo that looks like it was shot in the wild if you take the picture from a place where there is little or no evidence of manmade objects. Sometimes, finding such a location is difficult. Alternatively, you can look for a place where the manmade objects can be camouflaged by other objects.

2. **Zoom in, and then press the shutter button halfway to achieve focus.**

   If you're close to the animal, position the auto-focus point over the eye that's closest to the camera.

3. **Compose the picture.**

   Use the objects around the animal to draw your viewer's attention to your subject. If possible, photograph the animal from below or at the animal's eye level. You can also zoom in tight to minimize evidence of any objects in the background (see Figure 17-1).

4. **Take the picture.**

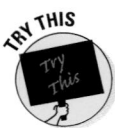

After you take a few pictures of an animal, hang around for a minute or two. You never know when the animal will do something amusing (as shown in Figure 17-2). Patience is worth developing for any photographer.

Troubleshooting

- **There's a reflection in my picture.** This situation happens when you photograph an animal through glass. Put your camera right up to the glass, and then take the picture.

- **The camera won't focus through the glass.** Switch to manual focus, focus on your subject, and then take the picture.

- **The lens motor makes noises but doesn't focus.** This problem happens when wire mesh is between you and the animal. In most instances, the camera has a hard time achieving focus on anything behind the wire. If the camera does achieve focus on the wire, your subject will be out of focus. When the camera hunts for focus, the only solution is to switch to manual focus, focus on your subject, and then take the picture.

- **I can see wires from the fence in my picture.** This problem happens when you photograph animals through a wire enclosure. The solution is to get as close to the wires as possible and zoom in. Switch to your largest aperture and then manually focus on the animal. The wires will melt into the animal and almost disappear. Figure 17-1 was photographed with a 200mm focal length at f/4.0. You can barely see a trace of the wires, and your attention is riveted toward the beautiful tiger.

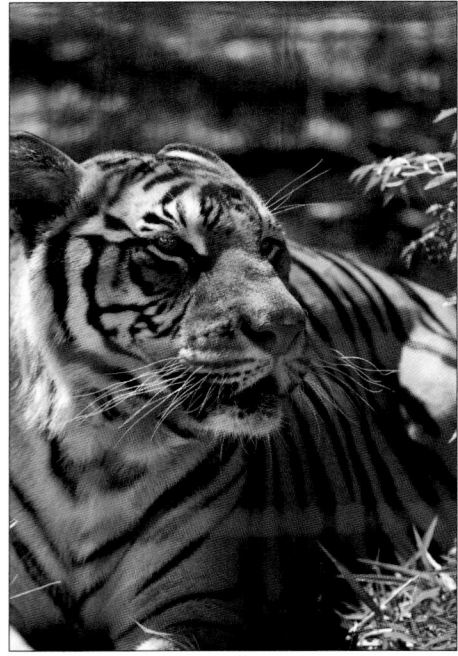

Big Cat Rescue www.bigcatrescue.org

Figure 17-1: Zoom in tight to crop out as much of the background as possible.

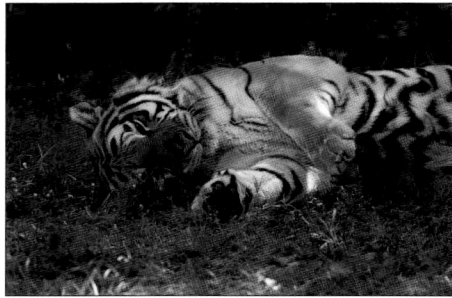

Big Cat Rescue www.bigcatrescue.org

Figure 17-2: Take a photo of the animal doing something interesting or amusing.

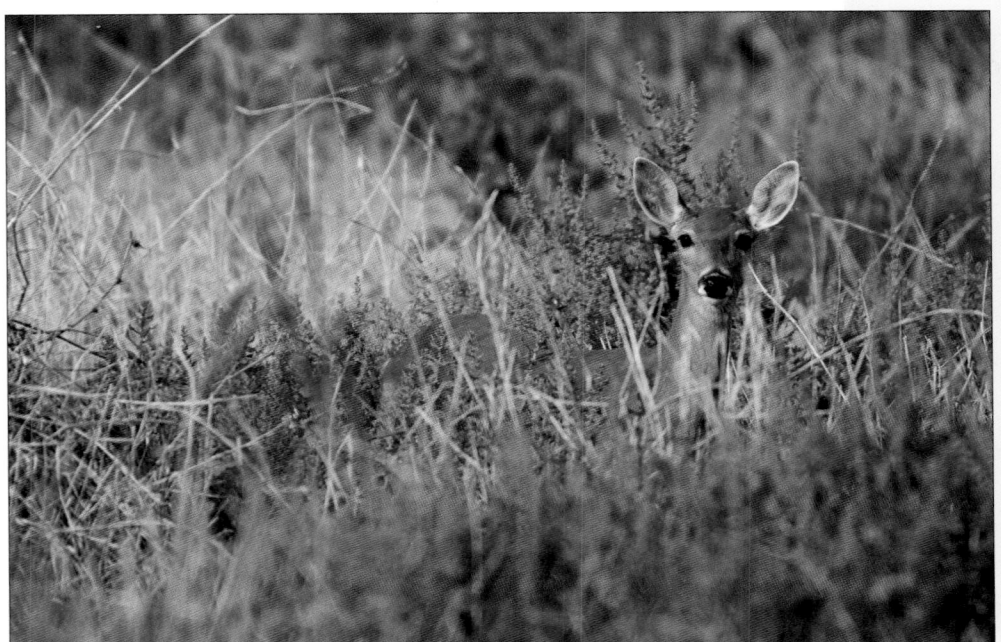

Camera Settings

- **Metering Mode:** Evaluative
- **Drive Mode:** Continuous
- **Shooting Mode:** Aperture Priority
- **Aperture:** f/3.5 (which gives you a shallow depth of field)
- **ISO Setting:** The lowest ISO setting for available light conditions that gives you a shutter speed fast enough that you can hand-hold the camera with the focal length you're using
- **Focus Mode:** Continuous Auto-Focus
- **Auto-Focus Point:** Single auto-focus point
- **Focal Length:** A long focal length so that you can take the photograph from a safe distance without endangering the animal or yourself. (See "Understanding focal lengths" in the appendix.)
- **Image Stabilization:** Optional

*I*f you live near a state park or wilderness area, you can capture some wonderful photographs of animals such as deer, raccoons, and otters in their natural surroundings. You can easily spook these kinds of wild animals because they're relatively low in the food chain. They have a natural fear of people, which means you have to be somewhat stealthy to photograph them; patience is a virtue. If you're patient and don't do anything startling, you can capture great images of animals such as the one shown here.

If you live near a state park, go there often to find out in which areas of the park you're likely to find your subjects and to get to know the habits of those animals — including their feeding habits. After you know the habits of the animals you want to photograph, get familiar with the lay of the land, and use the settings I recommend, you can capture some wonderful wildlife images.

Setting the Camera

The goal of this type of photography is to capture a photograph of an animal in the wild. You use Aperture Priority mode for this type of photography to control depth of field. The animal is the subject of your picture, therefore you use a large aperture to create a shallow depth of field and draw your viewer's attention to your subject. Continuous Auto-Focus mode enables the camera to update focus while the animal moves. You also use Continuous Drive mode to capture a sequence of images of the animal as it moves through the area. The focal length you use depends on how close you can safely approach the animal. Use image stabilization if you have to shoot at a slow shutter speed.

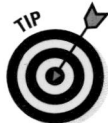

The slowest shutter speed you should use when handholding your camera is the reciprocal of the 35mm-equivalent focal length. For example, if your camera has a 1.6 focal length multiplier and you're using a 50mm lens, the slowest shutter speed you should use when holding the camera by hand is 1/100 of a second ($1 \div 50 \times 1.6$).

Taking the Picture

When you're taking pictures of animals in their natural habitat, you have to stay out of the open so that you don't frighten the animal. I also recommend wearing clothing that helps you blend in with the surroundings.

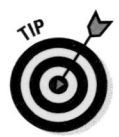

1. **Go to a place where you've previously sighted the species you want to photograph, hide behind some natural cover, and wait.**

   Photograph during the early morning or late afternoon when the light is better and animals are out foraging for food.

2. **Switch to the camera settings discussed earlier in this chapter.**

3. **When you see an animal, zoom in until the animal fills the frame, and then zoom out slightly.**

4. **Position the auto-focus point over the animal's eye, press the shutter button halfway to achieve focus, move the camera to compose the picture, and then press the shutter button fully to take the picture.**

   When you use Continuous Drive mode, the camera continues to capture images as long as you have your finger on the shutter button.

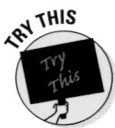

Zoom in tight on the animal to capture an intimate portrait and compose the image according to the Rule of Thirds. This kind of photo is as close as you'll get to shooting a portrait of a wild animal (see Figure 18-1). See the appendix for more about the Rule of Thirds.

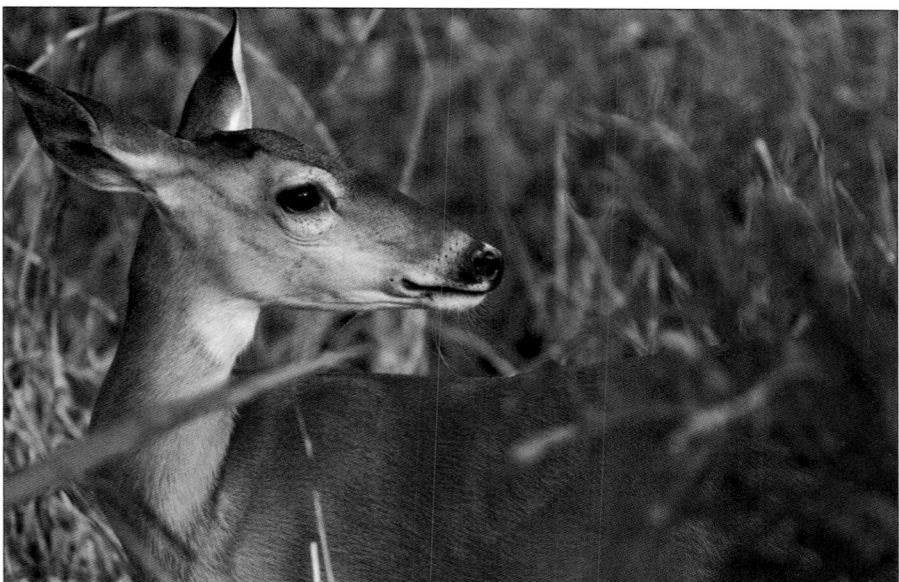

Figure 18-1: Zoom in close for an intimate animal portrait.

Troubleshooting

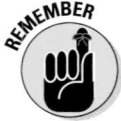

✓ **The image isn't sharp.** Make sure you're shooting at an ISO that's high enough to enable a relatively fast shutter speed, and use image stabilization if your lens or camera has this feature. If you don't have the image stabilization feature, mount your camera on a tripod or monopod.

Don't use image stabilization if the camera is mounted on a tripod because you may get undesirable results as the camera or lens attempts to compensate for operator motion when in fact the camera is rock steady.

✓ **The animal blends into the background.** The coloration of some animals causes those animals to blend into the background. Try shooting from a different angle. You can also use the largest aperture to blur the background as much as possible. If you use a large aperture, make sure you get the animal's eyes in focus. If you don't, the entire picture appears to be out of focus.

✓ **The animal disappears before I take the picture.** Make sure you're well hidden and not upwind from the animal.

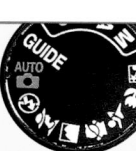

1n many parts of the world, you can photograph exotic and dangerous animals in their natural habitat. The resulting photos are much more rewarding than taking a picture of an animal in a cage.

However, you must be extremely careful when photographing any animal in its natural habitat. The goal of this type of photography is to take a photograph of the animal without endangering yourself or confronting the animal.

Animals have a natural fear of humans, but in many locations, such as national parks, they've become accustomed to people and are bolder than usual. As long as you're careful and use these settings, you can get some incredible pictures of potentially dangerous animals in their natural habitats.

Camera Settings

- **Metering Mode:** Evaluative
- **Drive Mode:** Single Shot or Continuous
- **Shooting Mode:** Aperture Priority
- **Aperture:** f/3.5
- **ISO Setting:** The lowest ISO that yields a blur-free image when hand holding the camera
- **Focus Mode:** Continuous Auto-Focus
- **Auto-Focus Point:** Single
- **Focal Length:** The longest available focal length so that you can distance yourself from the animal (See "Understanding focal lengths" in the appendix.)
- **Image Stabilization:** On

Setting the Camera

You want to create an image that draws your viewer's attention to the animal, so you use Aperture Priority mode and a large aperture to ensure a shallow depth of field. If you're photographing a large animal, such as a bear, you may have to use a slightly smaller aperture (a larger f/stop number) to ensure the entire animal is in focus. You also have to pick and choose your angle with care so that you have a natural and pleasing background. Set your camera to Continuous Auto-Focus mode so that the camera updates focus while the animal moves through the frame. You can photograph the animal using Single Shot Drive mode, or hedge your bet by using Continuous Drive mode to capture a sequence of images of the animal. Safety is paramount when photographing dangerous animal. Use the longest focal length you own so you can photograph the animal from a safe distance and make sure you're not upwind from the animal.

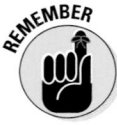

Here are a few more pointers to keep in mind:

- If you're using a long telephoto or telephoto zoom lens, you may not have the option to choose an aperture as large as f/3.5. If this is the case, choose the largest aperture (smallest f/stop number) that's available for the focal length at which you're shooting.

- If you're photographing in bright conditions, you may not be able to achieve a large aperture, even with your lowest ISO setting. If you take pictures in these conditions on a regular basis, consider investing in a neutral density filter, which lowers the amount of light entering the camera, thereby enabling you to shoot with a larger aperture.

- The slowest shutter speed at which you can hand-hold the camera is the reciprocal of the 35mm equivalent of the focal length you're using to shoot the picture. For example, if you're using a lens that is the 35mm equivalent of 80mm, the slowest shutter speed at which you can hand-hold the camera is 1/100 of a second.

Taking the Picture

When you're taking pictures of animals in their natural habitat, you have to blend in with the surroundings. If you walk out in the open, you may frighten the animal or, worse yet, provoke it. Wear clothing that blends in with the surroundings.

1. **Go to a place where you've previously sighted the species you want to photograph, and then wait.**

   Patience is a necessary virtue when you want to photograph wildlife. If possible, hide behind some natural cover and make sure you're not upwind from the animal.

Some animals are lethargic in the middle of the day. Go to your favorite place early in the morning or late in the afternoon when the animal you want to photograph is searching for food.

2. **Switch to the camera settings detailed previously in this chapter.**

3. **When an animal appears, zoom in.**

In many state parks, bears have become accustomed to humans and are quite bold. If you visit a park such as Yosemite, don't leave any open food containers in your car or tent. Bears have broken into cars to get a free meal before winter hibernation and caused considerable damage to the vehicle in the process. You can also take pictures of animals when they're feeding (see Figure 19-1). Just make sure you use a focal length that's long enough to keep you out of harm's way. Also, make sure you're under cover and not upwind of the animal.

4. **Position the auto-focus point over the animal's eye that's nearest the camera, press the shutter button halfway to achieve focus, move the camera to compose the picture, and then press the shutter button fully to take the picture.**

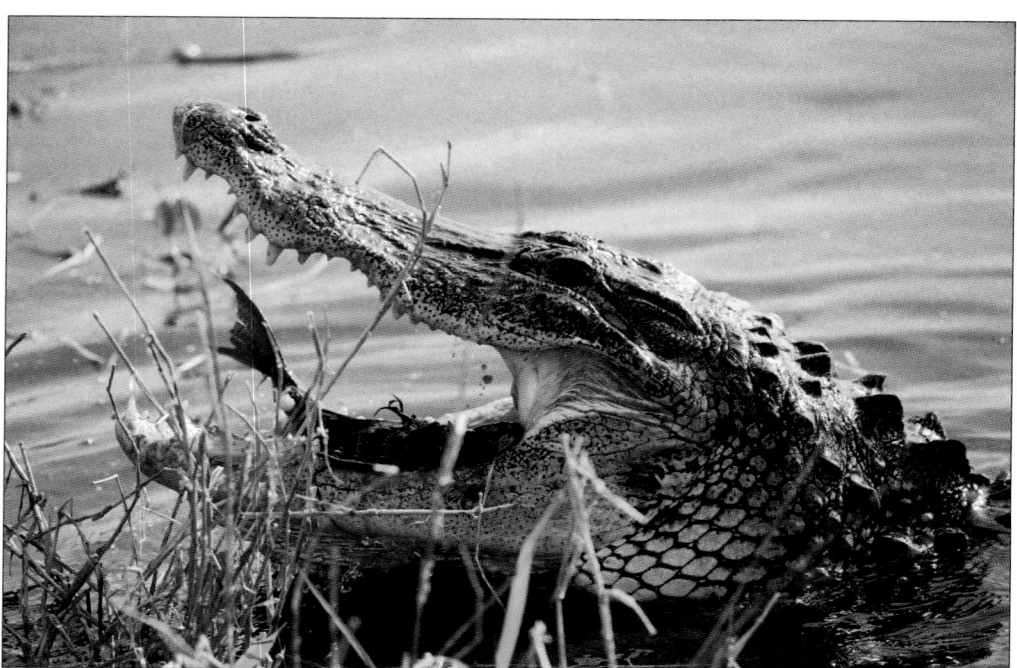

Figure 19-1: Take pictures of animals when they're feeding.

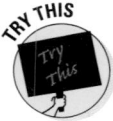

To take pictures of wild animals without endangering yourself, consider visiting a facility such as Big Cat Rescue (www.bigcatrescue.org) in Tampa, Florida, that protects exotic animals such as lions and tigers. You'll get some great shots of wild animals (see Figure 19-2) without putting yourself in harm's way.

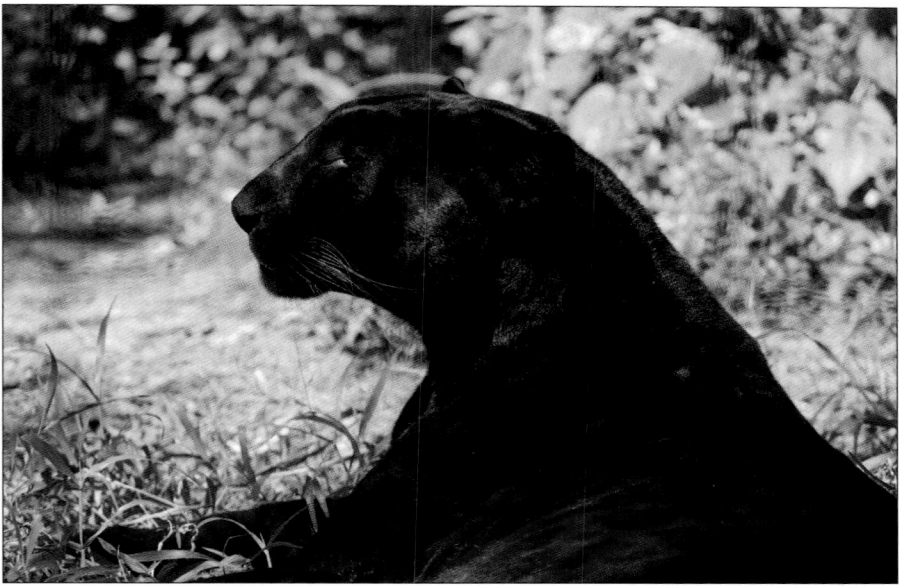

Figure 19-2: Take pictures of wild animals at exotic animal rescue organizations.

Troubleshooting

- **The animal doesn't appear to be in focus.** Make sure you position the single auto-focus point over the animal's eye and press the shutter button halfway until you hear a beep and/or see a green light in your viewfinder. The method used to indicate that focus has been achieved varies depending on the camera. Check your camera manual for details.

- **The animal blends into the background.** The coloration of some animals causes those animals to blend into the background. Try shooting from a different vantage point. You can also use the largest aperture to blur the background as much as possible. If you use a large aperture, make sure you have the animal's eyes in focus. If not, the entire picture appears to be out of focus.

20 Fish in a Public Aquarium

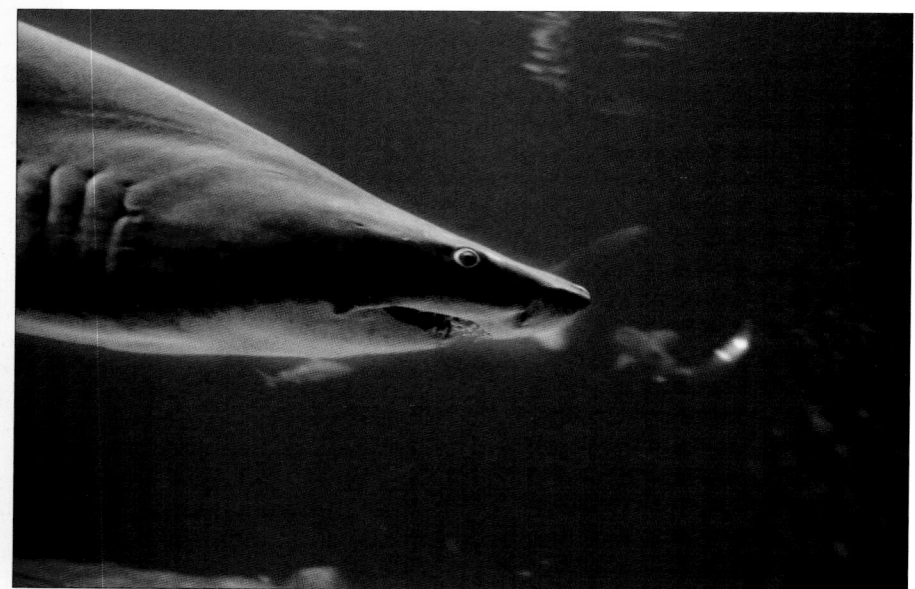

*E*ven seasoned photographers can have difficulty getting great photographs of fish in the ocean, a lake, or a stream. You have to be a scuba diver, and you need a water-proof housing for your digital camera. Of course, you can find disposable one-time-use underwater cameras, but those types of cameras don't deliver the best photographs. Fortunately, you can easily capture photographs of fish such as sharks swimming underwater by taking a trip to your local aquarium.

Like anything else worth doing, photographing fish in an aquarium does have a certain set of rules, and you must use certain settings to get interesting photos. But it's still a heck of a lot easier than jumping in the water with your precious dSLR protected — you hope — by an underwater housing and risking a close encounter with Jaws or one of his close relatives. By using these settings, you can get great shots of fish at your local aquarium.

Camera Settings

- ↩ **Metering Mode:** Evaluative
- ↩ **Drive Mode:** Single Shot
- ↩ **Shooting Mode:** Shutter Priority
- ↩ **Shutter Speed:** 1/125 of a second or faster
- ↩ **ISO Setting:** 100 or the lowest ISO that gives you an aperture of f/5.6 or larger (a low f/stop number)
- ↩ **Focus Mode:** Continuous Auto-Focus
- ↩ **Auto-Focus Point:** Single auto-focus point
- ↩ **Focal Length:** Depends on how close you can get to the fish, the size of the fish, and whether you're taking a picture of the fish from snout to tailfin or want a toothy-head-and-gill-plates portrait of a smiling barra-cuda or shark
- ↩ **Image Stabilization:** Useful, but not neces-sary with the suggested shutter speed

Setting the Camera

Shooting in Shutter Priority mode with a shutter speed of 1/125 of a second or faster freezes the motion of the fish. Choosing an ISO that allows you to shoot with a larger aperture (a smaller f/stop number) blurs out the background and camouflages any traces of mechanical devices, such as pipes or underwater pumps, which makes it look like you actually photographed the fish underwater instead of in an aquarium. Continuous Auto-Focus mode enables the camera to continuously track the fish while it moves through the frame, which means your subject is in focus when you take the picture.

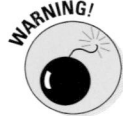

Unless your camera or lens is equipped with image stabilization, make sure you don't use a shutter speed that has a value lower than the reciprocal of the 35mm equivalent of the focal length you're using.

Switch to Continuous Shooting mode to capture a series of photos while the fish swims past your vantage point. When you use this mode, the camera continues taking pictures as long as you keep your finger on the shutter button.

Don't use a focal length less than the 35mm equivalent of 30mm or wider if the fish is swimming close to the glass. If you use a short focal length, the fish looks more like a cartoon character than a fish in your photos. (For more information, see "Understanding focal lengths" in the appendix.)

Taking the Picture

Taking pictures of fish in an aquarium is a lot of fun, but you also need a lot of patience. Visit the aquarium on a slow day so that you don't have to contend with throngs of people. You can also spend a lot of uninterrupted time in front of the tank that contains the fish you want to photograph.

1. **Choose a vantage point where you don't have a lot of distracting elements in the background, especially if you're photographing big fish in a big tank.**

2. **Press the camera lens against the tank.**

   If you don't press the lens against the tank, your photo includes a reflection from the ambient light shining on the glass, which distorts the image.

3. **Zoom in to compose the picture.**

   When you try to zoom in on moving fish, you have to make a best guess. You can zoom in to capture part of the fish or you can zoom to a focal length that can capture the entire fish and a bit of his surroundings (see Figure 20-1).

4. **When the fish you want to photograph comes into view, press the shutter button halfway to achieve focus, and then take the picture.**

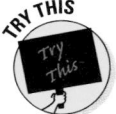

Your local aquarium has a lot of interesting sea life to photograph. Try photographing critters in some of the small tanks, such as sea horses, live coral, or nudibranchs (see Figure 20-2).

Troubleshooting

- **The photo is dark.** Some aquariums are a bit on the dark side. If your camera doesn't meter the scene to your liking, use exposure compensation to increase the exposure until you get a properly exposed image.

- **The fish is blurred.** You may run into this problem if you're photographing small fish that swim very fast. Increase the shutter speed until you freeze the motion of the fish that you're photographing.

- **The fish is out of focus.** Some cameras have this problem when they attempt to focus through thick aquarium glass. Switch to manual exposure and focus on the fish.

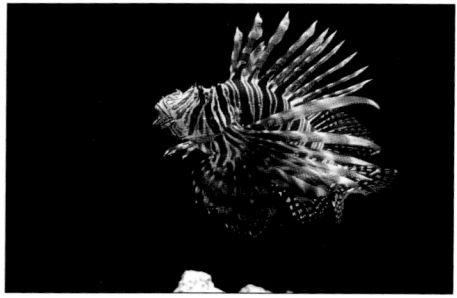

Figure 20-1: Zoom to capture the fish and his environment.

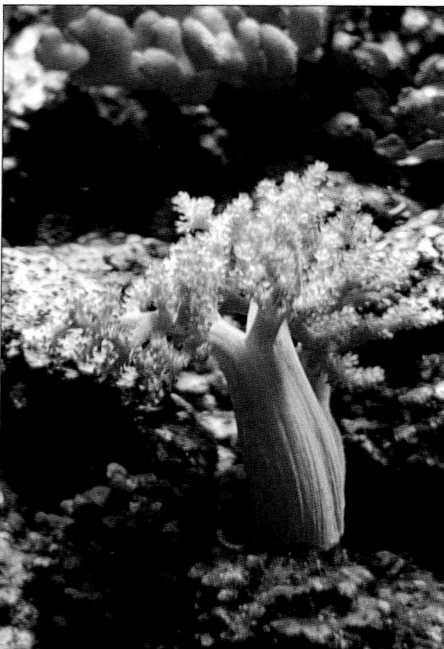

Figure 20-2: Photographing other inhabitants of the aquarium.

Part III
Landscapes and Nature

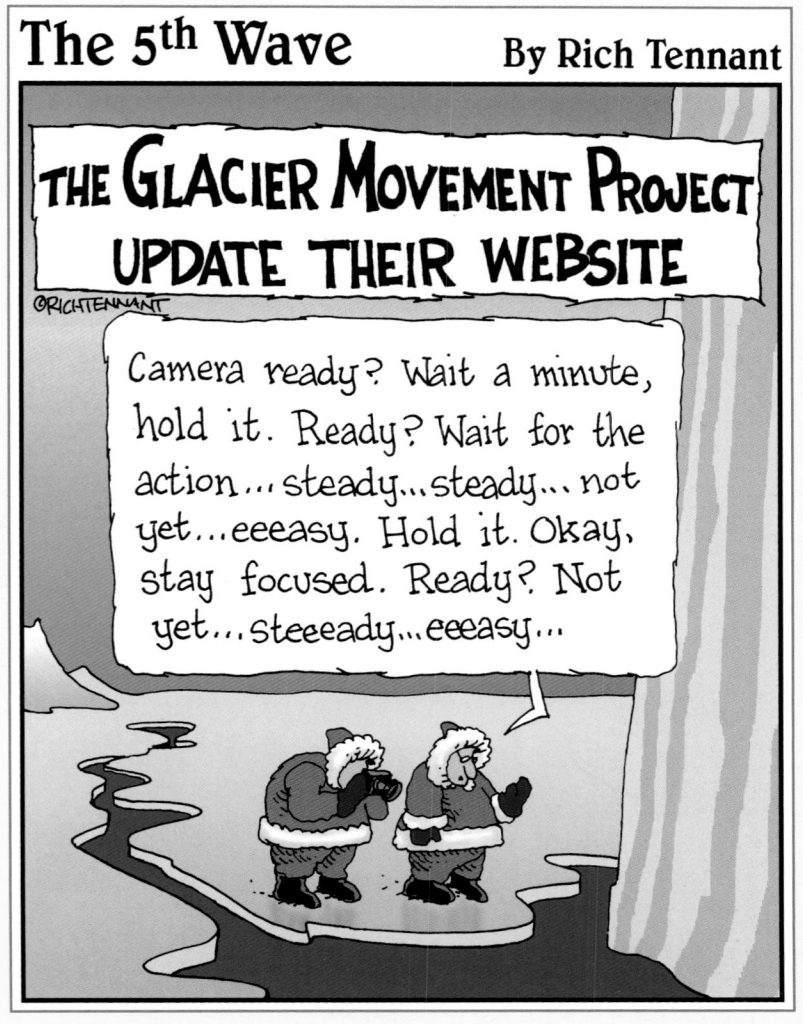

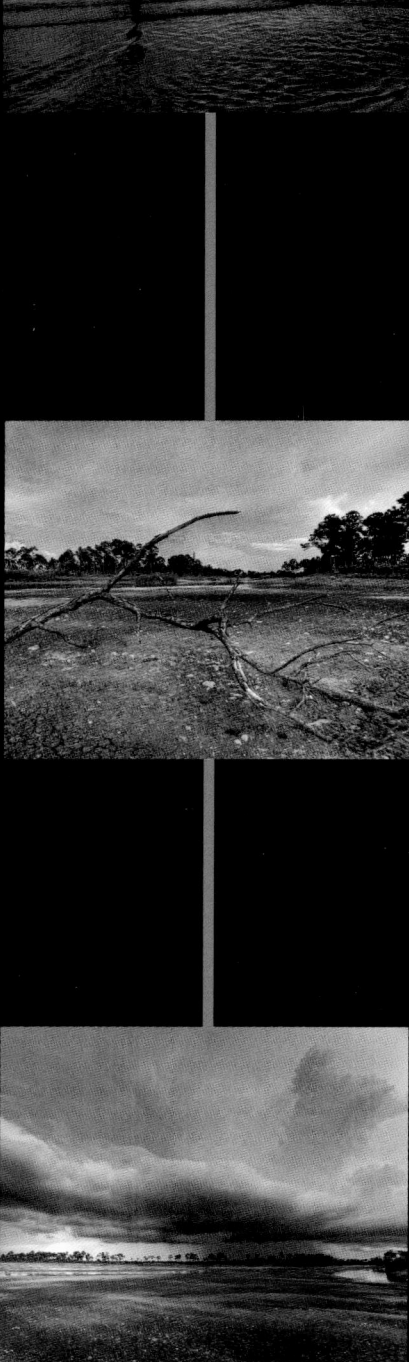

*M*ountains, streams, rivers and lakes, flowers, and other beautiful things you find in nature are excellent subjects for photographers. Beginning photographers rely on the Landscape scene mode to take pictures of nature. In this part, I show you how to break out of that mold and show you which settings and lens to use when photographing landscapes and nature. If you're intrigued by the lovely landscape work of photographers like Ansel Adams, Clyde Butcher, or David Muench, check out the chapters in this part.

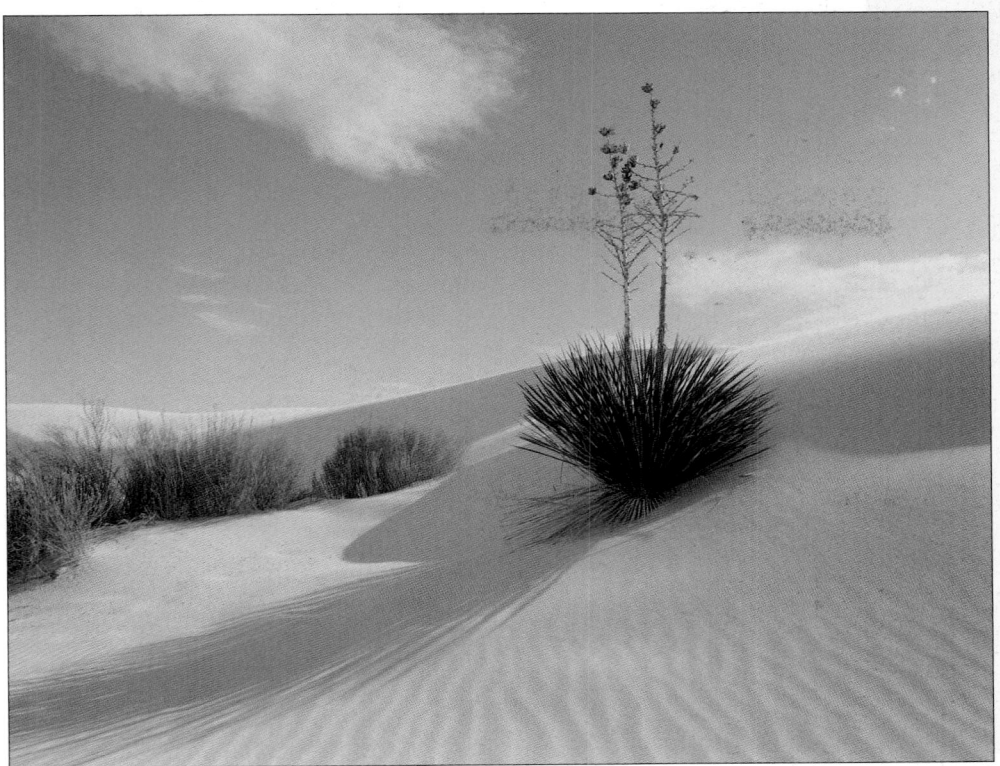

Digital Vision

Camera Settings

- **Metering Mode:** Evaluative
- **Drive Mode:** Single Shot
- **Shooting Mode:** Aperture Priority
- **Aperture:** f/16
- **ISO Setting:** 100 to 400
- **Focus Mode:** Single Shot
- **Auto-Focus Point:** Multiple auto-focus points
- **Focal Length:** 28mm or wider (35mm equivalent; see "Understanding focal lengths" in the appendix)
- **Image Stabilization:** Optional

Deserts are arid landscapes with bleak beauty. The wind sculpts the sand into artistic dunes that are sparsely populated with succulent plants such as cacti. You can also find diverse wildlife that have adapted to the harsh conditions.

For the patient photographer who doesn't mind a bit of heat, the desert can be a wonderful place to take pictures, using the settings in this chapter.

Setting the Camera

When you photograph a beautiful scene such as a desert, you want the largest depth of field possible, so you use Aperture Priority mode and a small aperture (a large f/stop number). Deserts are usually bathed in bright sun, which is why you should use the lowest ISO setting possible. I suggest using multiple auto-focus points because this gives the camera more options for finding areas of contrast upon which to focus. Just make sure the camera doesn't focus on a piece of tumbleweed 10 feet in front of the camera. A desert is a wide expanse of real estate, so always use a wide-angle focal length to capture the vastness of the landscape. You probably don't need to use image stabilization because you have plenty of light and end up with a shutter speed that's fast enough to capture a blur-free image if you hold the camera by hand.

Taking the Picture

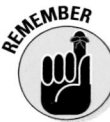

When you traverse desert terrain, you're traveling in hostile territory. First and foremost, make sure you have protection from the sun and an adequate supply of water. Next, protect your camera. Make sure that you've securely fastened your camera strap to your camera, and keep that strap around your neck at all times. Dropping your camera in the desert sand is the last thing you want to do. A couple of grains of sand can wreak havoc with the moving parts of your lens. Never change the lens when photographing in the desert unless you're in a building or closed vehicle. If sand blows in the camera body, your camera will probably need expensive repairs. Other than avoiding sand damage and a possible encounter with a scorpion, taking photographs in the desert is a breeze.

If you've prepared yourself for the heat, brought enough water for a thirsty camel or two, and protected your camera, you can get some interesting photos in the desert by following these steps:

1. **Enable the camera settings discussed earlier in this chapter.**

2. **When you find an interesting scene, move to a suitable vantage point from which to photograph the picture.**

   When you photograph a landscape such as a desert and have nothing but blue skies overhead, position the horizon line in the upper third of the image.

3. **Select the desired focal length, and then compose the scene.**

   Find something interesting to draw your viewer into the picture. Look for patterns in the sand or a large curving dune, which are ideal ways to get your viewer to spend some time with the image.

4. Press the shutter button halfway to achieve focus.

Several auto-focus points should illuminate. If an auto-focus point illuminates on an object that's close to you, release the shutter button, move the camera slightly, and press the shutter button halfway again.

5. Take the picture.

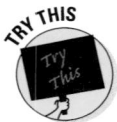

Look for interesting patterns in the sand and find a position that's higher than the patterns you want to photograph. Compose the picture so that the patterns make your viewer spend some time in the image (see Figure 21-1).

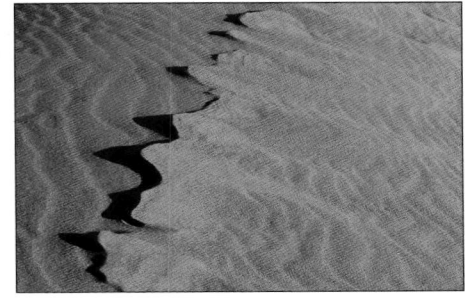

Corbis Digital Stock

Figure 21-1: Look for interesting patterns in the sand.

Troubleshooting

- **The photograph looks harsh.** This problem occurs when you take a picture with the sun directly overhead. Photograph the desert in the early morning or late afternoon. The sun is at a low angle then and produces softer shadows. The low angle of the sun also gives you a wonderful rendition of sand dunes and other elements in the scene. At these hours of the day, the sun also casts a wonderful golden hue.

- **The foreground is busy.** You encounter this problem when objects such as tumbleweed and small plants appear near the camera. Move a few feet until you can no longer see the objects in the viewfinder. You want to see the big view, but you also need to look in the viewfinder to make sure you don't have anything in the frame that would distract your viewer's attention.

- **Objects in the distance are hazy.** The atmosphere can distort distant objects. Placing a UV (ultraviolet) filter on your camera lens absorbs the UV rays, which gets rid of some of the haze in the image. This filter works its magic without affecting the color of the image. Some photographers leave UV filters on their lenses at all times to protect those lenses. After all, a UV filter is a lot cheaper than a new lens.

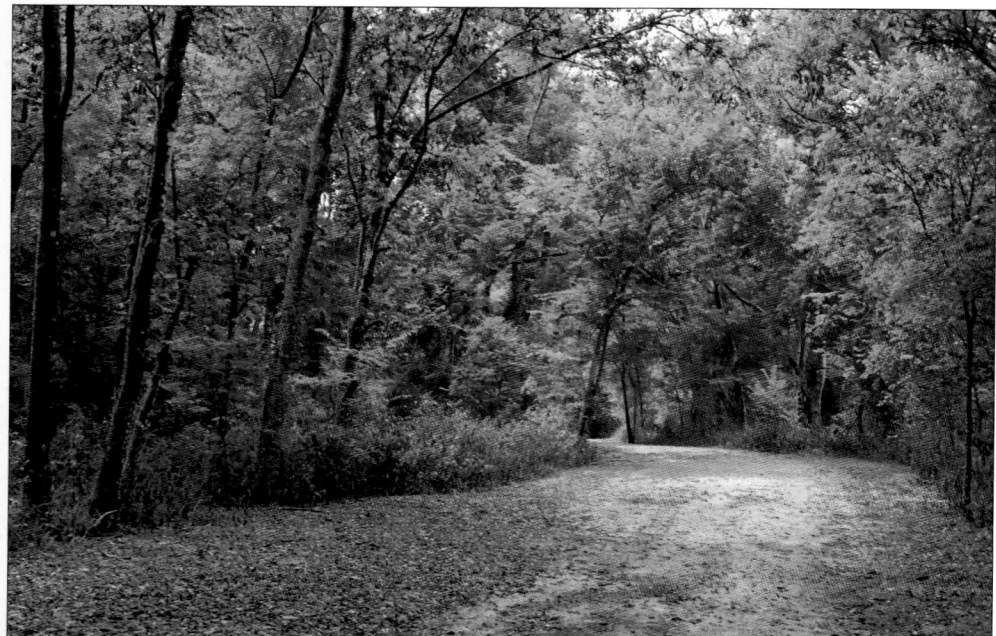

22 Forest

orests are green, and they have a lot of trees. It's one of nature's laws. If you live near a forest or vacation in a forested area, you know that forests provide great locations for you to take long walks while contemplating nature. They're also great places to photograph.

Some people shy away from photographing forests. After all, most people don't find a photo that shows nothing but a bunch of green leaves and sticks very interesting. However, if you have interesting elements to incorporate in your picture, such as the early morning sun shining through the trees or a winding path, you have everything you need for a great forest photo.

Camera Settings

- **Metering Mode:** Evaluative
- **Drive Mode:** Single shot
- **Shooting Mode:** Aperture Priority
- **Aperture:** f/16
- **ISO Setting:** 100 or the lowest setting that gives you a shutter speed of 1/30 of a second or faster
- **Focus Mode:** Single Shot Auto-Focus
- **Auto-Focus Point:** Multiple auto-focus points
- **Focal Length:** 28mm (35mm equivalent; see "Understanding focal lengths" in the appendix)
- **Image Stabilization:** Depends

Setting the Camera

Photographs of forests beg for a large depth of field, which is exactly what you get when you shoot in Aperture Priority mode with a small aperture (a large f/stop number) of f/16. A low ISO setting ensures that you get an image that's sharp and has little or no digital noise. If you're photographing in overcast conditions or dim lighting, you may have to increase the ISO setting in order to use the recommended shutter speed. Alternatively, you can mount your camera on a tripod. Forests don't move, which is why I recommend Single Shot Auto-Focus mode. I also recommend that you use multiple auto-focus points, which gives the camera a chance to scan the entire scene and find objects to focus on, such as tree trunks or branches. When you use a wide-angle focal length as I suggest, you can get the big picture. If your camera or lens is equipped with image stabilization, you can use it if you're photographing a forest in dim lighting conditions but don't want to increase the ISO rating. If you enable image stabilization with a 28mm focal length, you can get a sharp picture at a shutter speed as low as 1/15 of a second.

Some photographers think more is better and use the smallest available aperture, which on many wide-angle lenses is f/22. However, many lenses deliver pictures that are a bit soft at the largest and smallest apertures, which is why I recommend using these apertures only when absolutely necessary.

Taking the Picture

When you're strolling through your favorite forest with camera in hand, stay alert for interesting scenes, such as a path curving through the forest. Look for contrast, as well. Green on green on green doesn't make an interesting photograph. However, with some different colors to add contrast, or rays of sunlight creating an interesting aura, you have the recipe for a photograph that will catch the viewer's eye.

1. **Enable the camera setting discussed earlier in this chapter.**

2. **Compose the scene, and then press the shutter button halfway to achieve focus.**

   Note which auto-focus dots illuminate, as well as the objects over which they're illuminating.

3. **If the camera focuses on a nearby object, release the shutter button and press it again until the camera focuses on the objects that you want in focus.**

If you're photographing a scene that includes tall trees and a narrow path, rotate the camera 90 degrees for a more interesting composition (see Figure 22-1). When you take a picture that's taller that it is wide, you've taken that picture in *Portrait mode*.

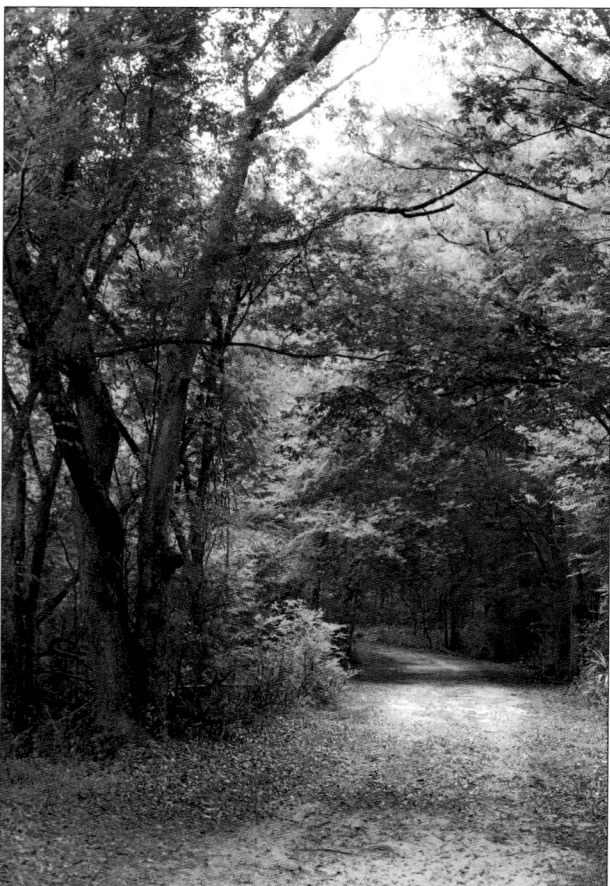

Figure 22-1: Photographing a forest in Portrait mode.

4. Take the picture.

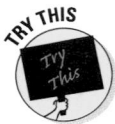

When you're in a forest of tall trees, switch the ISO to your lowest setting, switch to your smallest aperture (largest f/stop number), and then zoom out. Point the camera up to the sky, and then press the shutter button halfway to achieve focus. Press the shutter button fully while zooming in to create an artistic zoom blur (see Figure 22-2).

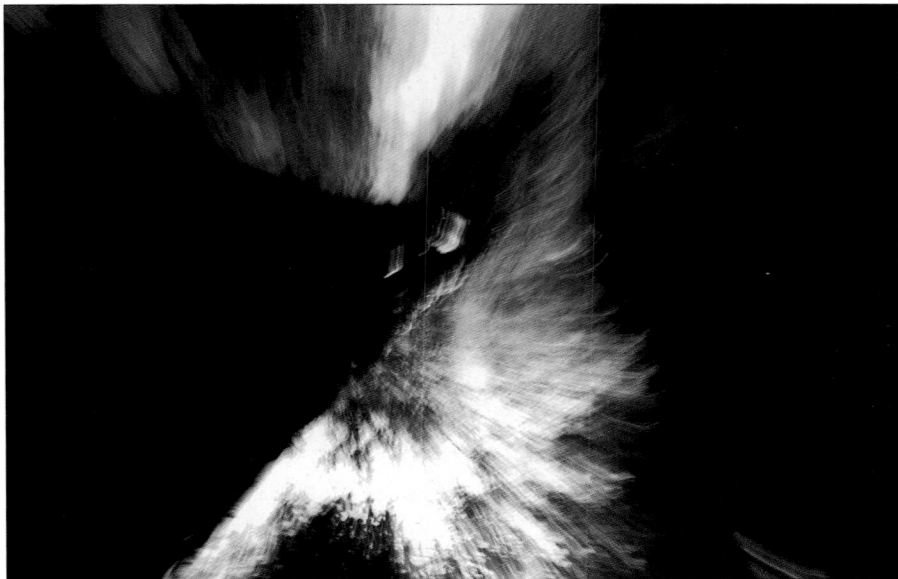

Figure 22-2: Creating artistic images of forests.

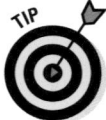

You can get some wonderful photos of forests on overcast days. Because of the lack of direct sunlight, the forest's colors appear muted, so be sure to photograph scenes that have contrasting colors, such as colorful flowers or an area with some leaves that are changing color.

Troubleshooting

✔ **The photo has no visual interest.** This problem often happens when you photograph the forest and nothing but the forest. If you don't like what you see on the LCD monitor, move around until you find something to add contrast and visual interest to the image, such as some rays of sunlight or a patch of colorful leaves.

✔ **Bright patches of sunlight are blown out to solid white.** If you photograph a forest in bright sunlight, you have areas of deep shade where the sun can't penetrate the dense foliage and areas of bright sunlight where the sun filters through the leaves. Your camera can't handle this dynamic range. Move to a slightly different position where the sun isn't shining directly at the camera and take another picture.

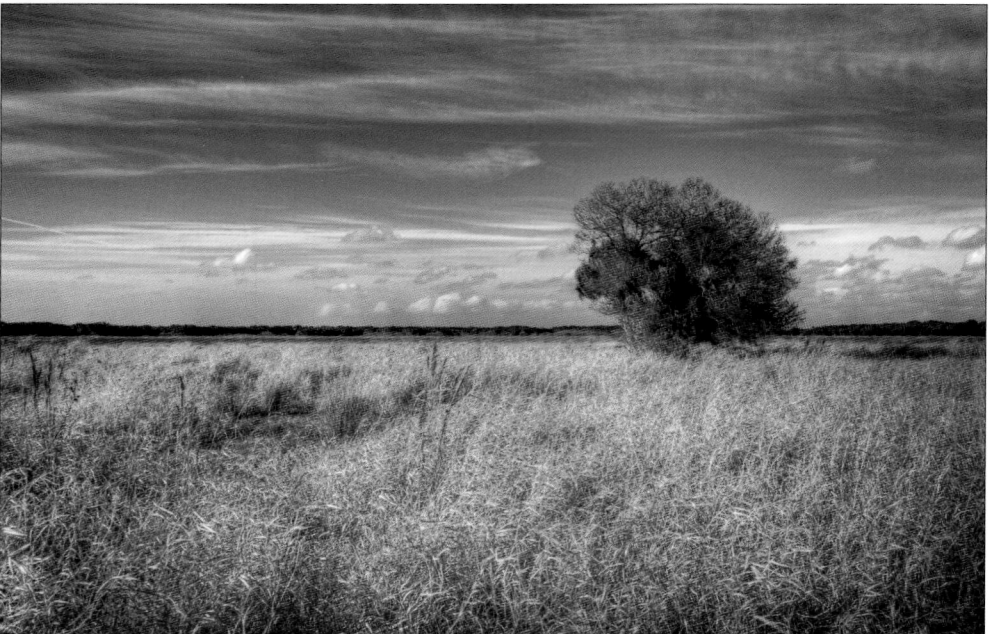

23 Landscapes

*N*o matter where you live, you can find lovely landscapes, usually within a few miles of your home. Landscape photography done right is stunning. It captures the mystery and grandeur of the place where you took the picture. When you photograph a landscape, your vantage point and the way you compose the photograph go a long way toward creating something that's a work of art and not just a snapshot. You want to draw viewers into the picture so that they take more than just a casual glance.

Camera Settings

- **Metering Mode:** Evaluative
- **Drive Mode:** Single shot
- **Shooting Mode:** Aperture Priority
- **Aperture:** f/11 to f/16
- **ISO Setting:** 100 to 200
- **Focus Mode:** Single Shot
- **Auto-Focus Point:** Single auto-focus point
- **Focal Length:** 24mm to 35mm (35mm equivalent; see "Understanding focal lengths" in the appendix)
- **Image Stabilization:** If your camera or lens has this option, enable it — especially if the shutter speed dips below 1/30 of a second.

Setting the Camera

When you photograph a beautiful landscape, you want to see every detail, which is why you use Aperture Priority mode and a small aperture. A wide-angle focal length lets you capture the majesty of the landscape in your photograph, and a low ISO setting gives you a noise-free image. However, if you're photographing landscapes on overcast days, you may have to increase the ISO setting to maintain a shutter speed of 1/30 of a second. If you don't want to increase the ISO setting, use image stabilization if your camera or lens has this feature, or mount your camera on a tripod.

When you photograph a landscape, you photograph the big picture: a wide sweeping brushstroke that captures the beauty of the area. So, you want every subtle detail to be in focus, which means you want a huge depth of field. In addition to a large depth of field, composition also plays a key role when you photograph a landscape. Notice the placement of the tree in the previous photo. The picture would not be as interesting if the tree was in the middle of the image.

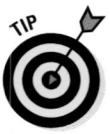

Being a great landscape photographer requires practice and a bit of study. Shoot landscapes whenever you have the chance and study the work of master landscape photographers, such as Ansel Adams, Clyde Butcher, and David Muench. Studying the work of the masters can help give you an eye for landscape photography and, after much practice, develop your own unique style. Google these photographers to see samples of their eye-popping work.

Taking the Picture

You can photograph a landscape whenever you see one that strikes your fancy. However, whether you're photographing landscapes on vacation or at home, try to set aside a block of time in which to photograph landscapes. Travel to your favorite area, or spice things up and travel to a place you've never visited before. Then, you just need to embark on your quest to capture the perfect photograph of the area you're in.

1. **Enable the camera settings discussed previously in this chapter.**

2. **When you find an area that you want to photograph, find the ideal vantage point.**

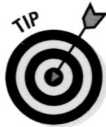

Don't place the horizon line in the middle of the picture. Place the horizon line in the upper third of the image when the most important part of the landscape you're photographing dominates the bottom of the scene, such as when you're photographing sand dunes in the desert. Place the horizon line in the lower third of the image when the most important part of the landscape dominates the upper part of the scene you're photographing, such as when you're photographing a mountain range.

3. **Press the shutter button halfway to achieve focus, and then compose the image.**

   If you're photographing with a zoom lens, zoom out until you see something you like in the viewfinder.

4. **Take the picture.**

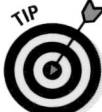

To get the best shot possible, keep these points in mind:

- When you find an interesting element in the landscape, such as a photogenic rock or dead branch, move close to the object, zoom in, and then move around it until you see an interesting composition in your viewfinder (see Figure 23-1).

- Many landscape photographers have tunnel vision and look straight ahead. Notice what's both above and below you. You may find an interesting photograph hiding there.

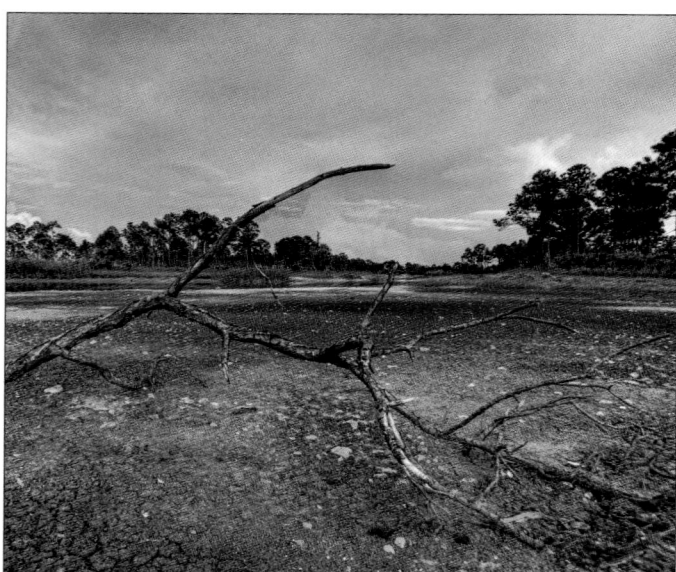

Figure 23-1: Use an interesting landscape element to create an interesting picture.

✒ Some people litter everywhere. Before taking your picture, take a good look at the area you have framed in the viewfinder to make sure there isn't any litter, such as empty soda cans or candy wrappers, that can ruin an otherwise great image.

✒ The best time to take great landscape pictures is early in the morning, just after the sun rises, or late in the afternoon, when the light is pleasing. The first hour and the last hour of daylight are known as the *Golden Hours,* times when you have great light for photographing landscapes because the light accentuates forms such as rocks and trees.

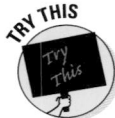

Barren landscapes can be saved with dramatic clouds. If you live near a place that's beautiful but stark, visit it when there are some moody clouds or thunderheads in the distance. Make this the focal point of your photograph by placing the horizon line in the lower part of the image (see Figure 23-2).

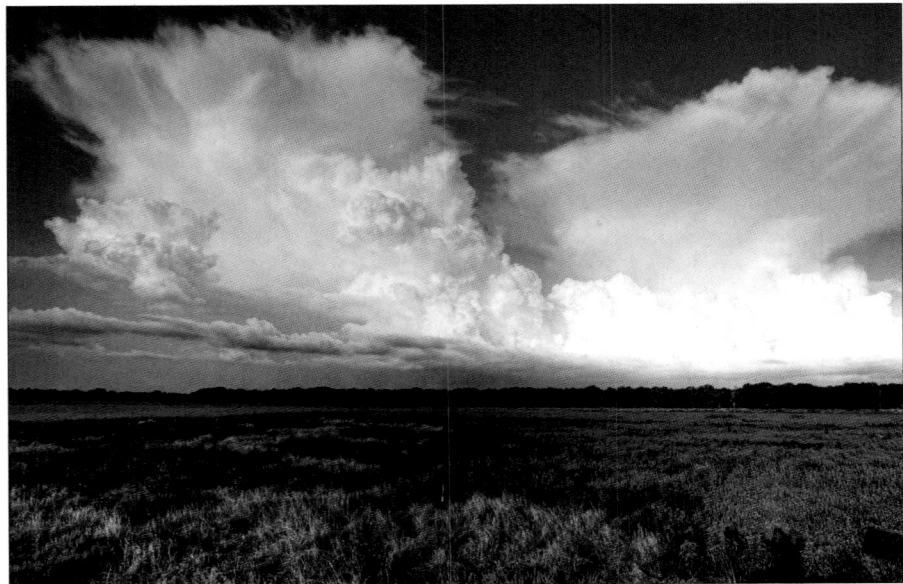

Figure 23-2: Barren landscape and brooding clouds equals a compelling photograph.

Troubleshooting

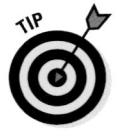

- ✔ **The foreground is too busy.** If the picture has details such as twigs, vines, or branches that detract from the overall picture, move to a slightly different vantage point to remove the offending details from the image.

- ✔ **The background doesn't seem sharp.** When you're photographing a huge landscape that goes on for miles and miles, atmospheric haze can cause distant details to look soft. If you encounter this problem, consider purchasing a UV filter for your lens.

  If your lenses have different accessory thread sizes, purchase filters for the largest-diameter lens you own, and then purchase a step-up ring for the smaller-diameter lenses. For example, if your biggest lens accepts 77mm filters and you also own a lens that accepts 58mm filters, buy a 58–77mm step-up ring, which is much cheaper than the cost of another filter.

- ✔ **There are telephone lines and houses in the picture.** Sometimes, you can't avoid getting a bit of civilization in your nature photos, but at other times, you can change your vantage point slightly to remove the offending elements from the picture. Alternatively, change your vantage point until a tree or other landscape element hides the objects.

- ✔ **The sky is boring.** If the scene you're photographing would benefit from a few clouds, patiently wait a few minutes for some clouds to drift into the scene. Alternatively, you can come back to the area on a different day, when atmospheric conditions are more conducive to a picture-perfect sky.

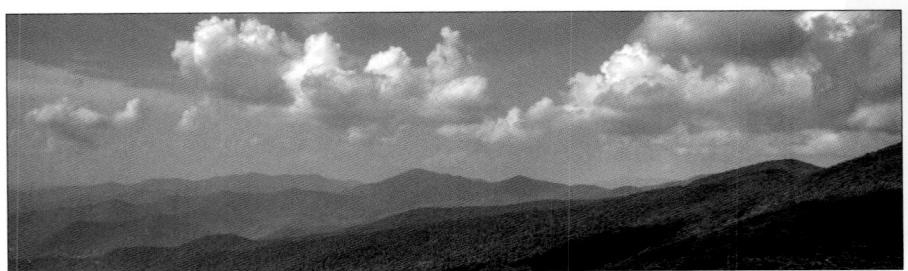

Camera Settings

- ✓ **Metering Mode:** Evaluative
- ✓ **Drive Mode:** Single Shot
- ✓ **Shooting Mode:** Manual
- ✓ **Aperture:** f/11 or f/16
- ✓ **ISO Setting:** 100
- ✓ **Focus Mode:** Single Shot
- ✓ **Auto-Focus Point:** Single auto-focus point
- ✓ **Focal Length:** 50mm (35mm equivalent; see "Understanding focal lengths" in the appendix)
- ✓ **Image Stabilization:** Off

*W*hen you find a stunning landscape, you want to capture as much of it as possible. A wide-angle lens lets you fit an impressive amount of real estate in a single picture, but you can record a majestic landscape in better ways. If your camera came with software such as a recent version of Photoshop Elements or software that enables you to stitch multiple images together, you can create a panorama. You create a panorama by giving the software four or five photographs, which the software then stitches into a single image. Although some software can recognize features and align images that you shot by holding the camera in your hand, you get better results if you mount your camera on a tripod and use these settings.

Setting the Camera

When you create a panorama of a landscape, you want everything to be in focus. Therefore, you use a small aperture. You shoot in Manual mode to prevent the camera from changing the exposure from one shot to the next. The camera takes the meter reading for you, as outlined in the following section. You plug in the exposure settings manually and use them for each panorama image. You also manually set the white balance to prevent a slight color shift that may occur when the camera automatically sets the white balance. The low ISO setting ensures the image will be crisp and noise-free. The focal length is important.

You may think that you should use a wide-angle focal length. However, wide-angle lenses can distort a scene and may cause *vignetting* (darkening at the corners of the image), which causes problems when the images are stitched together. The 50mm focal length lets you stitch together distortion-free images.

Taking the Picture

When you photograph images that you're going to stitch together into a panorama, you need to be meticulous when you set up for the shot. Make sure that you rotate your camera exactly 90 degrees to ensure proper stitching. Most tripods come equipped with a level. If your tripod doesn't have a spirit level, you can purchase an inexpensive level that attaches to the hot shoe of your camera.

1. **Switch to the settings mentioned previously in this chapter.**

2. **Switch to Aperture Priority mode, and then select to the desired f/stop from the range listed previously in this chapter.**

   For this technique, you use the camera to find out which shutter speed to use when you manually set the exposure, as I explain in Steps 5 through 8.

3. **Manually set the camera white balance.**

   Choose the white balance that matches the lighting conditions for the scene you're photographing. In most instances, you use the Sunlight or Cloudy setting. When the camera sets the white balance automatically, you may notice a slight difference from one image to the next, and the resulting stitched image doesn't look right. Refer to your camera manual for information on manually setting the white balance.

4. **Mount the camera on a tripod and use the tripod controls to rotate the camera 90 degrees (see Figure 24-1).**

5. **Rotate the tripod so that the camera faces the middle of the scene.**

   Typically, you want the middle of the scene to be the brightest part of the photograph.

6. **Press the shutter button halfway and note the shutter speed.**

7. **Rotate the camera to the left side of the scene, press the shutter button halfway, and note the shutter speed.**

8. **If the shutter speed at the left side of the scene is significantly slower than the shutter speed in the middle of the scene, reduce the shutter speed you noted in Step 6 by 2/3 of a stop (two speeds slower).**

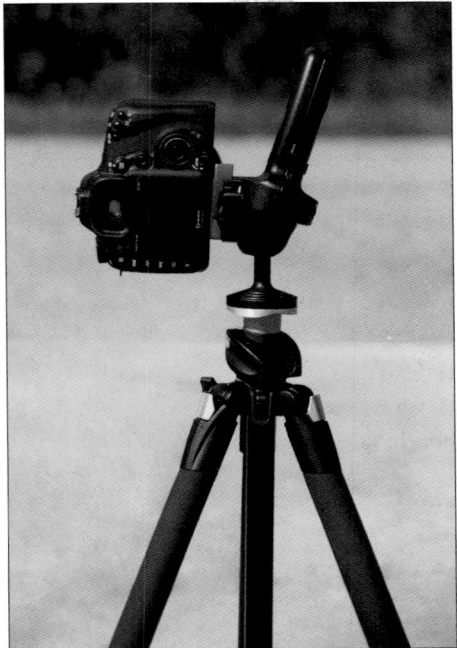

Figure 24-1: Rotate your camera 90 degrees on your tripod.

   If there's only a small difference, reduce the shutter speed by 1/3 of a stop (one speed slower).

9. **Switch to manual exposure, and then switch to the shutter speed that you determine in Step 8.**

10. **Rotate the tripod so that the camera is at the left side of the scene you want to photograph, and then take a picture.**

11. **Rotate the tripod so that the next image overlaps the one you just took by about 30 degrees.**

    Many tripods have markings similar to the points on a compass. You use these as a reference when overlapping the images that comprise your panorama. The details on the left side of each image overlap the details on the right side of the previous image.

12. **Take a picture.**

13. **Repeat Steps 11 and 12 to take two or three more pictures.**

14. **Stitch the images together in your image-editing application.**

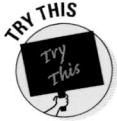

Create a panorama of a dynamic landscape that has a brooding thunderstorm in the distance. Remember to place the horizon line in the lower third of the image to draw your viewer's attention to the towering clouds (see Figure 24-2).

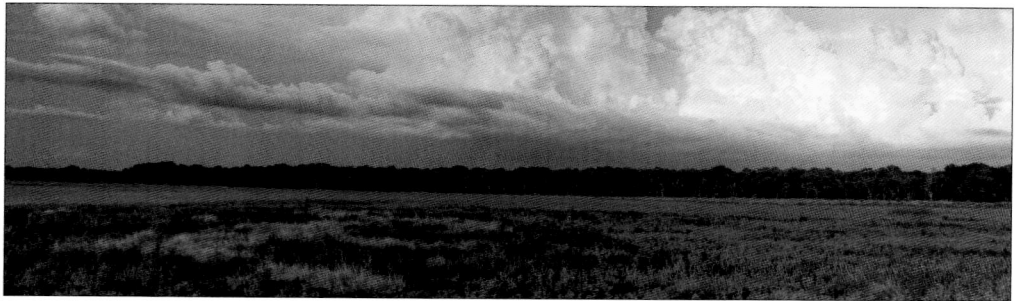

Figure 24-2: Create a panorama with a dynamic cloudscape.

Troubleshooting

- **The image isn't level.** You haven't rotated your camera exactly 90 degrees from level.

- **Each image for the panorama is a slightly different color.** You didn't manually set your white balance.

- **The stitching program can't align the images.** You didn't leave enough of an overlap between each image. Make sure you have about 30 degrees of overlap so that the image-editing program can find the edges it needs to stitch the images together.

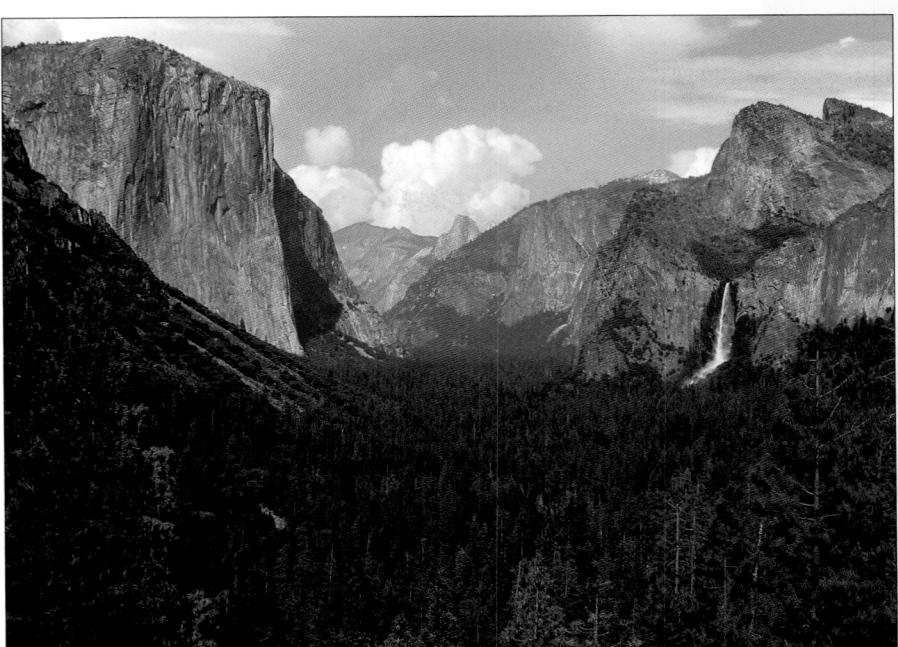

25 Mountains

Camera Settings

- **Metering Mode:** Evaluative
- **Drive Mode:** Single Shot
- **Shooting Mode:** Aperture Priority
- **Aperture:** f/16
- **ISO Setting:** 100 or the lowest setting that yields a shutter speed of 1/30 of a second or faster
- **Focus Mode:** Single Shot
- **Auto-Focus Point:** Multiple auto-focus points
- **Focal Length:** 28mm or wider (35mm equivalent; see "Understanding focal lengths" in the appendix)
- **Image Stabilization** (Optional): If you're shooting in low-light conditions and the shutter speed is faster than 1/30 of a second

If you live or vacation near a mountain range, you have a rich vein to tap for incredible photographs. Mountain ranges are like humans; they have their own distinct personalities. The Smoky Mountains are gently undulating, draped in evergreens, and often shrouded in mist. The Rockies and the California High Sierras are macho mountains with jagged granite outcroppings that have sparse vegetation sprouting from bare rock when you venture above timberline. (The fragile vegetation at these altitudes is similar to what you find in the Arctic Tundra, yet somehow survive against all odds.)

Many mountains are in state parks and readily accessible from your car, yet some mountains make you work a bit harder, requiring you to hike steep terrain to get to the best vantage points. When you arrive at a great mountain vista, you need only the right settings and the right equipment to capture a great photo that will be the envy of friends and family who think they're photographers.

Setting the Camera

When you photograph a mountain, you want to capture the wide majestic view and give your viewers a scene of the grandeur of the scene. So, you need to use a wide-angle focal length, such as 28mm or wider. This type of photography also cries for a depth of field that goes from the foreground clear into the next county. You want to see every subtle nuance of a mountain landscape, which is why you use an aperture of f/16 coupled with a wide-angle focal length to get a huge depth of field. Multiple auto-focus points are ideal for this type of photography. Just make sure that no auto-focus points illuminate over foreground objects, such as a twig. A low ISO setting is also ideal. However, if you're photographing in overcast conditions, you may have to increase the ISO setting. Alternatively, instead of increasing the ISO setting, you can mount the camera on a tripod.

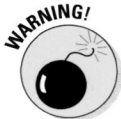

Don't use image stabilization if you mount the camera on a tripod. Doing so might lead to unpredictable results when image stabilization attempts to compensate for operator movement that isn't present.

Taking the Picture

If you're a seasoned mountain goat, you can hike to just about any good vantage point. If you're a city slicker vacationing in the mountains, you have the odds stacked against you and may need to rely on roadside vantage points or hikes that you're physically able to take. Ask park rangers or locals where the best vantage points are or buy a guide book prior to your vacation. When you find a great vantage point, bring the viewfinder to your eye and digitally capture the magic of the majestic scene before you; just follow these steps:

1. **Enable the camera settings discussed earlier in this chapter.**

   To become a better photographer of mountain landscapes, study the work of master landscape photographers, such as Ansel Adams and David Muench.

2. **Find a suitable vantage point from which to photograph the picture.**

   Look for objects to draw your viewer into the picture. You can also frame the mountain range by positioning the camera so a branch from a nearby tree appears at the edge of the image.

3. **Compose the picture, and then press the shutter button halfway to achieve focus.**

   You can take great pictures of mountains from low vantage points with the mountain range towering above you or from high vantage points to show the jagged details of the mountains that seem to go on forever (see Figure 25-1).

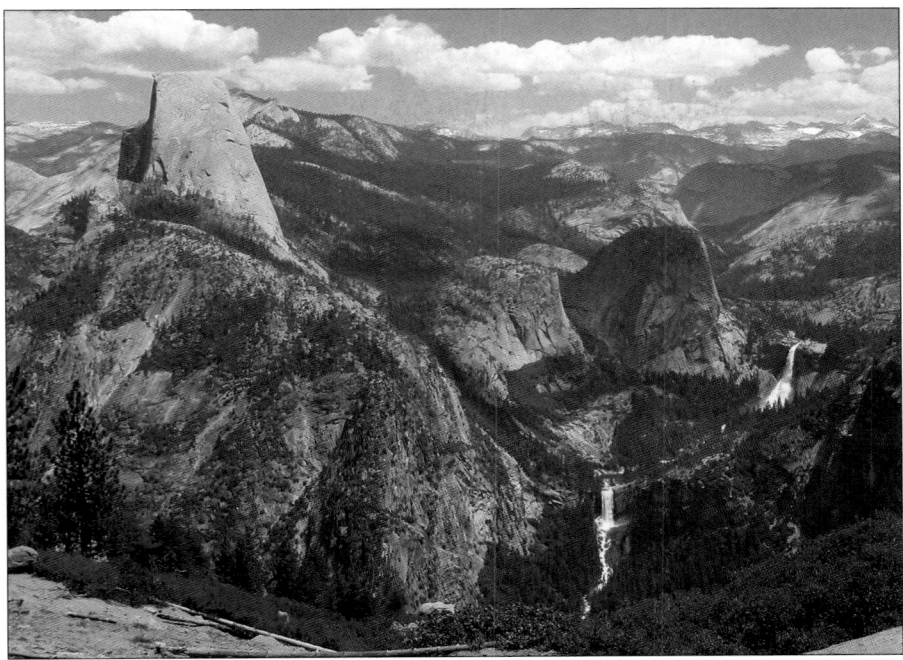

Figure 25-1: Find an interesting vantage point.

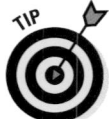

When you photograph a mountain from ground level, place the horizon line in the lower third of the picture. This compositional trick draws the viewers' attention to the mountains and clearly establishes the focal point of the photograph.

4. Take the picture.

Great mountain scenes need great light. When the sun's shining, you can get your best shots when you photograph mountains early in the morning or late in the afternoon. If at all possible, try not to photograph mountains in the middle of the day, when the light is harsh and unflattering.

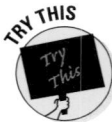

Look for interesting objects in the mountains, such as this old Jeffrey pine that Ansel Adams photographed in the 1940s when it was still alive (see Figure 25-2). Objects such as this pine provide the focal point of your scene, but you can also use them to frame other parts of the scene, such as a distant ridge of mountains.

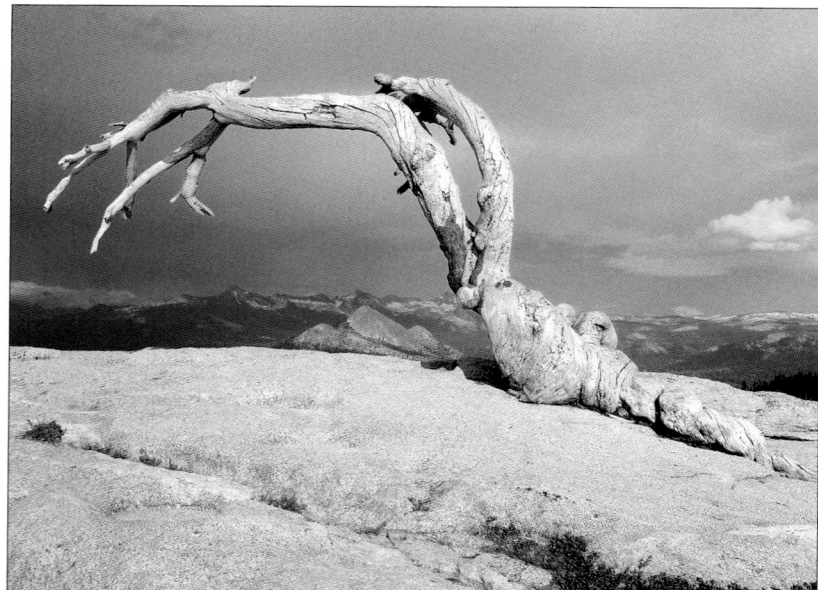

Figure 25-2: Using objects to capture your viewer's attention.

Troubleshooting

↳ **The mountains look flat and uninteresting.** This problem occurs if you take a picture when the sun is directly overhead. Photograph mountains in the early morning or late afternoon, when the low angle of the sun produces shadows that add depth to and model the mountains. The light is also a wonderful golden hue.

↳ **The foreground is busy.** Small objects littering the foreground, such as fallen leaves or pebbles, can create distraction. Often, you can cure this problem just by moving a few feet to a similar vantage point that has subtle foreground details, such as flowing grass, that enhance the picture. Alternatively, you can do a bit of landscape maintenance and re-arrange the elements to be more aesthetically pleasing. But if you do move things around, please be mindful of the environment. And if the details you want to remove are trash, place them in a trash receptacle rather than moving them to another spot.

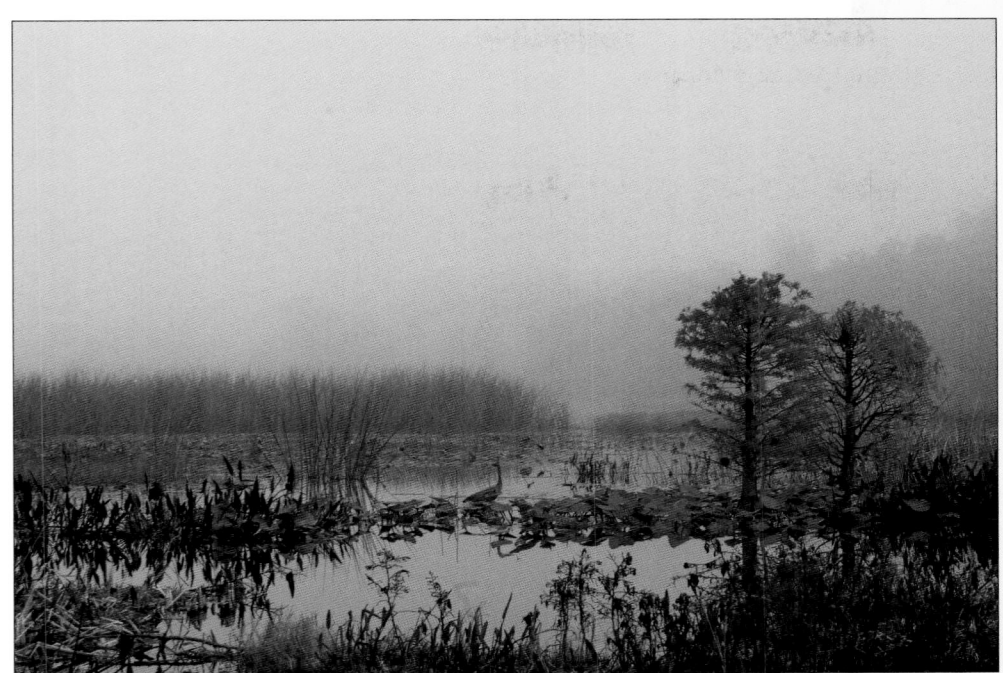

Camera Settings

- ✓ **Metering Mode:** Evaluative
- ✓ **Drive Mode:** Single Shot
- ✓ **Shooting Mode:** Aperture Priority
- ✓ **Aperture:** Varies, depending on subject
- ✓ **ISO Setting:** 100 or 200
- ✓ **Focus Mode:** Single Shot
- ✓ **Auto-Focus Point:** Single auto-focus point
- ✓ **Focal Length:** Varies, depending on subject (see "Understanding focal lengths" in the appendix)
- ✓ **Image Stabilization:** Optional

*S*wamps are mysterious areas, featuring dense foliage and not-altogether-friendly animals, such as alligators and spiders. Unless you're Clyde Butcher or you like to wade chest deep in water that's home to snakes and large reptiles that have nasty sets of teeth, I recommend you opt for the low-intensity swamp experience and visit a park, such as Corkscrew Sanctuary in Naples, Florida. In these parks, you have a wide diversity of subjects to photograph. You can opt for the wide view and photograph the entire swamp, photograph just the flora and fauna, or photograph the birds and reptiles that live there. Visit a swamp when it's foggy (see Chapter 45) for a truly mysterious-looking photograph.

Setting the Camera

You have a diverse range of subjects to photograph when you're in a swamp. Whenever you photograph a landscape, an object such as a flower, or a stationary creature such as a bird roosting or alligator on a log, Aperture Priority is the obvious choice. The aperture you choose determines the depth of field in your image. Remember to use a large aperture (a small f/stop number) when you want a shallow depth of field or a small aperture (a large f/stop number) when you want a large depth of field. Your focal length also varies, depending on your subject matter.

When you photograph the big picture, meaning a wide expanse of swamp, choose a small aperture (such as f/16) and a wide-angle focal length (such as 28mm). These settings let your camera capture an impressive amount of the scene in front of you, using a large depth of field.

If you're photographing a flower, zoom in to fill the frame with the flower by using a telephoto focal length of 100mm or longer. This focal length, coupled with an f/stop of f/4 or f/5.6, gives you a shallow depth of field. Alternatively, you can use a macro lens and a large aperture. You also use a large aperture and a long focal length when you photograph animals in a swamp.

Taking the Picture

When you photograph a swamp in a state park, you usually have only one option for your vantage point: a boardwalk. Keep your eyes open while you explore the park. You never know when a bird might be watching you from a tree or an alligator may decide to surface nearby.

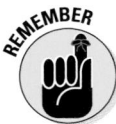

Before you lose yourself in the moment while photographing an ethereal swamp, make sure you take someone with you who can watch your back.

1. **Visit the swamp you want to photograph.**

   Visit the swamp early in the morning or late in the afternoon, when the light is a golden hue.

2. **Find a suitable vantage point.**

   When you photograph a swamp in a state park, you often have to photograph from a boardwalk. Make sure you can't see any manmade objects, such as telephone poles or other boardwalks, from your vantage point.

3. **Press the shutter button halfway to achieve focus.**

   Make sure the auto-focus point is over an object in the middle of the scene. Combined with the small aperture, this auto-focus point position ensures that you have a large depth of field with the entire scene in focus.

4. **Compose the picture.**

   Placement of the horizon line is important when you photograph a land-scape. Don't place the horizon line in the middle of the picture. If water is the dominant part of the scene, place the horizon line in the upper third of the image. If foliage is the dominant part of the scene, place the horizon line in the lower third of the image.

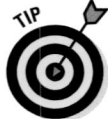

   Swamps have a tendency to be monochromatic. You can get a more interesting picture if you add a splash of color, such as golden rays of sun shining on foliage (see Figure 26-1).

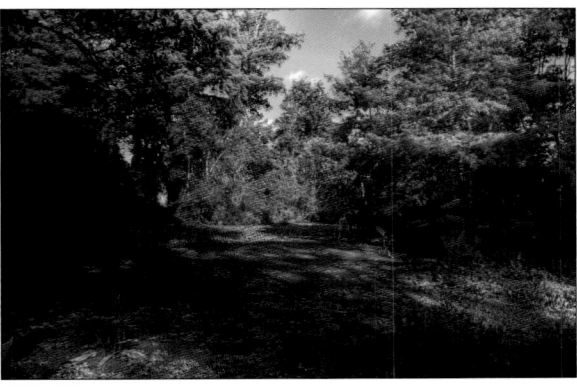

Figure 26-1: Using the sun to add a splash of color.

5. **Press the shutter button halfway to achieve focus, and then take the picture.**

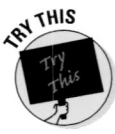

Visit a swamp early in the morning when the air contains a lot of moisture or fog. Photograph small objects such as berries, leaves, or spider webs that have beads of water glistening on them.

Troubleshooting

 ✔ **The image isn't interesting.** When you photograph a swamp, make sure you have a center of interest that draws the viewer into the picture. You can use a splash of color to act as the center of interest, or an animal such as a bird. Remember to compose the image so that the center of interest isn't in the middle of the image.

 ✔ **The image isn't colorful.** If you have only green foliage and green water in the image, convert the image to black and white in your image-editing program and pump up the contrast.

27 Sunrise

If you're a morning person, you can get some great sunrise shots of landscapes in the area in which you live or a place where you're vacationing. When the sun rises, the sky is bathed in wonderful hues of orange, pink, and violet. But many photographers make the mistake of showing up just minutes before the sun rises. To capture great pictures at sunrise, you need to allow yourself at least 30 minutes before the sun actually comes up. The extra time enables you to find a good spot and set up your equipment. In this chapter, I show you the settings and offer some tips on how to capture great pictures at sunrise.

Camera Settings

- **Metering Mode:** Evaluative
- **Drive Mode:** Single Shot
- **Shooting Mode:** Aperture Priority
- **Aperture:** f/8 to f/16
- **ISO Setting:** 400 to 800
- **Focus Mode:** Single Shot
- **Auto-Focus Point:** Single auto-focus point
- **Focal Length:** 28mm to 35mm (35mm equivalent; see "Understanding focal lengths" in the appendix)
- **Image Stabilization:** On

Setting the Camera

When you photograph a landscape at sunrise, you want a large depth of field, so use Aperture Priority mode and choose a fairly small aperture. Use the largest aperture (f/8) before the sun rises when you don't have as much light. Use the smallest aperture (f/16) when the sun is above the horizon, and you have more light to work with. The suggested ISO range helps you cope with the dim conditions before the sun rises. You end up using the lower ISO setting while the sun rises higher in the sky. The suggested focal length range is ideal for photographing landscapes. You can use image stabilization to ensure a blur-free photo, especially if you end up with a shutter speed slower than 1/30 of a second.

Taking the Picture

You get your best sunrise images when some clouds appear in the sky. The clouds give the sun a palette on which to paint wild and giddy colors just before and after the sun rises. Arriving early gives you plenty of time to set up and take a couple of pictures of the colorful clouds just before the sun rises. When you decide to photograph the sunrise, wake up early, grab a cup of your favorite coffee, pack your gear, and drive to your favorite location.

1. **Arrive on location at least half an hour before the sun rises.**

   You'll be working in near-dark conditions. Bring a flashlight with you and watch out for critters that may be lurking in the area where you're photographing. A flashlight also helps you see the dials on your camera and set up a tripod.

2. **Enable the settings discussed earlier in this chapter.**

   Start with a high ISO setting to compensate for the lack of light. This ISO setting gives you a shutter speed fast enough that you can hand-hold the camera. Better yet, mount the camera on a tripod and choose the lowest suggested ISO setting.

3. **Keep an eye on the clouds a few minutes before the sun rises.**

   When they start changing color, it's time to go to work.

4. **Press the shutter button halfway to achieve focus, and then compose the picture.**

   Just before the sun rises, look for the glimmer of light on the horizon, which is your visual clue to the position where the sun will actually appear when it rises. Compose the image so that you place the sun on one side (see Figure 27-1). Also, pay attention to where you place the horizon line. If you're taking a picture of a landscape in silhouette and the clouds are the predominant part of your image, place the horizon line in the lower third of the image. If you're photographing the reflection of the sun on a calm body of water, place the horizon line in the upper third of the image.

Figure 27-1: Position the sun to the right or left of center when you compose the image.

5. **Take the picture.**

   Continue taking pictures while the sun rises above the horizon. When the color starts disappearing from the clouds, pack up and grab breakfast.

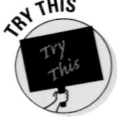

Wait until the sun is about 15 degrees above the horizon. Compose the photograph to position the sun behind a tree, and then take a picture. This technique works great on a foggy morning. You see shafts of light peaking from behind the tree, as shown in Figure 27-2.

Troubleshooting

✓ **The image is blurry.** If the light is very dim, even at a high ISO, you end up with a shutter speed that's less than 1/15 of a second. Choose a slightly larger aperture (a smaller f/stop number) until you have a shutter speed faster than 1/15 of a second. However, if you have a tripod and you're photographing a beach at sunrise, you can get a nice dreamy image that shows the water as a silky mist.

✓ **The foreground is too dark.** When you photograph the sunrise, your camera does the best it can to give you a properly exposed image. However, the dynamic range of a digital camera is less than that of the human eye. People can see more distinctions from dark to light than cameras can record, which is why the foreground appears dark.

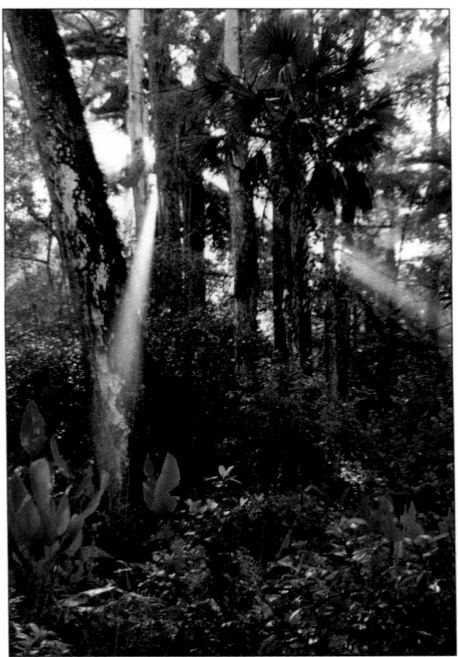

Figure 27-2: Capture rays of light on a foggy morning by placing the sun behind a tree.

Use a reverse-graduated neutral density filter. The gradient is darkest at the horizon, where the sun rises, so the shutter stays open longer and the camera does a better job of recording the scene the way you see it. A company called Singh-Ray makes a good reverse-graduated filter (www.singh-ray.com/reverse grads.html). You can also use a technique known as HDR (high dynamic range) photography to capture the full dynamic range of the landscape (see Chapter 100).

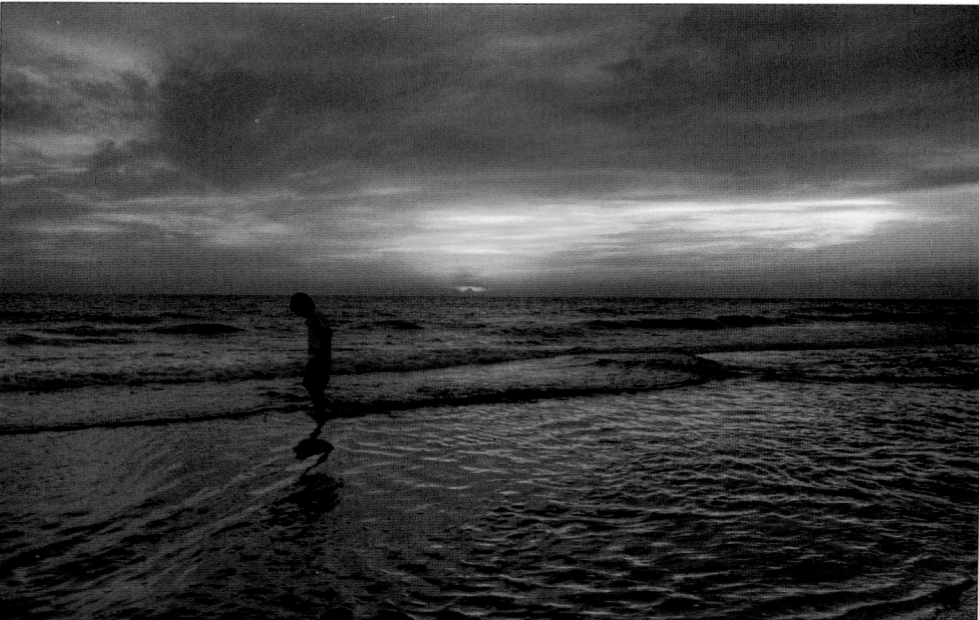

28 Beach at Sunset

Sunset is a wonderful time for photographers. The hour before sunset is known as "Golden Hour." The sun is low and diffused by the atmosphere. Clouds are bathed in wonderful hues of orange, pink, and purple. Add a sandy beach, ocean waves, and someone walking on the sand or in the water, and you have the recipe for a wonderful photograph.

The trick to getting a good sunset picture at the beach is having some interesting clouds in the sky. If you're vacationing or live near the beach, look toward the ocean 45 minutes before sunset. If you see some nice clouds, grab your camera and high tail it to the beach.

Camera Settings

- **Metering Mode:** Evaluative
- **Drive Mode:** Single Shot
- **Shooting Mode:** Aperture Priority
- **Aperture:** f/8 or smaller
- **ISO Setting:** The lowest ISO setting that enables you to achieve a shutter speed that's the reciprocal of the focal length you're using
- **Focus Mode:** Single Shot
- **Auto-Focus Point:** Single auto-focus point
- **Focal Length:** 28mm to 35mm (35mm equivalent; see "Understanding focal lengths" in the appendix)
- **Image Stabilization:** Enable this feature if your camera or lens has it

Setting the Camera

When you photograph a beach at sunset, you want everything in focus, from the vegetation in the sand dunes to the distant clouds, which is what you get when you shoot in Aperture Priority mode with a small aperture of f/8 or smaller (a larger f/stop number). A low ISO setting ensures that you get a sharp image that has little or no digital noise. The Single Shot Focus mode is perfect because landscapes don't move. When the camera achieves focus, you're ready to shoot the picture. The wide-angle focal length range provides you with a wide view that captures the clouds and landscape with a nice reflection of the sun on the water.

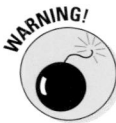

While the sun sinks and eventually drops below the horizon, the amount of available light changes. Therefore, you need to increase the ISO setting to keep the aperture at f/8 or smaller.

Taking the Picture

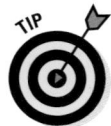

You can use a bit of science to pinpoint the direction from which the sun will rise and where it will set on any given day of the year by using a software application called the Photographer's Ephemeris (`http://photoephemeris.com`). As of this writing, the application is free for a PC or Macintosh desktop computer. You can also purchase the application for your iPod or iPhone from the iTunes store. With the application, you enter the day and the name of the place where you plan to shoot, or its longitude and latitude, to find out the direction from which the sun rises and the direction in which the sun sets.

After determining the precise details of where and when the sun will set, you're ready to follow these steps:

1. **Arrive at the beach about 20 minutes before sunset, find a suitable vantage point, and enable the camera settings discussed earlier in this chapter.**

2. **Start taking some pictures when the sun reflects on the bottom of the clouds and bathes them with a golden hue.**

3. **Move around and compose pictures with interesting objects between you and the sun.**

   Beach vegetation and people walking on the beach add interest to your image.

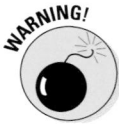

If you photograph beaches in sub-tropical or tropical paradises, be careful where you step. Small rattlesnakes often hang around vegetation such as sea oats.

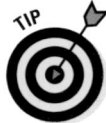

TIP

Switch to a medium telephoto focal length between 85mm and 100mm, and zoom in on a feature, such as a lifeguard station or some vegetation. Focus on the feature and use a slightly larger aperture (a smaller f/stop number), such as f/5.6. These settings give you a limited depth of field. Your subject is in silhouette and sharp focus, and the sun and clouds are a pleasant blur (see Figure 28-1).

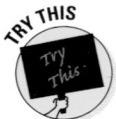

TRY THIS

Many photographers pack up their gear as soon as the sun goes down. If a lot of clouds are in the sky, wait 10 or 15 minutes. While the sun sinks lower, it still casts light on the clouds, and they turn giddy shades of orange, purple, and blue (see Figure 28-2).

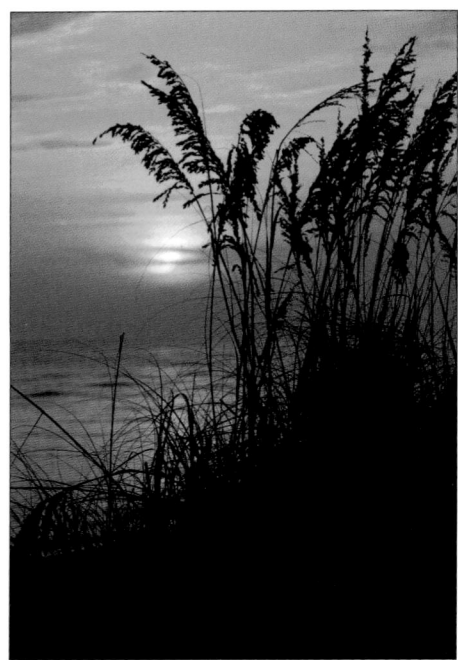

Figure 28-1: Take a silhouette sunset photo.

Figure 28-2: Photograph the scene 15 or 20 minutes after the sun sets.

Troubleshooting

✒ **The picture is brighter than the scene.** Cameras have a tendency to slightly overexpose scenes such as sunsets. Dial in enough exposure compensation until the picture you get matches the scene in front of you.

✒ **The sun is an orange blob.** Digital cameras can't record the brightness range in a scene like a sunset. If the sun is *blown out* (over-exposed, with no detail), use exposure compensation to reduce the exposure or compose the picture so that the sun is behind some vegetation or a tall tree.

✒ **The ocean is too dark.** Cameras can't record the same dynamic range of brightness that our eyes can see. Therefore, the exposure is often a compromise; you get a properly exposed sky but a dark ocean. If you like to photograph sunsets, consider investing in a graduated neutral density filter, which darkens the sky without affecting the rest of the picture.

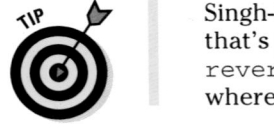

Singh-Ray makes an excellent reverse-graduated neutral density filter that's perfect for photographing sunsets (www.singh-ray.com/ reversegrads.html). The gradient is darkest at the horizon, which is where the sun will be when it sets.

29 Ocean Waves

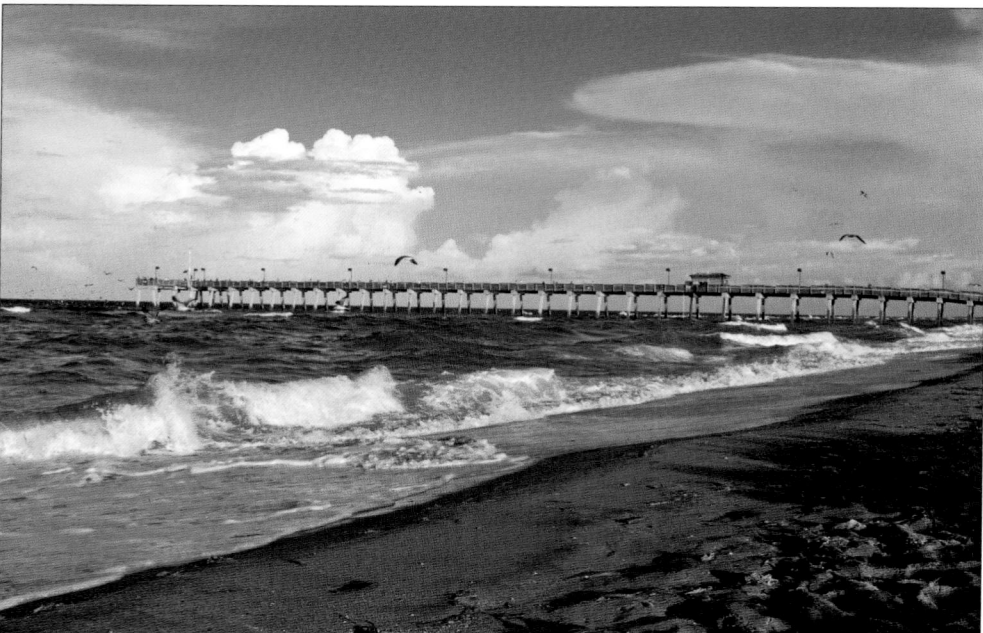

*H*umanity seems to have a love affair with the ocean. After all, our blood has roughly the same salinity as ocean water. Ocean waves crashing on a beautiful beach offers an invitation to grab your camera and start taking pictures. Some beaches, such as those on the west coast of the United States, almost always have big waves pounding the shoreline. Other beaches, such as those along the Gulf Coast of Florida, have fairly placid waves — sometimes, the Gulf of Mexico is almost dead calm. But add a storm at sea to the mix, and even the Gulf of Mexico can send some impressive waves to the Florida shoreline.

Camera Settings

- **Metering Mode:** Evaluative
- **Drive Mode:** Single Shot
- **Shooting Mode:** Shutter Priority
- **Shutter speed:** 1/60 to 1/250 of a second
- **ISO Setting:** 100 to 400
- **Focus Mode:** Single Shot
- **Auto-Focus Point:** Single auto-focus point
- **Focal Length:** 28mm to 70mm (35mm equivalent; see "Understanding focal lengths" in the appendix)
- **Image Stabilization:** Optional

Setting the Camera

When you photograph roiling waves on the ocean, your goal is to either freeze the waves or show some motion, which is why you use Shutter Priority mode for this type of photography. You can freeze the motion of a wave by using a shutter speed of 1/250 of a second, which shows individual droplets of water. If you opt for a shutter speed of 1/60 of a second, you see some of the motion of the wave and can still hand-hold the camera. The suggested focal length range lets you either capture the wide expanse of the beach and waves, or zoom in close to include birds and perhaps a fisherman in the shot. The suggested ISO range works for illumination from bright sunlight to slightly overcast conditions.

Taking the Picture

If you vacation or live near an ocean, you have wonderful opportunities for pictures. When the weather changes and the surf kicks up, grab your camera and walk along the beach. Use the following settings to get some compelling pictures of Mother Ocean.

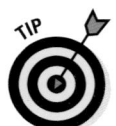

1. **Go to the beach you want to photograph and find a suitable vantage point.**

   Choose a location that includes something interesting, such as a pier in a background or a fisherman in the foreground (see Figure 29-1).

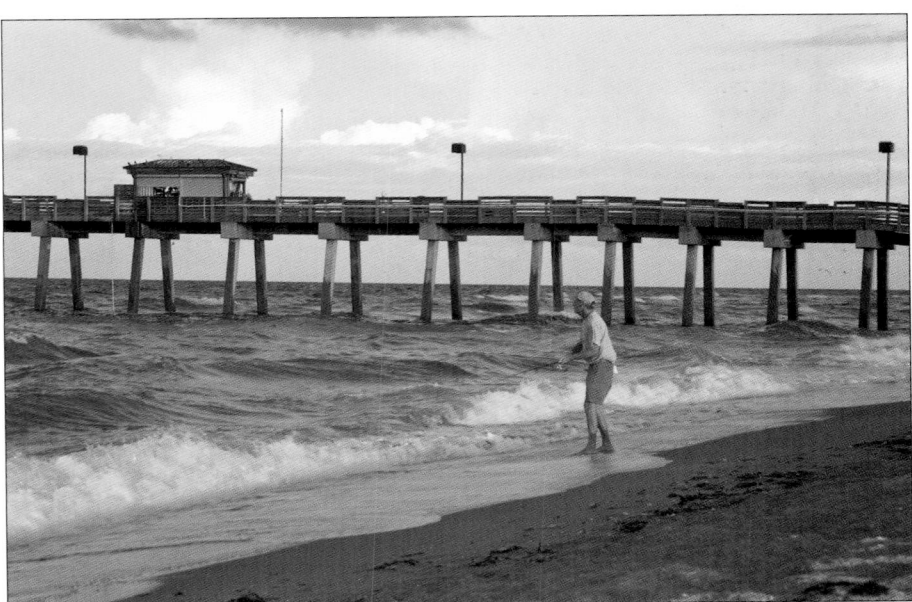

Figure 29-1: Add interest to the image with foreground and background objects.

2. **Zoom in and press the shutter button halfway to achieve focus.**

3. **Compose the picture.**

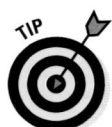

Place the horizon line in the upper third of the image if you want the ocean waves to dominate the image. If you have an interesting sky and you're shooting from a low vantage point, try placing the horizon line in the lower third of the image.

4. **Take the picture.**

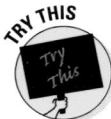

Place the camera on a tripod and select the slowest shutter speed possible. A shutter speed of 1/15 of a second or slower works great for this technique. If you're taking the picture in bright conditions, use a neutral density filter to reduce the amount of light reaching the sensor, which enables you to get a properly exposed picture with a slow shutter speed. Set the auto-timer for the lowest duration and take a picture. The waves look like smooth misty veils of water in your photograph (see Figure 29-2).

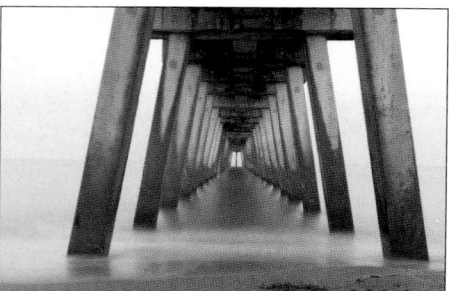

Figure 29-2: To create a mist effect, photograph ocean waves with a slow shutter speed.

Troubleshooting

- **The waves don't look as large as I remember.** You get this kind of an image if you take the picture standing up. You can see the full scale of the waves if you crouch down when you take the picture.

- **The background isn't in focus.** You used a high shutter speed in dim lighting conditions. To properly expose the image, the camera selects a large aperture, which gives you a shallow depth of field. You have two possible solutions: Select a higher ISO speed or select a slower shutter speed. If you're taking the picture on an extremely overcast day, you may have to do both.

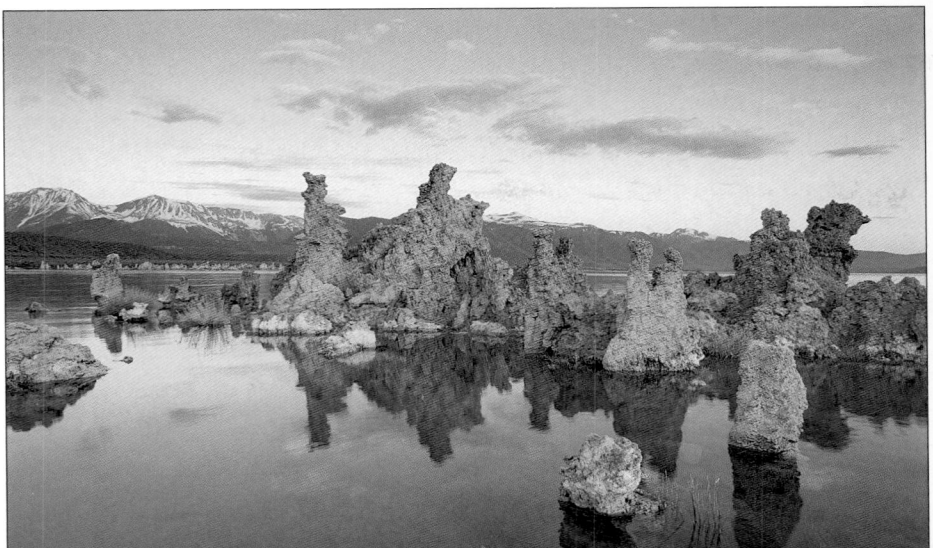

Camera Settings

- ✓ **Metering Mode:** Evaluative
- ✓ **Drive Mode:** Single Shot
- ✓ **Shooting Mode:** Aperture Priority
- ✓ **Aperture:** f/16
- ✓ **ISO Setting:** 100 to 400
- ✓ **Focus Mode:** Single Shot
- ✓ **Auto-Focus Point:** Multiple auto-focus points
- ✓ **Focal Length:** 28mm to 35mm (35mm equivalent; see "Understanding focal lengths" in the appendix)
- ✓ **Image Stabilization:** On

*B*odies of water are great subjects for photographers. You can photograph big bodies of water (oceans), small bodies of water (ponds and streams), and medium-sized bodies of water (lakes, which sometimes are so large that you can't see the other side, which makes them look like oceans minus the humongous waves).

Lakes can vary from almost swamp-like to something that looks like it's from the dark side of the moon, such as Mono Lake in California (shown here).

Setting the Camera

When you photograph any lake, you want to have as much in focus as possible, so you shoot in Aperture Priority mode and use a small aperture (a large f/stop number). The suggested ISO range gives you the option of photographing a lake in bright sunlight or in overcast conditions. The focal-length range lets you capture the big view. In this situation, multiple auto-focus points are helpful. Image stabilization ensures a blur-free image if you're photographing in dim conditions, and the suggested aperture yields a shutter speed slower than 1/15 of a second.

Taking the Picture

Any photograph of a body of water is more appealing when it includes clouds. If you're photographing a calm lake, the clouds reflect on the water. Lakes also have finer details, such as lily pads and reeds of grass along the shoreline. Make sure you photograph lakes early in the morning or late in the afternoon, when the sun shines wonderful golden rays and everything in its path casts soft, pleasing shadows.

1. **Travel to the lake you want to photograph.**

2. **Find a vantage point you like.**

   Look for interesting features on the shoreline, such as tall strands of grass.

3. **Enable the settings discussed earlier in this chapter and compose the picture.**

   If you're photographing a lake on a cloudless day, look for something — such as a tall stand of trees, as shown in Figure 30-1 — that reflects in the water. Place the horizon line in the lower third of the image if you have a mountain range in the background. Place the horizon line in the upper third of the image if the scene includes a shoreline and wonderful reflections in the water.

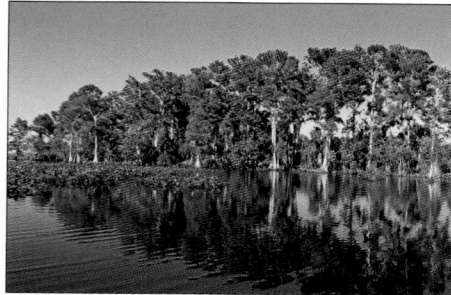

Figure 30-1: Reflections on calm water make wonderful images.

4. **Press the shutter button half-way to achieve focus.**

5. **Take the picture.**

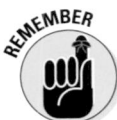

Never be satisfied with one picture. After you take your first picture of a scene, walk around the scene and put the camera up to your eye to see what a picture would look like from that vantage point. Your first shot isn't necessarily a good one.

6. **Move around the scene and take pictures from different vantage points.**

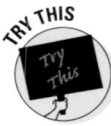

Taking pictures of a lake you find beautiful can give you a great way to spend a morning or afternoon. Use the same settings to photograph details of the lake, such as lily pads and grass along the shoreline (see Figure 30-2).

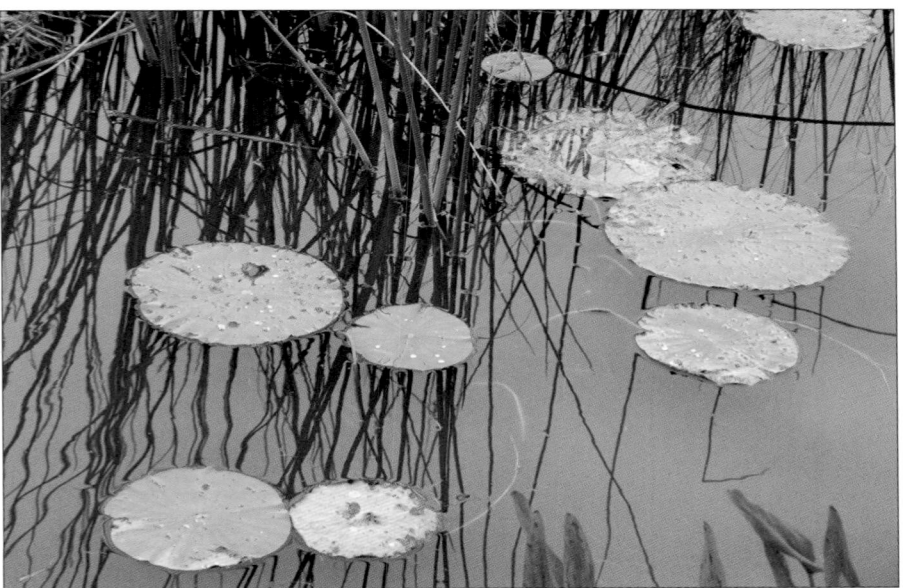

Figure 30-2: Photos of a lake's details are good candidates for framing.

Troubleshooting

✔ **The camera focuses on an object close to shore.** This problem definitely can cause the background to go out of focus. Release the shutter button, and then press it halfway again. If the camera still focuses on the nearby object, you might want to consider moving to a slightly different spot because this object may be too prominent in the final image.

✔ **The image is brighter than the actual scene.** If you photograph when it's late in the day or it's overcast, the camera tries to make the scene brighter than it actually is. Use exposure compensation to decrease the exposure by 1/3 to 2/3 a stop.

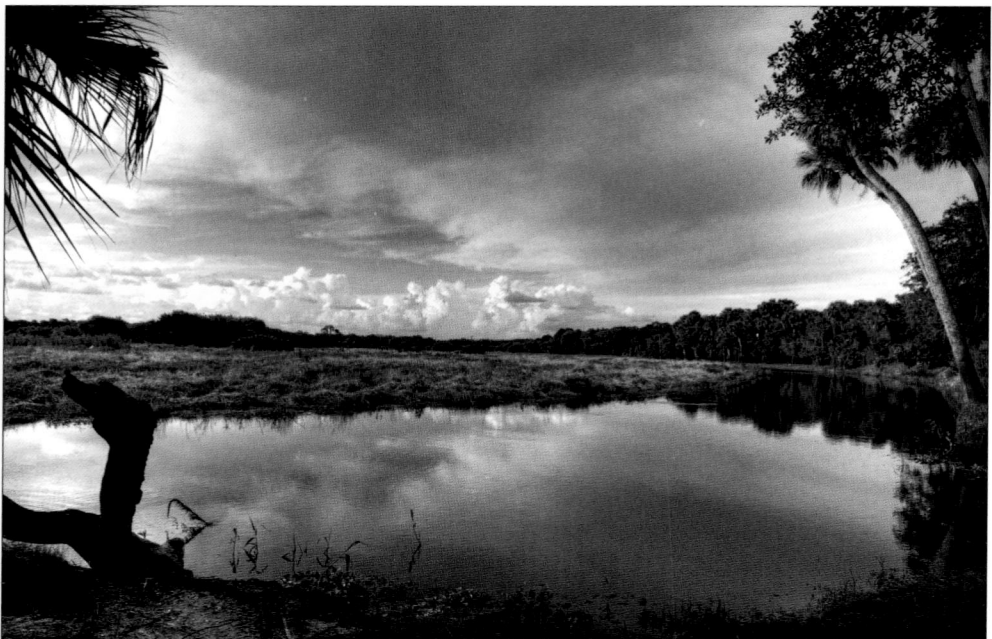

*R*ivers travel long distances, from misty mountaintops to the sea. A river can be docile, meandering slowly along its banks, or it can be a raging mass of white water cascading over rocks while it seeks its level. When you visit an area that includes a river, don't forget to take your camera along. You can photograph the river, the wildlife that lives in and around the river, or the surrounding foliage. When you come to a bend in the river that has a sky full of clouds reflected in the still water, you just need your camera and the settings in this chapter to create a great picture.

Camera Settings

- **Metering Mode:** Evaluative
- **Drive Mode:** Single Shot
- **Shooting Mode:** Aperture Priority
- **Aperture:** f/16
- **ISO Setting:** 100 to 400
- **Focus Mode:** Single Shot
- **Auto-Focus Point:** Single auto-focus point
- **Focal Length:** 28mm to 50mm (35mm equivalent; see "Understanding focal lengths" in the appendix)
- **Image Stabilization:** Optional

Setting the Camera

Photographing a river is similar to photographing a landscape. You want a large depth of field to capture all the subtle details of the river and surrounding terrain, which you achieve by using Aperture Priority mode and selecting a small aperture of f/16. The ISO range is suitable for taking pictures in bright sunlight and moderately overcast conditions. If you're photographing in low light, you can fudge down to an aperture as large as f/8.0, increase the ISO slightly, or use a tripod. The focal length you use depends on how close you can get to the river.

Taking the Picture

A river can be a raging torrent that rushes rapidly or a body of slowly flowing water that meanders along its banks. The trick to turning a body of water into an interesting photograph is what you include in the frame and what section of the river you photograph. If you photograph a straight section of the river and its uninteresting surroundings, you don't end up with an interesting photograph. However, if you photograph a bend in the river or a section of the river that features interesting foliage or wildlife, you have a pleasing image that people will want to view.

1. **Travel to the section of the river that you want to photograph.**

   If you're hiking along a river that has dense vegetation on its banks, you may get only brief glimpses of the river. If you're in this situation, look for trails that lead you to the riverbank and explore those trails to see what the river looks like.

2. **Find an interesting vantage point.**

   A bend in the river is a great spot to photograph a river. Many rivers offer vistas that include mountains, majestic trees, or waterfalls. If you have a great sky full of clouds that are reflected in the river, place the horizon line in the lower third of the image. If the river is cascading over boulders with frothy white water, place the horizon line in the upper third of the image.

3. **Press the shutter button halfway to achieve focus, and then compose the picture.**

   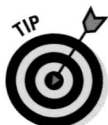

   Look for islands in the middle of wide rivers. They add visual interest and give your viewers a point of reference to determine the grandeur of the river. Alternatively, see whether you can include people canoeing down the river or people on the riverbank (as shown in Figure 31-1), which also helps define the size of the river.

4. **Take the picture.**

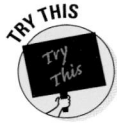

Look for places in the river where it drops. Inevitably, you can find rapids or a mini-waterfall. Place your camera on a tripod or steady it on something solid. Choose your smallest aperture to ensure a slow shutter speed. You may have to use a neutral density filter to reduce the amount of light reaching the camera. In the resulting picture, you get a silky-smooth flow of water, where the water cascades and then pools at the next lowest level, which is similar to photographing a waterfall (see Chapter 34).

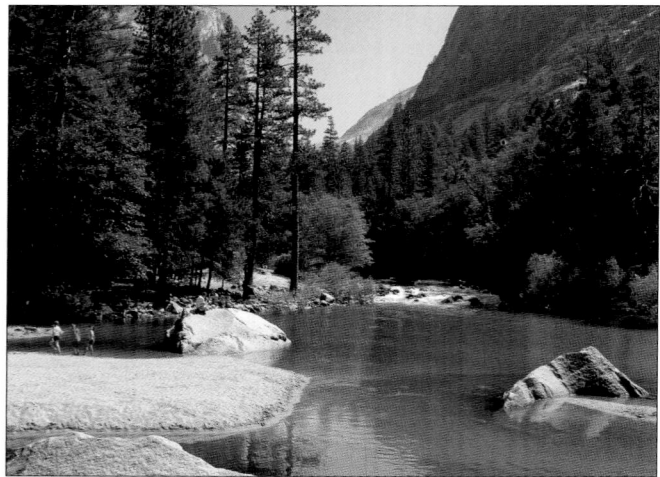

Figure 31-1: Use objects to define the scale of the river.

Troubleshooting

- **One side of the river is very dark.** You get this kind of image when the sun is low in the sky and shining over trees. The trees are in deep shadow, and the other side of the river is lighted perfectly. The only cure is to come back at a different time, when the sun is illuminating both the river and the banks.

- **The picture is too bright.** This problem happens when you photograph a river late in the day. The camera overcompensates and makes the resulting image too bright. Use exposure compensation to reduce the exposure by 1/3 to 2/3 of a stop. After you employ exposure compensation, review the image on your LCD monitor to make sure the image is faithful to the scene you see in front of you.

- **The sky is too bright.** This image problem pops up when the sky is much brighter than both the river and everything else below the horizon line. The camera can't cope with the wide dynamic range. Use a graduated neutral density filter that reduces the amount of light reaching the top of the sensor (where the sky is brightest) and gradually lets the full amount of light reach the sensor at the middle of the filter.

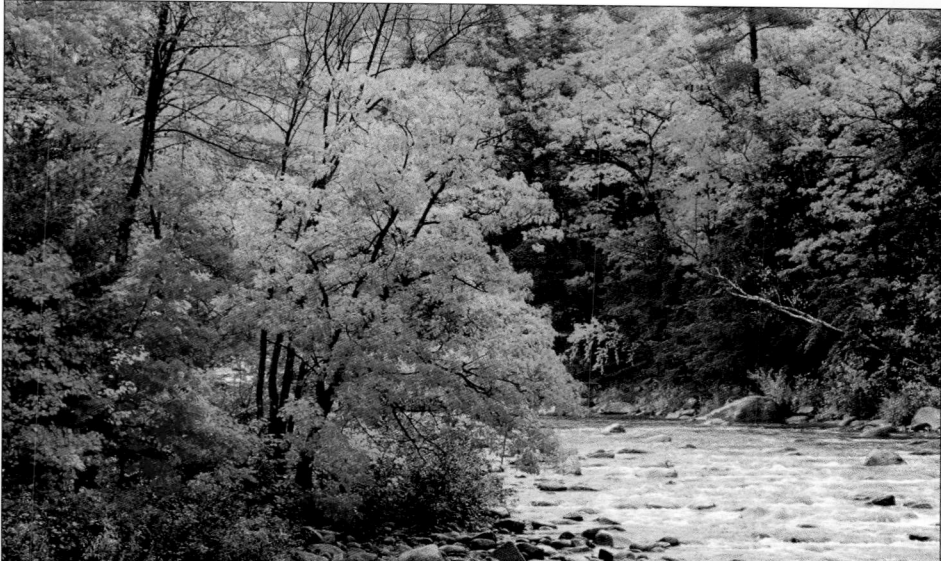

Corbis Digital Stock

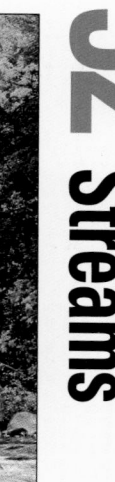

Camera Settings

- ✔ **Metering Mode:** Evaluative
- ✔ **Drive Mode:** Single Shot
- ✔ **Shooting Mode:** Shutter Priority
- ✔ **Shutter Speed:** 1/2 to 1/15 of a second or slower
- ✔ **ISO Setting:** 100
- ✔ **Focus Mode:** Single Shot
- ✔ **Auto-Focus Point:** Single auto-focus point
- ✔ **Focal Length:** 28mm to 70mm (35mm equivalent; see "Understanding focal lengths" in the appendix)
- ✔ **Image Stabilization:** On

Streams are small rivers that gently meander through a forest or mountainside. Streams can be placid or can cascade into small waterfalls while they drop over small rocks or boulders. When you photograph a stream, you use surrounding elements to draw the viewer's attention to the stream. For example, streams look very festive when the leaves change color (as shown here). If you live in an area that has streams, you have the raw material for some great photographs. You just need your creativity and the settings in this chapter to create compelling images of streams.

Setting the Camera

When you photograph a stream, you're photographing a body of water that's moving. Therefore, you photograph it using Shutter Priority mode. If you photograph a stream with a fast shutter speed, you freeze all the motion — but a stream doesn't look very interesting if nothing moves. However, if you shoot the scene by using a shutter speed in the suggested range, you end up with a dreamy rendition of the stream that immediately draws the viewer's attention to that stream. Use a low ISO setting to ensure that the camera can properly expose the scene when you use a slow shutter speed. As a rule use a wide-angle focal length when photographing landscapes. However, you may need to zoom in if the stream is far away and you can't walk to it.

Taking the Picture

When you're hiking in the woods, looking for interesting landscapes to photograph, you have to pack light. If you bring everything but the kitchen sink, you wind up being one very tired photographer. Also, you want to photograph landscapes that include streams at certain times of the day. Take your pictures early in the morning or late in the afternoon, when the light is a wonderful golden hue and the shadows are soft.

You can also capture great photographs of streams on overcast days. Typically, you need a zoom lens with a wide-angle–to–normal focal length. Many digital SLR kits ship with an 18mm-to-55mm lens, which is a great all-around lens for landscape photography because it covers wide-angle (18mm) to normal focal length. Because of the slow shutter speed, you need a tripod or some other means of stabilizing the camera.

So, pack light, grab a bottle of water if you're going to be out for a while, slather on some sunscreen, and get ready to take some great pictures of streams.

1. **When you find a stream that you want to photograph, enable the settings discussed previously in this chapter.**

   If you're taking the picture on a bright day, you may have to use a neutral density filter to properly expose the image when you use a slow shutter speed. A neutral density filter reduces the amount of light reaching the sensor but doesn't change the colors. At your favorite camera retailer, you can find neutral density filters that decrease the amount of light reaching the sensor in a range from 1 to 4 stops.

2. **Mount your camera on a tripod.**

   In lieu of a tripod, you can place your camera on a flat surface, such as a rock or bench.

3. **Set the auto-timer for the slowest duration.**

   The auto-timer delays the shutter opening, which allows time for any vibration that occurs when you press the shutter button to stop. You can skip this step if you have a very sturdy tripod.

4. **Zoom in to the desired focal length, and then compose the picture.**

   Find a vantage point where the stream curves or one that includes a splash of color (see Figure 32-1). If you're photographing a very small stream, crouch low and include a point of interest, such as a moss-covered rock or some leaves on the bank of the stream.

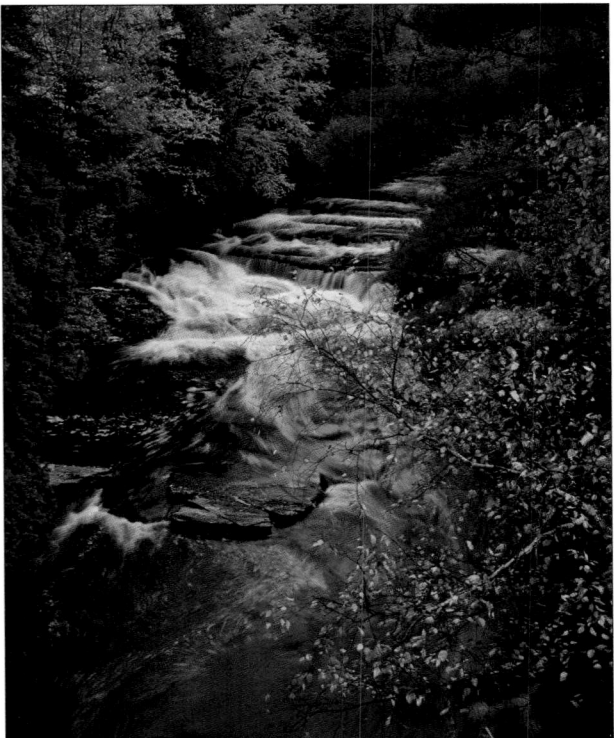

Corbis Digital Stock

Figure 32-1: Use a curve to compose your image.

5. **Press the shutter button halfway to achieve focus, and then completely press the shutter button to take the picture.**

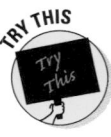

Find a stream that has a waterfall (as shown in Figure 32-2) and rotate the camera 90 degrees. Use the settings from earlier in this chapter to capture a photograph of the mini-waterfall.

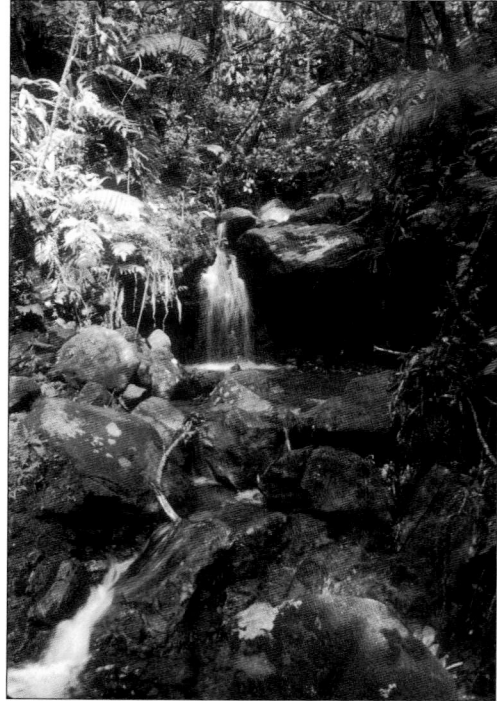

Robert Pierce

Figure 32-2: Photographing a mini-waterfall in a stream.

Troubleshooting

- ✓ **The depth of field is too shallow.** This problem occurs if you photograph on an overcast day or when a dense forest canopy blocks the sunlight. You get a shallow depth of field if your camera selects an f/stop value of f/7.1 or smaller (a large aperture). Switch to a higher ISO setting until you get a small aperture (a large f/stop number). An f/stop of f/11 or f/16 is ideal for photographing streams.

- ✓ **The camera doesn't achieve focus.** Your camera may have a hard time achieving focus unless the scene includes something that provides contrast. When your camera can't achieve focus, move the single auto-focus point over the edge of a tree or something else that has a sharply defined edge, and then press the shutter button halfway to achieve focus. With the shutter button still pressed halfway, use the tripod lever to move the camera to the desired position. Alternatively, you can switch to manual focus.

- ✓ **The image appears to be moving vertically.** This condition, which is known as *tripod creep,* happens when you exceed the load limit of your tripod. The weight of the camera and lens causes the tripod to sink slightly, which shows up as a motion blur in the image due the slow shutter speed. You can switch to a lighter lens or purchase a sturdier tripod.

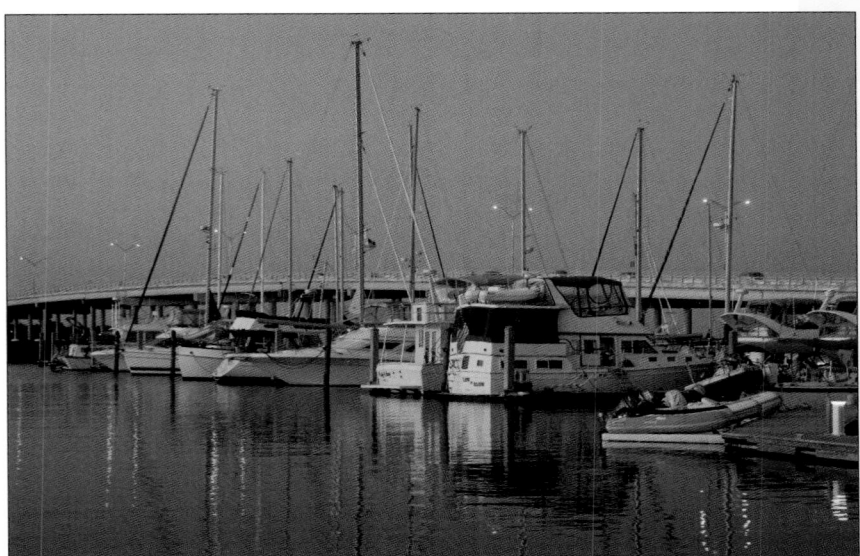

Camera Settings

- ✔ **Metering Mode:** Evaluative
- ✔ **Drive Mode:** Single Shot
- ✔ **Shooting Mode:** Aperture Priority
- ✔ **Aperture:** f/16 or smaller (larger f/stop number)
- ✔ **ISO Setting:** The lowest ISO setting that allows you to achieve a shutter speed of about 1/50 of a second or faster
- ✔ **Focus Mode:** Single Shot
- ✔ **Auto-Focus Point:** Single auto-focus point
- ✔ **Focal Length:** 28mm to 35mm (35mm equivalent; see "Understanding focal lengths" in the appendix)
- ✔ **Image Stabilization:** Enable image stabilization if it's available on your lens or camera, unless you're using a tripod

*I*f you live near a large body of water, you know it has a temperament, just like you. Sometimes it's turbulent, other times it's fairly calm, and sometimes (when no wind is blowing) the water is flat with absolutely no ripples. When you're near calm water, you can capture some wonderful images with the water reflecting the clouds, boats, and any objects that are nearby.

Like any other type of photography, you can find good times and bad times to take pictures of calm water. The best times to capture these types of images are early in the morning or late in the afternoon, when the sun is low on the horizon and the light has a wonderful golden hue.

Setting the Camera

This type of photography begs for a huge depth of field. When you have a scene that includes wonderful reflections, you want the objects that are reflecting on the water to be in sharp focus, as well as the water itself, which is why you choose Aperture Priority mode with a small aperture. A wide-angle focal length lets you capture the big picture. If you have one with you, a tripod ensures that you can keep the camera rock steady and produce a blur-free picture. If you don't have a tripod, steady hands and a relatively fast shutter speed can yield a crystal-clear image.

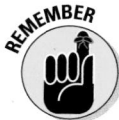

The slowest shutter speed at which you can hand-hold the camera is the reciprocal of the 35mm equivalent of the focal length you're using to take the picture.

Taking the Picture

When you want to capture an image that includes great reflections on still water, you have to be a little spontaneous and, at the same time, do a bit of planning. You can't get flattering light in the middle of the afternoon. Therefore, plan your photo shoot for early morning or late afternoon. Also, find out the direction from which the sun is shining. If you try to shoot directly into the sun, the reflections and the water look dark in the photo. You get the best pictures of reflections when the sun is shining at the objects casting the reflections.

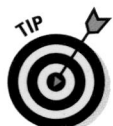

1. **Find a good vantage point, compose your image, and enable the settings discussed earlier in this chapter.**

   When you take this type of photograph, the reflections are the main focus of your image. Therefore, place the horizon line near the upper third of the image (see Figure 33-1).

   You can wait until a gentle breeze kicks up. The breeze causes small ripples on the water, which result in painterly reflections.

2. **Press the shutter button halfway to achieve focus.**

3. **Press the shutter button fully to take the picture.**

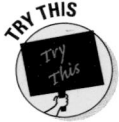

You can get compelling images of reflections from common objects such as mirrors and store windows. When you see a reflection that you find worthy of a photo, move around until you can see part of the reflection and part of what's behind the window (see Figure 33-2) and take a picture.

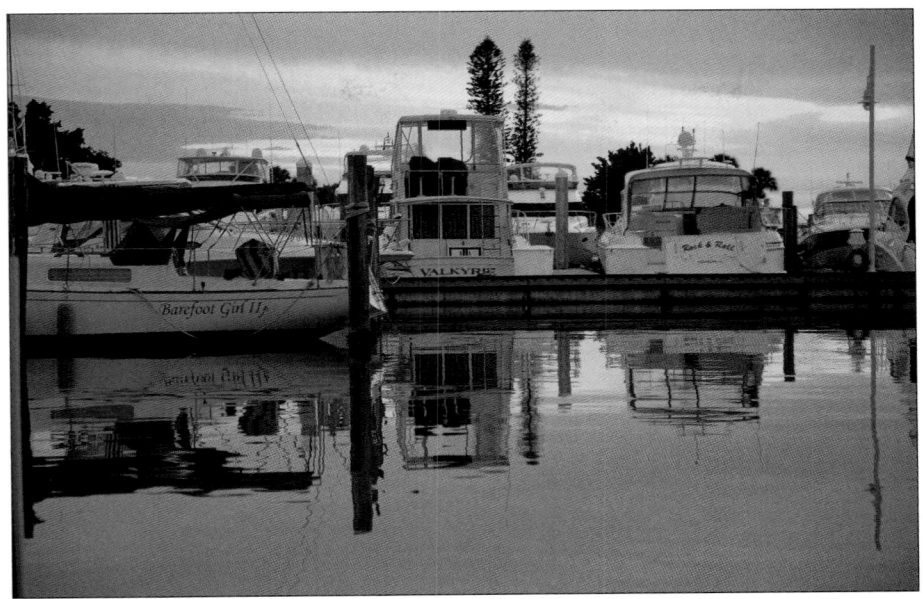

Figure 33-1: Place the horizon line in the upper third of the image.

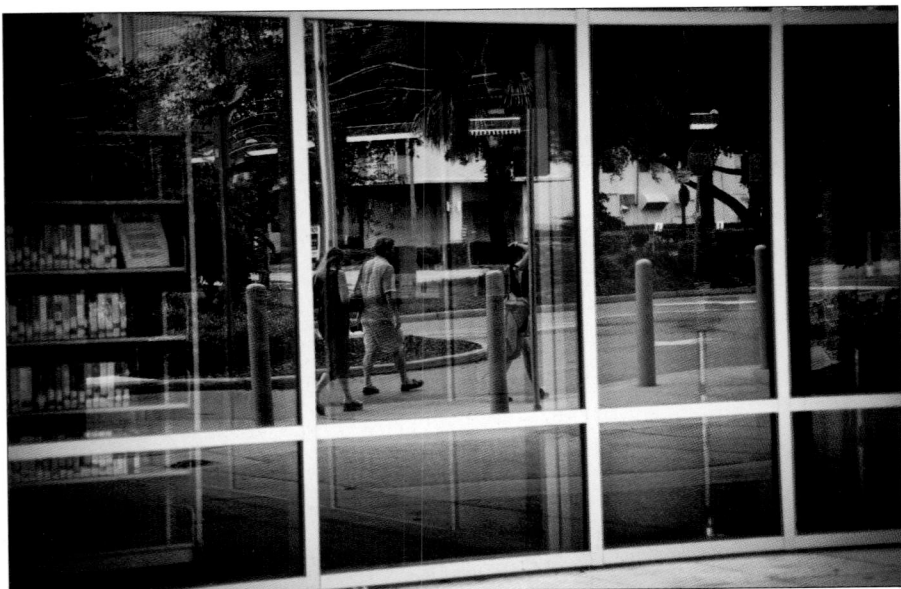

Figure 33-2: Capture reflections from a store window.

Troubleshooting

- ✔ **The reflection is dark.** This problem can occur when you photograph a scene that has a dynamic range that your camera can't capture, such as when the sun is in the image, along with deep shadows. Change your composition so that the sun is hidden behind a building or a tree. Alternatively, you can change your vantage point until the scene doesn't have a huge dynamic range from dark areas to bright areas.

- ✔ **The reflection doesn't have vibrant color.** You may have this problem when you're shooting in harsh light, such as mid-afternoon sun. You can also experience it when you have a lot of cloud cover in your scene. If you capture an image like this, wait until the lighting conditions change or return at a different time.

- ✔ **The entire image is too bright or too dark.** Digital camera metering systems do their best to give you a properly exposed image. If the image is too bright, use exposure compensation to decrease the exposure by 1/3 or 1/2 a stop. If the image is too dark, use exposure compensation to increase the exposure by 1/3 or 1/2 a stop.

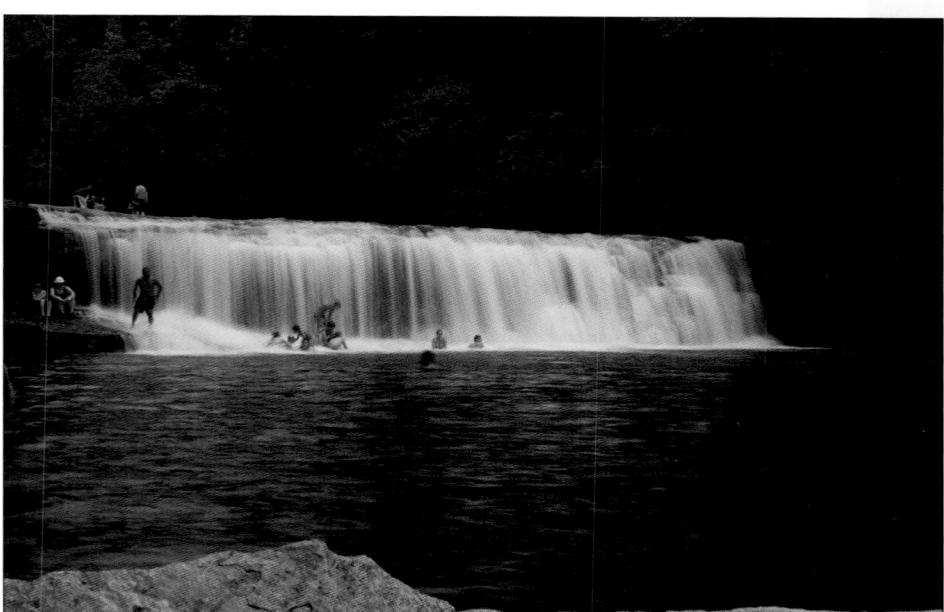

Camera Settings

- ✓ **Metering Mode:** Evaluative
- ✓ **Drive Mode:** Single Shot
- ✓ **Shooting Mode:** Shutter Priority
- ✓ **Shutter Speed:** 1/2 to 1/15 of a second or slower
- ✓ **ISO Setting:** 100
- ✓ **Focus Mode:** Single Shot
- ✓ **Auto-Focus Point:** Single auto-focus point
- ✓ **Focal Length:** Varies (see "Understanding focal lengths" in the appendix)
- ✓ **Image Stabilization:** Optional

*W*aterfalls can be conduits for thousands of gallons of water dropping from lofty mountains when warm spring weather melts the snow, or they can be gently flowing streams of water, dropping a few feet to meet the next level of a river. You can capture wonderfully artistic photos of waterfalls with your digital SLR. This technique — which requires some preparation, and one or two accessories — shows you how to capture a waterfall as a dreamy veil of water. But if you live in an area that has a lot of waterfalls or river rapids, this technique enables you to capture the true beauty of the rushing water.

Setting the Camera

To capture a waterfall as a misty stream of water, shoot in Shutter Priority mode and use a slow shutter speed. Taking a picture by using these settings records the flow of the water, instead of freezing every drop. The ISO setting coupled with the slow shutter speed gives you a small aperture (a large f/stop number), which ensures a large depth of field. The focal length you use depends on both how close you are to the waterfall and the height of the waterfall. If you're photographing water rustling down a river, you can use a wide-angle focal length. However, if you're photographing a distant waterfall, a telephoto focal length is in order.

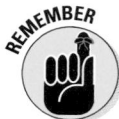

Because you're shooting at a slow shutter speed, you need to mount your camera on a tripod to stabilize the camera.

Taking the Picture

You can't take everything with you. Where would you put it? When you want to photograph a waterfall, get your gear ready the evening before or the morning of the shoot. When you photograph a waterfall in an area you know, you just need a lens that offers the focal length you want, a tripod, and perhaps a neutral density filter. The ISO setting and slow shutter speed give you a large depth of field. However, you need a tripod to stabilize the camera. Some waterfalls are easy to reach; you can park your car by the side of the road and take the picture. To photograph other waterfalls, you may have to hike. If you have to trek to the waterfall, make sure you wear sensible shoes that give you traction on slippery rocks. And pack only what you need — especially if you'll be hoofing it for a while.

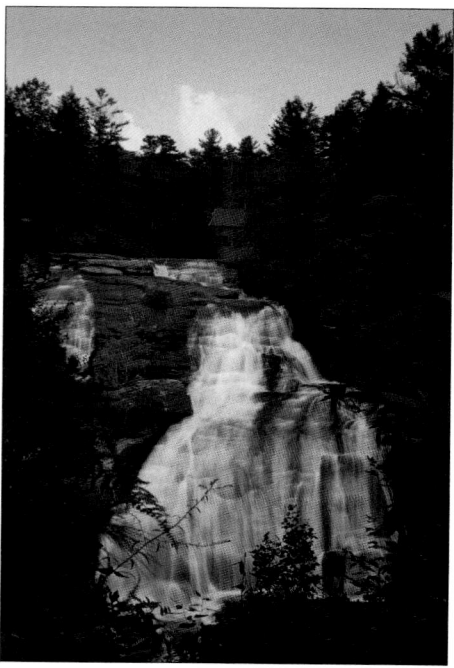

1. **With the proper gear in tow, travel to the waterfall you want to photograph.**

   If you're photographing a tall waterfall, rotate the camera 90 degrees (see Figure 34-1).

Figure 34-1: Photographing a tall waterfall.

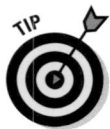

If you don't like the idea of lugging a heavy tripod around with you, consider investing in a Joby Gorillapod (`http://joby.com/gorillapod`). These versatile devices are lightweight, and you can attach them to almost anything. Joby offers several models for small point-and-shoot cameras up to heavy digital SLRs that have long lenses. These devices are great when you go on vacation because they easily fit in checked luggage.

2. **Find a suitable vantage point and mount your camera on a tripod.**

3. **Enable the camera settings listed previously in this chapter.**

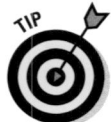

If you're photographing on a bright day, you may not be able to achieve a slow shutter speed. In that case, use a neutral density filter to reduce the amount of light that reaches the camera sensor. Neutral density filters can decrease the amount of light reaching the sensor in a range from 1 to 4 stops.

4. **Zoom in and compose the picture.**

When you compose the picture, make sure you leave some room in the foreground and around the sides of the waterfall so that the image gives your viewers an idea of what the area looks like, and show the roiling water where the waterfall merges with its adjoining body of water.

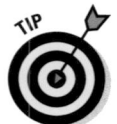

If you're photographing a waterfall at close range, the mist in the air can damage your camera. Keep an inexpensive shower cap in your camera bag that you can use to cover your camera when the air contains a lot of moisture. Cut small holes for your camera strap and a small hole for the lens. Use a rubber band to snug the shower cap to the lens. If you're really ambitious, cut a hole for the viewfinder, and then stick some clear packing tape over both sides of the hole. You don't get a crystal-clear viewfinder view, but it's better than nothing at all and definitely beats getting your camera damaged by moisture.

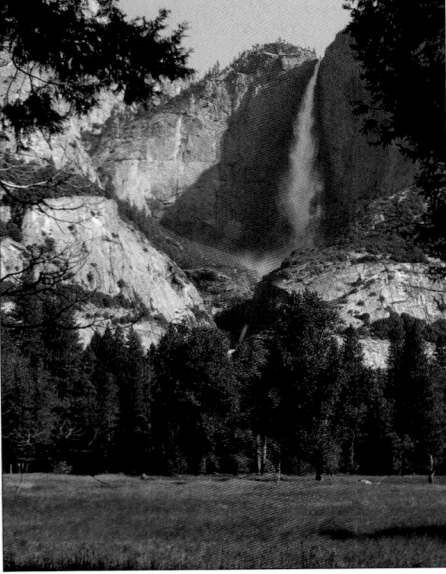

Figure 34-2: Freezing the motion of a waterfall.

5. **Press the shutter button halfway to achieve focus, and then fully press the button to take the picture.**

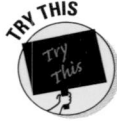

If you're photographing a towering waterfall, such as Yosemite or Bridal Veil Falls, switch to a shutter speed of 1/125 of a second or faster to freeze the motion of the water and mist. When photographing a tall waterfall, rotate the camera 90 degrees (see Figure 34-2).

Troubleshooting

- **The depth of field is too shallow.** This problem may occur if you photograph on an overcast day or in a densely wooded forest. If your camera selects an f/stop value of f/8 or smaller (a large aperture), switch to a higher ISO setting until you get a small aperture (a large f/stop value). An f/stop of f/11 or f/16 is ideal for waterfall photography.

- **The camera doesn't achieve focus.** Your camera may have a hard time achieving focus unless the waterfall includes some dark rocks to provide contrast. Move the auto-focus point over an object that's the same distance from your camera as the waterfall, press the shutter button halfway to achieve focus, and then move the camera to the desired position to compose the picture.

- **The sky above the waterfall is too bright.** On a bright day, the camera tries to compensate for the wide dynamic range. You can deal with this problem after the fact if you process your images in a program such as Lightroom or Photoshop. However, to handle this situation when you actually take the picture, use a graduated neutral density filter, which decreases the amount of light that reaches the top of the sensor and gradually gets lighter, graduating toward clear glass in the middle of the image.

- **The image isn't crystal clear.** You can run into this problem if you don't have a sturdy tripod. When you press the shutter button, vibrations are transmitted to the camera and amplified by an inexpensive tripod. Set the self-timer for its lowest duration. The lag between when you press the shutter button and when the shutter opens should provide time for the camera and tripod to stabilize.

- **The image appears to be moving vertically.** This condition, which is known as *tripod creep,* can happen when you exceed the weight limit of the tripod. The weight of the camera causes the tripod to sink slightly, which the camera picks up in the image because of the slow shutter speed. Switch to a lighter lens.

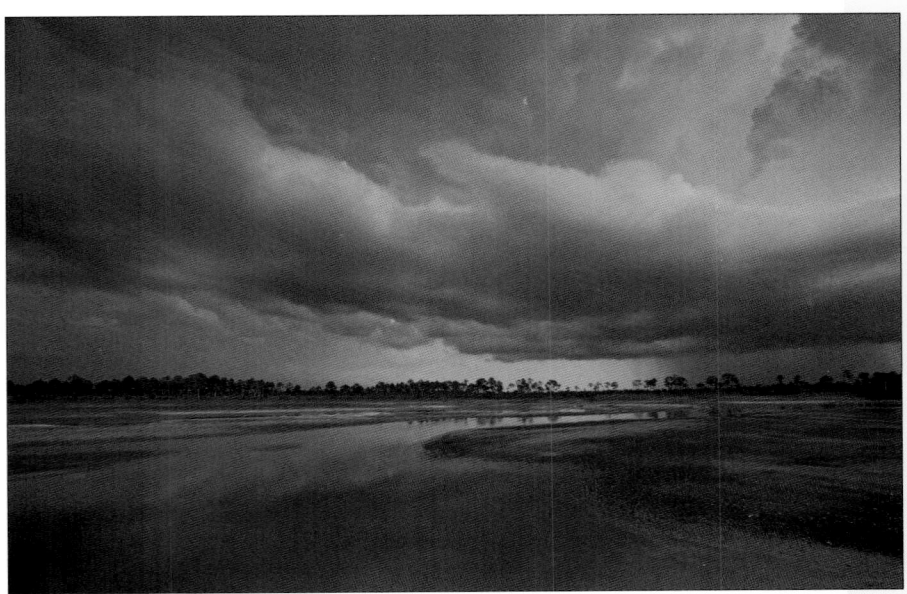

35 Landscapes in Stormy Weather

Many photographers don't like rainy weather. It's not fun to be out in the rain, especially if you live in Florida, where daily monsoons happen like clockwork in summer. And then you have to deal with your gear getting wet. Talk about your oil and water (that is, your camera gear and water definitely don't mix). But if you protect yourself — and don't take pictures during a thunderstorm — you can get some awesome photographs of landscapes in stormy weather.

Setting the Camera

When you photograph a landscape in stormy weather, the scene includes a lot of ominous clouds, which decreases the visibility considerably. Therefore, you have to set the ISO to 400. When you shoot landscapes, you want an incredible depth of field, so you use Aperture Priority mode. However, the dim conditions require that you use a medium aperture of f/8.0 to f/11.0. When you use this aperture with a wide-angle focal length of 28mm, you still get a tremendous depth of field, and unless the conditions are absolutely abysmal (dark and gloomy), you still can hand-hold the camera when you take this type of picture.

Taking the Picture

When you photograph during dubious weather, you need to be prepared for the worst. Never venture far from cover. A sudden storm could ruin your day and your camera. Manufacture a makeshift cover for your camera by using either a baggie or a shower cap. If you're serious about having a place to store you stuff, consider buying a camera bag that features a rain cover. As long as you're protected and you have protection for your camera, step outside your tent, cabin, or vehicle and take a different type of landscape photograph.

1. **When you find an interesting landscape to photograph, enable the settings discussed previously in this chapter.**

2. **Find a suitable vantage point.**

   Move around the scene and put the camera to your eye when you see something that looks interesting.

3. **Zoom out to about 28mm.**

   You don't have to use the focal length I recommend. When you zoom out, notice what's in the frame. If you see too much in the viewfinder (such as a tree stump appearing on either side of the picture), either zoom in or walk forward (*foot zoom* in photographer speak) until the offending element disappears from the frame.

4. **Compose the picture.**

   Make minute adjustments in your position until you like what you see in the viewfinder. As a rule, you don't want a symmetrical composition. Place an object of interest on a power point according to the Rule of Thirds. Also, when you photograph in stormy weather, you have a sky full of angry clouds. They should be the predominant part of your photograph, so place the horizon line in the lower third of the image (see Figure 35-1).

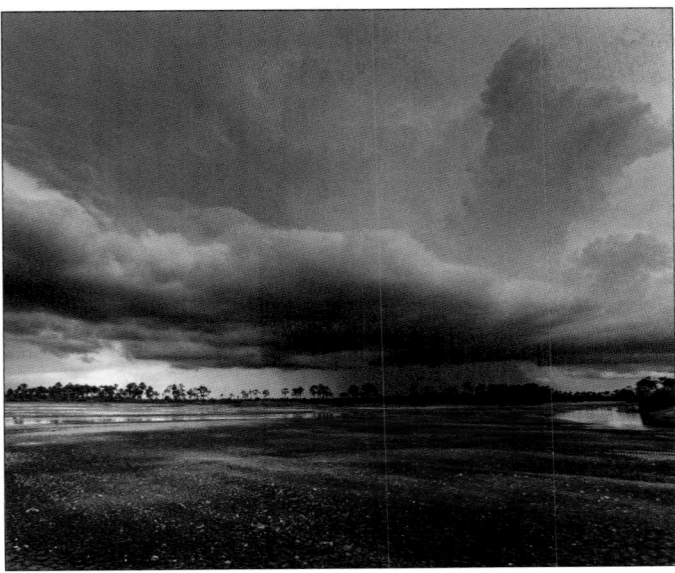

Figure 35-1: When you photograph a landscape that has ominous clouds, place the horizon line in the lower third of the image.

5. **Press the shutter button halfway to achieve focus, and then press the button completely to take the picture.**

   After you take the picture, review the image on your LCD monitor to make sure it's properly exposed.

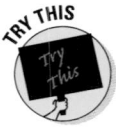

Wait until the storm starts to clear and take a picture when some blue sky and sun enter the equation (see Figure 35-2). One of Ansel Adams' most famous landscape photographs was taken when a storm was clearing and is aptly named "Clearing Winter Storm."

Troubleshooting

✔ **The image is brighter than the scene.** Cameras often overcompensate in gloomy weather and give you a picture that's much brighter than the actual conditions. Use exposure compensation to decrease the exposure. If you're photographing on a really dreary day, you may have to decrease the exposure by as much as 1 stop.

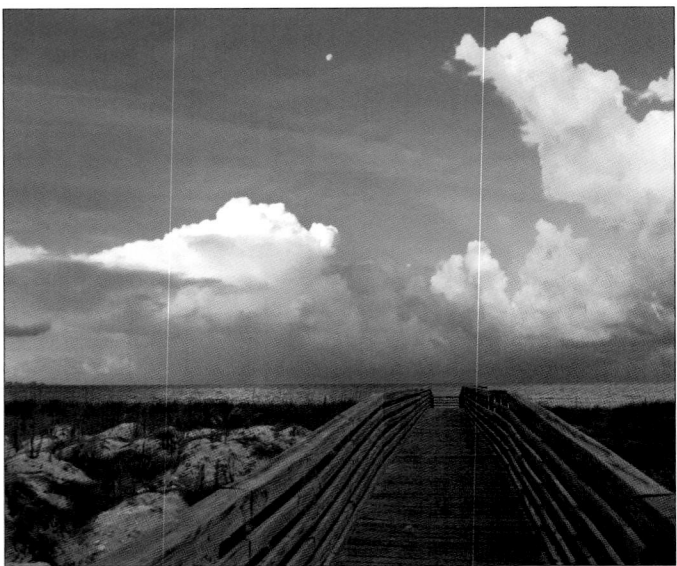

Figure 35-2: Photograph a clearing storm.

↙ **The sun is peaking through and looks like an orange blob.** Your camera can't handle the dynamic range of bright sun and dark shadows in the same image. You can bring things back into range by using a graduated neutral density filter. This filter is dark at the top and gradually becomes brighter until the filter is completely clear in the middle. The darker part of the filter decreases the amount of light reaching the sensor, which helps you capture a bit of detail in the sun and surrounding clouds.

↙ **The clouds are brighter than the scene.** This problem can occur when you have a fairly dark landscape, such as the image in Figure 35-1. When I took this shot, I added a graduated neutral density filter to my camera to darken the tops of the clouds.

↙ **Condensation forms on the camera.** This situation happens when you leave an air-conditioned building or car, and walk into humid conditions. Picture the condensation on the side of a can of soda during a hot summer day. Let your camera gradually acclimate to the humid conditions. If you're using a car for cover, turn off the air conditioner a couple of minutes before you venture outside. Plus, when the car fogs up inside, you can play tic-tac-toe on the windshield to pass the time. If you're going directly from an air conditioned building to humid conditions, leave your camera in the camera bag for several minutes until it's acclimatized.

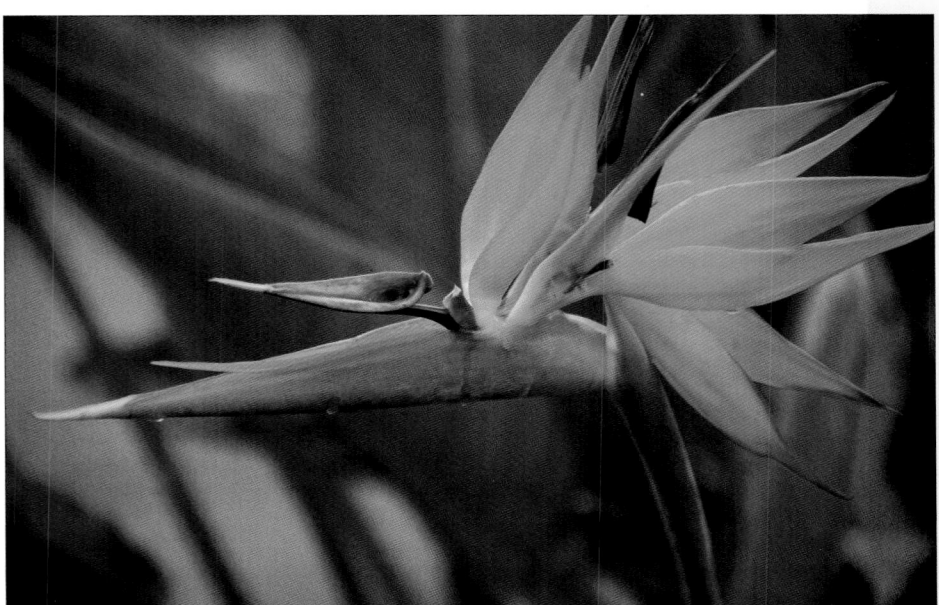

Camera Settings

- ✔ **Metering Mode:** Evaluative
- ✔ **Drive Mode:** Single Shot
- ✔ **Shooting Mode:** Aperture Priority
- ✔ **Aperture:** f/3.5 to f/5.6
- ✔ **ISO Setting:** 100, 200, or the lowest setting that gives you a shutter speed that's the reciprocal of the focal length you're using to photograph the flower
- ✔ **Focus Mode:** Single Shot
- ✔ **Auto-Focus Point:** Single auto-focus point
- ✔ **Focal Length:** 100mm or longer (35mm equivalent; see "Understanding focal lengths" in the appendix)
- ✔ **Image Stabilization:** Enable this feature if your camera or lens has it

*1*f you have lush flowers in your yard or live near a botanical garden, you have a rich resource for wonderful flower photographs. You can take a nice photograph of a flowerbed or create something really special by photographing a flower up close and personal. A close-up of a flower reveals beautiful architecture; elegant silky petals, spindly stamens, plus the wonderful vibrant colors.

When you see a compelling photograph of a flower, you can almost smell that flower. To create a similar photograph, you need great-looking flowers, the right light, and a good eye for composition. Add the settings and techniques discussed in this chapter, and you're well on your way to creating great photographs of flowers.

Setting the Camera

When you photograph a close-up of a flower, you take the picture almost like you're shooting a portrait of a person. In both cases, you carefully compose the image and choose the proper camera settings to get a great photograph. When you shoot in Aperture Priority mode and use a large aperture (a small f/stop number), you get a shallow depth of field that draws the viewer's attention to the flower. With a single auto-focus point, you can lock focus on any part of the flower so that you draw attention to the stamen, a flower petal, or an insect on the flower. A low ISO setting gives you a crisp image that has little or no digital noise. A focal length of 100mm lets you zoom in on the flower. However, you can get better results if you have a macro lens, which lets you get real close to the flower and capture wonderful detail. If your camera or lens has image stabilization, enable the feature. When you capture close-ups of any object, the slightest bit of operator movement can result in an image that doesn't look sharp. Don't use image stabilization if you mount your camera on a tripod.

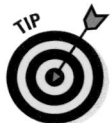 Many lenses come equipped with a Macro mode, which lets you get really close to your subject and still keep it in focus. If you don't have a macro lens, consider purchasing one if you enjoy photographing close-ups of objects such as flowers. This type of photography is known as *macro photography*.

Taking the Picture

You get your best images if you photograph flowers in flattering light, such as soft window light. You can photograph flowers indoors or outdoors. If you photograph flowers outdoors, take your photos early in the morning or late in the afternoon because the light is wonderfully soft and has a golden hue. Also, cloudy overcast conditions offer soft, diffuse light, which is great for this type of photograph.

1. **When you see a flower that you want to photograph, find a suitable vantage point and enable the camera settings previously shown in this chapter.**

   Photograph a light-colored flower against a dark background and photo-graph a dark-colored flower against a light background. If you're shooting a flower indoors, try placing it near a window that's not receiving direct sunlight so that you can get soft, diffuse light.

2. **Zoom in and press the shutter button halfway to achieve focus.**

3. **Compose the picture.**

   If you're taking a picture of the entire flower, make sure you leave a bit of breathing space around the flower.

4. **Press the shutter button fully down to take the picture.**

Use your on camera or auxiliary flash to add a kiss of light to the image. This extra light warms the image and adds light to the shadows (see Figure 36-1). If your camera has flash exposure compensation, use it to determine how much light the flash adds to the image.

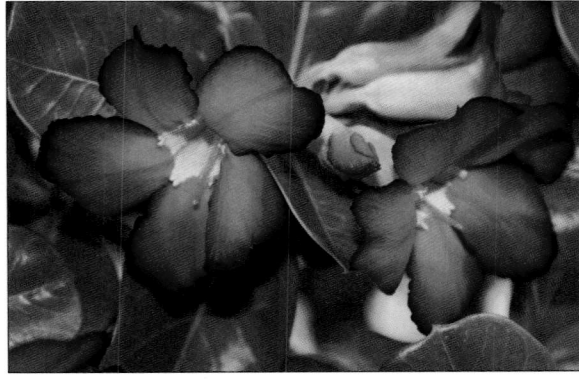

Figure 36-1: Using fill flash to illuminate the shadows.

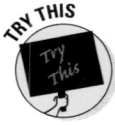

You can create a very intimate flower portrait if you zoom in tight and capture fine details of the flower (see Figure 36-2). When you zoom in this closely, remember to compose the scene in your viewfinder to create an aesthetically pleasing picture.

Troubleshooting

- ✓ **It's windy, and the camera won't focus on the flower.** First, you can try placing someone or something upwind from the flower to act as a windbreak. (A carefully positioned piece of cardboard can serve as an effective windbreak.) Second, you can set your camera to Continuous Auto-Focus mode, which tracks the flower while the wind moves it.

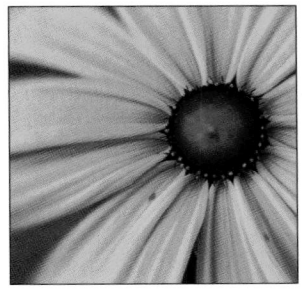

Figure 36-2: Zoom in tight to capture fine details of a flower.

- ✓ **The flower is too dark.** This issue can come up when you photograph a light-colored flower against a very dark background. Use exposure compensation to increase the exposure or use fill flash to brighten the flower.

- ✓ **The flower is too bright.** This problem occurs when you photograph a very dark flower against a bright background. Use exposure compensation to reduce the exposure until you get the desired result.

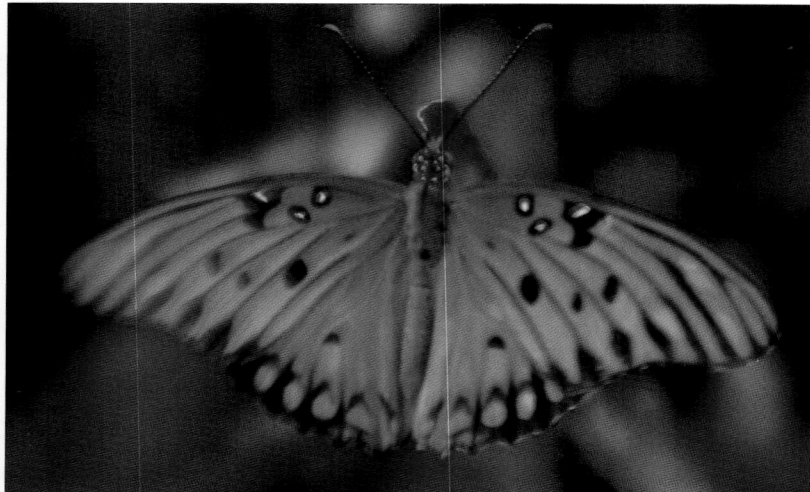

37 Insect and Other Creepy Crawly Close-Ups

You can find a wonderful world of small critters that fly through the air, crawl on the ground, or spin their own webs. If you're a nature lover, photographing insects is a natural. This type of photography requires you to get close to your subject — really close.

Photographing flying insects presents a unique challenge because they're always flitting from flower to flower. The constant movement can try your patience and tax your camera's focusing system. Insects that crawl on the ground or live in webs present challenges, as well. However, with a bit of patience and the following settings, you can capture rewarding pictures of insects.

Warning: A certain amount of caution is in order when photographing certain bugs. Don't get too close to an insect that can sting or cause you harm.

Setting the Camera

With the exception of large spiders, most of the insects you photograph are fairly small, which means you have to get close to your subject. Photographing insects by using Shutter Priority mode enables you to choose a shutter speed fast enough to freeze the motion of the insect's wings. Shooting with a fast shutter speed is also handy when you're photographing crawling insects because when you zoom in tight with a fairly long focal length, the slightest movement of the camera or subject is magnified, which means you get an image that isn't tack sharp.

If you're photographing small insects, you may need a macro lens to get close enough to your subjects. A low ISO setting gives you a relatively noise-free image. It also ensures a fairly large aperture, even in bright sun, which gives you a shallow depth of field. Enabling your camera's Continuous Auto-Focus mode lets the camera track the insect while it moves in the frame. This mode is also handy when you're photographing a subject such as a spider whose web is blowing in the wind because the camera updates focus as the spider's web moves to and fro in the wind.

If you try to photograph an insect by using a focal length of less than 100mm, you have to get very close to the bug in question, which may cause it to fly away. You may also be putting yourself in harm's way if you're photographing a potentially dangerous insect, such as a bee (see Figure 37-1).

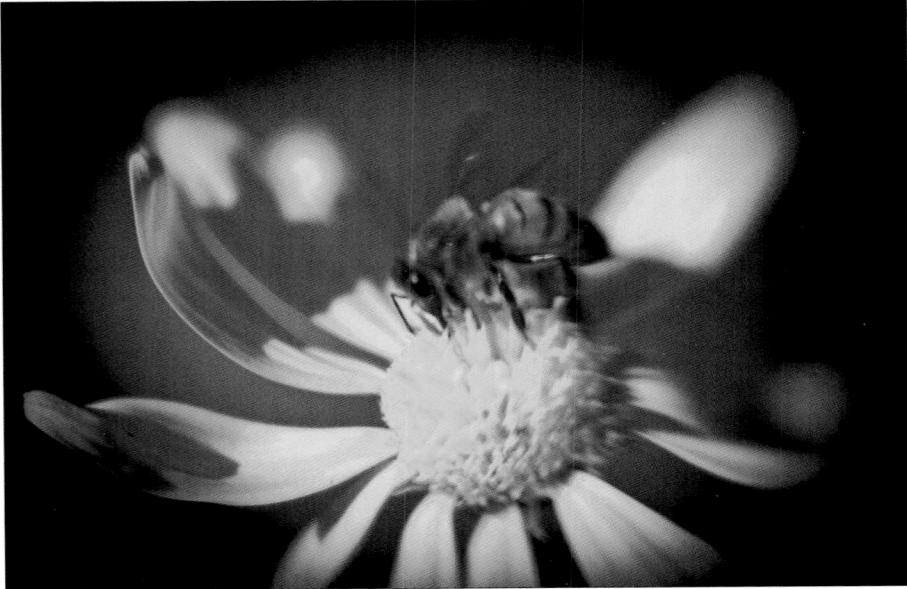

Figure 37-1: Use a long focal length to distance yourself from insects that sting.

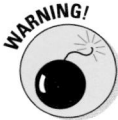

If you're photographing insects on an overcast day, you may need to increase the ISO. Unless you have one of the newer full-frame sensor cameras, don't exceed ISO 800. If you do, your photos will include noticeable digital noise that degrade the image.

Taking the Picture

If you have a butterfly garden in your back yard, you have all the elements you need for taking pictures of insects. The alternative is a stroll through a park or someplace that provides a home to a lot of insects.

1. **Enable the camera settings discussed earlier in this chapter.**

2. **Aim your camera at a flower or bush where you've seen the insect you want to photograph.**

   Patiently waiting for an insect to appear can be a lot easier than trying to chase insects. If you wait in a place frequented by the insect you want to photograph, your subject appears sooner or later.

3. **Zoom in.**

   You have to make your best guess for the actual focal length to use, based on your knowledge of the insect. Try to visualize the size of the insect. You can always fine-tune the focal length when the insect appears in the frame.

4. **When an insect appears, press the shutter button halfway to achieve focus; quickly fine-tune your focal length, and then fully press the button to take the picture.**

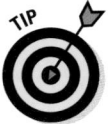

Try to leave some space around the insect (see Figure 37-2), especially if it's a kind of bug that constantly flits from flower to flower. If you don't leave enough space around the insect and it starts flying when you press the shutter button, you end up cutting off part of the insect in your picture. You can always crop out a bit of extra space when you edit the image.

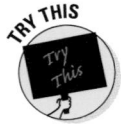

Enable your camera's Continuous Shooting mode to take several pictures of the insect in motion. Taking several pictures ensures that you capture at least a couple good images of the insect. You can also assemble the resulting images in an image-editing application that supports animation to create something that looks like a movie.

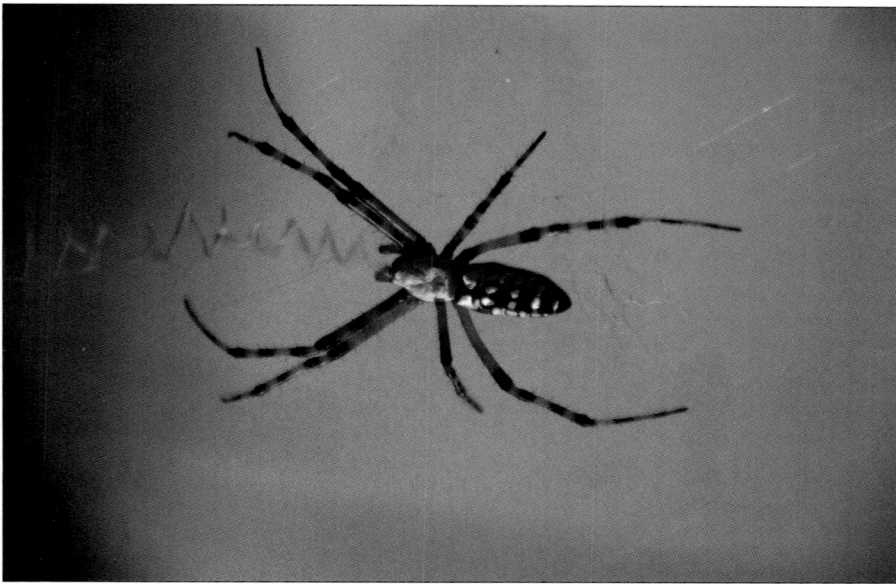

Figure 37-2: Leave some space around the bug.

Troubleshooting

✔ **The insect's wings are blurry.** This problem occurs when you photograph an insect such as a bee. Increase the shutter speed and take another picture.

✔ **The insect isn't in focus (#1).** Sometimes, photographers are a bit too quick to push the shutter button and end up with an image in which something other than the subject is in focus. If you jump the photo-taking gun, take the picture again and make sure the auto-focus point is over your subject before you press the shutter button halfway.

✔ **The insect isn't in focus (#2).** This problem may also occur if you don't position the auto-focus point over your subject when you achieve focus. Take the picture again, making sure the camera achieves focus on the insect before you move the camera to compose the image.

✔ **The camera doesn't achieve focus.** You have this problem when you zoom in too close. Move away from the subject, and then try again. You probably need a macro lens if you're photographing a very small insect.

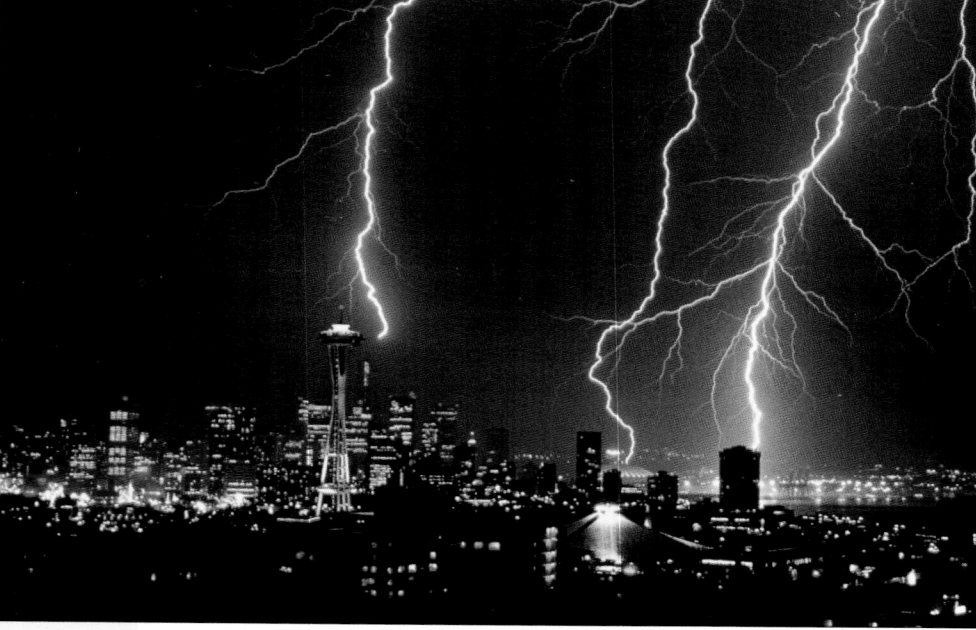

PhotoDisc, Inc.

38 Lightning

W eather is a wonderful thing to photograph, even when it turns ugly. When the clouds build, the temperature starts falling, and the wind starts blowing, you know that a storm is nearby. Soon, you'll hear the rumble of thunder and see streaks of lightning illuminate the sky. You can photograph lightning during the day if you have a sensor mounted to your hot shoe that triggers the shutter when the sensor detects lightning. These sensors cost a few hundred dollars. But you can get great pictures of lightning at night (as shown here) by using only a tripod or some other means to stabilize the camera, plus a remote trigger, in addition to your camera.

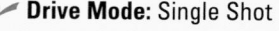

Camera Settings

- ✔ **Metering Mode:** Evaluative
- ✔ **Drive Mode:** Single Shot
- ✔ **Shooting Mode:** Bulb (B on most cameras)
- ✔ **Aperture:** f/16
- ✔ **ISO Setting:** 100
- ✔ **Focus Mode:** Single Shot
- ✔ **Auto-Focus Point:** Single auto-focus point
- ✔ **Focal Length:** Varies (see "Understanding focal lengths" in the appendix)
- ✔ **Image Stabilization:** Off

Setting the Camera

When you photograph a thunderstorm at night, you want to capture one or more streaks of lightning per exposure, which you can do by keeping the shutter open for a long period of time. When you take a photograph in Bulb mode, the shutter stays open as long as the shutter button is fully pressed. The small aperture (large f/stop number) and low ISO setting ensure that you have an exposure of ten seconds or longer, which is plenty if you're photographing a distant thunderstorm. Because you have your camera mounted on a tripod, turn image stabilization off.

Taking the Picture

When you hear the delicate sound of thunder in the distance, you'll soon see jagged streaks of lightning. You know how far away the storm is by how long it takes to hear thunder after seeing a streak of lightning. If it takes five seconds to hear the thunder, the storm is a mile away. You may think it's safe to stay outside and photograph a storm that's a couple of miles away, but it isn't. Lightning has been known to travel ten miles before striking ground. Therefore, pick the location (preferably under shelter) from which you want to photograph the storm ahead of time. If you know the pattern for storms in your area (and if you don't, watch local weather news to find out), you can almost predict at what time of the evening you can photograph lightning.

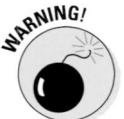

As long as you keep out of harm's way, you can capture some wonderful photographs during an electrical storm. You can create photos of familiar landscapes punctuated with artistic stabs of lightning.

With the necessary precautions in mind, pack up your gear and follow these steps:

1. **Travel to the place from which you're going to photograph the storm.**

   An excellent location is a hill from which you can see a city in the distance. Just make sure you're near your car or some other shelter in case the storm changes direction.

2. **Mount your camera on a tripod and attach the remote switch.**

3. **Enable the settings discussed earlier in this chapter.**

4. **Zoom in and compose the picture.**

   If you're photographing a city during a thunderstorm, compose the picture so that a prominent building or landmark is off to one side of the image. Doing so creates viewer interest, which makes your viewer want to spend some time with your image. If the prominent landmark is a tall building, you may get lucky and take a picture when lightning strikes it. Also, place your horizon line in the lower third of the image, which draws your viewer's attention to the lightning.

5. **Press the remote button halfway to achieve focus.**

6. **Press the remote button fully to take the picture.**

   The shutter remains open as long as you keep the remote button pressed.

7. **Count off about 20 seconds, and then release the remote.**

   With any luck, you have at least one streak of lightning in the photo. If you're photographing a violent thunderstorm, you may have several streaks of lightning in the image.

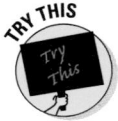

Photograph the countryside during a thunderstorm. The lack of ambient light renders the trees and other topography as silhouettes in contrast to the bright spears of lightning (see Figure 38-1).

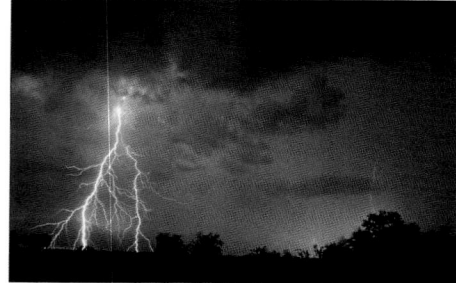

PhotoDisc/Getty Images

Figure 38-1: Photographing the countryside in a thunderstorm.

Troubleshooting

✓ **The camera doesn't achieve focus.** Many photographers have this problem when photographing distant scenes at night. Switch to manual focus and set the focus at infinity.

✓ **I can't see the camera controls.** Many cameras have a button that you can push to illuminate the LCD view. You may also want to carry a small penlight with you.

✓ **The nearby trees are bright.** When traffic passes by and car headlights briefly illuminate the trees, those trees look brighter. Photograph from a vantage point that doesn't have much traffic in the scene.

✓ **The image is too dark.** This problem occurs when the scene doesn't have a lot of ambient light. Hold the shutter open for another five or ten seconds to let more light reach the sensor.

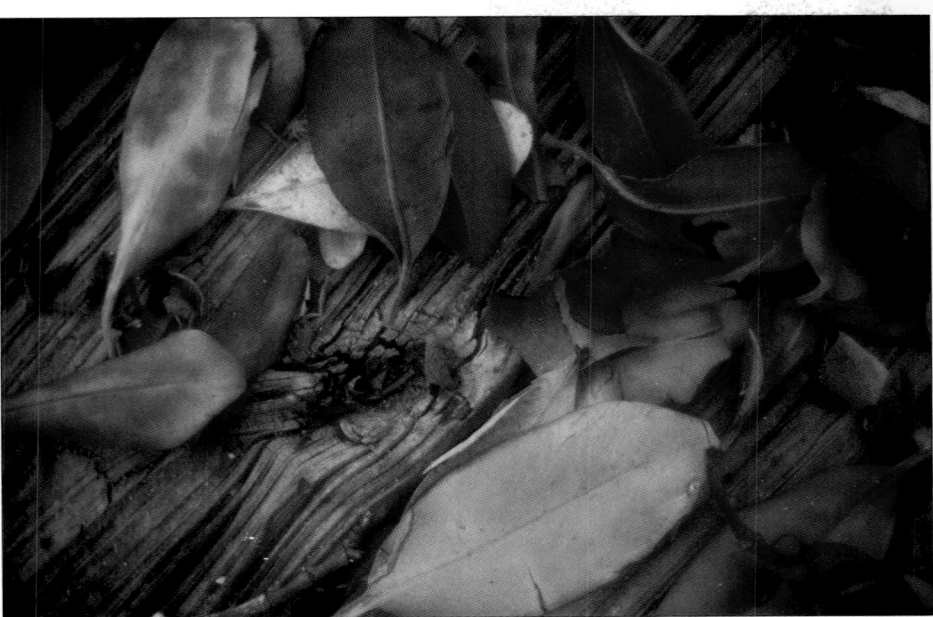

Camera Settings

- ✓ **Metering Mode:** Evaluative; this mode uses the entire scene for metering but emphasizes the middle of the scene
- ✓ **Drive Mode:** Single Shot
- ✓ **Shooting Mode:** Aperture Priority
- ✓ **Aperture:** The lens's largest aperture to f/4.0
- ✓ **ISO Setting:** 100, 200, or the lowest setting that gives you a shutter speed that's the reciprocal of the focal length you're using to photograph the image
- ✓ **Focus Mode:** Single Shot
- ✓ **Auto-Focus Point:** Single auto-focus point; with a single auto-focus point, you can lock focus on any part of the scene you're photographing
- ✓ **Focal Length:** 100mm or longer (35mm equivalent; see "Understanding focal lengths" in the appendix)
- ✓ **Image Stabilization:** Use this feature if your camera or lens has it

Some photographers are so busy looking at what's directly in front of their path, they often miss photo opportunities to the left, right, above, or below them. When you're photographing nature, take a photograph to capture the big picture, but then take a moment to stop and notice the lovely details around you.

This type of photography is similar to flower photography (see Chapter 36). You zoom in on your subject, and then use or break the rules of composition to create a compelling photograph.

Whether you're walking in a city park or hiking in a state park, you never know what you'll find when you start looking at the details around you — perhaps an artistic pile of leaves on a boardwalk (as shown here).

Setting the Camera

When you photograph details of the world around you, you're cutting to the chase, capturing an image of specific details that includes nothing else that would distract your viewer's attention. For this kind of photography, you need a telephoto zoom lens that has a maximum focal length of at least 100mm, which gets you close to your subject. When you photograph details, you use Aperture Priority mode, coupled with a large aperture and long focal length to limit the depth of field and draw attention to your subject. The low ISO setting gives you a noise-free image. Image stabilization helps ensure a sharp picture at slow shutter speeds (but disable image stabilization if you mount your camera on a tripod).

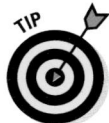

If you have a macro lens, you can use it for this type of photography. Your telephoto lens may also have a Macro mode. Either option lets you get very close to your subject.

Taking the Picture

This type of photography begs for flattering light. Early morning or late afternoon is the best time to photograph subtle details in nature due to the soft nature of the light and its golden hue. Cloudy, overcast conditions are another option for this type of photography because this type of weather gives you soft, diffuse light.

Go to the location where you've found something you want to photograph and follow these steps:

1. **Find an interesting vantage point and enable the camera settings discussed previously in this chapter.**

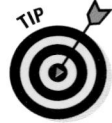

   When an object gets your attention, don't shoot from the position where you were when you noticed the object. Walk around the object until you find a vantage point that creates an interesting photograph. You may find a couple of different vantage points that look good. Shoot pictures from all of them.

2. **Zoom in on your subject and press the shutter button halfway to achieve focus.**

3. **Move the camera to a different position to compose the picture.**

   When you photograph details, the sky's the limit. You can create a straightforward shot, position your center of interest to the left or right of the photo's center, or tilt the camera to create an abstract image.

4. **Press the shutter button fully to take the picture.**

You can use auxiliary flash to add light to the shadow areas and warm the image.

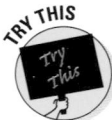

You can create a compelling image by zooming in on details such as vines (see Figure 39-1) or spider webs. Also, foggy mornings or immediately following a rainstorm are great times to photograph nature because the light is soft and diffuse, and shiny drops of water cover the leaves.

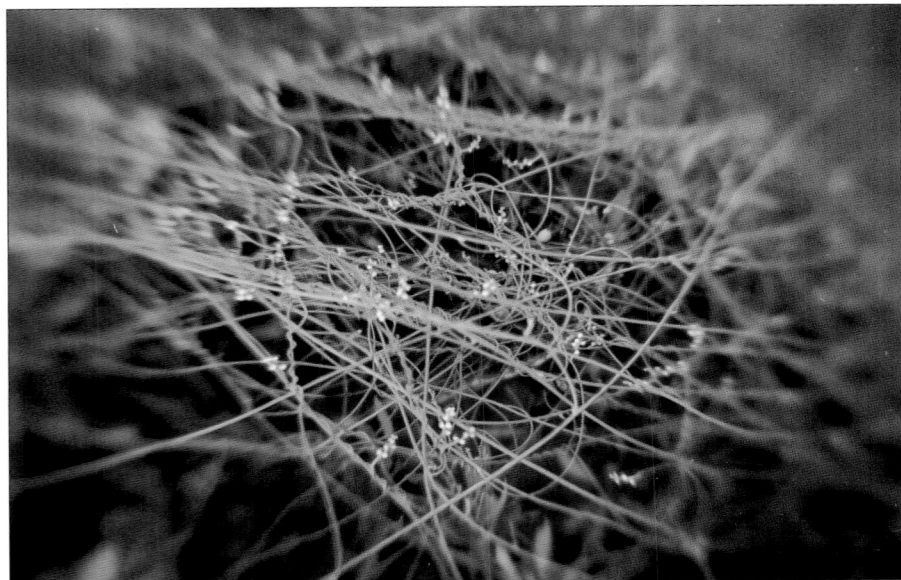

Figure 39-1: Zoom in on details, such as vines.

Troubleshooting

- **The subject looks great, but the image lacks interest.** When an image doesn't capture your attention immediately, the image probably isn't well composed. Move to a slightly different vantage point, tilt the camera, or zoom in until you see something interesting in the viewfinder.

- **The image isn't colorful.** Many objects in nature are monochromatic and therefore aren't good subjects for color photographs. For example, green leaves on a green background can't create a compelling image. Look for scenes that have a wide variety of colors to keep the viewer's eye dancing within the image. Remember the eye is attracted to warm colors (reds and yellows).

- **The camera doesn't focus on my subject.** If you try to get up close and personal with your subject by using a lens that's not a macro lens, you're standing too close, so the lens can't achieve focus. Back up a bit and press the shutter button halfway, then wait for the focus lamp to illuminate.

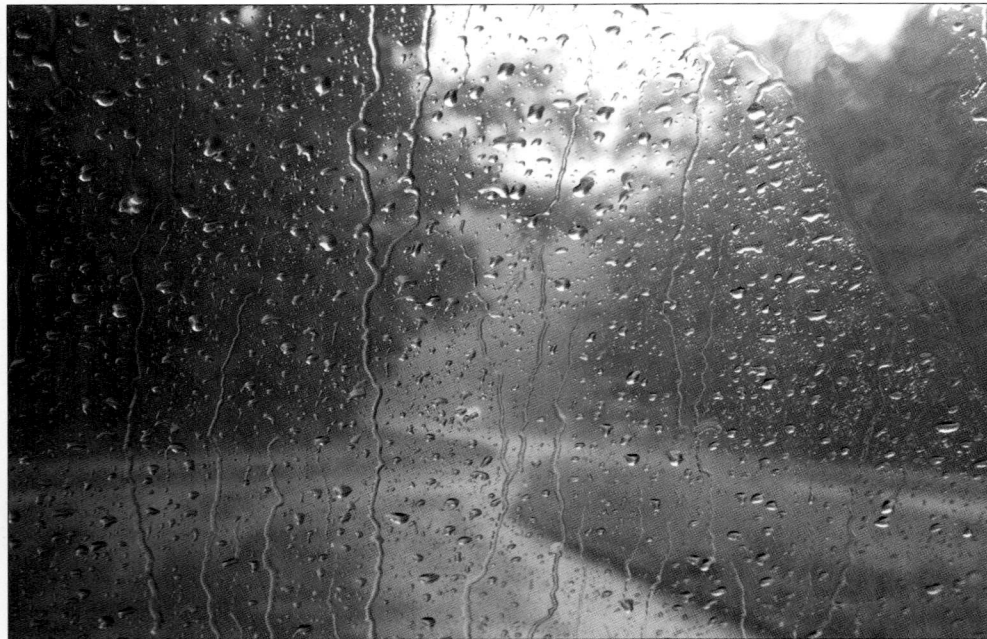

40 Rain

Your parents told you not to play in the rain. But most creative types don't take directions well, and prefer to work and play outside the envelope. The fact that you're reading this chapter means you probably played in the rain when you were a kid. And, to be honest, many of us are still kids at heart. When you photograph anything in the rain, you get soft, muted colors. If it's really raining hard, you can capture an interesting photo by focusing on the raindrops on your windshield, which makes everything outside look like a Monet painting.

You have to be careful when you photograph in the rain. As long as the rain doesn't come with lightning and you're dressed for the elements, you have no problem. Your camera, however, is another kettle of fish. If your camera gets wet, the water can damage the sensitive components and perhaps ruin the camera. In this chapter, I discuss the fine art of photographing in the rain and offer a tip for protecting your camera.

Camera Settings

- **Metering Mode:** Evaluative
- **Drive Mode:** Single Shot
- **Shooting Mode:** Aperture Priority
- **Aperture:** f/7.1 to f/11.0
- **ISO Setting:** 400 to 800
- **Focus Mode:** Single Shot
- **Auto-Focus Point:** Single auto-focus point
- **Focal Length:** 50mm (35mm equivalent; see "Understanding focal lengths" in the appendix)
- **Image Stabilization:** Optional

Setting the Camera

When you photograph in the rain, you can capture wonderfully muted colors thanks to the way that the clouds and rain diffuse the light. Rain and clouds are Mother Nature's soft box. The amount of rain is also a factor. If you try to photograph in an outright deluge, you end up with very dreamy pictures. If you photograph in a light drizzle, you get wonderful reflections of streetlights on pavement. If you're photographing in a light rainstorm, you can capture slashes of rain. The suggested aperture range gives you a decent depth of field. The suggested focal length should enable you to hand-hold the camera, in most instances. The higher ISO setting is a compromise between image quality and the ability to take pictures in overcast conditions without using a tripod. If the weather is very overcast and you can't achieve a shutter speed of at least 1/50 of a second (1/15 of a second if you use image stabilization), you have to use a tripod.

Taking the Picture

When you photograph in the rain, you need to protect yourself. Don't attempt to photograph outdoors in a thunderstorm. Photograph when the rain is abating or has stopped. If you photograph outdoors, you need to protect your camera. You can photograph from within a car through a clean windshield or through an open window. When the rain slows to a drizzle, you can get some great shots of reflections in puddles or on asphalt. You can even venture out of your vehicle or from under cover if you have some way to protect the camera. You can

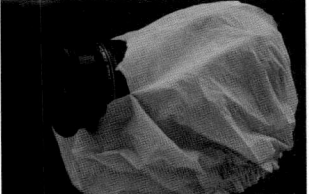

Figure 40-1: Protect your camera from the weather.

create a makeshift rain hood for your camera from a plastic bag or a shower cap. Use rubber bands to wrap the plastic bag or shower cap snugly around the camera (see Figure 40-1).

1. **Enable the camera settings listed previously in this chapter.**

2. **Compose the scene.**

3. **Press the shutter button halfway to achieve focus, and then press the shutter button fully to take the picture.**

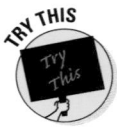

When the sun comes out, take pictures of reflections of scenery in puddles (see Figure 40-2). Photograph a scene like this from a low vantage point to make the puddle the predominant part of the image. You also want to make sure you can see part of the object making the reflection. But on second thought, if you have a reflection that is almost perfect, a picture of the puddle would also pique viewer curiosity.

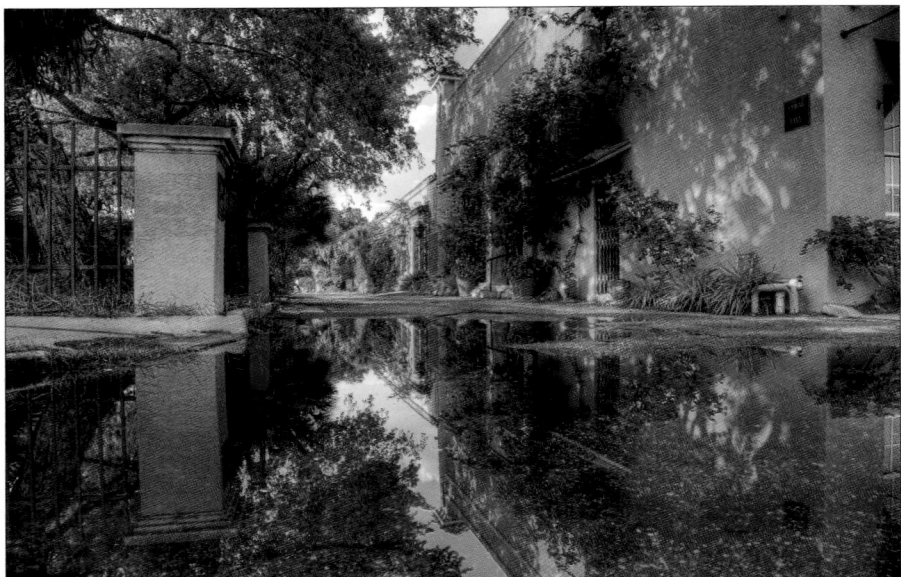

Figure 40-2: Take pictures of reflections in puddles.

Troubleshooting

✏ **The camera can't achieve focus.** This problem can occur when you attempt to take a picture of anything in a blinding rainstorm. If the camera can't achieve focus, your only option is to focus manually.

✏ **The camera lens fogs.** You can run into this problem if you leave a conditioned space and venture into very humid conditions. Try to clear the lens by using your lens cleaning equipment. However, the lens may fog up again immediately. The best option is to give the camera a few minutes to adjust to the new conditions.

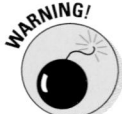

Don't change the lens, battery, or memory card when you move to an area that has different climatic conditions than the area you just left. Wait until the camera adjusts to the new conditions before you change lenses or open the camera. If you leave a conditioned space and immediately open your camera in humid conditions, condensation forms on the inside of your camera, which can potentially damage sensitive electronic components.

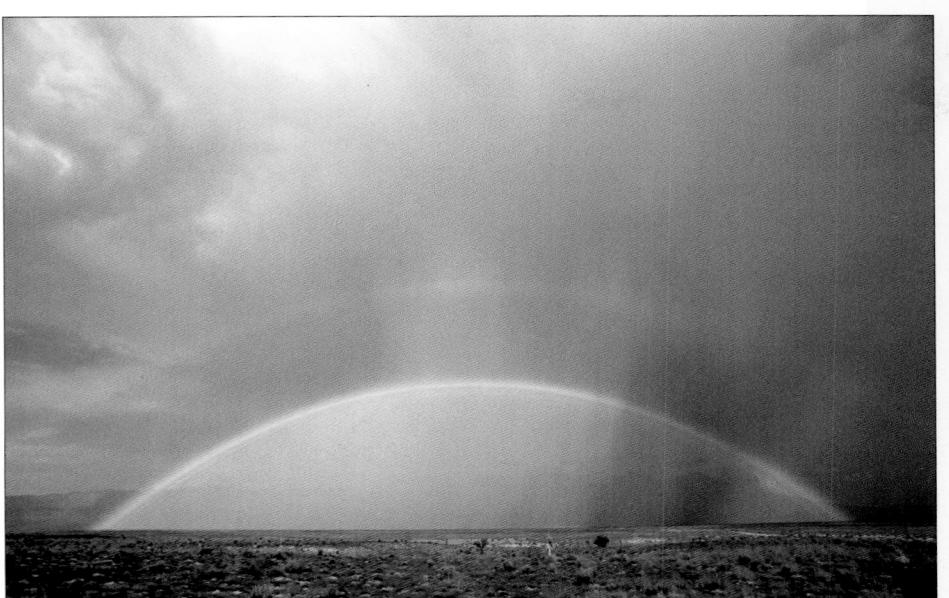

PhotoDisc/Getty Images

Camera Settings

- ✔ **Metering Mode:** Evaluative
- ✔ **Drive Mode:** Single Shot
- ✔ **Shooting Mode:** Aperture Priority
- ✔ **Aperture:** f/11 or smaller
- ✔ **ISO Setting:** 100 to 200
- ✔ **Focus Mode:** Single Shot
- ✔ **Auto-Focus Point:** Multiple auto-focus points
- ✔ **Focal Length:** 28mm to 35mm (35mm equivalent; see "Understanding focal lengths" in the appendix)
- ✔ **Image Stabilization:** On

*Y*ou may never find the mythical pot of gold at the end of the rainbow, but you can capture wonderful pictures of rainbows by using your digital SLR. Rainbows occur when the sun passes through droplets of water. You can find rainbows when a rainstorm clears, and you also can find rainbows near waterfalls.

When you see a rainbow, you need just your camera and the settings in this chapter to capture a compelling image.

Setting the Camera

Rainbows occur when you least expect them, so never leave home without a camera. When you do see a rainbow, you want to capture it, as well as the surroundings, in sharp focus. Therefore, use Aperture Priority mode and a medium to small aperture so that you can obtain a large depth of field. Use the suggested ISO range when you photograph rainbows because the sun is always shining when a rainbow is present. Multiple auto-focus points ensure that the camera finds objects with contrasting edges because your camera has a hard time achieving focus on the rainbow; it can achieve focus on objects that are near the rainbow. The wide-angle focal length lets you capture the grand vista and the entire rainbow without having to back up into the next county.

Taking the Picture

Rainbows occur after rainstorms. In fact, rain may still be falling when you first see the rainbow. If you hear thunder, you have to be a bit cautious — lightning can strike from a storm cloud that's miles away. As long as you protect yourself, as well as protecting your camera gear from any moisture (a baggie or a shower cap works great as an impromptu camera shield), you're ready to get some great images of rainbows.

1. **Enable the camera settings discussed previously in this chapter.**

2. **When you see a rainbow, find a suitable vantage point.**

    If possible, see whether you can photograph a rainbow from end to end. You can't move the rainbow, so you have to move yourself to find the ideal angle. If you can't photograph the rainbow from end to end, find an object, such as a tree, to signify the beginning or end of the rainbow (see Figure 41-1).

3. **Zoom to crop the rainbow to the frame.**

    You want to photograph the entire rainbow, making it the prominent part of your image. Include just a bit of the scenery on either side of the rainbow.

4. **Press the shutter button halfway to achieve focus and then compose the image.**

5. **Press the shutter button fully to take the picture.**

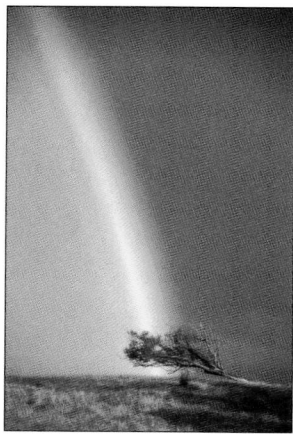

Image State

Figure 41-1: Find an interesting vantage point.

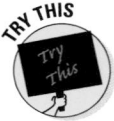

If you're in a state park that has waterfalls, ask the park ranger what time of day you can expect to see a rainbow by one of the waterfalls. With a bit of research and some patience, you can end up with a wonderful image of a waterfall and a rainbow (see Figure 41-2).

Troubleshooting

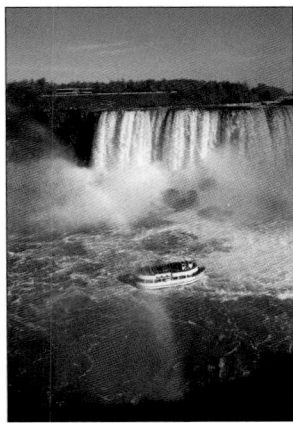

PhotoDisc/Getty Images

Figure 41-2: Photograph a rainbow caused by a waterfall.

✓ **The rainbow doesn't look as vibrant in the picture as it does in real life.** A polarizing filter can help solve this problem because this kind of filter helps saturate colors and makes the rainbow more prominent in the resulting image. Rotate the outer ring of the polarizing filter until you see something you like in the viewfinder.

✓ **The rainbow is hard to see in the final image.** Rainbows are transparent, so you can have trouble photographing them if the background is nothing but a mass of gray clouds. Try moving to a different angle until you can see the rainbow more clearly.

✓ **I'm too close to the rainbow to get it all in the frame.** Rotate the camera 90 degrees (to Portrait mode) to capture a picture of the rainbow arcing through the frame (as shown in Figure 41-1).

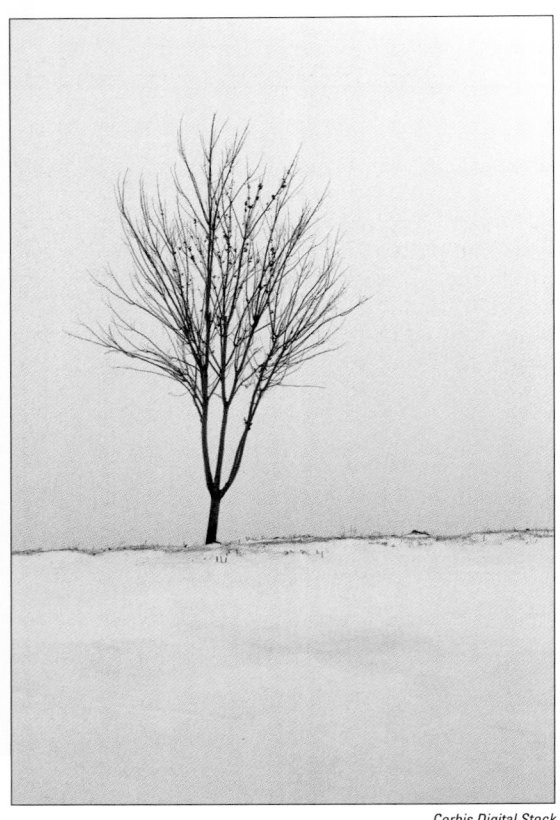

Corbis Digital Stock

42 Snow

*I*f you live or vacation in a winter wonderland, use your digital camera to get pictures of the landscape and buildings in the snow. You can even photograph a snowstorm. The possibilities are limited only by your imagination.

Photographing snow-laden winter landscapes can be a numbing experience if you're not wearing warm clothing. Be sure to bundle up and wear a pair of gloves that are flexible enough to operate the camera controls. Some photographers buy gloves just for photography. They cut the fingertips off so that they can feel the controls. In fact, you can even find gloves with fingertips that peel back (http://shop.freehands.com/). When not shooting pictures, put your hands in your pockets to warm them. If you're photographing in bone-chilling temperatures, wear a pair of mittens over your custom photography gloves. Take the mittens off when you want to photograph something, and then put them back on.

Camera Settings

- **Metering Mode:** Evaluative
- **Drive Mode:** Single Shot
- **Shooting Mode:** Aperture Priority
- **Aperture:** f/7.1 to f/16
- **ISO Setting:** 100 to 800
- **Focus Mode:** Single Shot
- **Auto-Focus Point:** Single auto-focus point
- **Focal Length:** 28mm to 85mm (35mm equivalent; see "Understanding focal lengths" in the appendix)
- **Image Stabilization:** On

Setting the Camera

When you photograph landscapes in the snow, you want a huge depth of field, therefore you shoot in Aperture Priority mode. The smallest suggested aperture (f/16) gives you a huge depth of field, especially when you're using a wide-angle focal length (28mm). The largest aperture (f/7.1) still gives you a decent depth of field, but it lets more light reach the sensor, which is a good thing if the conditions are overcast. The suggested ISO range lets you shoot in bright sunlight (by using ISO 100) to very overcast conditions (by using ISO 800). In fact, you can even photograph a snowstorm at ISO 800. You get photos that includes some noise, but that noise blends in with the flying snowflakes. The suggested focal length range lets you capture the wide expanse of a winter landscape at 28mm or zoom to 85mm to photograph details. You may be tempted to use a longer focal length, but you need a faster shutter speed to hand-hold a long focal length — which means a larger aperture, which means a shallow depth of field; and you really don't want a shallow depth of field when you photograph landscapes.

Taking the Picture

When you want to photograph landscapes during or after a snowstorm, the first order of business is to bundle up. The second order of business is to make sure your camera has acclimated to the cold, which I discuss in some detail in the "Precautions" section, later in this chapter.

1. **Prepare for your outing.**

   Make sure you have a fully charged battery in the camera, and carry a spare battery or two. Also, carry a small cotton towel in your camera bag in case any snowflakes land on your camera. Water and digital cameras are like oil and water: They don't mix. You can also protect your camera by keeping it under your coat, if there's enough room.

2. **Enable the settings discussed previously in this chapter.**

3. **When you find a landscape that you want to photograph, find a suitable vantage point.**

   When you see a scene that grabs your interest, explore it. Walk around. When the scene looks photo-worthy, put the viewfinder up to your eye.

4. **When you find a vantage point you like, zoom in and compose the image.**

   Remember to leave some room so that you can crop the photo to different image sizes than your digital camera's aspect ratio. When you compose the scene, remember that the eye is drawn from shadow to light, cold colors (blues and dark greens) to warm colors (yellows and reds). You can also place elements on power points according to the Rule of Thirds, like the tree at the beginning of this chapter.

You can also use diagonals to draw your viewer into the image, like the diagonal lines formed by the shadows in Figure 42-1, which leads the viewer's eye to the birch trees. For both images, the camera has been rotated 90 degrees because the trees in these images are taller than they are wide.

5. **Press the shutter button halfway to achieve focus, and then press the shutter button fully to take the picture.**

   Photographing a snowy landscape can be a bit tricky. Make sure you review your LCD monitor after you take a picture because the monitor can alert you to any exposure or white-balance problems (see the following section).

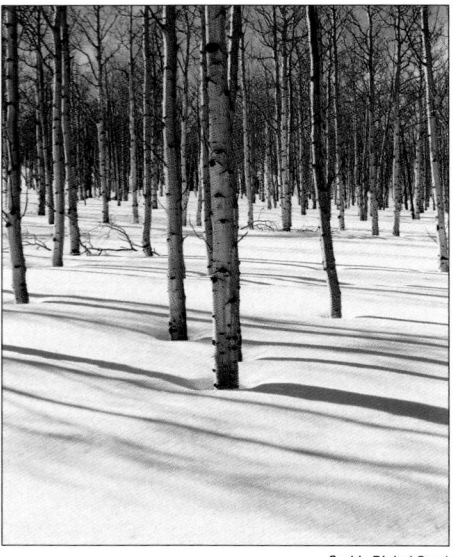

Corbis Digital Stock

Figure 42-1: Compose the picture to draw the viewer to your point of interest.

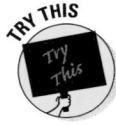

Snow melts, and then it freezes again. When you're photographing your winter wonderland, look out for artistic arrangements of icicles. When you see some icicles that you want to photograph, switch to a larger aperture (a smaller f/stop number) for a shallower depth of field, and then zoom in on the icicles.

Troubleshooting

- **The snow looks blue.** The camera is fooled by the abundance of white in the picture, and the automatic white balance makes the snow look blue. Switch to the Cloudy White Balance setting or manually set the white balance. Refer to your camera manual for more information on setting white balance.

- **The scene looks darker in the photograph than it actually is.** This problem can happen when you're photographing snow in bright sunlight. The bright light fools the camera into thinking the scene should be darker than it actually is. Use exposure compensation to increase the exposure.

Precautions

- ✔ **The batteries drain quickly.** Cold weather saps batteries quickly. Keep your spare batteries inside your pocket or, better yet, inside a shirt pocket if you're wearing a heavy overcoat. Your body heat prevents the batteries from losing some of their charge before you put them in the camera.

- ✔ **Don't change lenses or memory cards outside.** The inside of your camera is slightly warmer and considerably drier than the ambient conditions. If you change memory cards or lenses, you run the risk of condensation forming on the inside of your camera, which can damage the sensitive circuitry of your camera. Invest in a high-capacity memory card (8GB or 16GB) so that you have room for gobs of pictures before you fill the card.

- ✔ **Be careful when you take your camera outdoors.** If you leave a warm space and go out into the elements, condensation can form on the camera, and the lens fogs over. Place the camera in a baggie and zip it up tight before you go outside. In a few minutes, the camera acclimates to the conditions, and you can remove it from the baggie and start shooting up a storm.

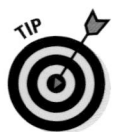

  If you're shooting a snowstorm, cut a hole for the lens in the baggie after the camera acclimates to the cold, and then use a rubber band to secure the baggie to the lens.

- ✔ **Be careful when you bring your camera indoors.** The camera needs to acclimate to the warmer and drier conditions inside. Condensation can form on the camera body (picture a can of ice-cold soda on a warm summer day) if you bring it inside without giving it time to warm up. Put the camera inside your camera bag before you come inside and leave it in the bag for at least 45 minutes before you bring it out. The camera bag warms gradually and gently acclimates the camera to the ambient conditions. Don't take the card out of the camera for at least 90 minutes after coming inside.

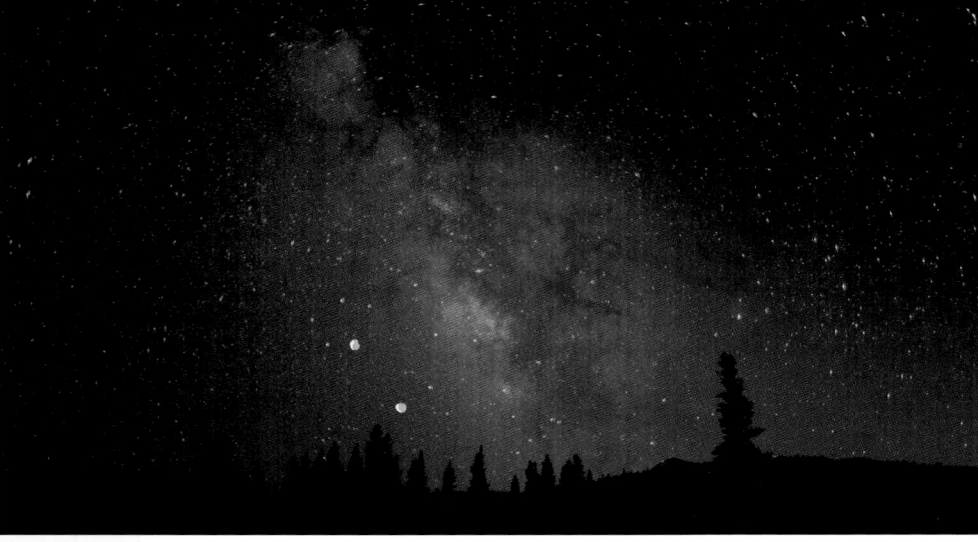
iStockphoto

43 Starry Skies

*W*hen the sun sets, many photographers pack up their gear and head home. If you do, you're missing some wonderful photo opportunities, especially if you're in an area that doesn't have much ambient light from nearby cities. In the fall and winter, the air has less humidity (unless you live in a tropical paradise), which means you can see a lot of stars. To capture a photograph of a scene complete with stars, you need to use a long exposure. You also need a tripod or some other means of steadying the camera, as well as a remote trigger to trigger the shutter. The trick is to find a great spot with next to no ambient light so that you can capture an image like the one shown here.

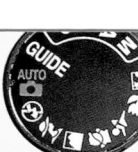

Camera Settings

- **Metering Mode:** Evaluative
- **Drive Mode:** Single Shot
- **Shooting Mode:** Bulb
- **Aperture:** f/16
- **ISO Setting:** 100 or 200
- **Focus Mode:** Single Shot
- **Auto-Focus Point:** Single auto-focus point
- **Focal Length:** 28mm to 50mm (35mm equivalent; see "Understanding focal lengths" in the appendix)
- **Image Stabilization:** Off

Setting the Camera

When you photograph a scene that includes starry skies, you want a huge depth of field to keep everything in focus, so use a small aperture that has an f/stop of f/16. If you rely on the camera to expose the scene, you don't see any stars at all. Therefore, shoot this type of picture by using the B (Bulb) shooting mode. When you use this mode, the shutter stays open until you decide to close it — you must remotely trigger the shutter button. You can find a remote trigger for your camera at your favorite camera retailer. I suggest two ISO settings because the lowest ISO setting on some older cameras and Nikons is ISO 200. But always use the lowest ISO setting available on your camera for this kind of photograph. The suggested focal-length range lets you either capture a wide expanse of landscape and stars, or zoom in for a tighter view.

Taking the Picture

Depending on where you live, you might have to travel some distance to find a good spot — which means an area that has little ambient light. Too much ambient light (from nearby cities) makes the stars hard to see.

1. **Find an interesting place that has little ambient light.**

   A scene that includes mountains or tall trees can add interest to this type of photograph.

2. **Mount your camera on a tripod and enable the settings discussed previously in this chapter.**

3. **Attach the remote trigger to your camera and set the lens to manual focus.**

4. **Set the lens focus to Infinity (see Figure 43-1).**

   This setting, combined with the small aperture, gives you a huge depth of field.

5. **Attach the hood to your lens.**

   The hood prevents any ambient sidelight from washing out the image.

6. **Compose the scene.**

   Because of the long exposure, you can readily identify some objects in the photo. If you have some tall trees in the scene, compose the scene so that they're on power points according to the Rule of Thirds.

7. **Press and hold the remote release.**

   Experiment with different exposure times. Start out with an exposure of about 30 seconds.

8. **Release the remote trigger and review the image.**

iStockphoto

Figure 43-1: Set the focus to Infinity.

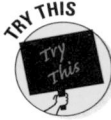

TRY THIS Take pictures of a starry sky from the same position at 5-minute intervals. The stars appear in slightly different positions each time. If you have an application capable of creating movies or slide shows from still images, you can create an animation of the nighttime sky.

Troubleshooting

- **The sky is too bright in the photo.** The image is overexposed. Decrease the exposure by about five seconds.

- **The photograph includes bright areas.** Find an area that has no ambient light at all. If a car turns a corner and the headlights flash on some nearby trees, this will be recorded as a bright spot in your image.

- **The silhouettes of the trees are blurry in the photo.** If you use this technique on a windy evening, the trees move back and forth, which appears in the image. The amount of blur depends on how windy it is. If you don't like this blur, photograph the scene on a calm evening.

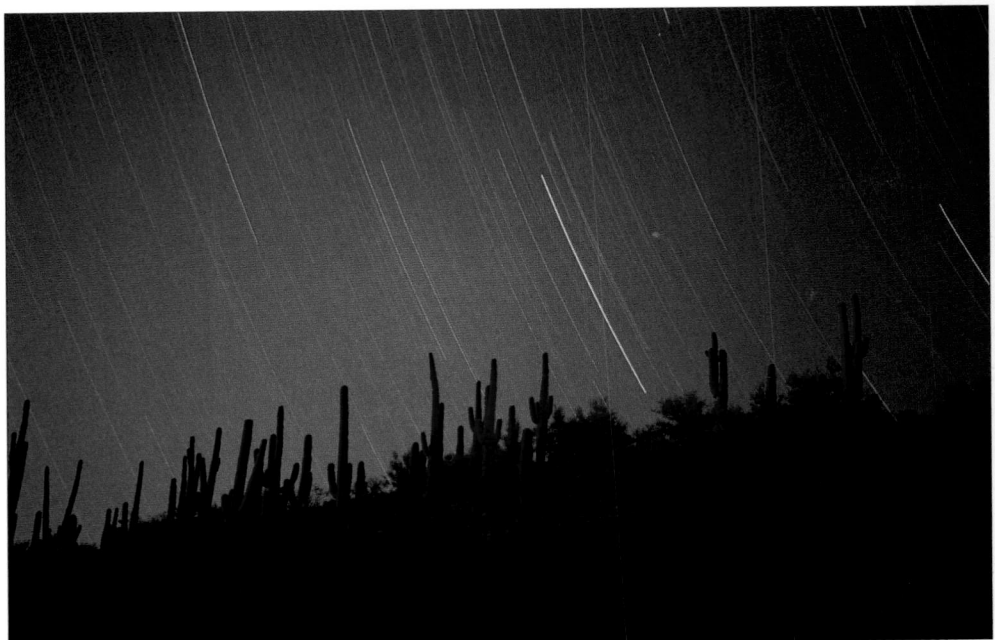

44

Star Trails

Camera Settings

- ✓ **Metering Mode:** Evaluative
- ✓ **Drive Mode:** Single Shot
- ✓ **Shooting Mode:** Bulb
- ✓ **Aperture:** f/16
- ✓ **ISO Setting:** 100 or 200
- ✓ **Focus Mode:** Single Shot
- ✓ **Auto-Focus Point:** Single auto-focus point
- ✓ **Focal Length:** 28mm (35mm equivalent; see "Understanding focal lengths" in the appendix)
- ✓ **Image Stabilization:** Off

*P*hotographs that include star trails just plain look cool. This technique requires an exposure of several minutes to possibly an hour or more. You absolutely must take this type of photograph in an area that has little ambient light. The image shows the scene brighter than the scene actually was when you took the photograph because of the long duration of the exposure. The trails appear because of the rotation of the Earth during the exposure: The stars are stationary, but the Earth is moving, which creates the trail effect (as shown here).

Setting the Camera

When you create a star-trail photograph, you want a huge depth of field, so you take this type of photograph by using a small aperture that has an f/stop of f/16 in Aperture Priority mode. This kind of photo requires a long exposure, so make sure you have a battery that's fully charged. If you're taking the photograph in cold weather, take the battery out of the camera and store it in your shirt pocket until you're ready to take the picture. Your body heat prevents the battery from going flat because of the cold. Use a low ISO setting, which gives you a relatively noise-free image. Of course, your photograph has more noise than normal because of the long exposure. You don't need to worry about the focus mode or auto-focus point because you focus the camera manually. The wide-angle focal length lets you capture a wide view of the landscape and the sky.

Taking the Picture

Many cameras have the option to illuminate the LCD monitor. However, when you're out taking this kind of shot, always carry a flashlight with you, which can help you see what you're doing when you're setting up and leveling the tripod. With flashlight in hand, follow these steps:

1. **Find an interesting place that has little ambient light.**

   A scene that includes mountains, tall trees, or a still lake works well for this type of photography. Make sure you're far away from any major metropolitan area.

2. **Attach your camera to your tripod and enable the settings discussed previously in this chapter.**

   Make sure you have the camera level. Most tripods have a spirit level that you can use to level the camera. Alternatively, you can purchase a spirit level that fits into the hot shoe of your camera.

3. **Attach the remote trigger to your camera and set the lens to manual focus.**

   Most lenses have a switch on the side that says AF (Auto Focus) or M (Manual). Push the switch to M.

4. **Set the lens focus to Infinity.**

   This setting, combined with the small aperture, gives you a huge depth of field that renders the stars and scenery in sharp focus.

5. **Attach your lens hood to the lens.**

   The lens hood prevents any ambient sidelight from spoiling the image. You may have to purchase a lens hood as an accessory.

6. Compose the scene.

Because of the long exposure, some objects appear readily identifiable in the photo. Make sure the sky dominates the frame. Place the horizon line very low in the image, unless you have a body of water. If the latter is the case, place the horizon line in the lower third of the image.

7. Press the remote switch to take the picture.

When you shoot in B (Bulb) mode, the lens stays open as long as you have the remote switch in the On position. Keep the shutter open for at least ten minutes to record star trails. Make sure your remote release has a position that enables you to hold the shutter open without having to hold the remote release. If you keep the lens open for longer than ten minutes, your photo displays longer star trails (see Figure 44-1).

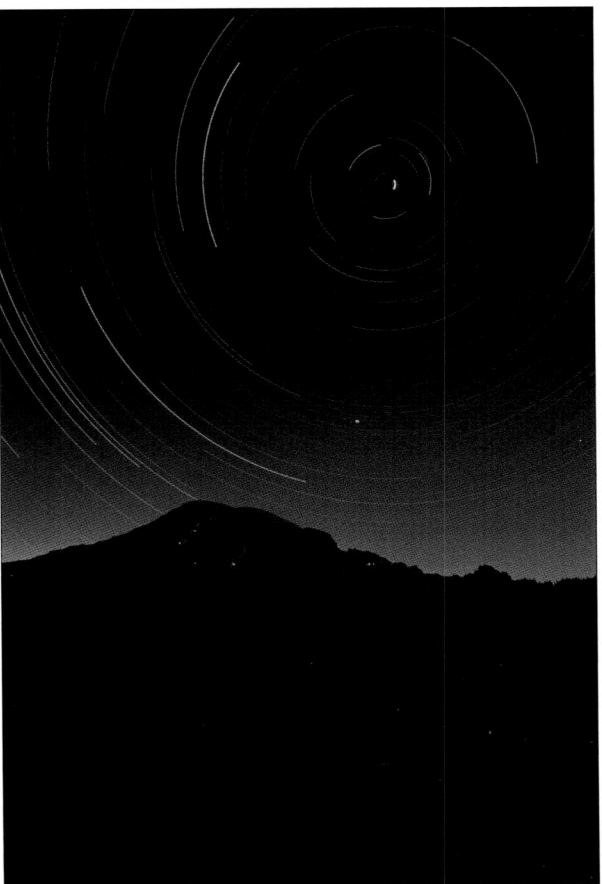

Figure 44-1: Keep the shutter open for long durations to capture long star trails.

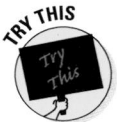

If you like this type of photography, consider purchasing a remote interval timer. An interval timer opens the shutter at precise intervals. You can also program the device to hold the shutter open for a pre-determined length of time. Contact your favorite camera retailer to see whether your camera can use a remote interval timer.

Troubleshooting

✔ **A bright rim of light appears on the horizon in my photo.** You run into this problem when you try to photograph star trails too close to a major city. Even when you're 100 miles from a city, the camera records the glow of city light on the horizon, even though you may not easily see it with your naked eye. The length of the exposure turns a dim glow into a bright flash of light, which distracts the viewer's attention from the star trails.

✔ **The image is very noisy.** When you keep the shutter open longer than 20 minutes, you get a lot of noise. If you want to take a star-trail photo for a longer period than 20 minutes, take several pictures in sequence that add up to the desired duration. For example, if you want a 60-minute star trail, take three 20-minute exposures. Combine the images in an image-editing program that supports layers.

✔ **I've seen images where the star trails form a perfect circle. How do I do that?** Align the camera to polar north, which puts the North Star in the center of the image. If you keep the shutter open long enough, the stars form a perfect circle around the North Star.

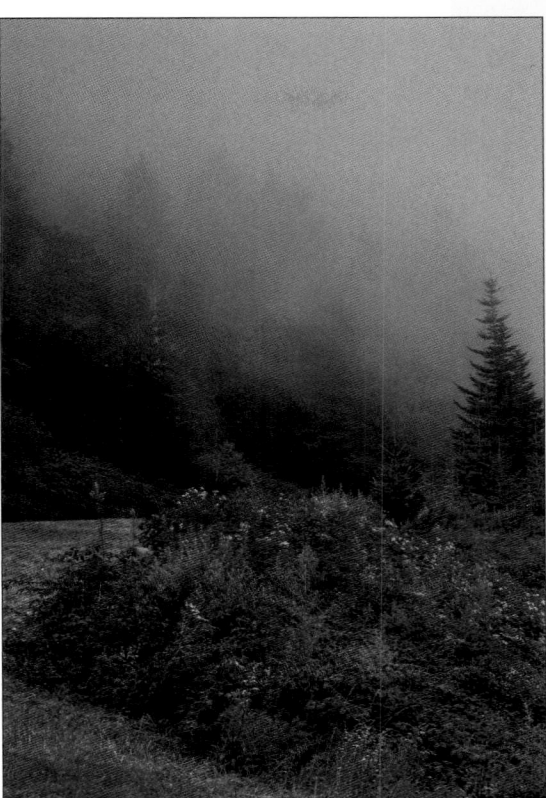

Camera Settings

- **Metering Mode:** Evaluative
- **Drive Mode:** Single Shot
- **Shooting Mode:** Aperture Priority
- **Aperture:** f/11 or smaller (larger f/stop number)
- **ISO Setting:** 200 to 400
- **Focus Mode:** Single Shot
- **Auto-Focus Point:** Single auto-focus point
- **Focal Length:** 24mm to 70mm; 100mm or longer if photographing wildlife (35mm equivalent; see "Understanding focal lengths" in the appendix)
- **Image Stabilization:** Optional

1 f you've never photographed during foggy conditions, you're in for a treat. The light is very even and wonderfully diffuse, the colors are muted, and distant details melt into the mist. If you have a favorite lake or river that's in a city, fog is a great equalizer. When it's extremely foggy, you may not be able to see the other side of the lake, which makes it look like you're in the middle of a beautiful wilderness and not in the city.

You can also find clouds masquerading as fog in places such as the higher spots in the Smoky Mountains (as shown here). The clouds drift in and out like ethereal tendrils. In addition to photographing beautiful landscapes in the fog, you can also photograph animals on foggy days. With a keen eye and the settings in this chapter, you can capture some great images on foggy days.

Setting the Camera

When you photograph landscapes on a foggy day, you have less light to work with than you do on a sunny day, so you need a slightly higher ISO setting than you'd use on a sunny day. The small aperture ensures that you get a large depth of field. Even though you have limited visibility on a foggy day, you want everything that you can see to be in focus. The focal length depends on what part of the scene interests you. You can cut to the chase and use a short telephoto focal length to zoom in to a specific part of the scene, or you can use a wide-angle focal length to capture the broad expanse of what you see in front of you. Image stabilization is useful if you're shooting in really dim conditions, and you don't want to switch to a higher ISO setting.

Taking the Picture

Unless dew is dripping from the trees, you photograph in the fog very much like you photograph on a sunny day. You just need to have a creative eye to carve a great picture out of the foggy conditions.

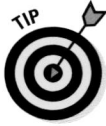

If you photograph a monochromatic color scheme, such as the green-on-green of a forest on a cloudy day, you get a boring picture (unless you convert it to a high-contrast black-and-white image in post-processing). Look for scenes that have a splash of color and use that color to draw your viewer's eye into the scene. In the image at the beginning of this chapter, the yellow wildflowers draw viewers into the image.

1. **Visit the area that you want to photograph and look for a scene you want to photograph.**

2. **Compose the picture, and then press the shutter button halfway to achieve focus.**

   Find a center of interest in the scene and position it to one side of the frame. Don't place the horizon line in the center of the image. Look for the predominant aspect of the scene and place the horizon line below it.

3. **Press the shutter button fully to take the picture.**

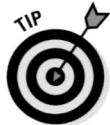

Birds in the fog make good subjects for a photo. Switch to Shutter Priority mode and choose a shutter speed of 1/200 of a second or faster. When a bird takes off from his foggy perch, snap the picture. If you photograph a bird on a lake on a foggy day, you also get a reflection of the bird in the still water (see Figure 45-1), which is a nice bonus.

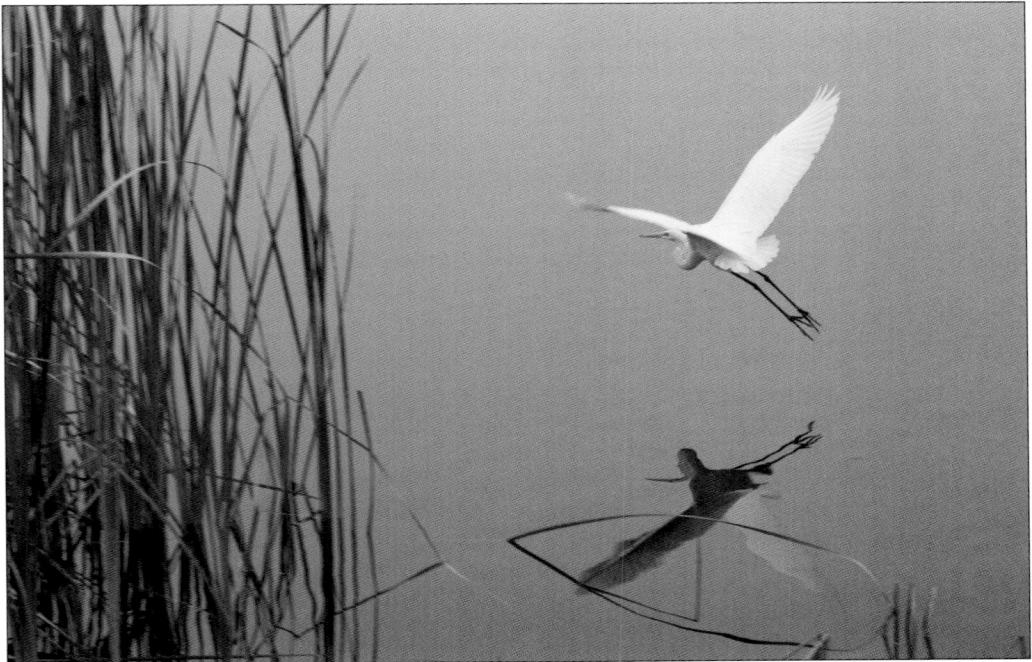

Figure 45-1: Photographing wildlife on a foggy day.

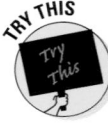

Be on the lookout for details such as leaves or spider webs. The humid conditions dapple these kinds of small items with pearls of moisture (see Figure 45-2). To photograph small details, switch to a longer focal length or a macro lens, and zoom in on the dew-covered items that you want to photograph.

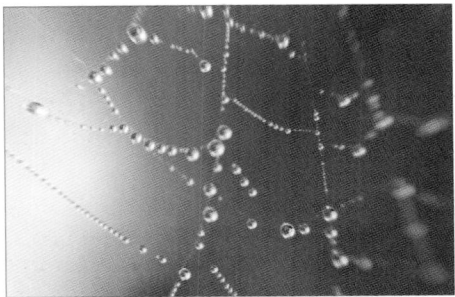

Figure 45-2: Photographing details on a foggy day.

Troubleshooting

✏ **The image lacks contrast.**
This problem often occurs when you photograph a scene on a foggy day. Make sure you have some contrasting colors in the scene.

✏ **The lens fogs over.** This issue happens when you leave a conditioned space, such as a building or your car, and step into a moisture-laden atmosphere. Wait for the camera to acclimate to the conditions, which causes the fog to clear.

✔ **The camera doesn't achieve focus.** On a very foggy day, the fog can blur the edges of objects. Position the auto-focus point over a well-defined edge, achieve focus, and then compose the picture. Alternatively, you can manually focus the camera.

✔ **The foggy areas are blown out to pure white.** You run into this problem when the camera can't cope with the wide range of brightness. Employ exposure compensation to reduce the exposure by 1/3 or 2/3 a stop. If the fog is at the top of the scene, you can use a graduated neutral density filter to reduce the amount of light reaching the sensor.

Part IV
People

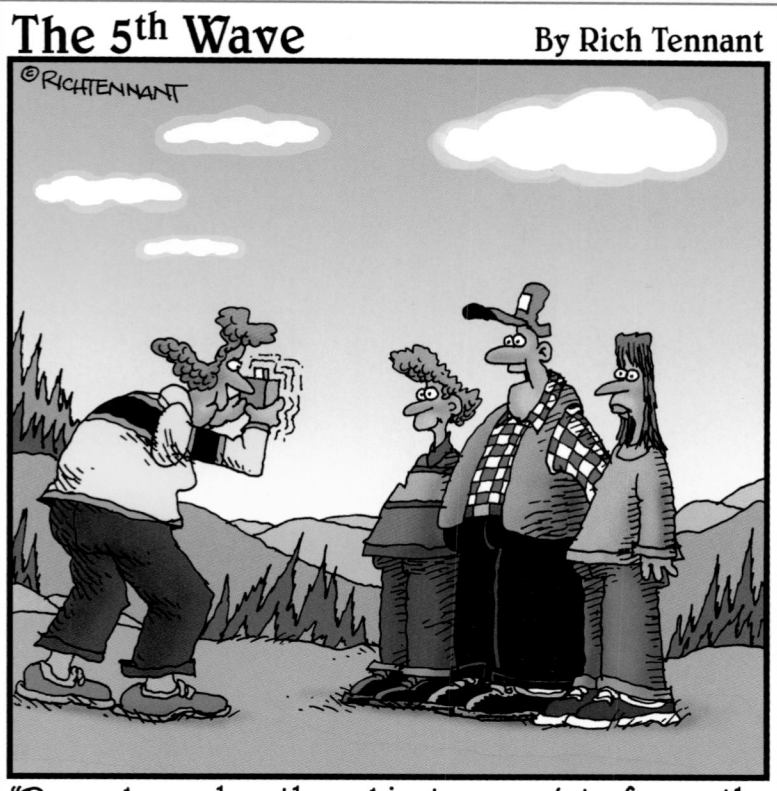

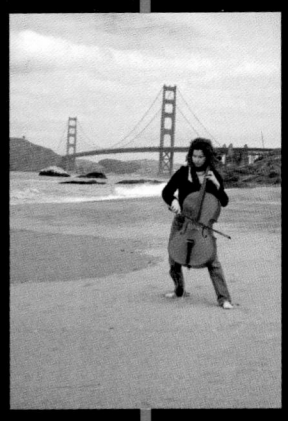

*P*eople come in all shapes and sizes. There are old people, young people, and infants. The sheer diversity of people and the types of photographs you can create makes choosing the proper settings a challenge for many photographers. Whether you want to take a photo of your husband playing basketball, your child's first birthday party, or a wedding, you'll find a chapter in this part with the settings you need to nail the photo. There are lots of other scenarios for photographing people that I cover in this part of the book as well.

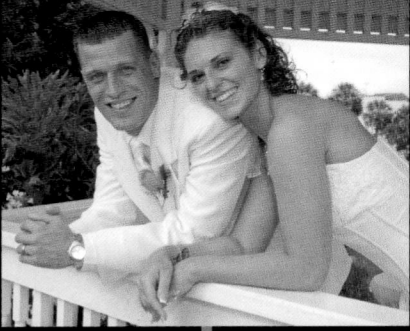

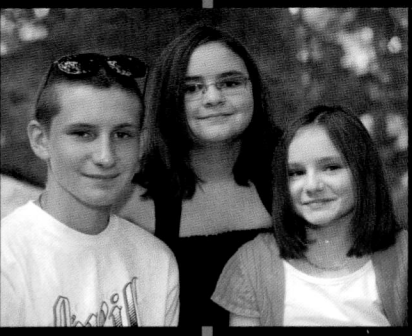

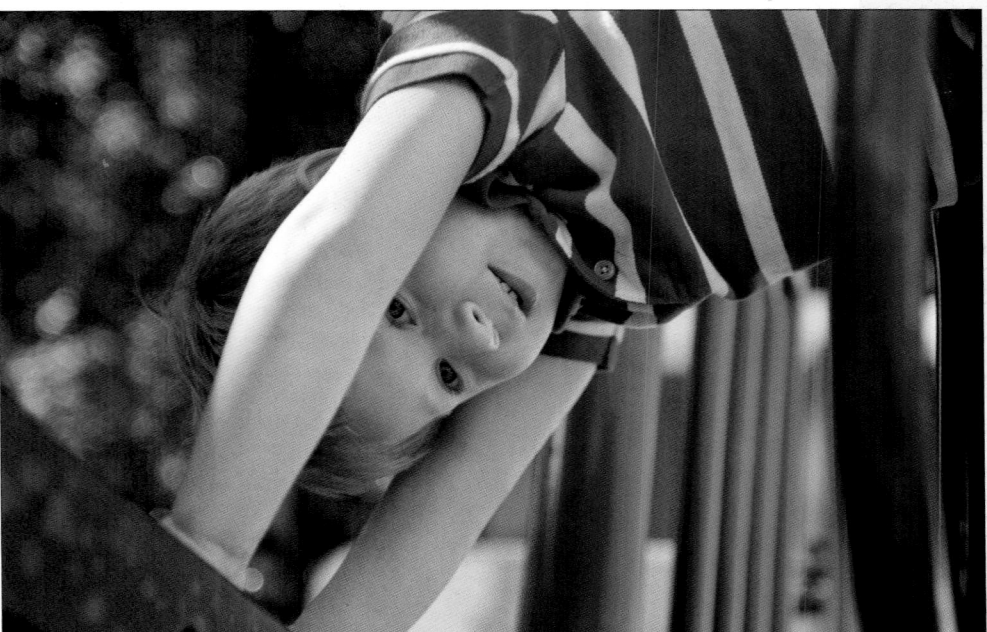

Camera Settings

- **Metering Mode:** Evaluative
- **Drive Mode:** Continuous
- **Shooting Mode:** Aperture Priority
- **Aperture:** f/3.5 or larger (smaller f/stop number)
- **ISO Setting:** 100 to 400
- **Focus Mode:** Continuous Auto-Focus
- **Auto-Focus Point:** Single auto-focus point
- **Focal Length:** 50mm to 105mm (35mm equivalent; see "Understanding focal lengths" in the appendix)
- **Image Stabilization:** Optional

*P*hotographs of kids being themselves are precious. Children grow up so quickly; they can change significantly during a few months. The best way to preserve memories is to photograph children often. You can take pictures of your children playing in the yard, at school, or at a local park. You can even capture interesting photos of them playing in the house. In future years, you and the child can look at the photographs and remember the wonderful times. When you photograph your child, you want to be a fly on the wall. If you're the only adult, the child may turn his attention to you. Have another adult or older child along when you photograph a young child. Your assistant can occupy the child's attention while you clandestinely take a lot of photographs of that child at play.

Setting the Camera

When kids are playing, they can be whirling dervishes of boundless energy, which is why you use Continuous Drive mode. You can capture a sequence of shots of your child at play. Continuous Auto-Focus mode means the camera updates focus while the child moves to different positions. You shoot in Aperture Priority mode and use a large aperture to limit your depth of field. The relatively short focal length means you have to be fairly close to the child — which means the child may interact with the photographer, and the resulting pictures may not be exactly what you're looking for. (Another adult or older child can come in handy in these circumstances because they occupy the child's attention, which results in more natural photos.) The ISO range gives you latitude for different lighting conditions. Image stabilization compensates for operator movement and comes in handy if you're moving around a lot to keep up with the child. So you may want to use it if you have this option on your camera or lens.

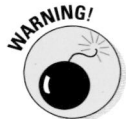

Unless your camera has a full-frame sensor or the camera's fairly new, don't exceed an ISO setting of 400 because digital noise can ruin the image.

Taking the Picture

Photographing young children playing definitely keeps you on your toes, especially if they're on a playground. You can get a workout keeping up with them while they move from the jungle gym to the slide and then to the swings. Pay attention to your angle with this type of photography: Don't photograph the child from above, but rather stoop down and photograph the child at his level as shown in Figure 46-1. You can also create unique shots by switching to a different vantage point, such as the bottom of the slide.

1. **Accompany the child to the playground with your camera.**

   Children have minds of their own. Don't expect them to wait around for you to get your camera set; they'll just

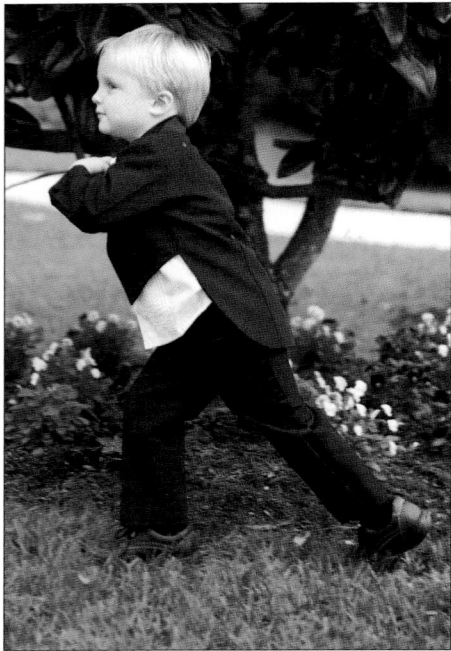

Figure 46-1: Photograph your child playing in his Sunday Best clothing.

be bored by that. Ask another family member to accompany you and engage the child, so you can focus on getting the photo.

2. **Be a fly on the wall and observe the child.**

3. **When the child does something worth capturing for posterity, zoom in, compose the picture, and then press the shutter button halfway to achieve focus.**

4. **Press the shutter button fully to take the picture.**

When you shoot in Continuous Drive mode, the camera continues to take pictures as long as you continue to press the shutter button.

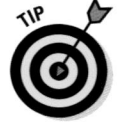

Photograph your child playing in his "Sunday Best" before going to church.

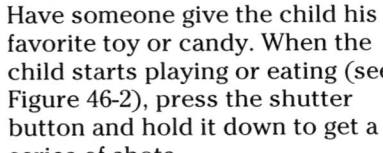
Have someone give the child his favorite toy or candy. When the child starts playing or eating (see Figure 46-2), press the shutter button and hold it down to get a series of shots.

Troubleshooting

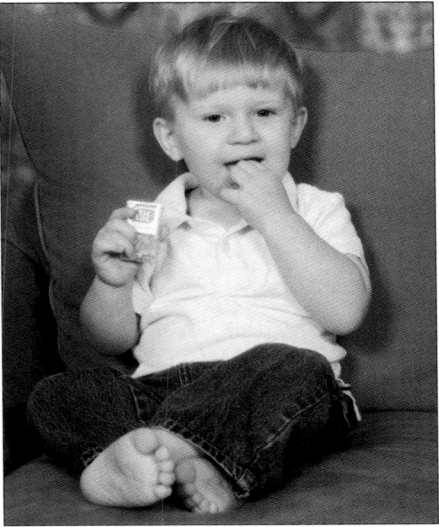

✔ **The child isn't in focus.** Make sure you're using a single auto-focus point; otherwise, the camera may focus on something other than the child. Also, make sure the auto-focus point appears over the child when you achieve focus.

✔ **The child is blurry.** Your camera is selecting a slow shutter speed because of dim lighting conditions. Increase the ISO until the shutter speed is the reciprocal of the focal length you're using.

Figure 46-2: Take a series of pictures of your child eating his favorite treat.

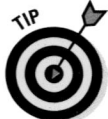
You can get an interesting image in dim lighting conditions by choosing the lowest ISO setting, which gives you a slow shutter speed that renders an artistically blurred image of your child at play.

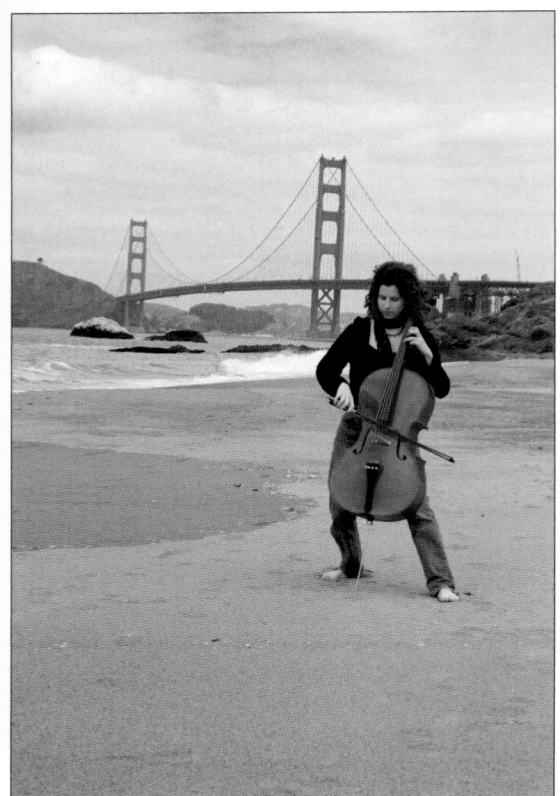

47 Artist Creating

*p*hotographers are artists. When you photograph, you take objects, and mix in shadow and light to create compelling images. So it's no wonder that photographers often like to photograph other artists. Whether you photograph a musician, sculptor, or painter, the settings in this chapter can help you create an interesting photo of an artist plying her craft. You can photograph the artist either at her place of work or in a picturesque locale.

Camera Settings

- **Metering Mode:** Evaluative
- **Drive Mode:** Single Shot
- **Shooting Mode:** Aperture Priority
- **Aperture:** f/4.0 to f/7.1
- **ISO Setting:** 100 or 200
- **Focus Mode:** Single Shot
- **Auto-Focus Point:** Single auto-focus point
- **Focal Length:** 28mm to 85mm (35mm equivalent; see "Understanding focal lengths" in the appendix)
- **Image Stabilization:** Optional

Setting the Camera

When you photograph an artist at work, you give your viewers a glimpse of the creative process. You do this by selectively focusing on the artist while blurring out other details such as the background. You can easily accomplish this by controlling the depth of field using a fairly large aperture in Aperture Priority mode. The ISO setting works for bright lighting conditions and cloudy days. The focal length you use depends on whether you want to capture the artist and a large portion of the surroundings, or take an up-close and intimate picture of the artist at work. You don't have to use image stabilization, but it hedges your bet by compensating for any operator movement or a slow shutter speed when the scene is very overcast. If you have a slow shutter speed and don't have the luxury of image stabilization, your only alternative is to increase the ISO setting.

Taking the Picture

You can take a picture of an artist at work fairly easily. Just let the artist do his thing. You simply need to observe and create. Give the artist a few minutes to get engrossed in his work while you silently observe. When the artist seems like he's totally in the moment, it's time for you to get in the moment and create.

However, any artist may get a bit preoccupied and stop working if he sees you with a camera. If he does, just smile and tell him you'd like to take a picture of him at work.

1. **Enable the settings discussed previously in this chapter, and quietly walk around the artist.**

   While you walk, observe the different vantage points available to you.

2. **Choose a vantage point where you feel you can get a good shot.**

   The best vantage points include the artist, the tools of her trade, and the work in progress.

3. **Press the shutter button halfway to achieve focus, and then compose the picture.**

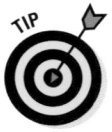

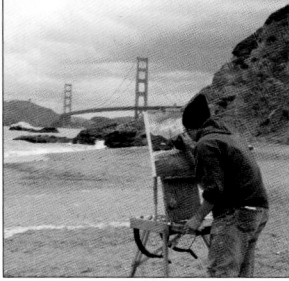

   Rules are made to be broken, and that includes the settings I suggest. If the artist is painting a landscape, switch to a small aperture (a large f/stop number) and zoom out to about 35mm. Walk up to the artist and compose the picture to include the artist and his easel, plus the scene he's painting (see Figure 47-1).

4. **Fully press the shutter button to take the picture.**

Figure 47-1: Photographing a painter and the scene he's painting.

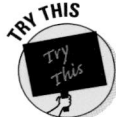

Many towns have sidewalk artists who create and sell their work outside of restaurants and cafes. You can capture interesting photographs of sidewalk artists (see Figure 47-2) while you walk through your city or town. Just be sure to ask first.

Troubleshooting

Photographing an artist at work isn't rocket science. Just be observant and creative, like the artist you're photographing. No particular problems are common to only this genre of photography. After you take a picture, review it on your camera LCD monitor. Check to make sure you have a photograph you're pleased with. Also, make sure the camera has properly exposed the image. Check the histogram to make sure you don't have any blocked shadows (a spike on the left side of the histogram) or blown out highlights (a spike on the right side of the histogram).

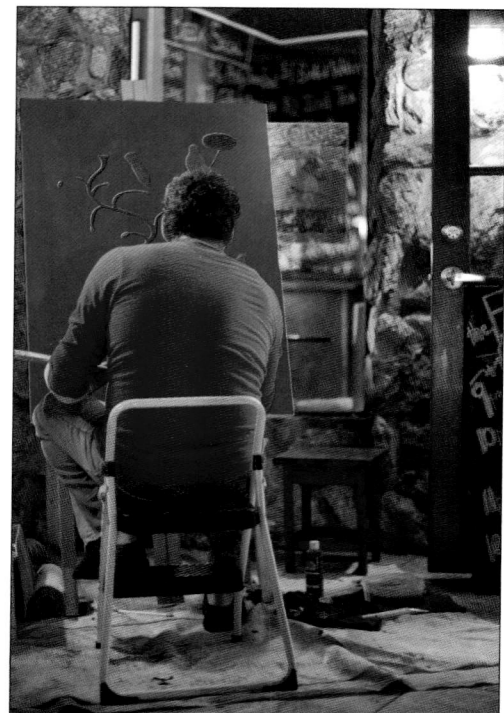

Figure 47-2: Photographing a sidewalk artist.

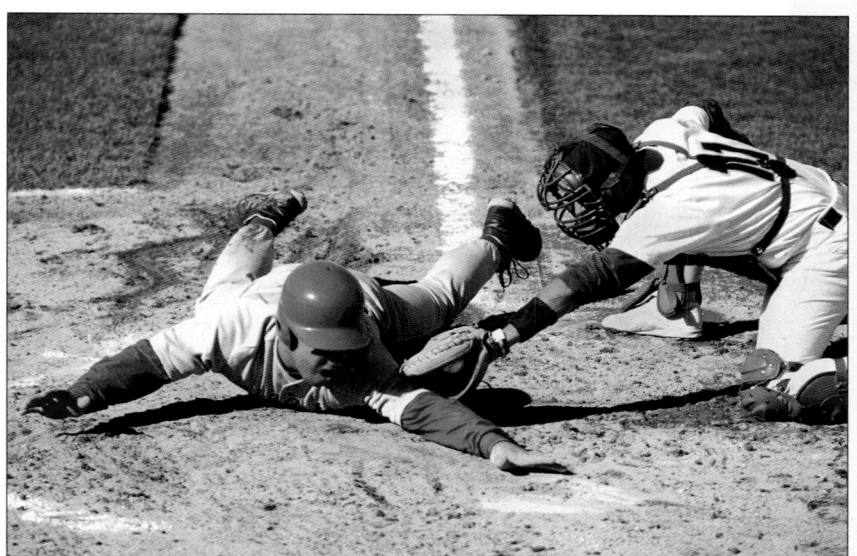

Corbis Digital Stock

Camera Settings

- **Metering Mode:** Evaluative
- **Drive Mode:** Single Shot or Continuous
- **Shooting Mode:** Shutter Priority
- **Shutter Speed:** 1/250 to 1/500 of a second
- **ISO Setting:** The lowest ISO setting for the available light conditions
- **Focus Mode:** Continuous Auto-Focus
- **Auto-Focus Point:** Single auto-focus point
- **Focal Length:** 100mm or longer (35mm equivalent; see "Understanding focal lengths" in the appendix)
- **Image Stabilization:** On

*P*hotographing a professional athlete playing a sport requires a press pass to get a decent vantage point, and getting a press pass is akin to parting the waters. If you're a mere mortal who doesn't work for *Sports Illustrated* or a major newspaper, you have to satisfy your desire by photographing amateur athletes. You can get closer to amateur athletes than you can pros, and you don't have to fight crowds, either. If you have a friend who plays tennis, basketball, or baseball, grab your camera and get ready to capture some great images by using the settings in this chapter.

Setting the Camera

Photographing athletes is fun. Of course, it helps if you know something about the sport. I give you a choice of drive mode in the preceding section because sometimes you can get the job done with just one shot. But when the action's hot and heavy, you can use Continuous Drive mode to capture a sequence of images in a situation such as two basketball players jumping up to the basket at the same time. I'm not recommending an ISO setting for this type of photography because of the wide range of lighting scenarios with which you may have to work. The suggested shutter speed can freeze most action, except for a baseball pitcher's fastball. If you do notice a bit of motion blur, you can either keep it as an artistic effect or change the shutter speed to 1/500 of a second or faster. The suggested focal length gives you the option of zooming in without getting close enough to the action to put yourself in harm's way. Image stabilization helps you get a blur-free image when you photograph athletes in motion because it compensates for any operator movement. And you may get operator movement when your hands aren't steady because you sprinted 10 yards with your camera to capture an image of a football player scoring the winning touchdown.

Taking the Picture

When you photograph athletes, you have to be on your toes. If you know the athletes and the sport, you can anticipate what's going to happen. If you don't know the sport, arrive early and watch the athletes go through their warm-up rituals. If you know the players well, ask them what to expect. A heads-up from the people you're photographing and the following steps tell you all that you need to know to get some great shots of adults playing sports.

1. **Enable the camera settings discussed previously in this chapter.**

2. **Patiently wait while the athletes begin playing.**

3. **When it looks like something exciting is getting ready to happen, zoom in on the athlete you want to photograph, and then press the shutter button halfway to achieve focus.**

   When you take pictures with Continuous Auto-Focus enabled, the camera updates focus when the athletes move as long as you have your finger pressed halfway on the shutter button. Do your best to compose the image. You may find composition difficult when athletes are moving at full-tilt speed. Choose an unusual vantage point or angle to create a unique image.

4. **Press the shutter button fully to take the picture.**

   If you choose the Continuous Drive mode, the camera continues taking pictures as long as your finger depresses the shutter button.

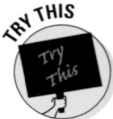

Zoom in tight when the athlete is making a decisive move, such as catching a pass or returning a serve (see Figure 48-1). Shoot in Continuous Drive mode and capture a series of images of the athlete doing what she does best.

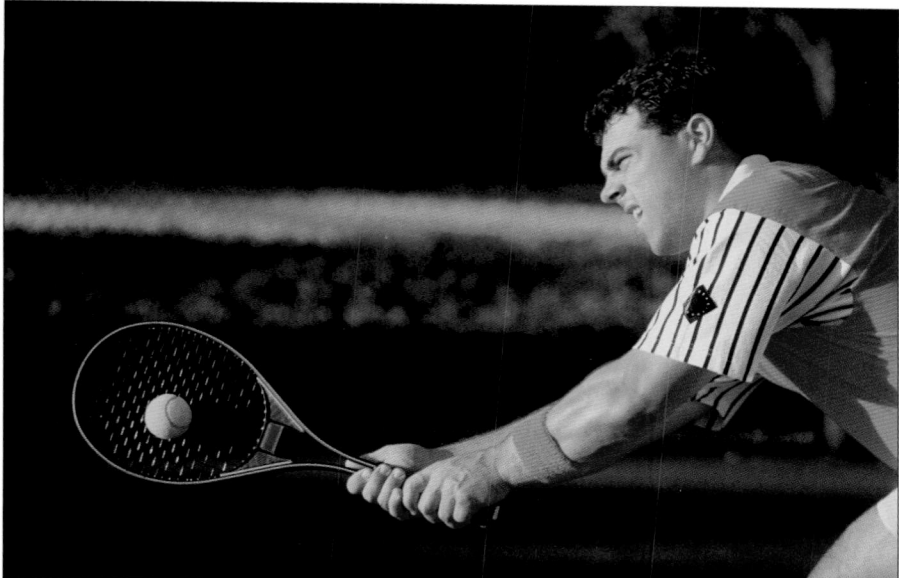

Corbis Digital Stock

Figure 48-1: Photograph an athlete making a key play.

Troubleshooting

✔ **The athlete isn't in focus.** Make sure the auto-focus point is over the athlete when you press the shutter button halfway, and make sure the auto-focus point illuminates to signify that the camera has achieved focus.

✔ **The depth of field is too shallow.** This problem can happen when you photograph in low-light conditions. To compensate for the low light, the camera chooses a large aperture, which results in a shallow depth of field. In some instances, such as when you're photographing one athlete, you want a shallow depth of field because it blurs distracting details and draws the viewer's attention to your subject. When you're photographing several athletes in action, you need a large depth of field to keep all of them in focus. To increase the depth of field, increase the ISO rating.

49 Candid Portrait

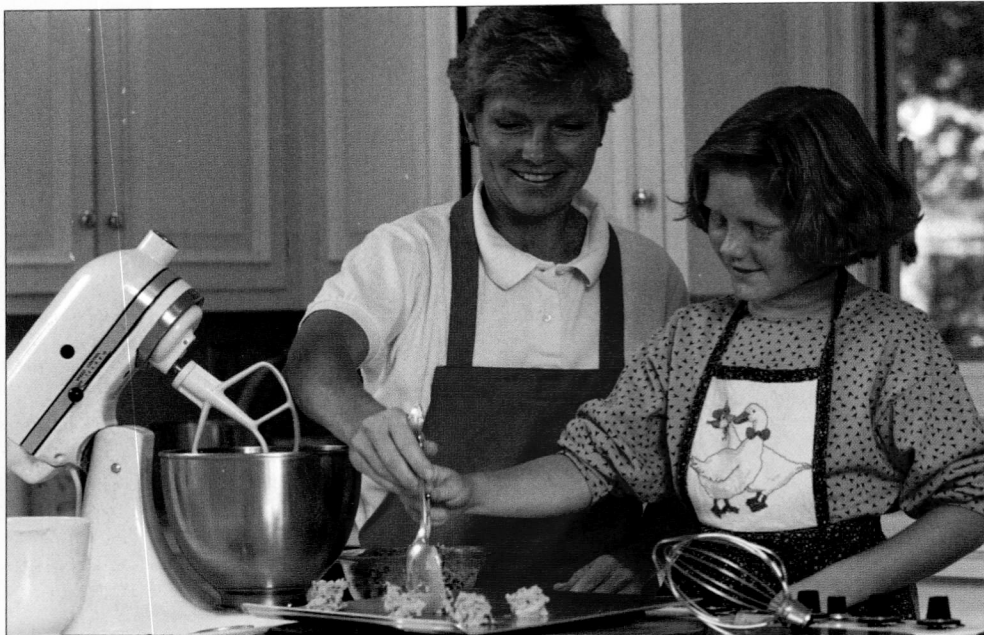

PhotoDisc, Inc./Getty Images

Candid photography is a lot of fun. But you have to be careful. When family members and friends know you're the photographer geek in the family, they have a tendency to keep their distance when you show up with a camera. Therefore, make sure that when family and friends see you, you always have your camera. If you carry the camera with you wherever you go (or, at least, frequently), friends and family get used to seeing it around your neck, and they let their guard down and act naturally. Catch them in the act of being themselves — when they take care of everyday chores, such as a mother and daughter baking cookies. You can take natural photographs when your subjects are preoccupied, not thinking about you and the camera you have around your neck.

Camera Settings

- **Metering Mode:** Evaluative
- **Drive Mode:** Continuous
- **Shooting Mode:** Aperture Priority
- **Aperture:** f/4.0 to 7.1
- **ISO Setting:** 100 to 800
- **Focus Mode:** Single Shot
- **Auto-Focus Point:** Single auto-focus point
- **Focal Length:** 50mm to 85mm (35mm equivalent; see "Understanding focal lengths" in the appendix)
- **Image Stabilization:** On

Setting the Camera

When you take a candid photograph of a friend or family member, your subject is the center of attention, which means you need to control depth of field. Aperture Priority mode is the obvious choice for this type of photography. You use a large aperture when you zoom in on your subject, and a slightly smaller aperture when you zoom out and want to include some of the background in the image. You can use the suggested ISO range for outdoor photography in bright light (ISO 100) or indoor photography (ISO 400 to 800). A single auto-focus point allows you to focus precisely on your subject. The focal-length range is suitable for a picture of your subject and a bit of the environment around her (50mm) or a close-up candid shot (85mm). You shoot in Continuous Drive mode so that you can capture a series of pictures when your subject starts doing something interesting. Image stabilization is always a plus when you're photographing a person because any movement you make can result in a picture that's not tack sharp.

Taking the Picture

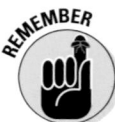

Taking a candid photograph of a friend or loved one involves patience. When you show up with your camera around your neck, your friends and family know they're fair game – which is why I recommend that you have your camera around your neck most of the time they see you. The camera becomes a fixture, and you can get natural-looking photos of them.

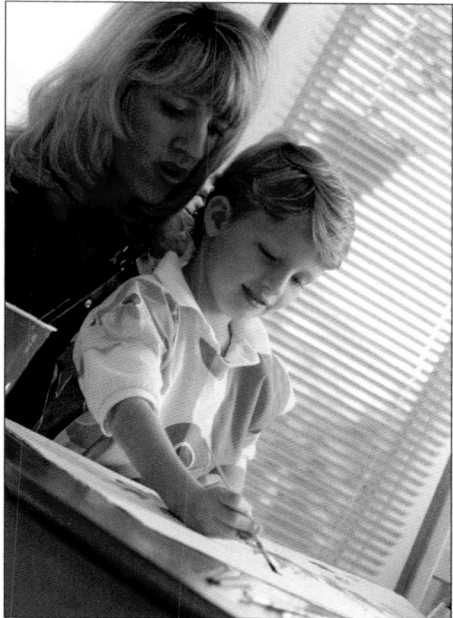

Corbis Digital Stock

Figure 49-1: Capture a candid photo of family members doing something.

1. **Visit the friend or relative you want to take candid photos of.**

   The best time for candid photography is when your subject is preoccupied. Visit him when other people are there.

2. **Stay near your subject and let her get involved with another friend or relative.**

   Don't get involved in the conversation or make any comments at all. Pretend to be bored, but keep an eye on your subject out of the corner of your eye. You can also be an interested participant when one of your children and spouse are doing something (see Figure 49-1). You may notice the camera was tilted when the picture was taken. It's perfectly okay when you shoot a candid photo. Have fun. Let your inner child run amuck.

3. **Pretend to be fiddling with your camera while you actually enable the settings discussed previously in this chapter.**

    Candid photography is just that. You catch your subject doing something interesting or funny. But you get a truly candid photo only if you catch him off guard.

4. **When your subject starts doing something interesting, quickly point the camera at her, press the shutter button halfway to achieve focus, and then press the button fully to take the picture.**

    You can get a couple of good shots before your subject pouts or sticks out his tongue. (Those reactions provide a different type of candid shot.)

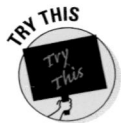

Walk into a room with your camera to your eye, prefocus on the first person you see and say, "Hi." Snap a picture when your unsuspecting subject looks up. You never know when you might end up with a winner (see Figure 49-2).

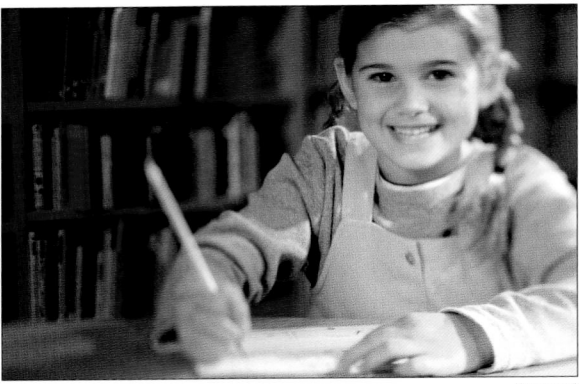

Purestock

Figure 49-2: Walk into a room and say, "Hi."

Troubleshooting

⌐ **My friends and family stop what they're doing when I point the camera at them.** You get this reaction when you take a lot of candid photos of the same people. They know what you're up to, and they're on guard. When your subject starts doing something you want to capture, point the camera at an object that's the same distance from the camera as your subject. Press the shutter button halfway to achieve focus, and then quickly move the camera toward your subject and press the shutter button.

⌐ **The faces of my subjects are a little dark.** This problem happens when you have a bright light source, such as light fixtures, above them. Use fill flash to fill in the shadows.

⌐ **The shot didn't turn out.** That's the way the ball bounces sometimes. You have to be on your toes and correctly apply your settings before you take a candid picture. You can't tell the people you just photographed that you made a mistake and want them please to adopt the adorable pose they had a few seconds ago.

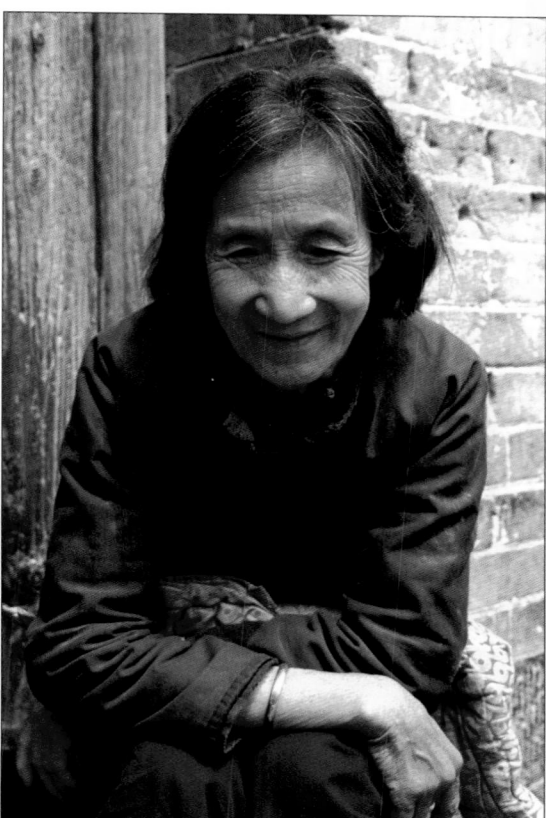

Flat Earth

Camera Settings

- **Metering Mode:** Evaluative
- **Drive Mode:** Single Shot
- **Shooting Mode:** Aperture Priority
- **Aperture:** f/7.1
- **ISO Setting:** 100 to 800
- **Focus Mode:** Single Shot
- **Auto-Focus Point:** Single auto-focus point
- **Focal Length:** 28mm to 85mm (35mm equivalent; see "Understanding focal lengths" in the appendix)
- **Image Stabilization:** On

1 f you travel to a foreign country without your camera, it's like going to a five-star restaurant and not eating dessert. Some things are just not done; leaving your camera at home when you go on vacation is one of them. When you go on vacation, you photograph the usual: landscapes, buildings, and whatnot. But if you're going to an exotic location where the local people dress differently than people do where you're from and have different belief systems and customs, take pictures of them.

When you get home, you can relive the vacation and have fond memories of the people, as well. However, you can't just point the camera at them and shoot. You have to respect your subjects. The language barrier may cause problems, but if you have a tour guide or cab driver who speaks the language, you have an interpreter.

You can also photograph people of other cultures if you visit an area such as Chinatown in San Francisco or New York. Many people in ethnic areas of U.S. cities look and act like they still live in their homeland.

Setting the Camera

When you photograph a person in a country you're visiting, you want to include some of the surroundings to give viewers a sense of the area. Aperture Priority is the perfect shooting mode for this type of photograph as it gives you precise control over your depth of field. You use a medium aperture, which gives you an adequate depth of field, but because the surrounding area isn't tack sharp, the viewer's attention focuses on your subject. The ISO range gives you the option of photographing the locals in bright sunlight or overcast conditions. You may think Continuous Drive mode would be the answer, but your subject may get startled when he hears the shutter open time after time. The suggested focal range lets you capture a picture of your subject and a lot of the surroundings (28mm), or zoom in for an intimate portrait. Just make sure you never photograph your subject at close range with a wide-angle focal length, which would distort the body parts of your subject closest to the camera. You may want to use image stabilization if your camera or lens has it because it helps you get a blur-free picture, especially when the aperture and ISO combination yield a slow shutter speed.

Taking the Picture

You can find people to photograph when you're taking pictures of other things. While you walk down a picturesque street in a foreign country, maybe you notice a local craftsman creating the items he sells or a woman walking to work.

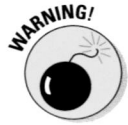

When you travel abroad, a high-tech camera case is a dead giveaway that something expensive is inside. Many photographers pack their gear in a diaper bag. Also consider getting a very sturdy camera strap that no one can easily cut.

1. **When you see someone you want to photograph, approach the person.**

   You may find approaching someone difficult if you're with a tour group. The locals tend to look the other way or scatter when a group with cameras comes into view. When you want to photograph people, travel in a small group or by yourself, if it's safe.

2. **Even if you don't speak the native language, communicate with your subject.**

   Keep eye contact with your subject and smile. If you don't know the language and don't have anyone to act as an interpreter, smile at your subject and hold your camera in the air. If your subject shakes her head, smile and move on.

3. **If your subject smiles back, quickly compose the picture.**

   Your subject may try to pose for you. If he does, do what you can to get him to go back to what he was doing.

If you have a language barrier, an interpreter comes in handy in this situation. If you don't have an interpreter, hand gestures are a universal language. Make a gesture similar to what your subject was doing when you arrived on the scene. When your subject continues what he was doing, compose the image. Place your subject on one side of the frame and use any object he's carrying to draw viewers into the picture. Work quickly. Your subject is giving you a gift. Don't abuse it.

4. **Press the shutter button halfway to achieve focus, and then fully press the button to take the picture.**

   Take a couple of pictures of your subject, but work quickly. When you're done, smile at your subject. If a handshake is customary in the country you're visiting, shake your subject's hand.

 Ask your hotel's concierge or desk clerk which areas of town are safe for tourists; you can even ask whether the concierge or clerk would accompany you in your travels for a small fee. Of course, make this request only if you find that person trustworthy.

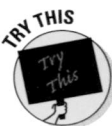 Stand on a corner and observe. Use a wide-angle focal length of about 28mm, put your camera to your eye, and frame the scene in the viewfinder. Include interesting architectural elements. Lean on a wall and relax. Before you know it, someone interesting will walk into the scene; raise the camera and take a few pictures (see Figure 50-1).

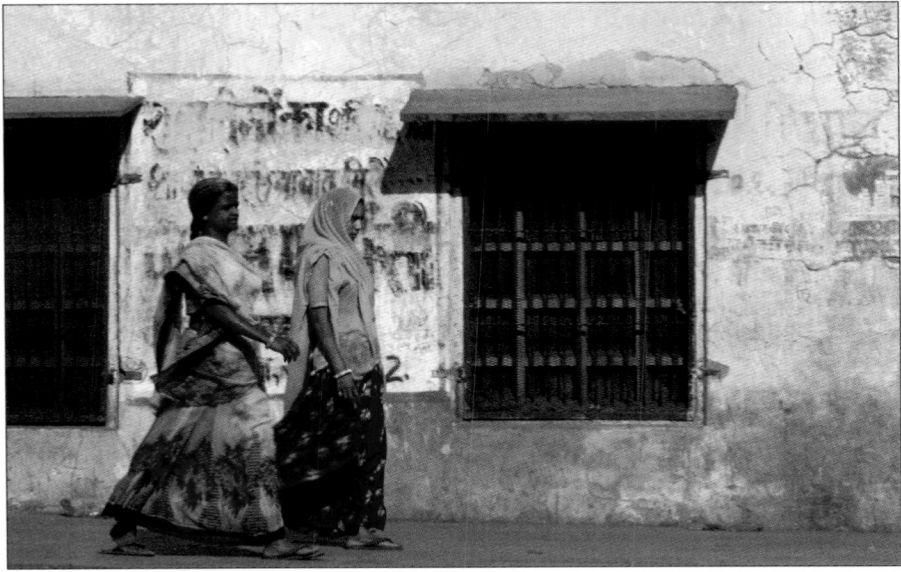

Figure 50-1: If you wait patiently, photo subjects walk into your scene.

Troubleshooting

⌐ **I'm photographing a dark-skinned person, and the camera doesn't capture detail on her face.** This problem happens when the light shines directly into your subject's face. Ask your subject to move so that the light is hitting her face from the side. The resulting shadows show the detail in your subject's face.

⌐ **My subject disappears in the background.** When you photograph people who have dark skin, get them to move to a brightly colored background, if possible. Alternatively (and if you can), have someone hold a white piece of fabric and angle it to bounce some light into the subject's face.

⌐ **My subject wants money for a photograph.** If you have some local currency, you can give your subject a small pittance for his trouble. If you know a little bit about the area before you visit, you can find out what's considered fair trade for a photograph. You can also do some research online, or find a photography forum and post a question about photographing people in the country you're visiting.

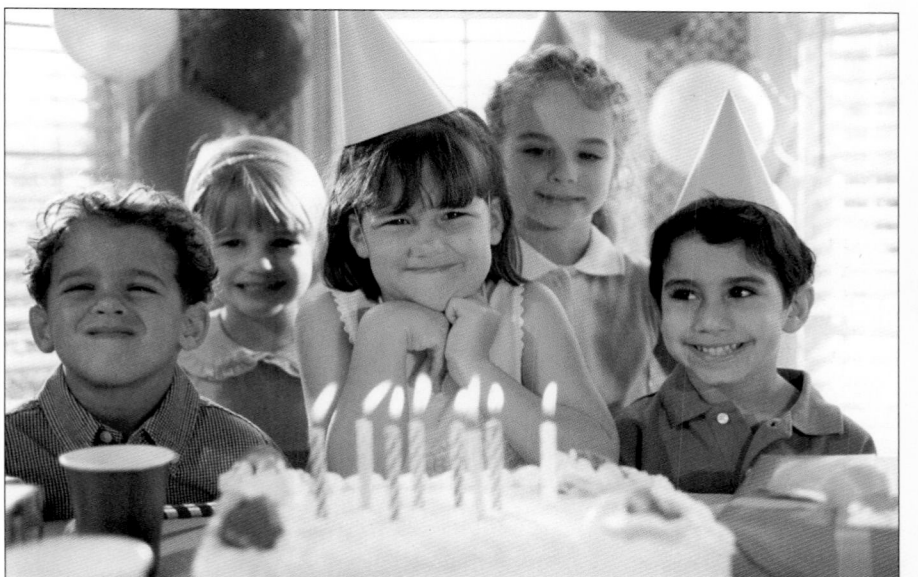

Purestock

- **Metering Mode:** Evaluative
- **Drive Mode:** Single Shot or Continuous
- **Shooting Mode:** Aperture Priority
- **Aperture:** f/3.5 to f/8.0
- **ISO Setting:** 100 to 400
- **Focus Mode:** Single Shot
- **Auto-Focus Point:** Single auto-focus point
- **Focal Length:** 50mm to 100mm (35mm equivalent; see "Understanding focal lengths" in the appendix)
- **Image Stabilization:** On

*B*irthday parties are wonderful opportunities for photographers to get great photos, especially when the party includes younger people. At this kind of event, you can use photos to tell a story. When you tell a story, you photograph everything at the event: party favors, the setting, and most importantly, the children at the event. And, of course, you need a lot of photos of the birthday girl. So, the next time a child in your family or a close friend's family has a birthday party, grab your camera and use the settings in this chapter to create great photos.

Setting the Camera

Photographing a child's birthday party can be a lot of fun. You can capture some wonderful pictures of exuberant children having a great time. I recommend that you use Aperture Priority mode for photographing a birthday party because it gives you complete control over the depth of field. When you photograph the entire party, you want a large depth of field, so you use a medium aperture that has an f/stop value of f/8.0. When you're photographing the birthday girl, you use a large aperture that has an f/stop of f/3.5, which gives you a very shallow depth of field and draws the viewer's attention to the honored guest. The suggested ISO range works great for outdoor parties (ISO 100) or indoor parties (ISO 400). The focal-length range lets you capture a picture of the entire gang (50mm) or zoom in to capture a picture of the birthday girl opening her presents (100mm). If you want to capture sequences of events, such as a child opening her gifts, you have the option to shoot in Continuous Drive mode.

Taking the Picture

If you want to tell the story of a child's birthday party, you can begin by photographing the setting, the guests arriving, and then the party itself. If you're photographing the birthday of a very young person, you may have to be on the lookout for flying cake and other sundry missiles of destruction. Other than that, photographing a child's birthday party is a piece of cake.

1. **Enable the settings discussed previously in this chapter.**

2. **If you're telling a story, photograph the settings and the party favors.**

    You can take these photographs in two ways. You can use a small aperture to get everything on the table in apparent focus or use a large aperture. If you choose the latter option, focus on something significant, such as a party hat with the birthday girl's name on it, and use a focal length of about 100mm. The hat is in sharp focus, the rest of the table is soft, and the objects in the near foreground and distant background are blurred.

3. **When you see something or someone you want to photograph, move the auto-focus point over your subject, and then press the shutter button halfway.**

4. **Compose the picture.**

    In most instances, you get a better photograph if you compose the shot so that it's not symmetrical. You can also use elements in the scene to draw your viewers into the photo.

5. Take the picture.

Continue taking photographs of everything that's important. You may get some wonderful candid shots of the birthday boy with a hair full of frosting.

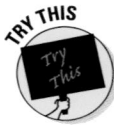

Before the birthday girl blows out the candles on her cake, switch to the largest suggested aperture (f/3.5) and a focal length of about 100mm. Rotate the camera 90 degrees (from Landscape to Portrait mode), and then compose the picture so that only the girl and the cake are in the viewfinder. Take the picture when she blows out the candles. To capture a sequence of pictures, switch to Continuous Drive mode and keep the shutter button pressed while she takes a deep breath and then blows out the candles (see Figure 51-1).

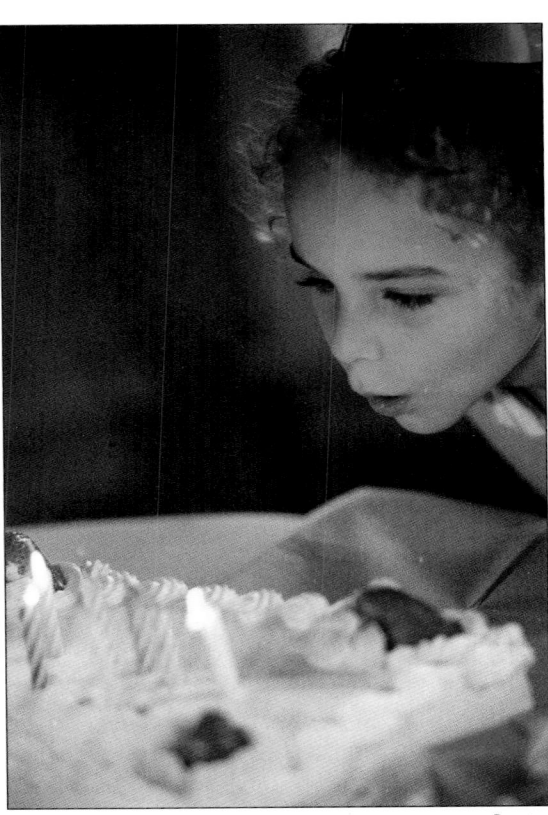

Purestock

Figure 51-1: Take a close-up shot of the birthday girl blowing out the candles.

Troubleshooting

- **The candle flames don't have detail.** You can't avoid this lack of detail. The camera can't capture the same dynamic range of bright and dark shades that our eyes can. As long as the rest of the image is properly exposed, don't worry about the candle flames.

- **The photo has too much detail.** This problem can happen when you take a picture by using a small aperture. To get rid of some foreground or background clutter, switch to a larger aperture (a smaller f/stop number). Most cameras have a depth-of-field preview button on the front of the camera that you can use to stop the lens down and preview the depth of field prior to taking the picture.

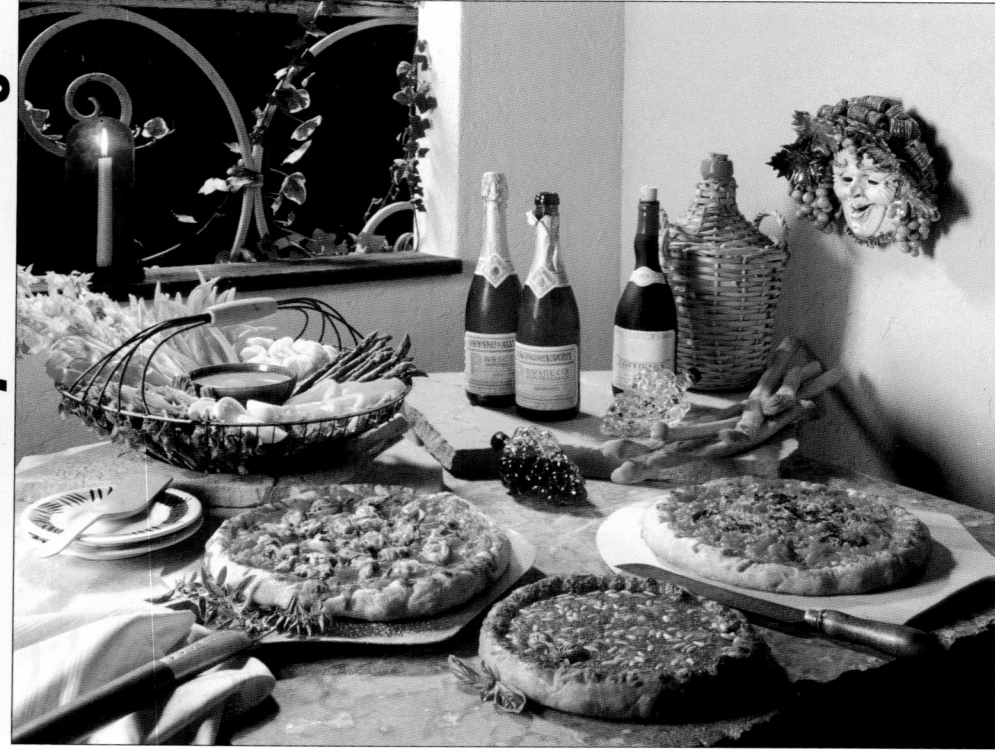

Kevin Sanchez/Cole Group/PhotoDisc

*W*hether you're part of a big family or a small family, it's a special occasion when everyone gets together to celebrate something. For a joyous event, such as a wedding anniversary, it's worth recording. And the onus of that task falls on you, the family photographer. Some photographers just take an odd shot or two to commemorate a special gathering, such as a baby shower. But any event worth photographing is worth photographing from start to finish. This technique requires a variety of pictures and settings. You want to photograph everything that can trigger a memory of the event — even the food served.

Camera Settings

- **Metering Mode:** Evaluative
- **Drive Mode:** Single Shot or Continuous
- **Shooting Mode:** Aperture Priority
- **Aperture:** f/3.5 to f/8.0
- **ISO Setting:** 100 to 400
- **Focus Mode:** Single Shot
- **Auto-Focus Point:** Single auto-focus point
- **Focal Length:** 50mm to 100mm (35mm equivalent; see "Understanding focal lengths" in the appendix)
- **Image Stabilization:** On

Setting the Camera

When you tell the story of a special family gathering, you want viewers to see the subjects you're photographing. The best way to draw attention to your subject by controlling depth of field, so use Aperture Priority mode. Use a large aperture when you photograph one person or object from the party and a medium aperture when you photograph several people. If you anticipate a lot of quick action, with people dancing and expressing a lot of emotions in a short period of time, shoot in Continuous Drive mode to capture an action sequence. Otherwise, Single Shot mode is fine. The suggested ISO range works well for outdoor parties (ISO 100) or indoor parties (ISO 400). The suggested focal-length range lets you capture an image of several guests (50mm) or zoom in on the party girl (100mm). Image stabilization can help you nail a blur-free shot.

Taking the Picture

When you want to tell the story of a party by taking pictures, make sure you arrive early. Start by photographing the preparations for the party.

1. **Enable the settings discussed previously in this chapter.**

2. **Photograph the place settings, any food that will be served, and so on.**

   When you photograph a table setting, you can use a small aperture to keep everything in focus or a large aperture to selectively focus on a single object, such as a place setting with the featured guest's name. When you selectively focus on a specific object, use a focal length of about 100mm, which gives you a shallow depth of field when coupled with a large aperture.

3. **Photograph the guests while they arrive.**

4. **Photograph the guests interacting with the featured guest.**

   To get these kinds of photos, you need to be patient. At first, the guests notice you and the camera, but when the event starts kicking into high gear, they start enjoying each other's company and interacting with the party girl. You can also create portraits of the special guest using the techniques in Chapter 65.

5. **Choose an interesting vantage point and compose the image.**

   When you tell the story of a family event, you want to draw the viewer's attention to the person for whom you're having the event. Figure 52-1 shows the entire party, but the interaction is between the lady with the purple blouse and the mom-to-be. They're both in sharp focus, and the rest of the people and gifts aren't. Also, the two ladies' eyes form a diagonal line.

6. **Press the shutter button half-way to achieve focus, and then fully press the button to take the picture.**

   Continue taking photographs of everything that seems to be important. You can eliminate the duds when you edit the photos in your image-editing application.

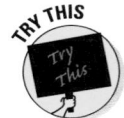

If the place where the party is being held has a second floor, you can get some wonderful candid shots by zooming in from above.

Troubleshooting

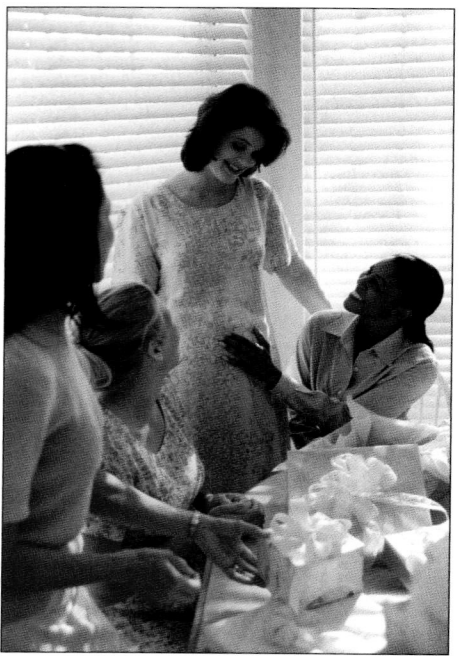

Purestock

Figure 52-1: Find an interesting vantage point and compose the image.

↳ **The people in the photo appear dark.** This problem happens when you have a bright light source behind your subjects, such as the light filtering through the blinds in Figure 52-1. Use fill flash (see Chapter 59) to fill in the shadows.

↳ **The background is in focus, and my subject isn't.** Make sure your camera is in Single Shot focus mode. If you inadvertently change to a different focus mode, the camera refocuses when you move the camera to compose the image. Also, make sure that the auto-focus point is over your subject and illuminates before you move the camera to compose the shot.

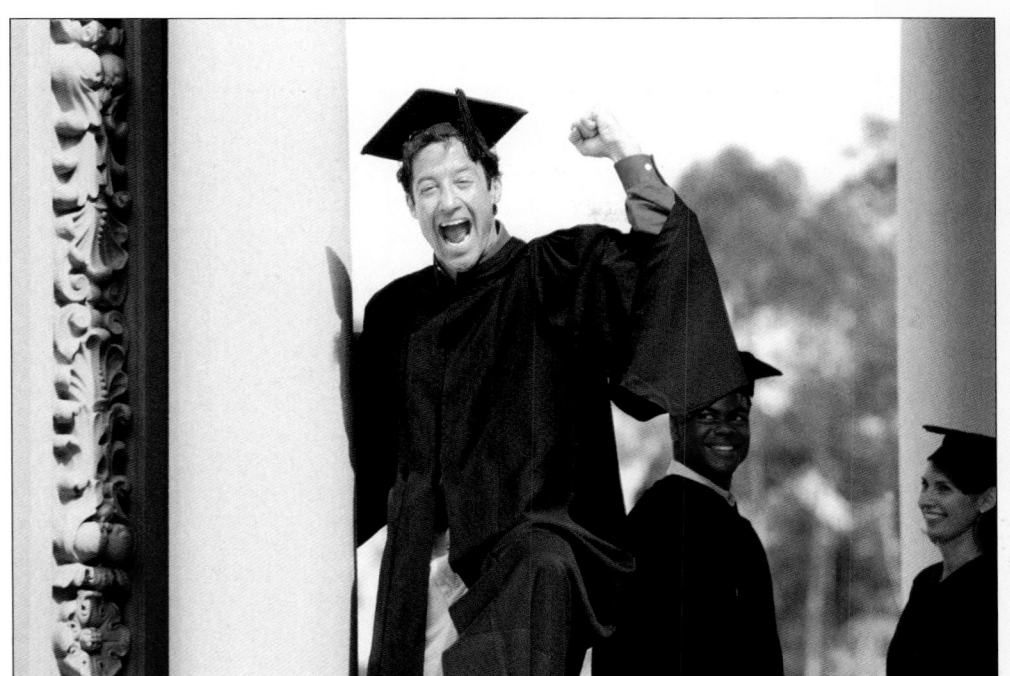

100 Ltd.

Camera Settings

- ✔ **Metering Mode:** Evaluative
- ✔ **Drive Mode:** Single Shot
- ✔ **Shooting Mode:** Aperture Priority
- ✔ **Aperture:** f/4.0 to f/8.0
- ✔ **ISO Setting:** 100 to 200
- ✔ **Focus Mode:** Single Shot
- ✔ **Auto-Focus Point:** Single auto-focus point
- ✔ **Focal Length:** 50mm to 100mm (35mm equivalent; see "Understanding focal lengths" in the appendix)
- ✔ **Image Stabilization:** On

A graduation is a wonderful day in both your child's and your life. It's a rite of passage that you should record by taking a lot of photographs. Your job as the family photographer/historian is to capture the graduation ceremony and take some great shots of your son while he celebrates his momentous achievement. By all means, enjoy the ceremony, but try to keep your emotions somewhat in check so that you can operate the camera. Your son will appreciate the pictures (and your efforts) when he looks at them many years from now.

Setting the Camera

When you photograph a graduation, you take many different types of pictures. Your subjects aren't moving, therefore you use Aperture Priority mode to take the pictures. I suggest a large range of aperture settings because of the different types of pictures you want to take. When you photograph a group of graduates, you need a depth of field large enough that you can capture the entire group in focus, so you use the smallest suggested aperture that has an f/stop of f/8.0. When you photograph a small group, your photos can benefit from a slightly smaller depth of field, which you can achieve by using an f/stop of f/6.3 or f/5.6. When you photograph one person, you want a very shallow depth of field and thus use the largest suggested aperture that has an f/stop of f/4.0. The suggested focal-length range gives you the option to photograph a group or zoom in to photograph one or two people. The suggested ISO range is perfect for a bright day. If you're photographing an indoor graduation ceremony, use on-camera flash, as well as a high ISO setting. On-camera flash gives you plenty of light, albeit harsh light, when you photograph a group, but if you photograph one or two people, diffuse the flash (see the appendix) to bathe your subjects in a soft light that doesn't cast harsh shadows.

Taking the Picture

At a graduation, you want to tell a story with your photography. You're not doing yourself or your family justice if you take just a few pictures. Therefore, in this section, I include some basic steps, and then list kinds of photos you might want to take the next time a family member graduates.

1. **Arrive early.**

   You don't want to show up at the last minute and get a seat that's far away from the ceremony. If you can get a seat up front, you don't have to shoot over people who are in front of you — or, worse yet, get a couple of rows of heads in your photo.

2. **Enable the settings discussed previously in this chapter.**

3. **Have a family member hold your seat, and then take photos of the graduate before the ceremony.**

   Before the ceremony is a great time to get pictures of your daughter donning her gown or chatting with her friends. Come back to your seat a few minutes before the ceremony begins.

4. **When you see something you want to photograph, press the shutter button halfway to achieve focus.**

   Make sure the auto-focus point is over your subject if you're photographing one person or in the center of the group if you're photographing several people. If the people aren't in a single row in front of you, use the f/8.0 aperture and focus on someone in the second row. When you use the relatively small aperture, two rows are in sharp focus, and the rest of the group is recognizable. If you're photographing in an auditorium, you have to use flash, a large aperture, and an ISO of 800.

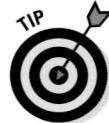

5. **Take the picture.**

Here's a list of photos you may want to consider:

- The graduate arriving at the event
- The graduate donning his cap and gown
- Any commencement speeches
- The graduate walking up to receive the diploma
- The graduate shaking hands with the dean or whoever's handing out diplomas
- The entire graduating class
- The graduate celebrating after the event
- The graduate with her best friend (see Figure 53-1)
- The graduate with family
- A close-up photo of the graduate holding the diploma in his hand

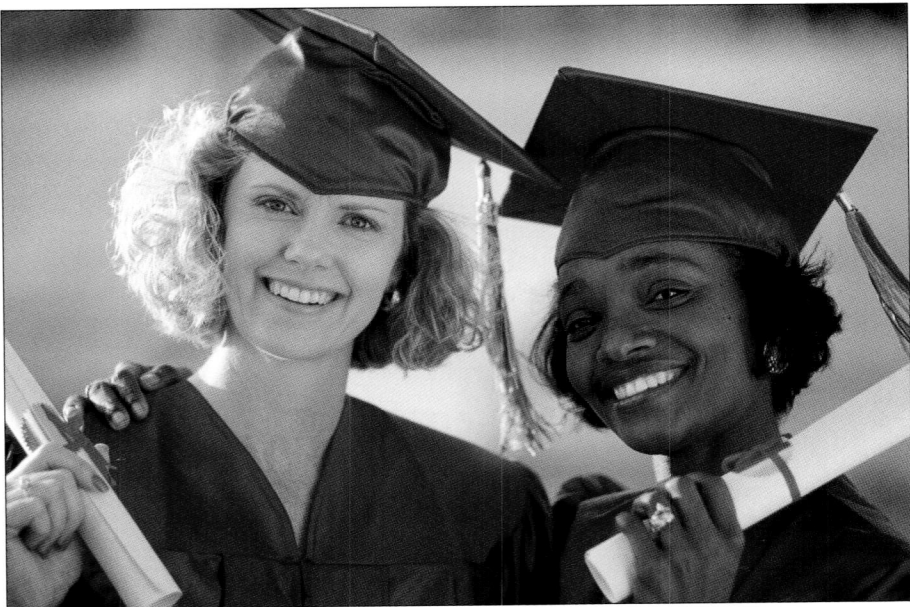

Dynamic Graphics Inc.

Figure 53-1: Photograph the graduate with her best friend.

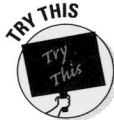

Take a close-up photo of the diploma and graduation cap on a plain background. Take the photo from a distance and zoom in to fill the frame (see Figure 53-2).

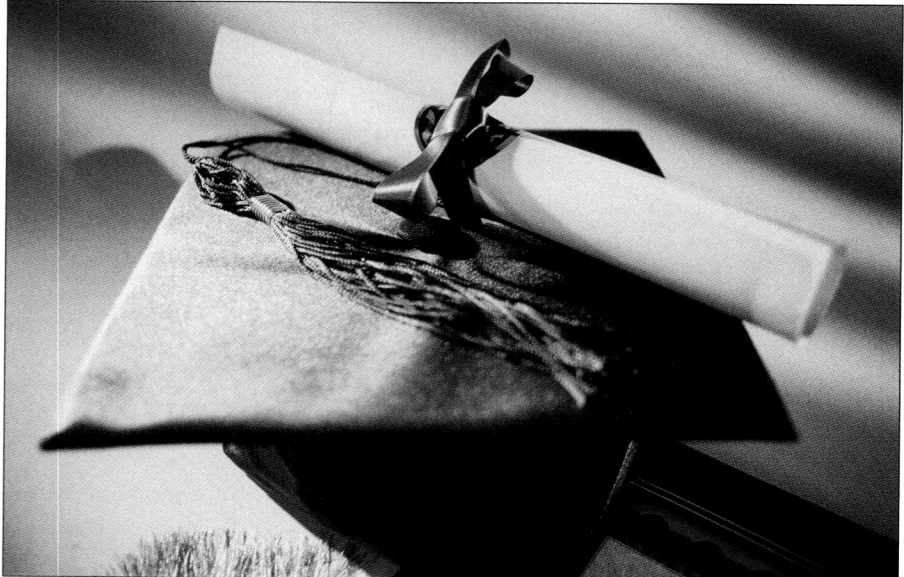

PhotoDisc, Inc./Getty Images

Figure 53-2: Take a close-up shot of the diploma and graduation cap.

Troubleshooting

↳ **The graduate's face has harsh shadows.** This problem can happen when you photograph a graduation on a bright day with the sun almost directly overhead. If you're taking a photo of the graduate accepting the diploma, you don't have any options. However, if you're taking a photo before or after the ceremony, position everyone in an area that's shaded and take the picture again. Alternatively, you can use fill flash.

↳ **I can't fit the entire graduation class in the photo.** This is one of the few instances when you can photograph people by using a wide-angle focal length. Just be sure you're not too close to the first row and that you're at eye level with the group so that you can avoid any distortion.

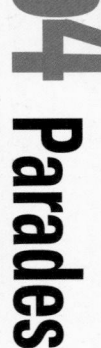

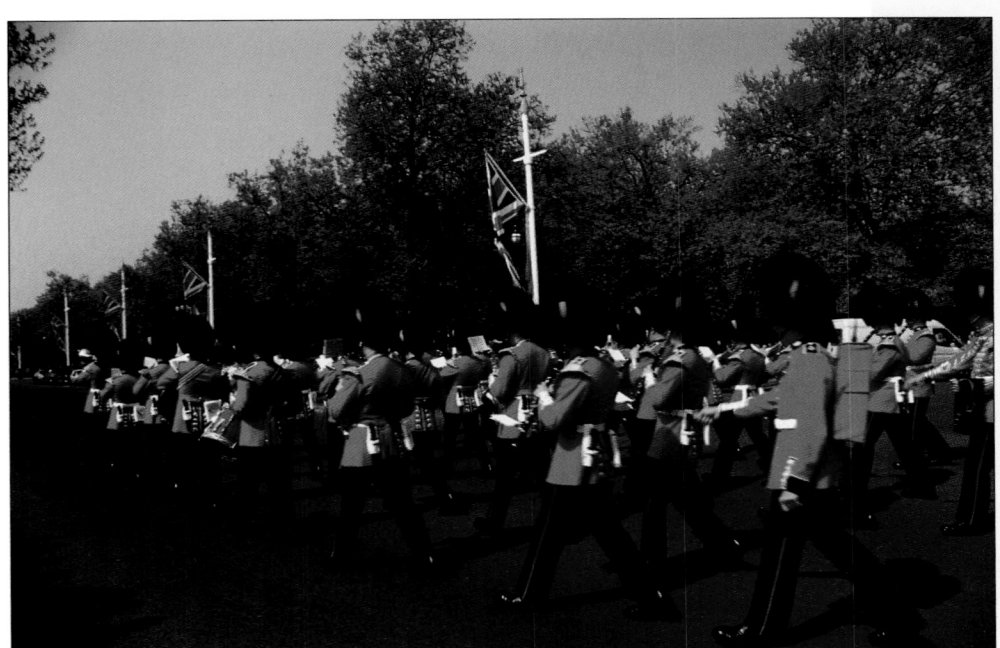

Camera Settings

- **Metering Mode:** Evaluative
- **Drive Mode:** Single Shot
- **Shooting Mode:** Aperture Priority
- **Aperture:** f/5.6 to f/8.0
- **ISO Setting:** 100 to 800
- **Focus Mode:** Single Shot
- **Auto-Focus Point:** Single auto-focus point
- **Focal Length:** 28mm to 100mm (35mm equivalent; see "Understanding focal lengths" in the appendix)
- **Image Stabilization:** On

A parade can be a solemn procession carried out with pomp, circumstance, and precision, such as the changing of the guard at Buckingham Palace, or a festive occasion, such as the Macy's Thanksgiving Day Parade. If you love photography — that's why you're reading this book — and you like parades, photographing a parade is right up your alley.

Setting the Camera

When you photograph a parade, your subjects are moving, but they're moving slowly. You want to control the depth of field to some degree, so you shoot this type of picture in Aperture Priority mode. When you photograph individuals in a parade, you use a large aperture for a shallow depth of field. When you photograph a group in the parade, you use the smallest suggested aperture for a large depth of field, which gives you a photo in which all the people are in focus. When you photograph a large group in the parade, you use a wide-angle focal length to get the entire group in the picture while they parade past. Coupled with a small aperture, you get a depth of field that ensures you can recognize everyone in the photos. The suggested ISO settings work for parades on bright sunny days or winter days that may be a bit on the gloomy side. Use image stabilization, if your camera or lens has it, so that you can ensure a blur-free shot.

Taking the Picture

When you photograph a parade, you take a wide variety of pictures, including interesting faces in the crowd. Be alert when you photograph a parade: You never know when an interesting photo opportunity will present itself.

1. **Arrive early.**

   When you arrive early, you can claim a spot by the curb. Also, pack light. If you try to photograph a parade with everything in your camera bag but the kitchen sink, you annoy people in the crowd when you reach into your bag for gear. You also present a prime target to any thieves who hope to profit from the parade.

2. **Enable the settings discussed previously in this chapter, before the parade begins.**

   The only settings you have to adjust are the f/stop and focal length. Use a large aperture (a small f/stop number) and zoom in when you want to photograph one or two people in the parade. Use a small aperture (a large f/stop number) and zoom out to photograph several people in the parade.

3. **When you see something you want to photograph, press the shutter button halfway to achieve focus.**

   Position the auto-focus point over the center of interest.

4. **To take the picture, fully depress the shutter button.**

   Review the image on the LCD monitor.

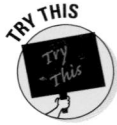

Zoom in close to crop to just the uniforms of people marching in the parade, then switch to manual focus. Move the focus ring until the subject is slightly out of focus to create a Monet-like picture of the parade (see Figure 54-1).

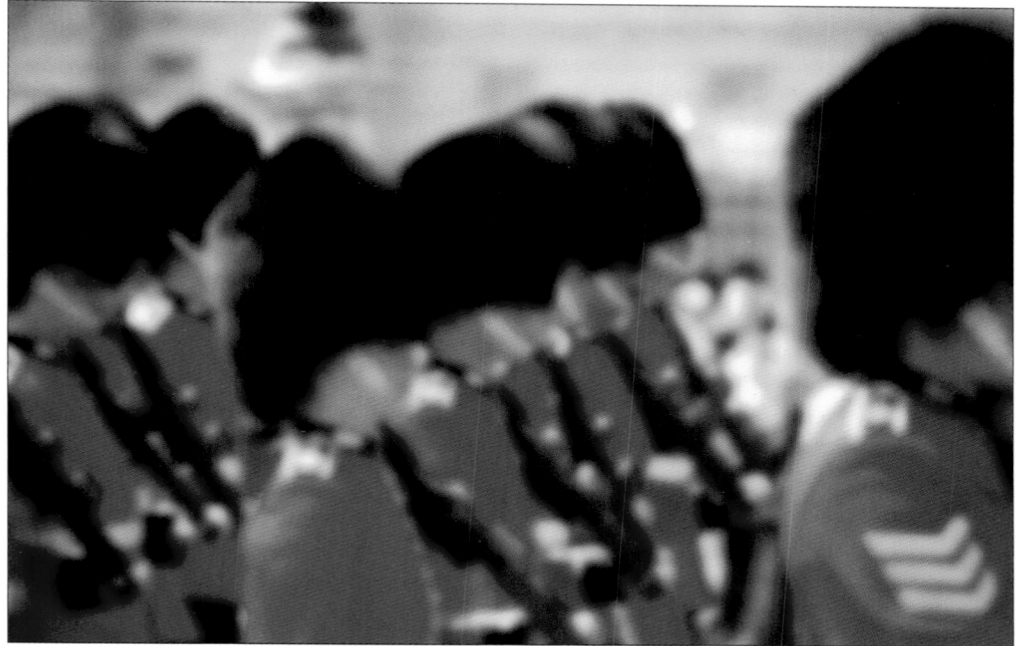

Image State

Figure 54-1: Take an artistic photo of the parade.

Troubleshooting

⬐ **My picture includes shadows of the crowd.** Move until the shadows don't appear as prominently in the viewfinder. If you know the area in which the parade will be held and where the sun will be during the parade, you can find a spot on the shadow-free side of the street before the parade starts.

⬐ **The people in the photos appear dark.** This problem happens if the sun is behind the people marching in the parade. Your only cure is to use exposure compensation to increase the exposure.

55 Wedding (Journalistic)

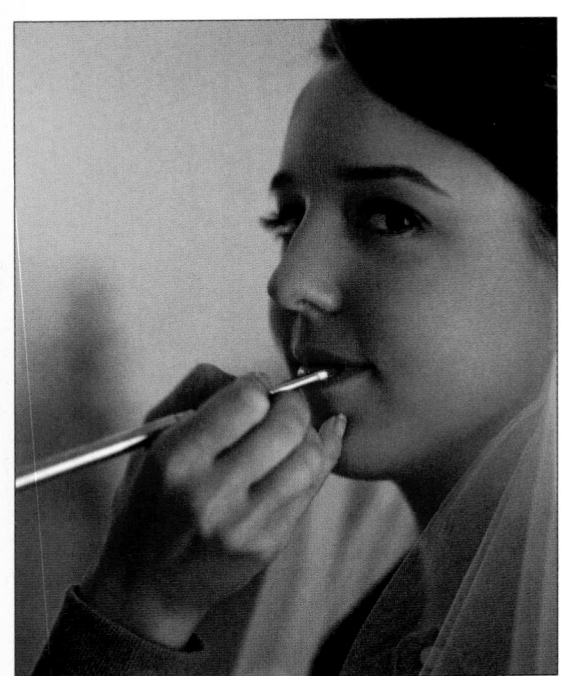

*p*hotographers have two schools of thought on wedding photography: journalistic and traditional styles. I cover the journalistic approach in this chapter. (I discuss how to go traditional in Chapter 56.) Journalistic coverage of a wedding means you include everything, from the program with the couple's names and wedding party to the soggy handkerchief Grandma left on the church pew. Some people like the journalistic style of wedding photography because it helps them remember everything about the day. When you photograph a wedding in the journalistic style, you actually use an array of settings. In this chapter, I give you a starting point for journalistic wedding photography. When you photograph a wedding by using this technique, have a photographer friend of the opposite gender help you out: The male photographer photographs the groom getting ready, and the female photographer photographs the bride getting ready.

Camera Settings

- ✔ **Metering Mode:** Evaluative
- ✔ **Drive Mode:** Single Shot
- ✔ **Shooting Mode:** Aperture Priority
- ✔ **Aperture:** f/4.0 (details and close-ups) to f/8.0 (the church and large groups)
- ✔ **ISO Setting:** 100 to 800
- ✔ **Focus Mode:** Single Shot
- ✔ **Auto-Focus Point:** Single auto-focus point
- ✔ **Focal Length:** 35mm (large groups and the church), 85mm (portraits), and 100mm or macro (details)
- ✔ **Image Stabilization:** On

Setting the Camera

When you photograph a wedding in journalistic style, you wear many hats. You photograph portraits, take candid pictures, and photograph details. Controlling depth of field is important in this type of photography, which is why you use the Aperture Priority shooting mode. When you're photographing the church or a group of people, you use a small aperture that has an f/stop of 8.0, which draws the viewer's attention to your subject. When you're photographing the couple with the officiant or details such as the wedding programs, the pastor's Bible, and so on, use a large aperture that has an f/stop of 4.0 to get a shallow depth of field. A single auto-focus point lets you pinpoint the object or person that you want the camera to focus on. Use the wide-angle focal length to photograph the church or a large group, and the long focal lengths to photograph the couple or details. (For more information, see "Understanding focal lengths" in the appendix.) The ISO range allows you to photograph a bright, outdoor wedding (ISO 100) or a wedding in a dimly lit church (ISO 800).

Taking the Picture

When you photograph a wedding journalistically, you have to keep your eyes open for everything. Capture pictures of the bride and groom heading down the aisle and also scan the pews for people smiling, crying, and so on. If you bring a friend or family member who's interested in photography, that person can help you capture the emotions of the event because you can't be everywhere at once.

1. **When you photograph any wedding, arrive early (and plan on staying late).**

    You can get some wonderful shots of the organist or pianist warming up before the wedding starts. You can also get shots of the church before the guests start arriving. For these pictures, use a combination of wide-angle focal lengths for shots of the church and medium telephoto focal lengths (of about 85mm) to photograph the details and the musicians warming up.

2. **Photograph the guests while they arrive.**

    You can get some wonderful shots of guests being ushered into the wedding. Pay attention to the emotions when the parents are escorted to the wedding. Photograph the guests by using medium telephoto focal lengths (of up to 100mm). Make sure you use a large aperture (a small f/stop number), to blur the background and foreground. You want your viewers to see the emotions and not be distracted by the background.

3. **Photograph the wedding party while they wait for the bride.**

    Be a fly on the wall. Keep your radar tuned to what's happening: You may see spontaneous outbursts of emotion while the wedding party assembles. Usually, you focus on the person who starts crying or laughing. However, sometimes you get lucky. In Figure 55-1, the photographer focused on the blonde lady holding the flowers, but it's obvious that another member of the wedding party is getting very emotional. And the blonde lady is looking right at her. Photograph everything.

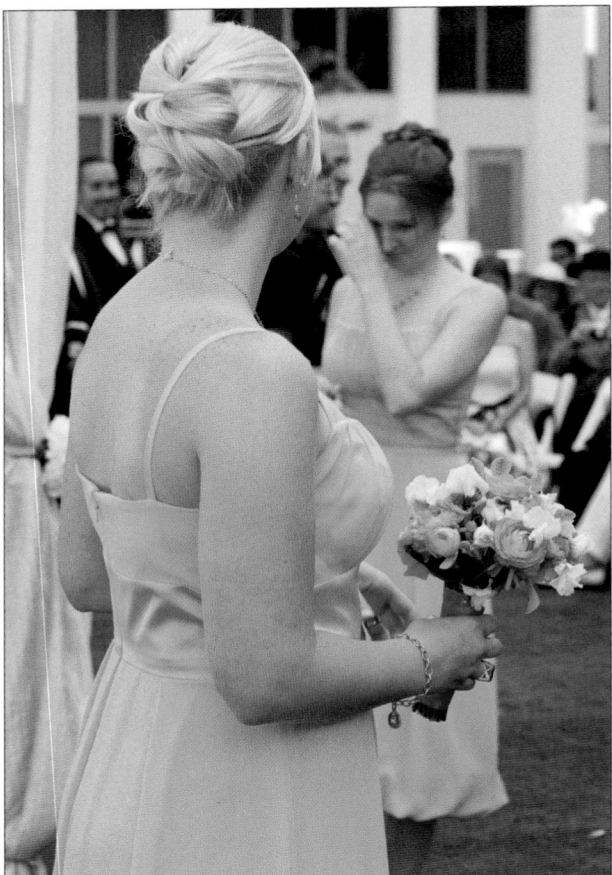

Figure 55-1: Keep an eye out for emotional guests.

4. Photograph the ceremony.

Photograph the bride coming down the aisle at the ceremony, but keep your eye on the groom and the other members of the wedding party. You're sure to see several watery eyes. Whenever you see emotion, point the camera, zoom in, and shoot the picture. Photograph everything during the ceremony, including any special segments such as the lighting of a unity candle or a sand ceremony.

5. Photograph the end of the wedding.

When the wedding officiant publicly introduces the couple as man and wife, stay on your toes. You're bound to see an outpouring of emotion and perhaps a few priceless moments, such as the bride and groom celebrating. And make sure you get a photo of the first kiss!

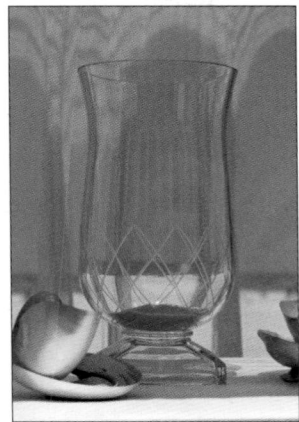

Figure 55-2: Photograph everything.

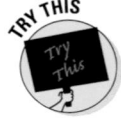

Take a close-up photo of any objects that can trigger fond memories when the bride and groom look at the photos many years from now. For example, if the couple has a sand ceremony, photograph the filled vessel after the ceremony (see Figure 55-2).

Troubleshooting

✓ **I'm getting a lot of blurry shots during the ceremony.** You do have to work fast at a wedding, but not that fast. If you become a bundle of nerves and your photography suffers, take a deep breath and regain your composure. When you want to photograph a specific person or group of people, make sure you're holding the camera steady and that the auto-focus point is over the people who are the center of interest. Make sure the auto-focus point illuminates before you compose the picture.

✓ **The couple is too dark in the photo.** This problem can happen when you photograph an outdoor wedding and the couple is *backlit* (a bright light source, such as the sun, is behind the bride and groom). Use exposure compensation to increase the exposure or use fill flash to fill in the shadows.

✓ **The camera focuses on the wrong objects.** Make sure the camera is in Single Shot focus mode. If you accidentally change to Continuous Auto-Focus mode, the camera updates focus when you compose the picture, and the camera focuses on objects that have edges with a lot of contrast, such as the blinds behind the happy couple walking down the aisle.

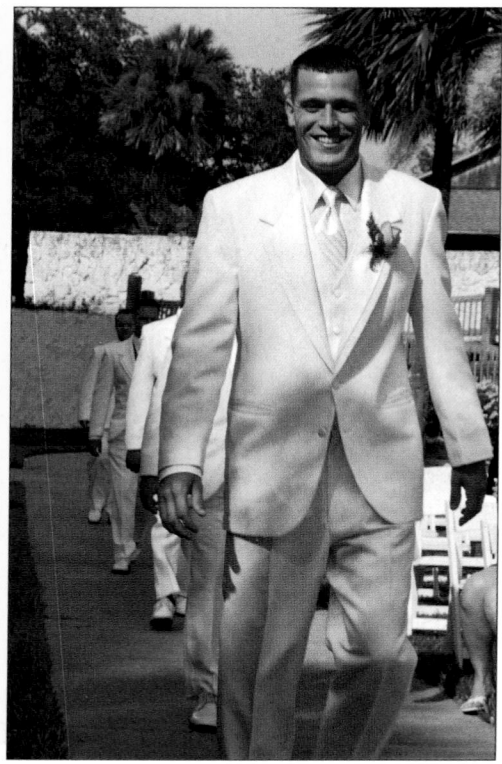

56 Wedding (Traditional)

Traditional wedding photography has been around for a long time. When you photograph a wedding in the traditional manner, you concentrate on the bride, the groom, and the wedding party. But that doesn't mean your photos have to be rigid. In fact, many photographers do a crossover between journalistic wedding photography (which I talk about in Chapter 55) and traditional wedding photography. Before photographing a wedding, read all the wedding chapters in this section. When you photograph a wedding traditionally, you begin with the wedding party marching down the aisle and take a series of photos of the ceremony, such as the bride and groom exchanging vows and the groom putting the ring on his bride's finger.

Camera Settings

- **Metering Mode:** Evaluative
- **Drive Mode:** Single Shot
- **Shooting Mode:** Aperture Priority
- **Aperture:** f/5.6 to f/8.0
- **ISO Setting:** 100 to 800
- **Focus Mode:** Single Shot
- **Auto-Focus Point:** Single auto-focus point
- **Focal Length:** 50mm to 100mm (35mm equivalent; see "Understanding focal lengths" in the appendix)
- **Image Stabilization:** On

When you photograph a wedding, check with the church to make sure you're not violating any rules the church or religion may have regarding photography. This chapter assumes that you're the official photographer. If the couple has hired another photographer to photograph the wedding, don't get in their way.

Setting the Camera

When you photograph a wedding in the traditional style, you take a time-honored series of pictures. Whenever people are your subject, you need to control depth of field; therefore, use Aperture Priority shooting mode. When you photograph the groom putting the ring on the bride's finger, use a large aperture, which gives you a shallow depth of field and draws the viewer's attention to the bride and groom. When you photograph the wedding party and the officiant, use a medium aperture to capture a larger depth of field, which gives you a photo that has everyone in the picture in focus. A single auto-focus point lets you pinpoint the person you want to make the center of attention. Use a short focal length to photograph the wedding party and the officiant. When the groom puts the ring on his bride, zoom in. The suggested ISO range allows you to photograph a bright outdoor wedding (ISO 100) or a wedding in a dimly lit church (ISO 800).

Taking the Picture

If you're photographing a traditional wedding, talk with the couple well in advance of the ceremony and ask them which shots are important to them. Their list may require a bit of movement on your part. Before the ceremony, make sure you and the groom (or bride) talk with the officiant so that he's not taken off guard when you start moving around. Just make sure you don't talk to the officiant with both the bride and the groom. After all, you're photographing the wedding in a traditional style, and it's a time-honored tradition for the bride and groom not to see each other before the ceremony on the wedding day.

1. **Arrive early at the place where the ceremony is being held and get your gear ready.**

   When you're cleaning your lenses, look for an ideal vantage point from which to photograph the procession. (You can better prepare yourself if you know what's going to happen. Attend the rehearsal if at all possible.)

2. **Photograph the wedding party while they walk into the venue.**

   Zoom in to capture a single shot of the groom walking down the aisle.

3. **Photograph the bride and her father walking down the aisle.**

   Take several pictures to capture the joy while the father gets ready to give his daughter in holy matrimony. The bride will be beaming, as well.

4. **Photograph the ceremony.**

   Photograph the wedding party and the officiant conducting the ceremony. Make sure you photograph the couple exchanging their vows. You just can't miss this traditional shot.

5. **Photograph the groom while he puts the ring on his bride's finger (see Figure 56-1).**

   You have to move around a bit and get creative. Make sure the officiant knows you'll be on the move. When you do move, be as quiet as the proverbial church mouse. You don't want to attract any more attention than you have to.

6. **Photograph the end of the wedding.**

   Get a photograph of the couple's first kiss and the wedding party celebrating.

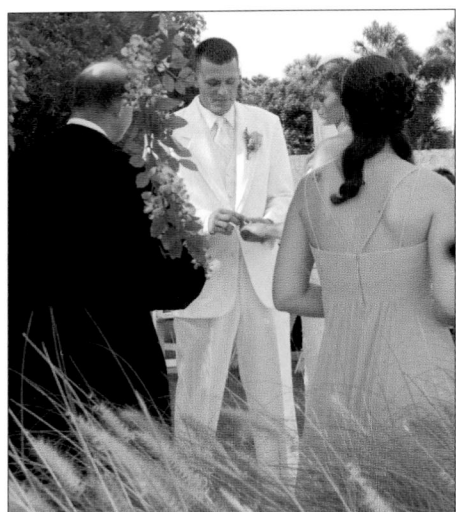

Figure 56-1: Photograph the groom putting the ring on his bride's finger.

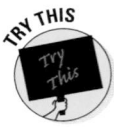

After the ceremony is over, photograph the wedding procession while they leave. You have to be quick on your feet and get to the end of the aisle right after you photograph the couple's first kiss. The bride and groom are the first to leave, and they get a lot of attention from the guests attending the ceremony. Photograph the other members of the wedding party, as well.

Troubleshooting

✏ **I'm photographing an outdoor wedding and the sky is too bright.** You need to make your exposure spot-on for the wedding party. Specifically, make sure your camera properly exposes the bride's dress. If the camera blows out a detail on the dress to pure white, you can have a hard time recovering the detail in your image-editing program. You can leave the camera settings so that the sky is pure white in the photos, as long as the wedding party is properly exposed.

✏ **People's faces include areas of bright light.** You have to deal with this problem when you shoot an outdoor wedding. Use exposure compensation to reduce the overall exposure by 1/3 EV. Your pictures still include areas of bright light, but those areas aren't as noticeable.

✏ **The officiant is in the shade, and the couple is in the sun.** When you're faced with this dilemma, underexpose the officiant. Your picture should show detail in the bride's dress. If you nail that, the bride will be happy.

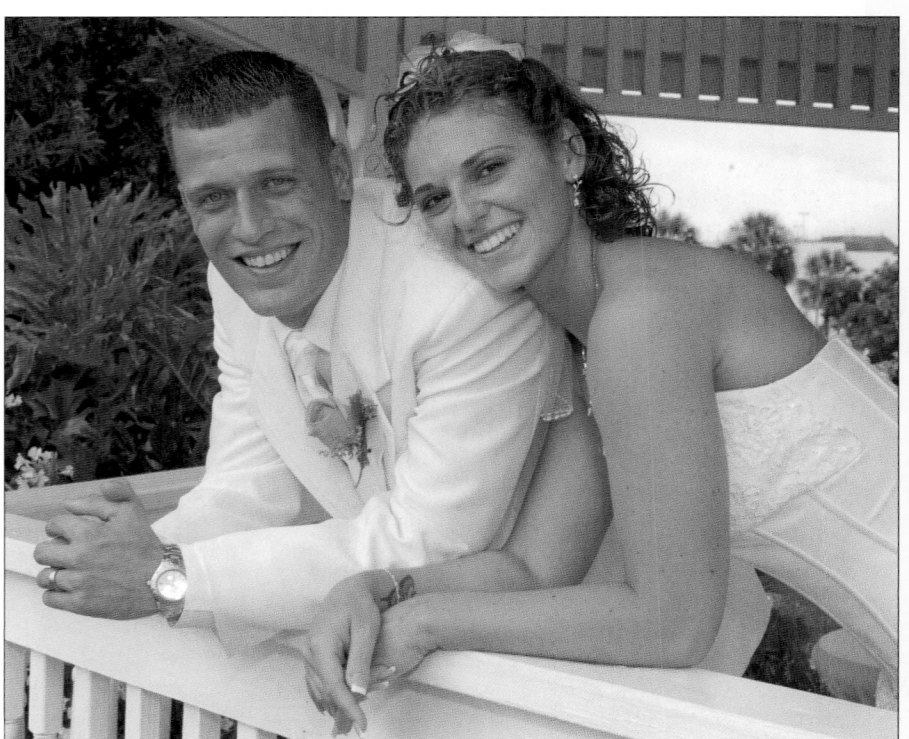

Camera Settings

- ✔ **Metering Mode:** Evaluative
- ✔ **Drive Mode:** Single Shot
- ✔ **Shooting Mode:** Aperture Priority
- ✔ **Aperture:** f/4.0 to f/7.1
- ✔ **ISO Setting:** 100 to 800
- ✔ **Focus Mode:** Single Shot
- ✔ **Auto-Focus Point:** Single auto-focus point
- ✔ **Focal Length:** 35mm to 85mm (35mm equivalent; see "Understanding focal lengths" in the appendix)
- ✔ **Image Stabilization:** On

After the happy couple ties the knot, you still have two hurdles to jump as a photographer: the formals and the reception. (I talk about reception photos in Chapter 58.) The formals are the shots that the family sends to their friends and other family members. You take pictures of the entire wedding party; the couple with the best man and maid of honor; the flower girl; and the happy couple on their own. Also take pictures of the newlyweds with any special members of the wedding party, such as a best friend from college, the oldest member of the family, and so on. To hedge all bets, just ask the couple before the ceremony to describe the pictures they want to have.

Setting the Camera

When you take formal pictures of the wedding party, you want to make the people the center of attention. You also want the viewer to be able to recognize the immediate area, but you don't want to include any distracting background elements. Aperture Priority shooting mode is the obvious choice. A medium aperture that has an f/stop of f/7.1 draws the viewer's attention to the members of the wedding party. When you take the formals of the bride and groom, switch to the largest suggested aperture with an f/stop of f/4.0 for a shallow depth of field that draws viewer attention to the happy couple. You can use a couple of different focal lengths. How close you can get to the party while including all the members determines the shortest focal length you use. When you take a formal picture of the happy couple, a focal length of 85mm is perfect. If at all possible, don't use a focal length of less than 35mm when you photograph the entire group. If you do, you end up with some distortion in your photos. The suggested ISO range lets you take pictures in bright sunlight (ISO 100) or dimly lit church interiors (ISO 800). You can also use fill flash to help fill in the shadows. Image stabilization is definitely a plus.

Taking the Picture

When you photograph wedding formals, you'll have to take on the role of director, in addition to being the photographer. If possible, ask another member of the family to assist you.

1. **Tell the wedding party to assemble at the place you picked to photograph the formals immediately after the ceremony ends.**

   If you've employed the services of a family member as an assistant, have her help you round up the group. Find the ideal location for the wedding formals *before* the ceremony. If you're photographing the formals in a church, the altar (which, in most churches, is an elevated area) provides an excellent choice. If the church has impressive architecture and steps leading to the front door, you can use that location to take some excellent photos. Floral gardens and gazebos also offer excellent backdrops for photographing wedding formals.

2. **Take a picture of the entire group, including the wedding party and family members (see Figure 57-1).**

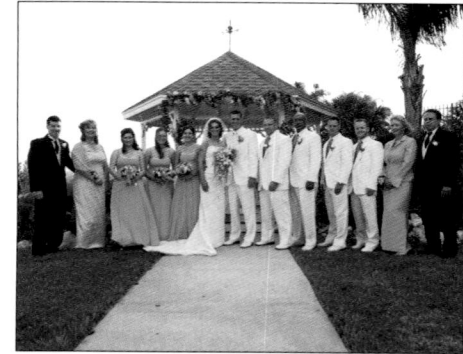

Figure 57-1: Your first formal picture includes the entire wedding party.

Use the widest suggested focal length for the entire group. Look through the viewfinder and make sure that no distracting elements appear in the background. A utility pole growing out of the groom's head doesn't make a good picture. If you find something distracting, move around until something hides the distracting element or until it's a minimal distraction. Of course, if you do your homework ahead of time, you won't have any distracting elements to contend with.

3. **Review the image on your LCD monitor.**

Make sure the image is properly exposed and that everyone is smiling. Also, make sure that you can see everyone's face. You may have to ask some people to move slightly after reviewing the image.

4. **Take another picture of the entire group.**

Always take multiple images from which you can later choose.

5. **Ask the family members who weren't directly involved in the ceremony to go to the reception.**

You're left with the bride, groom, flower girl, ring bearer, best man, and so on.

6. **Take a picture of the wedding party.**

Zoom in to include just the group in the picture. Leave a little breathing room so that you can crop to standard image sizes in your image-editing program. The standard aspect ratio of a digital picture is wider than standard image sizes such as 8 x 10 inches. If you don't leave some space around the subjects, you can cut out some of the wedding party when you crop to print sizes.

7. **Review the image, and then take another picture of the wedding party.**

Before you dismiss the rest of the wedding party, ask the bride and groom whether they want any other pictures.

8. **Photograph the bride and groom with the officiant.**

9. **Ask everyone but the bride and groom to go to the reception.**

10. **Take a picture of the bride and groom.**

Spend some time with the bride and groom. This is the most important day of their lives, and they've asked you to document it. Instead of grabbing just a couple of shots and then hurrying off to the reception, get creative and photograph them in different places. Ask the groom how he feels now that he's married the love of his life and then stand back and be prepared to capture the emotion.

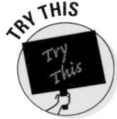

Take a close-up picture of the bride and groom's hands on top of the bride's bouquet (see Figure 57-2). Switch to a large aperture that has an f/stop of f/4.0, which gives you a shallow depth of field and draws the viewer's attention to the couple's hands and rings. If you have a macro lens, use it because you can get very close to get detailed shots.

Troubleshooting

✔ **The people are in shadow.** This problem happens because the light source is behind the subjects. Try to photograph the group with the light shining on their faces (but not directly into their faces). If you have to photograph the group when they're backlit, use fill flash to fill in the shadows. Alternatively, you can use exposure compensation to brighten the image, but this approach blows out areas of the background.

✔ **Some people in the group aren't smiling.** For this reason, you take several pictures of each group in the wedding party. If you notice someone who's not smiling when you review the image, call the person by name and tell him he's not smiling. If you're a funny photographer — after all, you are reading a *For Dummies* book — tell a joke, and then take the picture again. Knowing everybody in the group by name is a big help. You can holler at Uncle Fred and tell him to look at the camera and smile.

✔ **The pictures look static.** Spice up the pictures by photographing each group slightly differently. For example, when you photograph the bride with the best man and groomsmen, get a little creative and have the guys sit down on the floor and gaze up at the blushing bride. Or you can have the guys lie down on the floor like spokes of a wheel, with the bride standing up in the middle. Photograph this scene from a ladder and have everyone look up at you. Get creative and have fun. Just because they're called formals doesn't mean the photos need to be rigid and stodgy.

✔ **I can't fit all the people in the photo.** You may have to get creative. If you have access to a wide staircase, have the shortest people stand on the first step, have the next group stand on the second step, and so on, with the bride and groom at the top of the photo. You need to use a smaller aperture (a larger f/stop number) to have a depth of field large enough to keep everyone in focus.

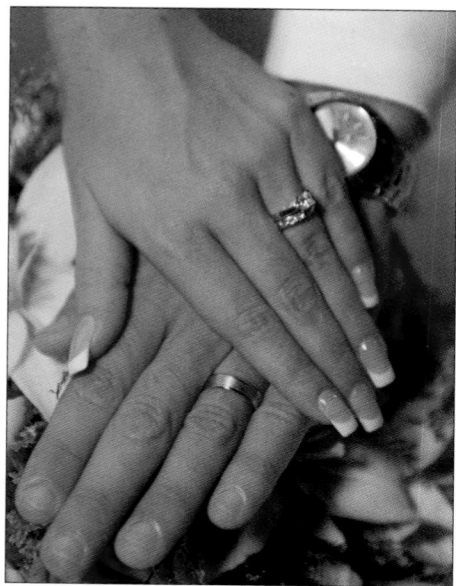

Figure 57-2: Zoom in on the bride and groom's hands.

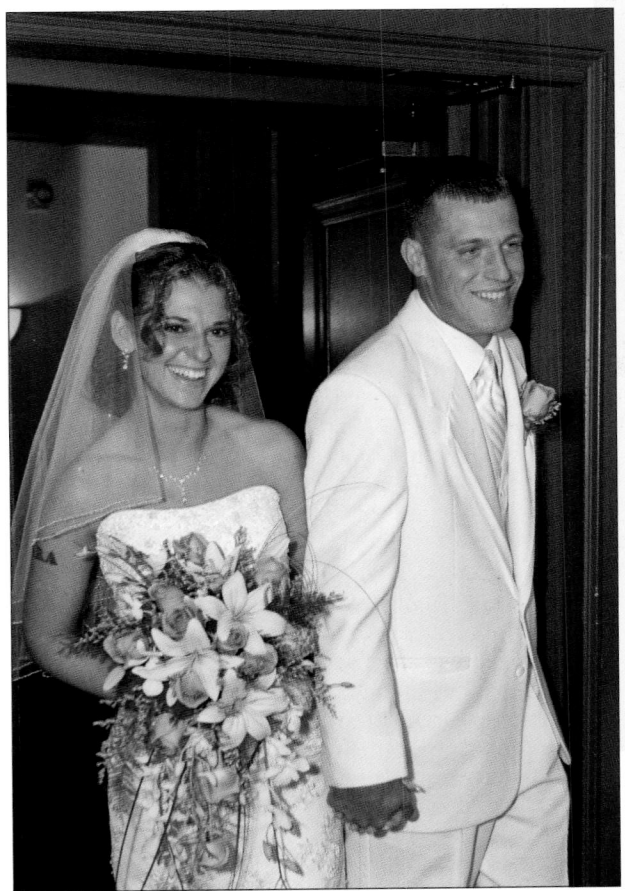

Camera Settings

- **Metering Mode:** Evaluative
- **Drive Mode:** Single Shot
- **Shooting Mode:** Aperture Priority
- **Aperture:** f/4.0
- **ISO Setting:** 1000 or higher
- **Focus Mode:** Single Shot
- **Auto-Focus Point:** Single auto-focus point
- **Focal Length:** 35mm to 70mm (35mm equivalent; see "Understanding focal lengths" in the appendix)
- **Image Stabilization:** On

*W*edding photography can be tedious. Even when you're not being paid for photographing a wedding, the onus is still on you, the family photographer, to deliver stellar pics of the bride, groom, and family. Fortunately, digital photography makes it possible for you to see instantly whether you nailed the shot. After the wedding's over, you can breathe a sigh of relief and enjoy yourself a little at the wedding reception. But you still have to document what goes on and capture the events while they unfold. After the formal dances are over and the dinner is served, the party starts, and you can capture the guests being themselves.

Make no mistake about it; you have to flash the guests (with your camera, I mean). Most receptions are held in dungeon-like conditions, so you need to use on-camera flash and a high ISO. You may want to try some of the flash diffusers mentioned in Chapter 59. Sure, you probably have some noise in the images, but you still can document the event.

Setting the Camera

Being a fly on the wall at a wedding reception is fun. You're photographing people in motion, but you're also photographing in dim light. Therefore, you shoot in Aperture Priority mode and use a large aperture. The large aperture gives you a shallow depth of field, so you have to focus carefully to make sure the camera focuses on your subject instead of Fred the Bartender. The large aperture — combined with your flash unit — gives you a fighting chance of capturing the image. The suggested focal-length range enables you to capture intimate exchanges between the bride and groom, as well as group shots. You may be tempted to choose a long focal length, but a long focal length and slow shutter speed (because of the dim light) makes it hard for you to get blur-free images if you hand-hold the camera. Use image stabilization, if you have it, because it enables you to capture sharp images at slower shutter speeds than normal.

Taking the Picture

When you photograph a wedding reception, you're working like a photojournalist. You capture the standard shots, such as the bride and groom arriving at the reception, and the formal stuff, such as the dances and cake cutting. After that, you blend into the background and capture pictures of the guests having a good time.

1. **Enable the settings discussed previously in this chapter.**

2. **Wait by the door for the newlyweds to arrive at the reception.**

   Find out ahead of time when the happy couple will arrive and make sure you get to the reception room early. Ask another couple to walk through the door so that you can do a dress rehearsal to figure out what focal length you need and exactly where you need to stand to get the best picture. Also, try to get one of the guests to agree to enter the room just before the couple so that you know to get ready.

3. **Take a picture of the newlyweds entering the room.**

   If you followed the advice in Step 2, you can nail the shot. Get another in the bank, just to be on the safe side.

4. **Photograph the formal part of the reception.**

   The bride and groom have their first dance together. The groom also dances with his mom, and the bride dances with her dad. Tears have been known to flow at this part of the reception (see Figure 58-1), so don't put the camera down until the dances are over.

5. **After the cake cutting, photograph the guests enjoying themselves at the party.**

   Stay on the sidelines, but watch the action. You can get some great shots of the bride and groom having a good time with their friends and loved ones.

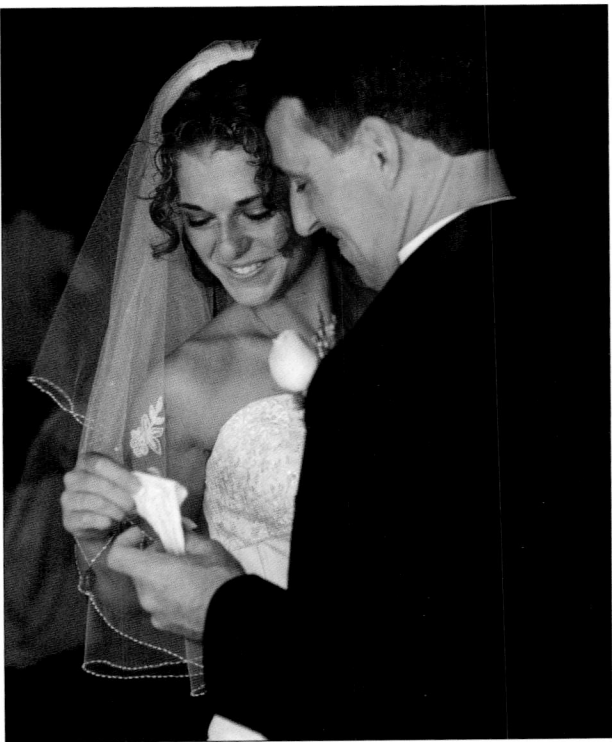

Figure 58-1: Capture the emotion at the wedding reception.

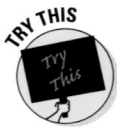

Capture a sequence of images of the bride and groom cutting the cake (see Figure 58-2), and be sure to get a shot of the bride feeding the groom and vice-versa.

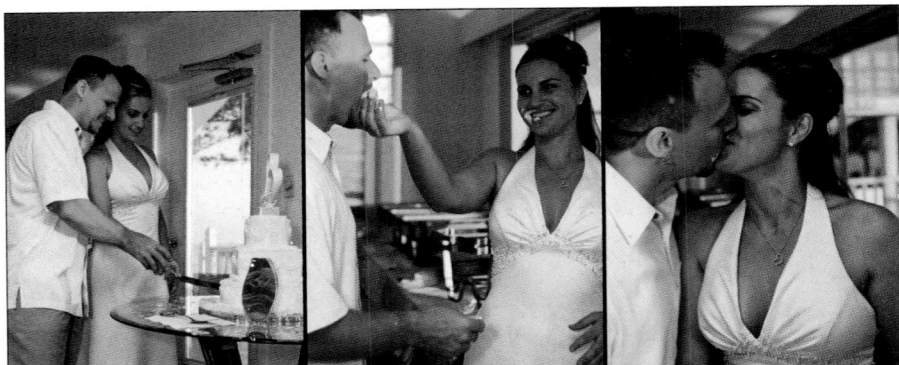

Figure 58-2: Photograph the bride and groom cutting the cake.

Troubleshooting

⌐ **The camera won't focus.** This problem can happen when you photograph a reception in a dimly lit room. Find a well-defined edge on the person you're photographing, such as the edge of the groom's jacket, and position the auto-focus point over it before you press the shutter button halfway to achieve focus. In extreme conditions, you may have to manually focus the camera. If you notice this problem before the festivities start, ask the event planner to bring up the room lights before the important parts of the reception, such as the first dance and the cake cutting.

⌐ **The photo shows a ghost image moving away from each person.** You can have this issue when you shoot in a dimly lighted room in Aperture Priority mode. Your camera uses a slow shutter speed, but the flash freezes the action. Your subjects are still moving after the flash fires, and the motion appears on the image as those ghosts. The ghost images (technically known as *motion trails*) are moving away from your subjects, like those people are having out-of-body experiences. Switch to 2nd Curtain Flash (also called 2nd Shutter Flash), which makes the flash fire at the end of the exposure, rather than the beginning of the exposure. Refer to your camera manual to see whether your camera offers this option.

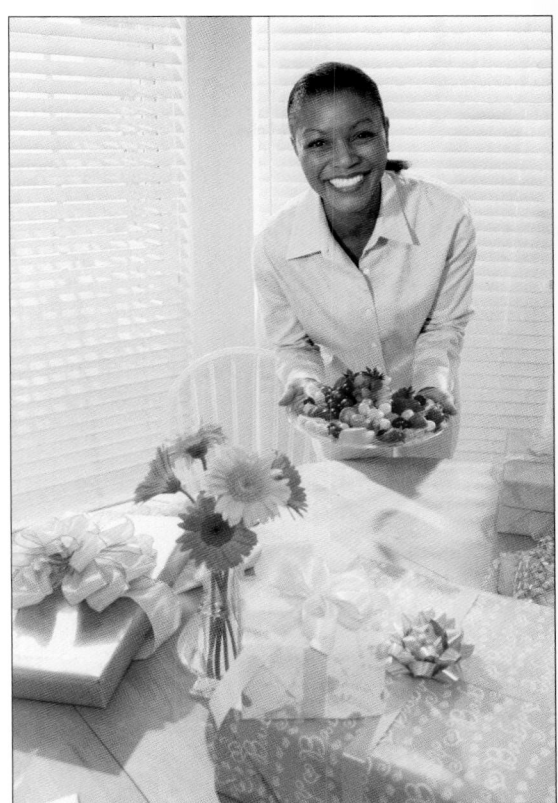

Purestock

Camera Settings

- ✔ **Metering Mode:** Evaluative
- ✔ **Drive Mode:** Single Shot
- ✔ **Shooting Mode:** Aperture Priority
- ✔ **Aperture:** f/4.0 to f/7.1
- ✔ **ISO Setting:** 100
- ✔ **Focus Mode:** Single Shot
- ✔ **Auto-Focus Point:** Single auto-focus point
- ✔ **Camera Flash:** On
- ✔ **Focal Length:** 50mm to 85mm (35mm equivalent; see "Understanding focal lengths" in the appendix)
- ✔ **Image Stabilization:** On

When a powerful light source is behind your subject, you have your work cut out for you. The camera meters for the bright light source, so your subject appears too dark in the photos you take. Therefore, you have to shed some light on your subject. You can most easily illuminate your subject by using the flash on your camera to fill in the shadows. But on-camera flash is quite harsh and causes a problem known as red-eye. Whenever you use on-camera flash to augment lighting, also use a diffuser, a device you place over your flash that gives you nice diffuse light instead of the usual harsh blast you get from an on-camera flash. When you use on-camera flash and a diffuser to fill in the shadows, you end up with a properly lighted photograph of your subject.

Setting the Camera

Aperture Priority mode is the ideal mode to use when creating a portrait. Using a large aperture, you have a shallow depth of field, which is ideal for a head and shoulders portrait. When you're creating a head to toe portrait of someone and you want to include some of the background in the shot, use a smaller aperture to render your subject in sharp focus with a recognizable background but not as sharp as your subject. The ISO setting is ideal for a noise-free image. You may end up with a very slow shutter speed if the light is dim, but the flash will freeze the motion. A single auto-focus point lets you focus precisely on the person you're photographing. The focal-length range is perfect for a full-body portrait (50mm) or a head and shoulders shot (85mm). Image stabilization is helpful especially if you're shooting in less than ideal lighting conditions.

Taking the Picture

With the exception of filling in the shadows, you don't have to do anything differently when you photograph a person who's backlit when compared to photographing a person in ideal lighting. You still need to create a rapport with the subject, get the person to strike a pleasing pose, and then compose the image creatively. With those minor tasks out of the way, you need to augment the lighting by following these steps:

1. **Enable the settings discussed previously in this chapter.**

   After you choose the flash option, your flash unit pops up and is ready for action.

2. **Place the diffuser over the flash unit.**

   A flash diffuser spreads the light out, which makes the light source appear bigger than it actually is. Flash diffusers are relatively inexpensive. Lumiquest makes an on-camera flash diffuser (shown in Figure 59-1) that sells for less than $15, as of this writing. For more information, visit www.lumiquest.com/products/softscreen.htm.

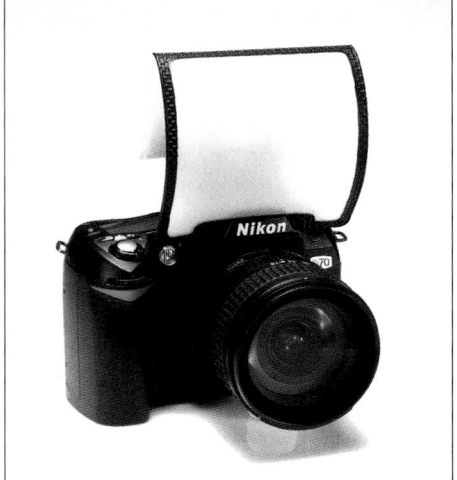

Figure 59-1: Place a diffuser over your camera flash.

3. **Find the ideal vantage point.**

   Get to your subject's eye level. While you get closer to your subject, the flash becomes a larger light source — and if you use the diffuser, you get a large, diffuse light source. However, don't get so close that you have to use a wide-angle focal length to photograph your subject; you have to get very close to your subject to photograph a portrait with a wide-angle lens. This distorts the features closest to the camera. Unless you want to give your mother-in-law a portrait where she has a really big nose, stick with the suggested focal lengths.

4. **Press the shutter button halfway to focus and compose the picture.**

   Don't place your subject in the middle of the frame because this results in a static and frankly, boring image. Also, you can make the picture more interesting if your subject is doing something with his hands. For more information on composing portraits, see Chapters 65, 66, and 67.

5. **Press the shutter button fully to take the picture.**

   After you take the picture, review the image on your LCD monitor. You probably have to take several shots to get a pleasing portrait. People who don't spend a lot of time in front of the camera take a while to relax and look natural.

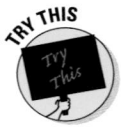

If your camera has a hot shoe, consider purchasing an auxiliary flash unit and a diffuser to fit it (see Figure 59-2). They're more powerful than on-camera flash units. Purchase a flash unit that's made by the manufacturer of your camera or a third-party flash that's dedicated to the brand of camera you own. When you get a flash that's compatible with your camera, the camera meters the scene and then communicates with the flash to determine how much additional light is needed for a properly exposed image.

Figure 59-2: Purchase a more powerful flash unit.

Troubleshooting

✓ **My subject is sharp, but a blurry area appears around her.** The combination of ISO setting and aperture yield a slow shutter speed. The camera flash freezes your subject, but the shutter stays open much longer than the duration of the flash. Operator movement creates the halo around your subject. You can either live with the result as a creative special effect or increase the ISO setting until you obtain a shutter speed that's at least 1/50 of a second, or mount your camera on a tripod.

✓ **The image looks too bright.** The ambient lighting conditions can fool your camera. If your on-camera or auxiliary flash unit has a feature known as flash compensation, use it to reduce the power of the flash. *Flash compensation* is similar to exposure compensation; it reduces the flash power in increments of 1/3 a stop on most cameras. If your camera doesn't have flash compensation, use exposure compensation.

60 Self-Portrait

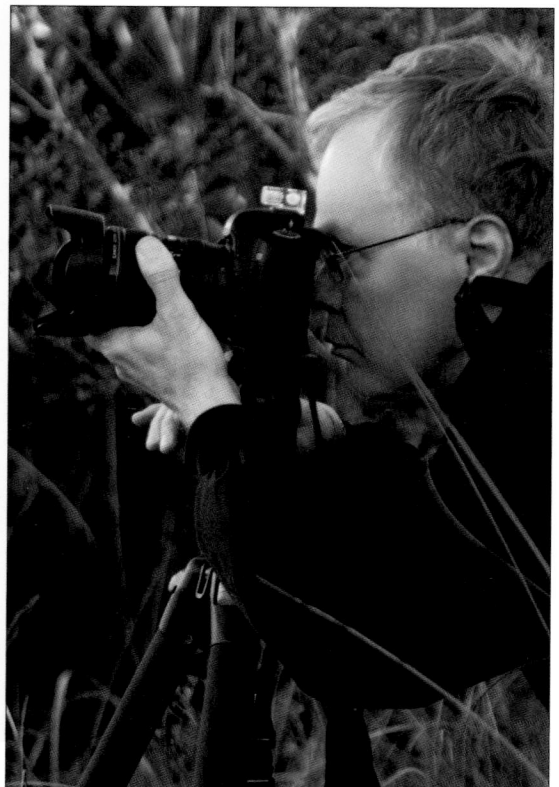

Many photographers don't like to have their picture taken. I know I always cringe when someone points a camera at me. However, even a photographer needs a picture of himself from time to time. Instead of asking someone to take a picture, you can set up and create your own self-portrait. This kind of photography comes in handy if you need to supply an image of yourself to someone on the fly. Taking your own picture involves a couple of tricks that I discuss in this chapter.

Camera Settings

- ✔ **Metering Mode:** Evaluative
- ✔ **Drive Mode:** Auto-Timer
- ✔ **Shooting Mode:** Aperture Priority
- ✔ **Aperture:** f/5.6
- ✔ **ISO Setting:** 100 to 400
- ✔ **Focus Mode:** Single Shot
- ✔ **Auto-Focus Point:** Single auto-focus point
- ✔ **Focal Length:** 80mm to 100mm (35mm equivalent; see "Understanding focal lengths" in the appendix)
- ✔ **Image Stabilization:** Off

Setting the Camera

Creating your own self-portrait isn't brain surgery. You do, however, need to find a way to stabilize the camera by using a tripod or setting the camera on a solid surface. Also, if you let the camera automatically focus the image, you'll almost certainly appear out of focus in the photo because the camera has no idea where you're standing. Therefore, you have to manually focus the image. You also have to delay the shutter opening to give yourself some time to get in the picture.

In portrait photography, you want to draw attention to your subject, so you use Aperture Priority mode and a large aperture to create a shallow depth of field. The suggested ISO range is ideal for bright light to moderately overcast days. The fact that you're mounting the camera on a tripod means that you don't have to go any higher than ISO 400. The focal-length range is ideal for portrait photography. Image stabilization should always be disabled when you're supporting the camera.

Taking the Picture

When you need to take a self-portrait, get your gear ready and find both a suitable backdrop and a suitable place to set up the camera. You have to be a bit patient when you take your own portrait. Unless you're good at putting on a smile or professional face at a moment's notice, you may have to take several pictures before you get one that you like.

1. **Find a suitable background for your picture.**

   If you're shooting the picture indoors, find a solid-colored wall for your backdrop. If you're taking the picture outdoors, find a simple background that won't distract your viewer's attention. After all, you're the star of the show.

2. **Find a suitable place from which to take the picture.**

   You may have to do a bit of experimenting. Zoom to a focal length in the suggested range that you think will be sufficient to capture a portrait of yourself, and then zoom out slightly. You have to visualize approximately where you'll be so that you can get the proper focal length. I find it helps to place a chair in the position you'll be in when you have the camera take the picture. For the image on the first page of this chapter, I placed my second camera on a tripod, which I used for my frame of reference. (Yes, I do have a lot of gear.)

3. **Enable the camera settings discussed previously in this chapter; place the camera on a tripod; and adjust the tripod to the proper height.**

   Again, you have to visualize where you'll be for the photo. As I mention in the preceding step, a chair or some kind of prop can help you set the tripod at the proper level.

4. **Switch your lens to manual focus, and then focus on the place you'll be when the camera takes the picture.**

   Focus on the chair or prop, and then move the focus toward the camera by about 6 inches. The suggested aperture gives you a bit of a fudge factor. As long as you're close, you'll appear to be in focus in the photo.

5. **Press the shutter button, walk into the picture, and then assume the desired pose.**

6. **Smile for the camera (if that's the kind of portrait you want) and stay still.**

   A red flashing light blinks on the front of your camera, representing the auto-timer counting down. On most cameras, the light flashes faster just before the shutter opens.

7. **After the camera takes the picture, review the image on the LCD monitor.**

   At this point, you may have to adjust the focal length, and the position and height of the tripod, and then take another picture.

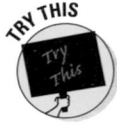

You can take a surreal self-portrait by shooting at night. Switch to a small aperture (an f/stop number of f/22 or larger) and an ISO setting of 100. These settings give you a large depth of field and long exposure. Press the shutter button and walk into the frame. Move a flashlight back and forth to create a pattern, and then walk out of the frame before the shutter closes. You end up with a surreal self-portrait and an interesting light pattern (see Figure 60-1).

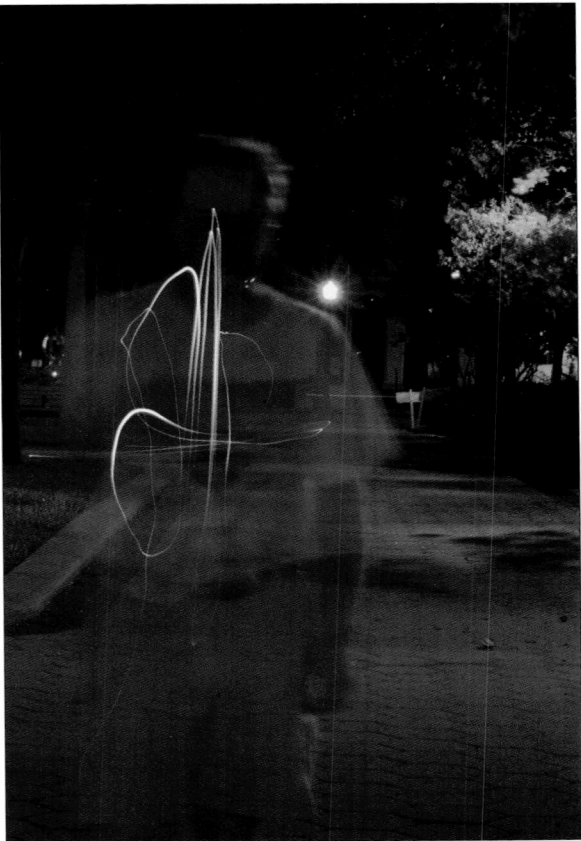

Figure 60-1: Be alert for any photographic opportunity.

Troubleshooting

- ✓ **The image is blurry.** This problem happens if you don't get your focus just right. If the image includes other objects, you can determine whether you focused behind or in front of the place you sat when your camera took the photograph. If you're taking your self-portrait against a plain-jane backdrop, prop something up in the chair that's about at your eye level in the right location, and then focus the camera.

- ✓ **The image isn't level.** You didn't get your tripod perfectly level or put your camera on a surface that's not level. Use the spirit level on your tripod to create a level platform for your camera. Alternatively, you can purchase an inexpensive spirit level that mounts in the hot shoe of your camera, which you can more easily see than the spirit level on most tripods. You'll see a spirit level mounted in the hotshoe of my camera if you look closely at the image at the beginning of this chapter.

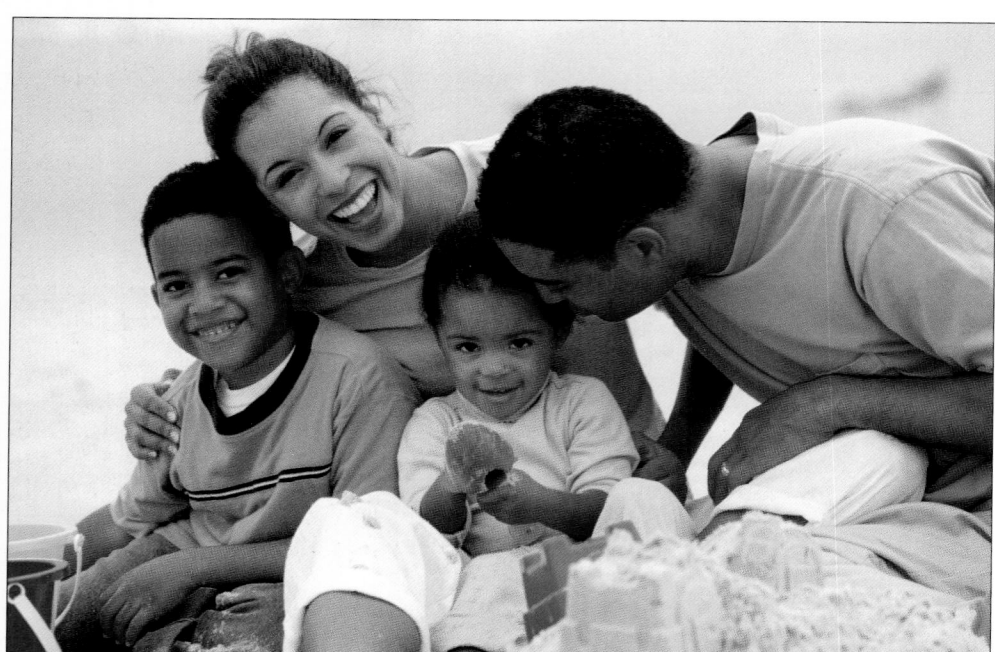

Purestock

A beach or a lake gives you an ideal place to create an intimate portrait of friends or family, as shown here. You have a photogenic background, where you can photograph your photogenic friends or family members. You just need some good light (early in the morning or late in the afternoon), some subjects to photograph, and the settings in this chapter.

Camera Settings

- **Metering Mode:** Evaluative
- **Drive Mode:** Single Shot
- **Shooting Mode:** Aperture Priority
- **Aperture:** f/5.6 to f/7.1
- **ISO Setting:** 100 to 400
- **Focus Mode:** Single Shot
- **Auto-Focus Point:** Single auto-focus point
- **Focal Length:** 50mm to 85mm (35mm equivalent; see "Understanding focal lengths" in the appendix)
- **Image Stabilization:** On

Setting the Camera

When you take a portrait of a couple or group on the beach, you want to make them the center of attention, but you also want to give your viewers an idea of where the photo was taken. Therefore, you photograph a beach portrait with Aperture Priority mode and a fairly large aperture because this combination gives you a soft foreground and background and your subjects are the center of attention. The suggested ISO range gives you the option of photographing in either bright light or slightly overcast conditions. The suggested range renders your subjects in sharp focus, while the foreground and background are soft (blurry) but still recognizable. The suggested focal-length range creates flattering portraits. Use the 50mm focal length if you're photographing a group of four or more, and use a focal length of about 85mm to photograph a couple or one person. Image stabilization is useful.

Taking the Picture

Sun, sand, and water make for a wonderful combination. But if you're taking someone's portrait on the beach, have your subject dress in casual attire. Save the swimsuit stuff for the action and candid shots.

1. **Find a suitable location on the beach for your portrait.**

   You want a background that shows people you took the picture at the beach, but not one that has so much detail it distracts viewers from your subject.

2. **Arrange the group (or person).**

   When you photograph a large group, place the tallest people near the back. Because it's the beach and you want to show some of the surrounding area, ask the people in the back to kneel and the people in the front to sit.

3. **Press the shutter button halfway to achieve focus.**

4. **Compose the picture.**

   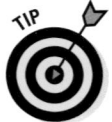

   When you photograph a group at sunset, position them with the sun shining in their faces (see Figure 61-1) to prevent the group from appearing as dark silhouettes. This positioning gives you even, warm lighting, but it can cause a problem because your subjects have to squint. Tell them to close their eyes and open them on the count of three. Press the shutter button on the count of three.

5. **Fully press the shutter button to take the picture.**

   Review the photograph to make sure everyone was smiling and that nobody was squinting when you took the picture.

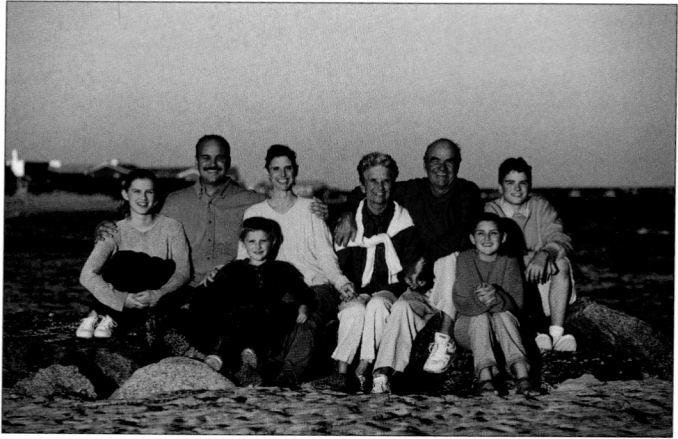

Figure 61-1: Photograph a group with the late afternoon sun shining on their faces.

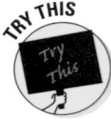

Create a portrait with the sun at your subjects' backs. Place a diffuser over your flash unit to fill in the light (see Figure 61-2) so that your group doesn't appear in silhouette. If your on-camera or auxiliary flash unit has exposure compensation, experiment with it to get just the right balance of light between your subjects and the background.

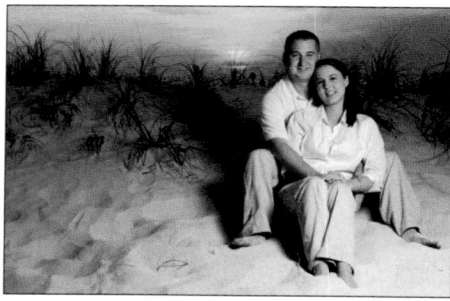

Figure 61-2: Use flash to illuminate a beach portrait.

Troubleshooting

- **The people's faces are too bright in the photo.** If the people you're photographing are lying down with their faces above the sand, that sand reflects light back into their faces. Use exposure compensation to reduce exposure by 1/3 to 2/3 a stop.

- **My subjects' faces seem too red.** This problem happens when you photograph in late afternoon sun. Many photographers prefer the warm look. If you don't, you can adjust the white balance to a slightly cooler setting, such as Cloudy. Alternatively, adjust the white balance in an image-editing program such as Photoshop Elements.

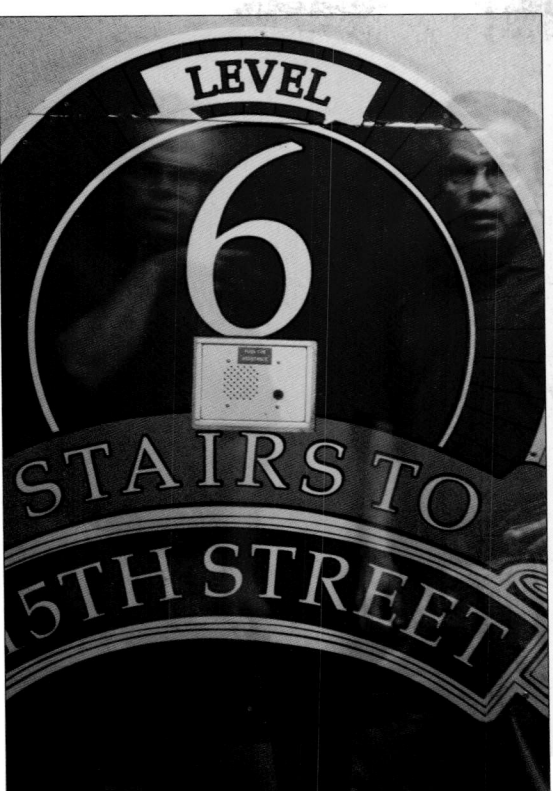

Camera Settings

- **Metering Mode:** Evaluative
- **Drive Mode:** Single Shot
- **Shooting Mode:** Aperture Priority
- **Aperture:** f/22
- **ISO Setting:** 100
- **Focus Mode:** Single Shot
- **Auto-Focus Point:** Single auto-focus point
- **Focal Length:** 28mm to 50mm (35mm equivalent; see "Understanding focal lengths" in the appendix)
- **Image Stabilization:** No

If you ever want to be beside yourself, you can do so by taking a double exposure. A traditional double exposure is two images on one frame of film. There are less than a handful of digital cameras that can achieve this technique, so this chapter shows you how to fake it. This technique requires a couple of accessories, but it's a fun way to create a unique picture of yourself that you can share with friends and relatives. This technique works better at night or in a dimly lit area because the shutter needs to be open for a long time, which doesn't happen in bright light. When you create a double exposure, pick a unique background and use the settings and techniques in this chapter.

Setting the Camera

This technique doesn't technically create a double exposure. Instead, you create two or more ghost-like images of yourself on a single picture. The shutter needs to be open for 20 seconds or longer, which is why you use the low ISO setting and the small aperture recommended in "Camera Settings." The small aperture also gives you a tremendous depth of field, which enables you to move about freely in the frame without the worry of being out of focus. The wide-angle to normal focal length also gives you a large depth of field. If you use a moderate to long telephoto focal length, your depth of field diminishes. You need to mount the camera on a tripod or solid surface to stabilize it during the long exposure, which means you don't need image stabilization.

Taking the Picture

Creating multiple iterations of you or a friend in a single image requires a bit of planning. You have to compose the picture before and know exactly where you want the subject to be when the shutter closes. When you compose the shot through your viewfinder, you see the boundaries within which you can move while taking the picture.

1. **Mount the camera on a tripod.**

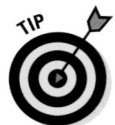

   If you don't have a tripod, set the camera on a table or other flat surface. You can also stabilize the camera by placing it on some wadded up cloth. When you create a makeshift tripod, make sure the camera is level. You can purchase a spirit level that fits in the hot shoe of your camera for a reasonable price.

2. **Enable the camera self-timer.**

   Most cameras have a ten-second self-timer, which gives you time to walk into the frame.

3. **Compose the picture, and then press the shutter button halfway to achieve focus.**

   Focus on something in the middle of the scene. The small aperture gives you a huge depth of field, so you appear in focus anywhere in the frame.

4. **Press the shutter button fully.**

   The self-timer starts counting down. On most cameras, a flashing red light starts blinking on the front of the camera. It starts flashing faster when the camera is about to open the shutter.

5. **Walk into the frame or ask the person you're photographing to walk into the frame.**

6. **When the light stops flashing and the shutter opens, count slowly to ten while holding perfectly still.**

7. **At the count of 11, walk to another area in the frame and hold position until the shutter closes.**

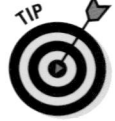 Try this technique at night. With a small aperture of f/22, the lens stays open for about 30 seconds (see Figure 62-1).

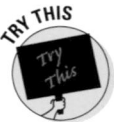 Try this technique with a friend and significant other in the same picture. Use a wide-angle focal length, such as 28mm. When the timer counts down, move into the frame with your friend and strike a pose. After ten seconds, move to another spot and strike a pose.

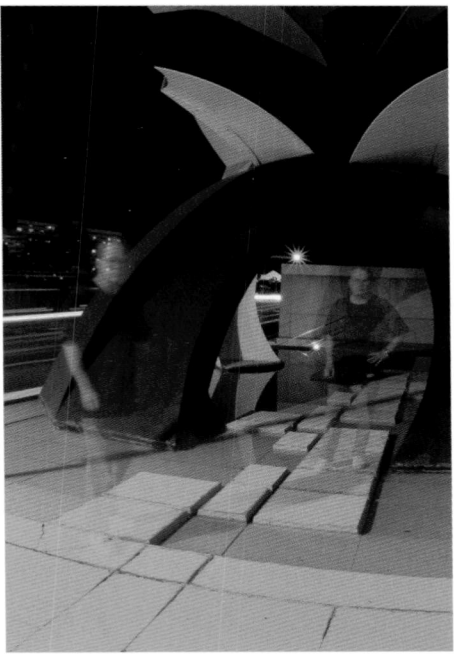

Figure 62-1: Creating a double exposure at night.

Troubleshooting

✔ **The shutter doesn't stay open long enough.** It's not dark enough for a long exposure. You can move to a darker area, stay in the same position and wait until it gets darker, or use a neutral density filter to decrease the amount of light reaching the sensor, thereby increasing the duration of the exposure.

✔ **The people in the image are barely visible.** This technique does create somewhat of a ghostly image. But if it's too hard to see the person, switch to an area that has a darker background. Also, make sure the person in the picture wears clothing that contrasts with the background.

✔ **The people in the image look small.** If you're taking the picture, tell the person where to stop.

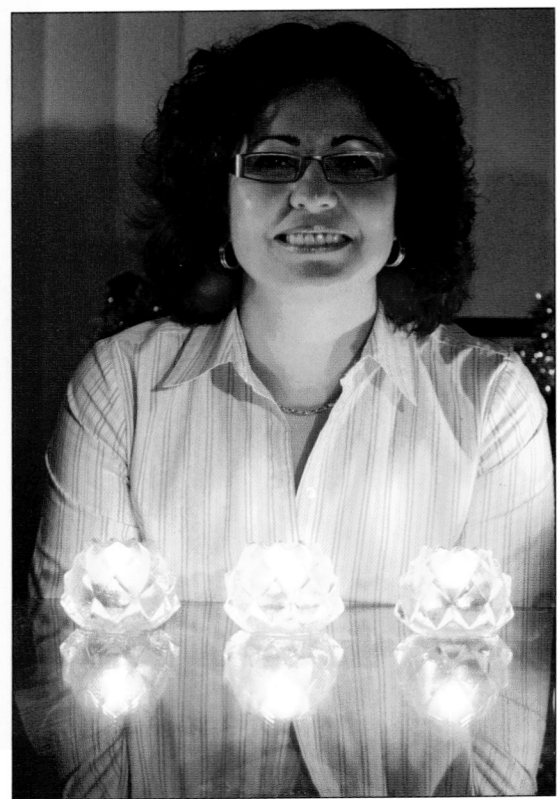

The light from a candle is warm and imbues your subject with a golden glow. Candles provide both ambiance for romantic dinners and light sources for romantic portraits. This type of photography requires a long exposure; therefore, you need to mount your camera on a tripod. Your subject also needs to be perfectly still during the exposure.

Camera Settings

- ✓ **Metering Mode:** Evaluative
- ✓ **Drive Mode:** Single Shot
- ✓ **Shooting Mode:** Aperture Priority
- ✓ **Aperture:** f/4.0 or larger (smaller f/stop number)
- ✓ **ISO Setting:** 100
- ✓ **Focus Mode:** Single Shot
- ✓ **Auto-Focus Point:** Single auto-focus point
- ✓ **Focal Length:** 70mm to 85mm (35mm equivalent; see "Understanding focal lengths" in the appendix)
- ✓ **Image Stabilization:** Off

Setting the Camera

You can get some pleasing results in a candlelight portrait. You want to control depth of field so that your subject is in clear focus, and the candles and any background aren't, which means you shoot this type of picture by using a large aperture of f/4.0 or larger (smaller f/stop number) in Aperture Priority mode. The suggested ISO setting gives you a relatively noise-free image. You could shoot the image hand-held by using a higher ISO setting, but the shadow areas of the image would contain noise. The suggested focal-length range is perfect for portrait photography. I recommend you keep image stabilization off because you have your camera mounted on a tripod. (Remember, using image stabilization when your camera is on a tripod sometimes yields unexpected results because the image stabilization feature is attempting to compensate for camera movement, which doesn't happen when your camera is locked and loaded on a tripod.)

Taking the Picture

When you photograph someone's portrait by the light of one or more candles, you get a dreamy portrait that has wonderful light. If you use only one candle, you end up with considerable shadow on the sides of your subject's face.

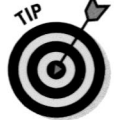

When you shoot a one-candle portrait, you can place two candles out of frame to augment the light of the single candle that appears in the image.

1. **Find a spot to take the portrait.**

   You want a spot that has a neutral background. You also want a spot where your subject feels comfortable. You need her to sit perfectly still for the duration of the exposure, which may be a second or more if you're using only one candle. A polished dining room table gives you a mirror reflection of your subject and the candles.

2. **Light the candles and ask your subject to sit down.**

   Because your subject has to be still for a while, she will likely be more comfortable seated.

3. **Mount the camera on a tripod and turn off the room lights.**

4. **Adjust the tripod and compose the image.**

   In this kind of photograph, you put your subject in the center of the frame.

5. **Press the shutter button halfway to achieve focus, and then press the button fully to take the picture.**

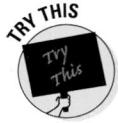

You can also use this technique when photographing a birthday party. Place the birthday boy in front of the cake, dim the room lights, and follow the steps in this chapter to capture a portrait by the candles of his birthday cake (see Figure 63-1).

Troubleshooting

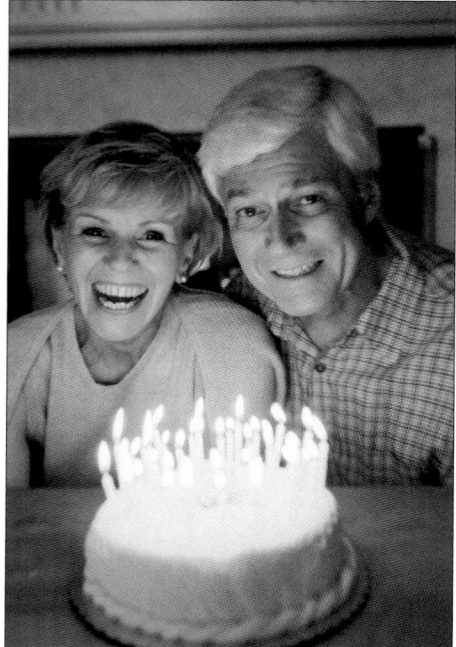

Purestock

Figure 63-1: Shoot a portrait by using the lights from birthday-cake candles.

- ↙ **The candles are blown out in the picture.** The candles are the brightest light source, and they flicker for the duration of the exposure. You can't avoid this outcome.

- ↙ **My subject's skin looks yellow.** This problem happens when the camera doesn't adjust the white balance correctly. Adjust the white balance in your image-editing program if you shoot in your camera's RAW format or adjust the white balance manually by using your camera's menu commands. Refer to your camera manual to figure out the procedure for manually adjusting white balance.

- ↙ **The image is too bright.** Cameras detest dark images for some reason. If the image you see on the LCD monitor is brighter than the scene before you, use exposure compensation to reduce the exposure of the image.

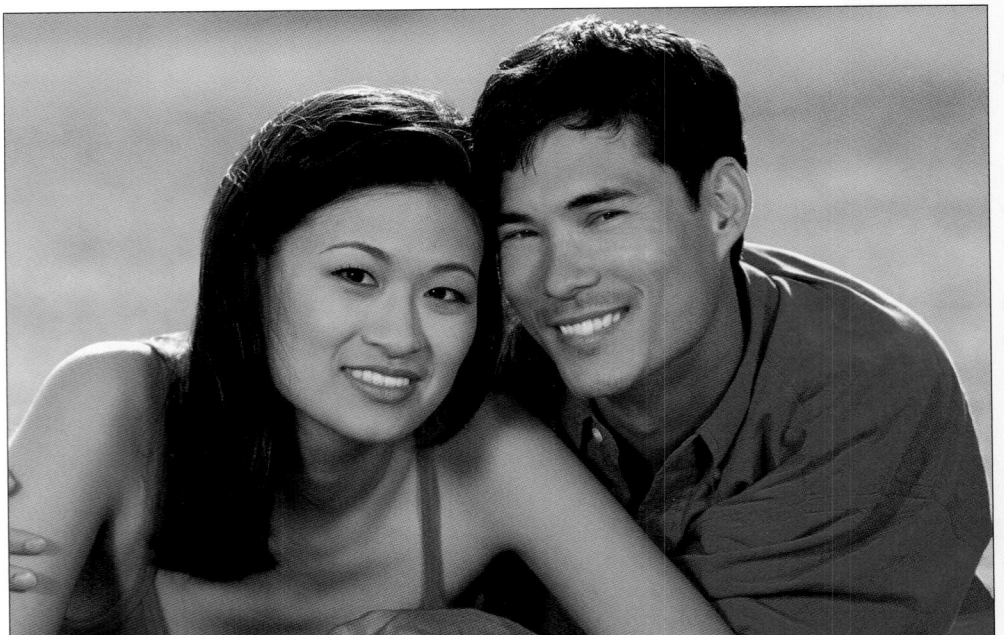

Corbis Digital Stock

Camera Settings

- **Metering Mode:** Evaluative
- **Drive Mode:** Single Shot
- **Shooting Mode:** Aperture Priority
- **Aperture:** f/2.8 to f/3.5
- **ISO Setting:** 100 to 400
- **Focus Mode:** Single Shot
- **Auto-Focus Point:** Single auto-focus point
- **Focal Length:** 80mm to 100mm (35mm equivalent; see "Understanding focal lengths" in the appendix)
- **Image Stabilization:** On

*P*hotographing a couple is a challenge. You want to capture a pleasing rendition of the couple, yet at the same time, you want to show the relationship between them. When you photograph a couple, position them very close to each other or, better yet, touching each other. The picture should show viewers that the couple has more than just a passing relationship with each other. Use your rapport with the couple, your photo-composing skills, and the settings in this chapter to create compelling images of the couple.

Setting the Camera

When you photograph a couple, they're the stars of your photograph. Therefore, you photograph this type of image by using Aperture Priority mode and a large aperture (a small f/stop number) so that you get a shallow depth of field. The suggested ISO range is suitable for either bright-light or overcast conditions. The single auto-focus point lets you precisely focus on your couple. The suggested focal length range gives you pleasing renditions of your subjects. Image stabilization gives you a sharper picture in most instances.

Taking the Picture

You can photograph a happy couple anywhere they happen to be: at the beach, at the zoo, in their home. Have a game plan before the shoot. Take control of the situation and tell the couple where you want them to meet you, suggest some clothing colors based on the area in which you'll be photographing them, and so on. Lighting is very important with this type of photography. Photograph your couple early in the morning or late in the afternoon, when the sun bathes them in soft, warm light. If the only window of opportunity is in the afternoon, make sure you photograph the couple in a shaded area. Soft window light is perfect if you're photographing a couple indoors (see Chapter 73).

1. **Tell your couple how you want them to pose.**

   When you photograph a couple, you need to be the director and tell them how you'd like them to pose. You also have to establish rapport so that they don't appear stiff and lifeless in the photos. You can use a standard pose, with the couple standing beside each other, or get a bit creative and have them lie down. You can also ask the woman to move in front of the man.

2. **Find the ideal vantage point from which to photograph your couple.**

   If you use a standard side-by-side pose, make sure you photograph the couple at eye level. If you're photographing a couple lying on the beach, photograph them from above (see Figure 64-1).

3. **Press the shutter button halfway to achieve focus, and then compose the picture.**

   You can use elements to draw the viewer into the picture. In Figure 64-1, the shoulders of the couple lead you into the picture. In Figure 64-1, the man's arms lead you to the woman's face. The man's face is also located on a power point according to the Rule of Thirds.

4. **Press the shutter button fully to take the picture.**

   After you take the picture, review it on your LCD monitor to make sure the image is properly exposed and that your couple had their eyes open and were smiling.

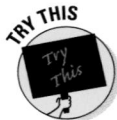

Photograph a couple who are looking into each other's eyes, with the man lying on his side, looking up at his wife (see Figure 64-2). When you use this pose, make sure you're at eye level with the woman.

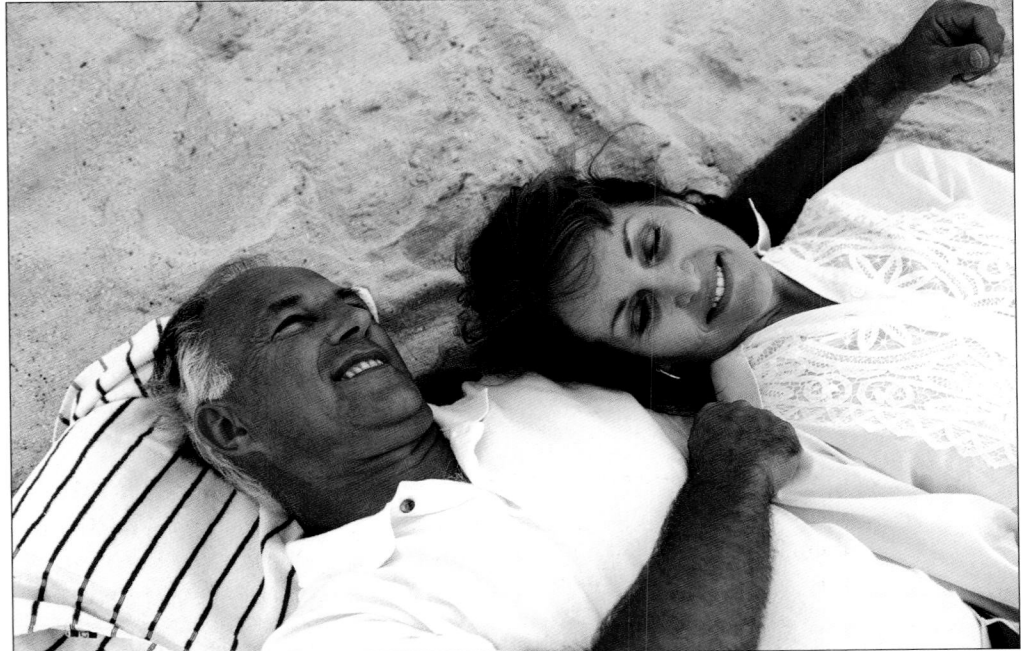

Corbis Digital Stock

Figure 64-1: Compose the image.

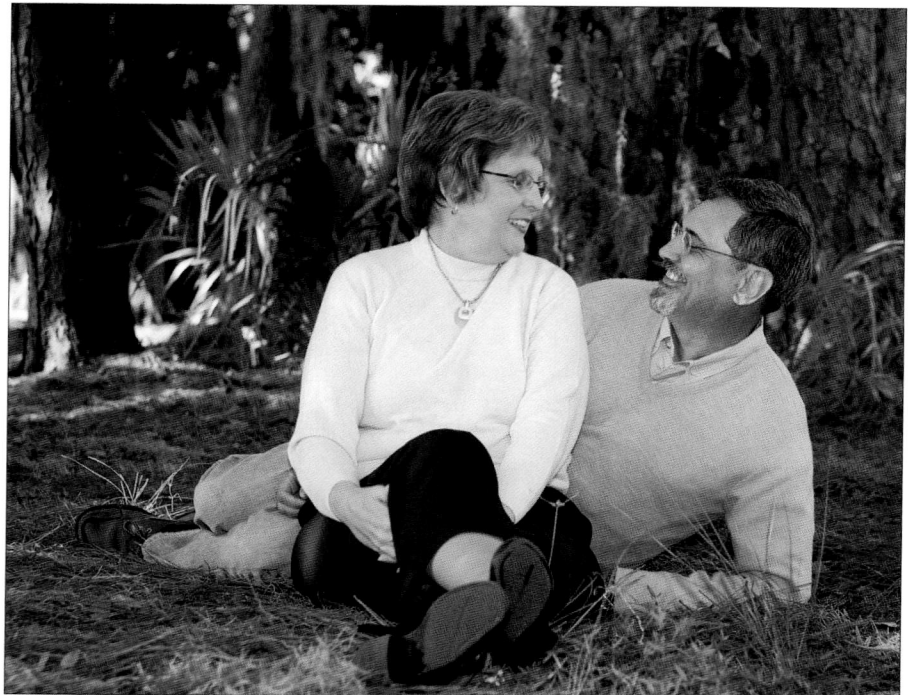

Figure 64-2: Photograph a couple looking into each other's eyes.

Troubleshooting

✓ **The couple is dark.** You have a bright light source, such as the sun, behind your subjects. If you use exposure compensation to increase the exposure, you blow out the background. You can use fill flash to add a splash of light, or you can have someone hold an object (such as a car sunshade or large T-shirt) to bounce some light into the shadow areas of your subjects.

✓ **The couple doesn't seem relaxed.** Use your social skills to make the couple comfortable. You generally don't get them to relax until you've taken several pictures. Try to engage the couple in conversation while you're setting up the camera. You generally get your best shots at the end of the photo shoot, when the couple has adjusted to being in front of the camera.

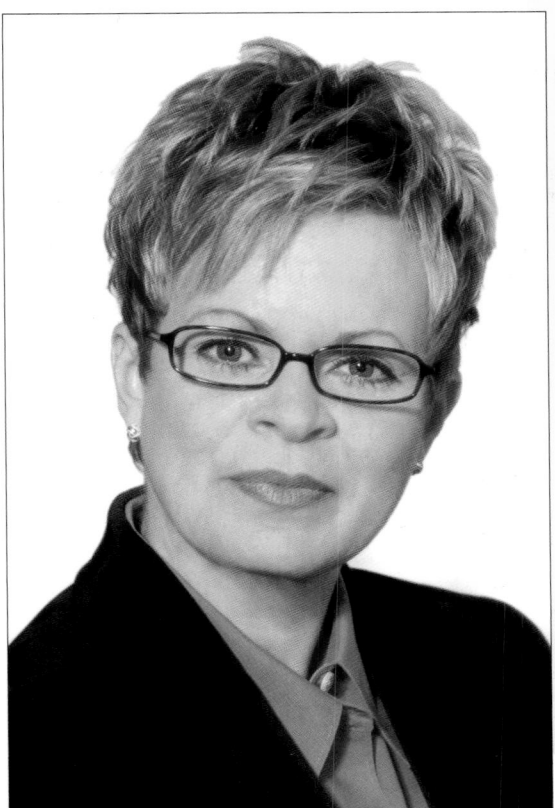

Camera Settings

- **Metering Mode:** Evaluative
- **Drive Mode:** Single Shot
- **Shooting Mode:** Aperture Priority
- **Aperture:** f/4.0 or smaller f/stop number (larger aperture)
- **ISO Setting:** 100 to 400
- **Focus Mode:** Single Shot
- **Auto-Focus Point:** Single auto-focus point
- **Focal Length:** 80mm to 100mm (35mm equivalent; see "Understanding focal lengths" in the appendix)
- **Image Stabilization:** On

*M*ost adults spend a lot of time earning money to support their lifestyle. Some people love what they do, but other people think their 9-to-5 routine is torture. If you have a friend who fits in the former category and needs a picture of herself for business cards or passports, grab your camera and use the settings in this chapter.

Setting the Camera

When you create a portrait for someone, you want to make him the center of attention, so you photograph the scene in Aperture Priority mode and use a large aperture (a small f/stop number) to create a shallow depth of field that draws the viewer's attention to your subject. The ISO setting is perfect for shooting in a bright room or outside. If you photograph the person in overcast conditions, use the highest ISO setting I recommend. The narrow focal-length range renders a pleasing portrait without distorting your subject's features. Use image stabilization if available because the slightest operator movement results in a photo that's less than tack sharp.

Taking the Picture

You photograph the typical formal portrait against a solid-colored background although some professional photographers use a painted muslin background. You can get good results if you photograph your subject against a solid-colored wall. Just make sure your subject is a few feet in front of the wall.

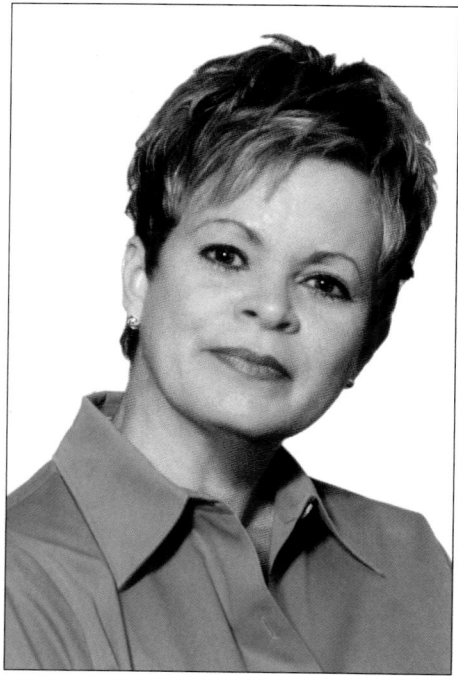

Figure 65-1: Tell your subject how you want her to pose.

1. **Turn off any unnecessary lights in your portable studio.**

   Overhead lights are fine. If you turn on lights on your subject's desk, you run the risk of throwing the camera white balance off and adding hotspots to your subject's face.

2. **Position your subject a few feet in front of your backdrop.**

3. **Tell your subject how you want her to pose.**

   Posing is beyond the scope of this book. However, a good generic pose involves having your subject turn her head to one side and tilt her chin up (see Figure 65-1).

4. **Press the shutter button halfway to achieve focus, and then compose the image.**

   When you compose the picture, use natural elements to draw the viewer into the picture. In Figure 65-2, the subject's right shoulder draws the viewer into the image. Her left eye is on a Rule of Thirds power point (see the appendix for more about this rule).

5. **Fully press the shutter button to take the picture.**

After you take the picture, review it on your LCD monitor. Make sure the image is properly exposed and your subject looks relaxed. In a typical portrait session, you have to take several pictures before the subject relaxes and you get some good images.

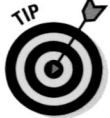 If you're photographing a model or an aspiring actress, use some props to draw the viewer into the image. In Figure 65-2, your eye is first drawn to the rose, which leads you to the woman's lips, and then her eye. The red earring adds a third red visual element, forming a triangle with her lips and the rose.

Troubleshooting

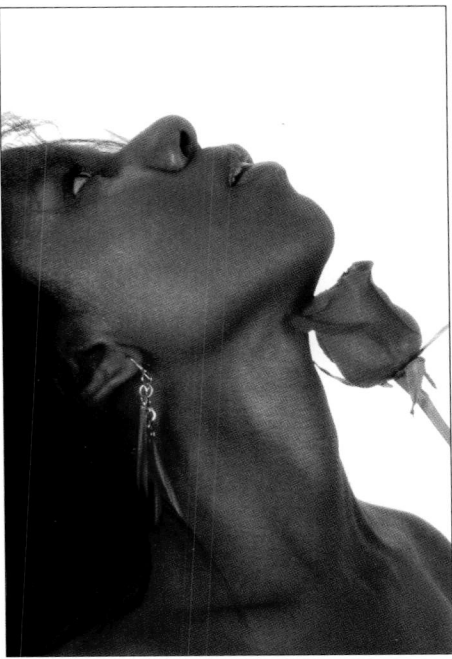

Figure 65-2: Add a prop to create visual interest.

✔ **The image is dull and lifeless.**
The lighting you have available usually causes this problem. Portrait photographers illuminate their subjects with multiple light sources. Working with multiple light sources is a subject for an entire book. However, you can add some life to your portraits by illuminating your subjects with a diffused flash (see the appendix).

✔ **The backdrop is dark gray.**
Even a white background looks gray if you don't use illumination. I took the images in this chapter by using multiple flash units. I placed two flash units behind the subject and triggered them by using the camera (a Canon EOS 7D). The flash units behind the subject were powerful enough to blow out the background to pure white. Some Nikon cameras also have the ability to trigger external flash units. If your camera doesn't have this option, you can use an image-editing application to create a careful selection around your subject and then replace or brighten the background.

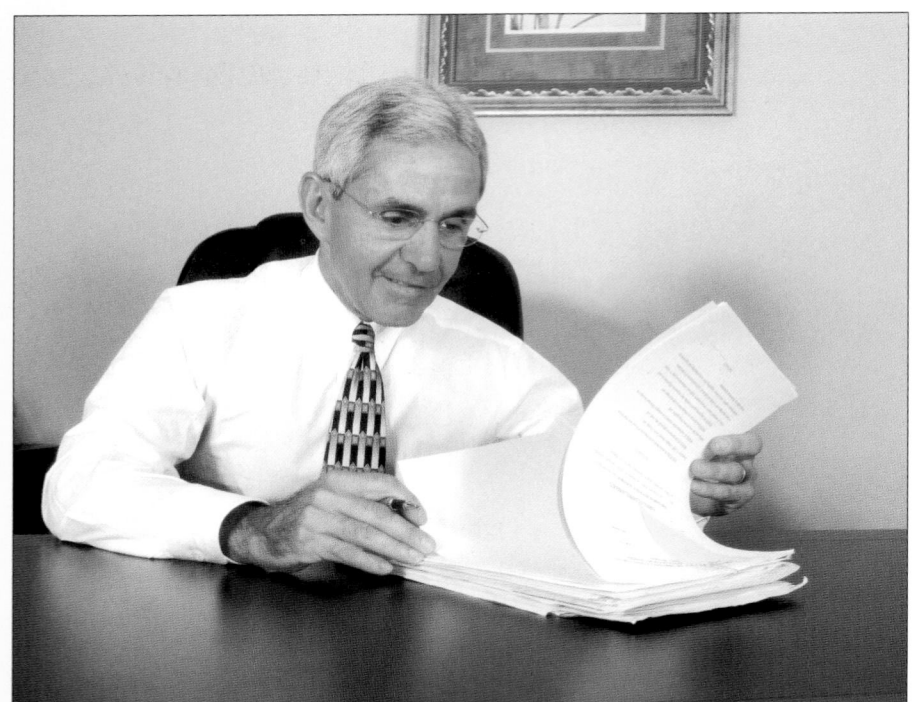

1 f you have a friend or relative who needs photos of himself while he's at work, you can easily do the job with your digital SLR. Just accompany the person to his place of employment and be a fly on the wall. Fiddle with your gear and let the person get engrossed in what he does. When he's totally in the moment, you can start taking pictures. The trick is to be creative and get some natural pictures that don't look posed.

Camera Settings

- **Metering Mode:** Evaluative
- **Drive Mode:** Single Shot
- **Shooting Mode:** Aperture Priority
- **Aperture:** f/5.6 to f/7.1
- **ISO Setting:** 100 to 400
- **Focus Mode:** Single Shot
- **Auto-Focus Point:** Single auto-focus point
- **Focal Length:** 80mm to 100mm (35mm equivalent; see "Understanding focal lengths" in the appendix)
- **Image Stabilization:** On

Setting the Camera

When you photograph someone at work, you want to control the depth of field, which means you shoot in Aperture Priority mode. A fairly large aperture draws attention to your subject but shows a bit of the surroundings. You want to show your friend in her environment. The ISO range works for many office-lighting scenarios. The suggested focal lengths are perfect for portrait photography. Image stabilization is useful if you photograph in low-light situations.

Taking the Picture

When you photograph someone at work, you want a natural setting, but you don't want a lot of clutter. Ask your friend to clean his desk and remove any items he doesn't use frequently. If possible, you also want a personal item on the desk, such as a photo of your friend and his family. Of course, you can work with a number of other environmental portrait scenarios, such as the salesperson on the road (see Figure 66-1).

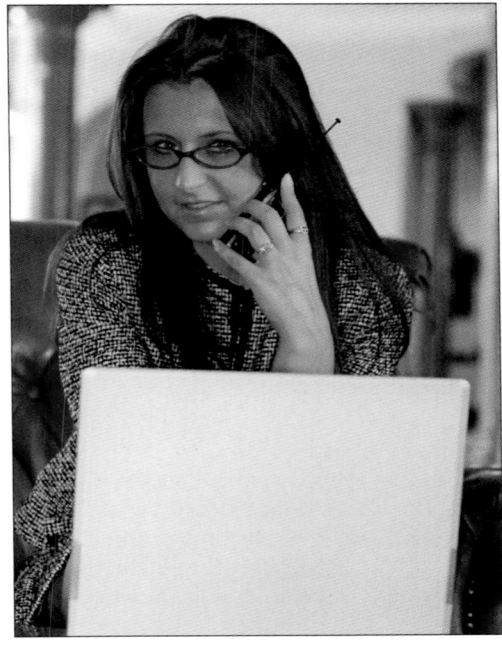

Figure 66-1: Take photos of a person who has a mobile office.

1. **Turn off any unnecessary lights in the office.**

   Overhead lights are fine. If you add lighting on the desk, you run the risk of throwing the camera white balance off and adding hotspots to your subject's face.

2. **While your subject is busy working, enable the settings discussed previously in this chapter.**

3. **When your subject starts doing something interesting, zoom in to the desired focal length.**

   Capturing a good photo of someone while she works involves getting your subject engaged with her work while you remain a silent observer.

   If your subject has diplomas or other certifications on her wall, make sure you include them in a few of the photos. To make the document recognizable, use the smallest suggested aperture.

4. **Press the shutter button halfway to achieve focus, and then compose the picture.**

   When you compose the picture, use natural elements to draw the viewer into the picture. For example, the papers in the picture on the first page of this chapter draw the viewer's eye to the attorney's face.

5. **Take the picture.**

   After you take the picture, review it on your LCD monitor. Make sure the image is properly exposed and your subject has her eyes wide open and a pleasing expression on her face.

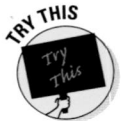

Photograph someone while he's using the tools of his trade, such as the photographer in Figure 66-2.

Troubleshooting

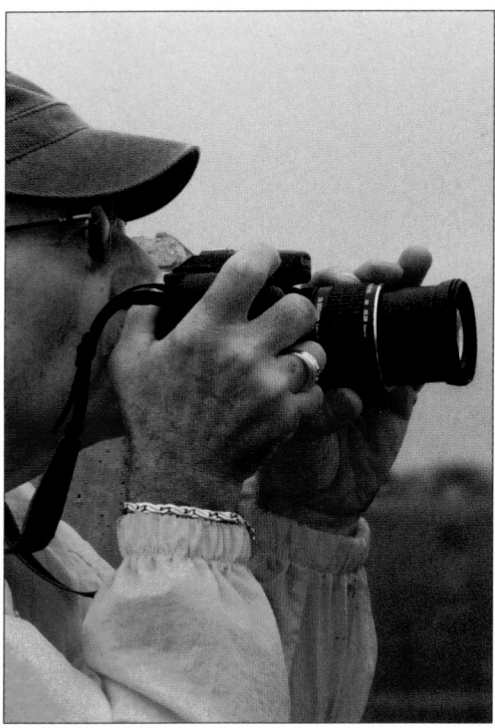

Figure 66-2: Photograph someone while he's using the tools of his trade.

- ✔ **My subject's face has a lot of shadows (#1).** This problem occurs when you photograph in a place that doesn't have a uniform lighting source to distribute light evenly to all areas of the room. You can use fill flash (see the appendix).

- ✔ **My subject's face has a lot of shadows (#2).** Photograph your subject in an area that includes light shining through an outside window that can provide soft, natural-looking light. For more information about using window light for portraits, see Chapter 73.

- ✔ **My subject's face includes shiny areas.** This problem occurs when you photograph someone who has oily skin. The light reflects off the oily skin to create shiny areas, known as *hot spots*. If your subject is male, ask him to wash his face. If your subject is female, ask her to wash her face and apply some light makeup. Before you make your request, tell your subject there is a problem with the photos and show him one on the LCD. He may ask how the problem can be solved. When he does, make your request.

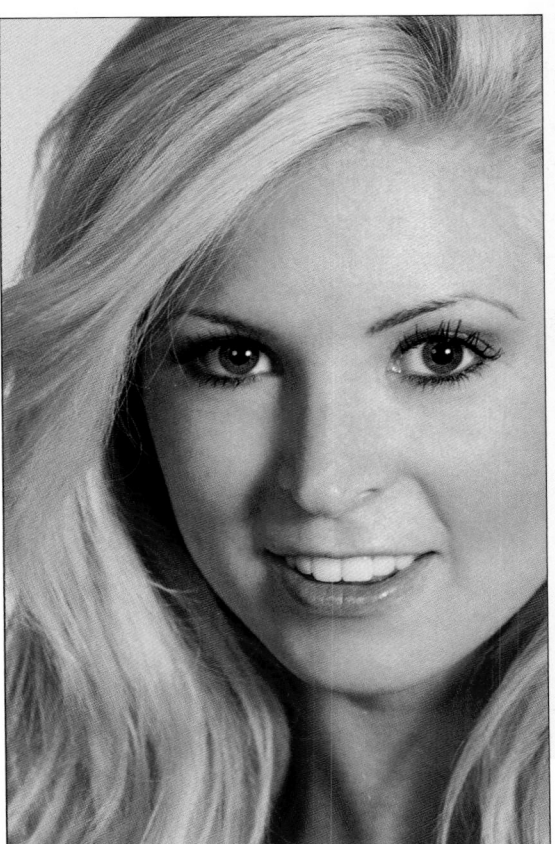

67 Extreme Close-Up Portrait

Camera Settings

- **Metering Mode:** Evaluative
- **Drive Mode:** Single Shot
- **Shooting Mode:** Aperture Priority
- **Aperture:** f/2.8 to f/7.1
- **ISO Setting:** 100
- **Focus Mode:** Single Shot
- **Auto-Focus Point:** Single auto-focus point
- **Focal Length:** 100mm to 150mm (35mm equivalent; see "Understanding focal lengths" in the appendix)
- **Image Stabilization:** On

When you photograph a person who has a beautiful face, the photo shoot's not over until you get an extreme close-up. This technique is an extension of the head-and-shoulders portrait. When you take an extreme close-up portrait, you zoom in tight on your lovely subject. Because you zoom in tight, you want to use this technique on someone who has flawless skin. So unless your mother-in-law has a peaches-and-cream complexion, don't use this technique on her. When you take an extreme close-up portrait, you don't include all of the person's head in the frame.

Setting the Camera

Good settings take the fear out of being close. The smallest suggested aperture prevents your subject's hair from being out of focus and works great if your subject's eyes are not equidistant from the camera. However, if you want a soft, dreamy look, use the largest suggested aperture. The single auto-focus point lets you precisely focus on your subject's eyes, which some have said are the windows to the soul. The suggested focal length lets you get a nice close-up without distorting your subject's features. Image stabilization ensures a blur-free image, so use it if your camera or lens has this feature. (Without image stabilization, the slightest operator movement results in an image that's not tack sharp. If you don't have image stabilization, consider using a tripod for this type of photo unless you have a very steady hand.)

Taking the Picture

You want soft light when you're shooting an extreme close-up. Try to do this type of photography on an overcast day or near diffuse window light (see Chapter 73). If you don't have overcast weather, take the photographs in a shaded area. Alternatively, you can use light from a diffused on-camera flash (see the appendix).

1. **Enable the camera settings discussed earlier in this chapter.**

2. **Zoom in tight, position the auto-focus point over one of the subject's eyes, and then press the shutter button halfway to achieve focus.**

3. **Compose the picture.**

   When you compose the picture, look through the viewfinder and give your subject instructions. Make sure she's giving you a lovely smile. You can also use jewelry, such as the earrings in Figure 67-1, as a compositional element to draw your viewer into the picture.

4. **Fully press the shutter button to take the picture.**

   After you take the picture, ask your subject to hold the pose while you examine the image for any problems.

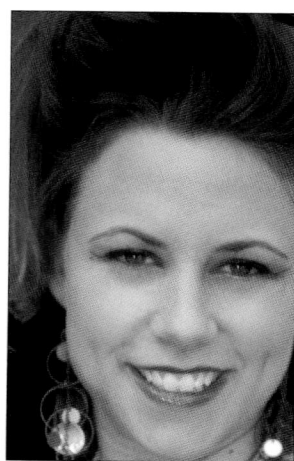

Figure 67-1: Use jewelry to draw your viewer into the image.

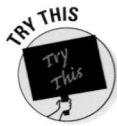

Ask your subject to turn away from the camera and then look toward it. Focus on the eye nearest the camera and compose the picture. Ask your subject to tilt her head down and smile (see Figure 67-2).

Troubleshooting

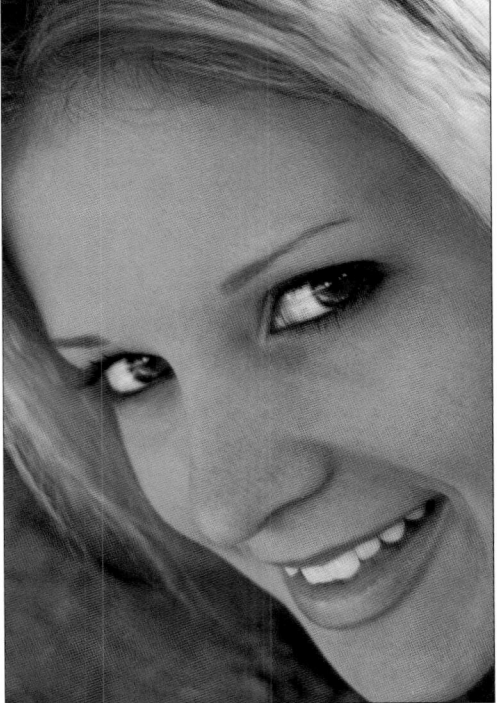

Figure 67-2: This portrait has an extremely shallow depth of field.

⤳ **One of my subject's eyes is out of focus.** Your subject isn't squarely facing the camera, and her eyes aren't equidistant from the camera. This composition is worth keeping, so here's the solution: Switch to a smaller aperture (a larger f/stop number) and take the picture again.

⤳ **My subject has a wonderful complexion, yet I see some wrinkles in the photograph.** Most modern lenses are so sharp that they capture character lines. You can minimize or remove character lines, such as crow's feet, in an image-editing program.

Alternatively, you can use a soft-focus filter, which minimizes character lines and adds a soft, dreamy look to the image. You can find soft-focus filters at your favorite camera retailer. They come in varying strengths, and many filter manufacturers rate them by number. The number 1 filter is the least powerful and works well for young subjects. If you decide to try this technique with an older person (for example, your mother-in-law), buy one of the stronger soft-focus filters. Ask your favorite camera retailer for more information about soft-focus filters to find the right one for your photography.

Head-and-Shoulders Portrait

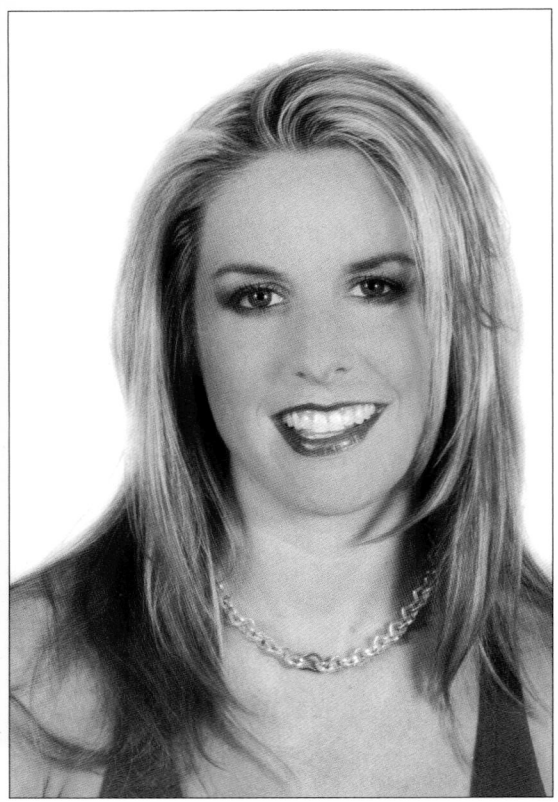

The traditional head-and-shoulders portrait has many uses. You can take this kind of photo for a friend or relative who needs a passport picture, a picture for a business card, or a portrait that you can hang on the wall (such as the one shown here). You can photograph a head-and-shoulders portrait indoors or outdoors.

When you shoot someone's portrait, be prepared to spend a little time with your subject, especially if she's not used to having her picture taken. Your subject may be tense and self-conscious when you shoot the first images. Start talking to your subject to loosen her up. Talk about something she likes and get her to smile. When your subject's at ease, you're ready to start photographing by using the settings in this chapter.

Camera Settings

- ✔ **Metering Mode:** Evaluative
- ✔ **Drive Mode:** Single Shot
- ✔ **Shooting Mode:** Aperture Priority
- ✔ **Aperture:** f/4.0
- ✔ **ISO Setting:** 100
- ✔ **Focus Mode:** Single Shot
- ✔ **Auto-Focus Point:** Single auto-focus point
- ✔ **Focal Length:** 85mm to 105mm (35mm equivalent; see "Understanding focal lengths" in the appendix)
- ✔ **Image Stabilization:** On

Setting the Camera

When you create a portrait, your subject is the star of the show. You don't want the background distracting the viewer's attention; therefore, you shoot in Aperture Priority mode and use a large aperture (a small f/stop number). An 85mm focal length gives you a portrait photo that has a pleasing, undistorted rendition of the person you're photographing. The sharpness of the image depends on the quality of your lens. An ISO setting of 100 gives you a noise-free image and, in good lighting conditions, a shutter speed of about 1/125 of a second. If your camera or lens has image stabilization, enable it: Otherwise, the slightest operator movement gives you a blurry photo. If you're taking the picture in dim lighting conditions, image stabilization enables you to use a shutter speed of approximately 1/50 of a second while you hold the camera by hand.

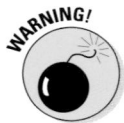

Never use a focal length that's the 35mm equivalent of less than 50mm to photograph someone's portrait. To shoot a head-and-shoulders portrait by using a wide-angle focal length, you'd have to be very close to the person, which would make the feature closest to the camera — the person's nose — look larger than it actually is.

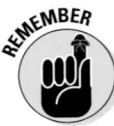

If you're taking the photograph in a low-light situation, you may have to increase the ISO to achieve a shutter speed of 1/125 of a second (1/50 of a second if you use image stabilization) or faster. Alternatively, you can use a tripod.

Taking the Picture

It's not easy to photograph people. You have to gain rapport with your subject and get your camera settings right. Also, you need soft diffuse light when you photograph a person. You want even illumination that gives you a pleasing picture. If you're photographing your subject on a bright day, find a spot that offers even shade. Overcast days are great for portrait photography. You can also get a great portrait when your subject is illuminated by window light (see Chapter 73).

1. **Enable the camera setting discussed earlier in this chapter.**

2. **If necessary, tell your subject how you want her to pose.**

   If your subject's a ham and naturally photogenic, just let her act naturally and take the pictures. However, if your subject is camera-shy, you have to tell her how to pose.

   A good garden-variety pose is to tell her to drop one shoulder and tilt her head (see Figure 68-1).

3. **Press the shutter button halfway to achieve focus.**

4. **Compose the picture, and then press the shutter button fully to take the picture.**

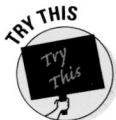

If you have a fast 85mm prime lens that has a maximum aperture of f/2.8 or larger (smaller f/stop number), shoot a head-and-shoulders portrait *wide open* (photographer speak for using your largest aperture). Focus on your subject's eye that's nearest the camera, then compose and take the picture. You end up with a great portrait that has a soft foreground and background. Of course, if you're zoomed in tight, you'll have a nice soft background (see Figure 68-2).

Troubleshooting

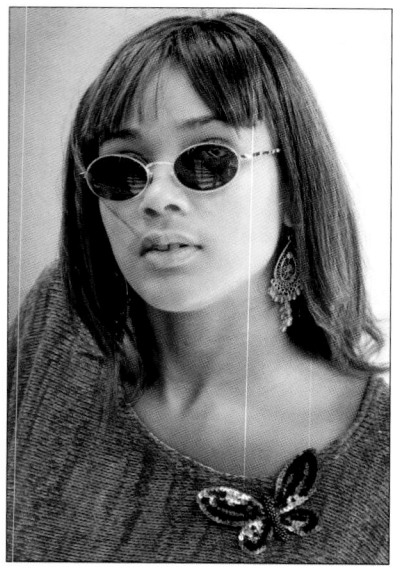

Figure 68-1: In portrait photography, the pose is everything.

- **Deep shadows appear around the subject's eyes.** This problem happens when you take a photograph in an unevenly illuminated area. Bounce light back into the shadows of your subject's face by using the sunshade from a car, a sheet, or a large white T-shirt.

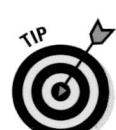

  If you're using a car sunshade to reflect light back into the shadow areas of your subject, use the gold side to reflect warm light onto your subject.

- **My subject doesn't look like himself.** This issue pops up when you photograph people who aren't used to being in front of the camera. Some people can't give you a natural smile. Stop for a few minutes, and then resume when your subject is more relaxed.

- **The image isn't sharp.** The camera focuses on an area other than the subject's eyes. Position the autofocus point over the eye that's closest to the camera when you achieve focus. If the eyes are in focus, the entire picture appears to be in focus.

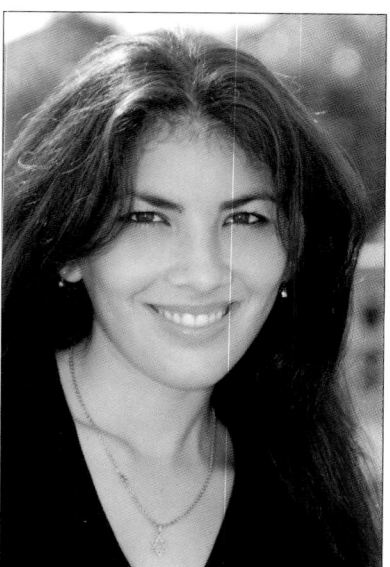

Figure 68-2: Shooting a portrait by using an extremely shallow depth of field.

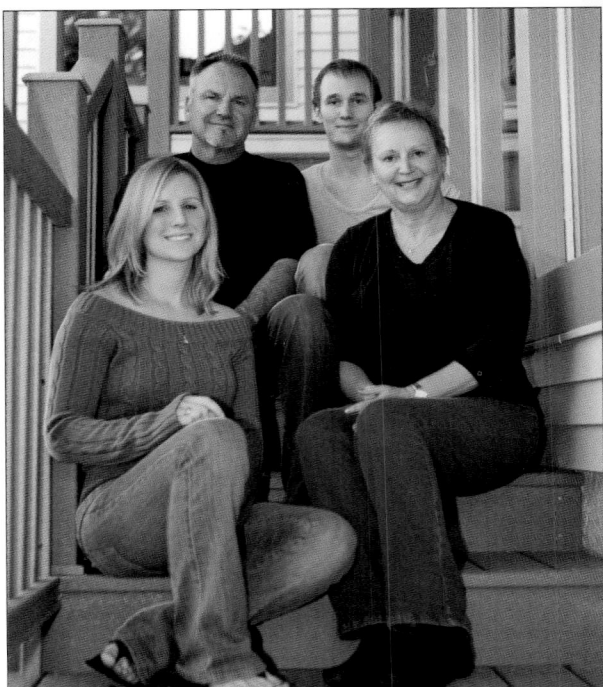

Camera Settings

- **Metering Mode:** Evaluative
- **Drive Mode:** Single Shot
- **Shooting Mode:** Aperture Priority
- **Aperture:** f/3.5 to f/5.6
- **ISO Setting:** 100 to 400
- **Focus Mode:** Single Shot
- **Auto-Focus Point:** Single auto-focus point
- **Focal Length:** 28mm to 100mm (35mm equivalent; see "Understanding focal lengths" in the appendix)
- **Image Stabilization:** Optional

You're the family photographer and historian, all in one neat little package. The fact that you own the magic box that captures digital images means that you get pressed into service to create pictures of your family, your friends' families, and perhaps the people with whom you work. When you photograph a group, you have tall people, small people, slim people, and wide people. You, as the photographer, need to turn a potential hodge-podge of humanity into a pleasing portrait. Your rapport with the group, your creative eye, and the settings in this chapter give you the ingredients for a pleasing group portrait.

Setting the Camera

Shooting in Aperture Priority mode and using a large aperture (a small f/stop number) gives you a shallow depth of field, which draws the viewer's attention to the group you're photographing. If you're photographing a group that's several rows deep, switch the aperture to f/5.6 or f/6.3, which gives you a larger depth of field so that you can keep everyone in the group in focus. The suggested ISO range gives you a noise-free image, although you can bump up to a higher ISO setting in low-light conditions if the shutter speed is too slow. The focal-length range lets you capture either a large group without having to back up into the next county or a small, intimate group of three or four people. If the lighting conditions yield a shutter speed slower than you normally use when you hand-hold the camera, use image stabilization, if available. Image stabilization also prevents you from having to use an ISO higher than the suggested range, which would result in a noisy image.

Taking the Picture

A group portrait can be a tricky picture to take. You must arrange the group (not line up people in the police sense of the word), and you also need to make sure everyone's smiling and no one has their eyes closed. You guessed it: You have to take several pictures to get a couple of keepers. In addition to getting the camera settings right, you also have to tell the group what to do. It's a tough job, but you're the family-photography guru, and the onus is on you to perform.

1. **Find a suitable location to photograph the group.**

   The best location has a background that doesn't distract the viewer's attention from the group.

2. **Arrange the group.**

   The typical group shot has the tall people in the back and the short people in front. Make sure nobody's mouth or eyes are blocked by other people in the group.

   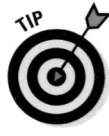

   If you have a tall person in the group, have him lie on his side on the ground and the rest of the group kneel behind him. This positioning is definitely an improvement on the police-lineup type of shot.

3. **Compose the photograph.**

   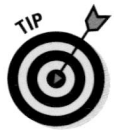

   To create a unique portrait, photograph the group from a high vantage point and have them look up at the camera before you take the picture (see Figure 69-1).

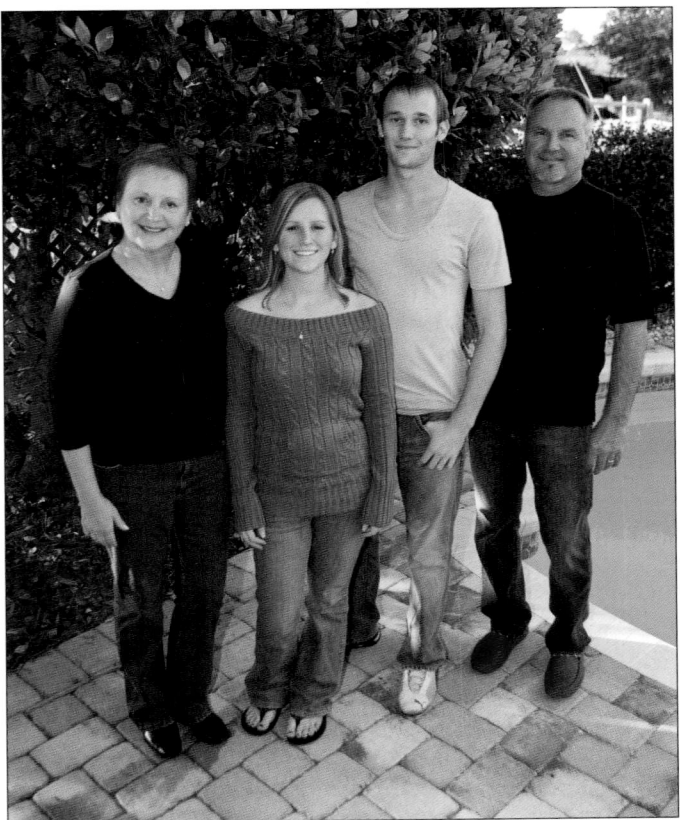

Figure 69-1: Photograph the group from a high vantage point.

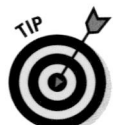

4. **Press the shutter button halfway to achieve focus.**

   If you're photographing a group that's a couple of rows deep, position the auto-focus point over someone in the middle of the group, and then press the shutter button halfway so that the group will be in focus from front to back.

5. **Look in the viewfinder and make sure everyone is looking at the camera and smiling.**

   You may have to use an old cliché (such as "Say cheese!") to get the group to cooperate.

6. **Take the picture, and then tell the group to stay put in case you don't like the image you recorded.**

7. **Review the picture and take another if you don't like what you see.**

   When you review the picture, make sure everyone's smiling and no one's doing anything like yawning or closing their eyes.

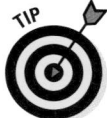

If you're photographing several generations and you want to draw attention to the grandparents, aunts, and uncles, position them in the front row and focus on that row. The other people in the group are slightly blurry in the photo, which draws the viewers' attention to the seasoned veterans of the group.

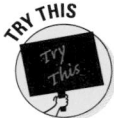

Photograph a group of three and position them so that their eyes form a semi-circle, which keeps your viewer in the image for more than just a brief glimpse. The viewers' attention switches from one person's eye to the next (see Figure 69-2).

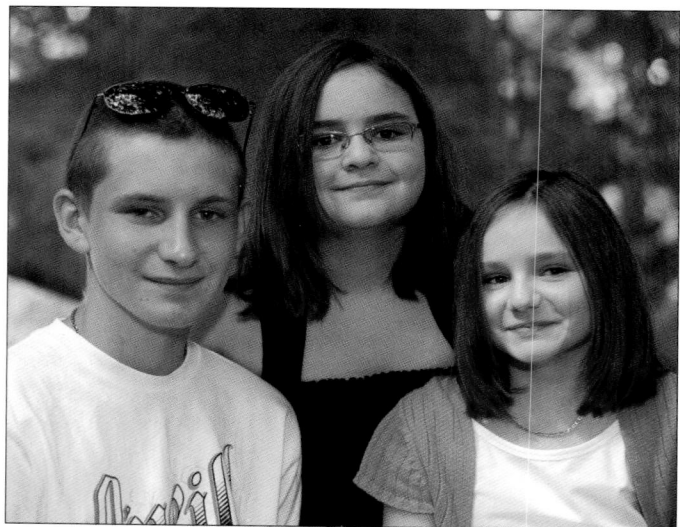

Figure 69-2: Composing the picture to draw viewer's attention to your subjects.

Troubleshooting

🖛 **One group member looks heavier than she actually is.** This problem occurs when you have a diverse group of people. The heaviest person in the group appears heavier than she actually is because she's surrounded by thin people. You can prevent this problem from occurring by sandwiching anybody who's not svelte behind two thinner people.

🖛 **A couple of people aren't smiling.** Keep taking pictures until you have one in which everybody's looking at the camera and smiling, and nobody has their eyes closed. Patience is a virtue when you're photographing a group of people.

🖛 **The back rows aren't in focus.** This problem occurs when you aim the auto-focus point over someone in the front row when you press the shutter button halfway to achieve focus. Aim the auto-focus point over someone's eyes in the middle row of the group.

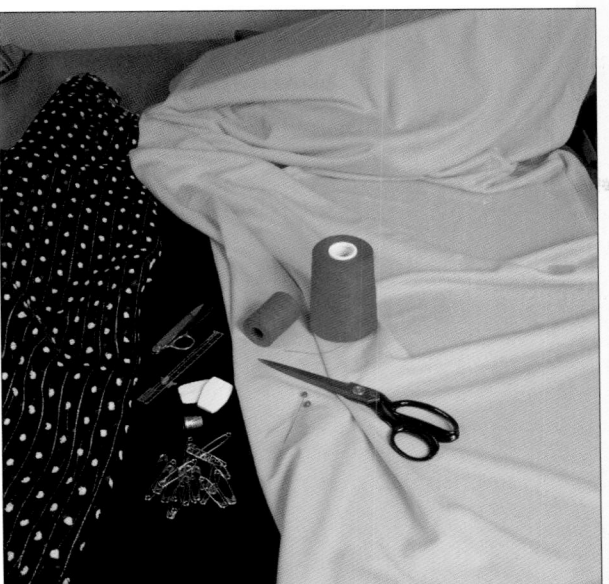

PhotoDisc, Inc./Getty Images

Camera Settings

- ✔ **Metering Mode:** Evaluative
- ✔ **Drive Mode:** Single Shot
- ✔ **Shooting Mode:** Aperture Priority
- ✔ **Aperture:** f/4.0 to f/6.3
- ✔ **ISO Setting:** 200 to 400
- ✔ **Focus Mode:** Single Shot
- ✔ **Auto-Focus Point:** Single auto-focus point
- ✔ **Focal Length:** 100mm or longer (35mm equivalent; see "Understanding focal lengths" in the appendix)
- ✔ **Image Stabilization:** On

*W*hen you see a loved one's prized possessions, you immediately connect with the person. A photo of the stuff that's important to a person is in a way of portrait of that person. As the family historian and photographer, you'll want to take photos of the stuff that's important to people who are important to you. If your father is a woodworker, you can take a photograph of the tools of his trade. The members of your family and your father's friends can immediately identify the things in the photograph that are an important part of his lifestyle. Your father and the entire family will cherish the photograph. You can create a great lifestyle photograph by using the settings in this chapter.

Setting the Camera

When you create a photograph of a family member's prized possessions, you want to selectively focus on the most important object. Therefore, you take the picture in Aperture Priority mode and use a large aperture of f/4.0. If your composition includes a lot of objects, use the smaller suggested aperture. Use a single auto-focus point so that you can achieve focus on the most significant item in your arrangement. The suggested ISO range enables you to shoot in most interior-lighting situations. However, try to photograph this type of arrangement in soft, diffuse light from a window. Any operator movement shows up as a less-than-sharp image, which is why I highly recommend enabling image stabilization, if your camera or lens has it.

Taking the Picture

Window light (see Chapter 73) is soft and almost shadowless, which makes it the ideal light for this type of photography. You set up an impromptu studio, and then decide which items to photograph and which of those items you want as your center of interest.

1. **Set up an impromptu studio on a table that faces a window.**

   When you create a lifestyle photograph, you create a little stage for the stuff you're going to photograph. You can create a stage where your loved one actually does her work, and neatly arrange the tools of her trade on a workbench. Or you can create your own stage and backdrop by using a white cloth.

2. **Arrange the objects on the table.**

   Create an artistic arrangement that draws your viewer's eye into the picture. For example, if the loved one you're creating the lifestyle photo for is in the building trade, arrange some of his tools and add some of the objects he uses, such as nails and wire-nuts (see Figure 70-1).

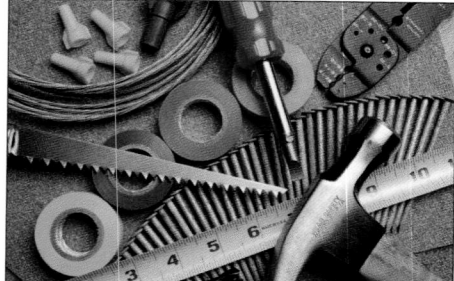

PhotoDisc, Inc./Getty Images

Figure 70-1: Create an artistic arrangement to draw your viewer into the picture.

3. **Enable the settings discussed previously in this chapter.**

   A macro lens comes in handy for this type of photography, so use it if you have one.

4. **Zoom in on your arrangement.**

   Leave some space around the edge of your composition so that you can crop to specific sizes in your image-editing program to create prints that are not the same aspect ratio as your camera.

5. **Compose the picture.**

You can create a more interesting photo if you compose it so that objects point to your center of interest. In Figure 70-1, the wire stripper, screwdriver, and saw all point to the hammer. The tape measure is at a diagonal, which also creates interest and gives the viewer another path to follow.

6. **Press the shutter button halfway to achieve focus, and then press the button fully to take the picture.**

After you take the picture, review the image to make sure it's properly exposed and that it has no obvious problems.

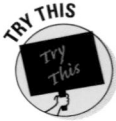

Mix in some items related to your loved one's passion in life. If you're creating a lifestyle portrait for a writer, for example, include a book written by one of her favorite authors, along with a couple of personal items (see Figure 70-2).

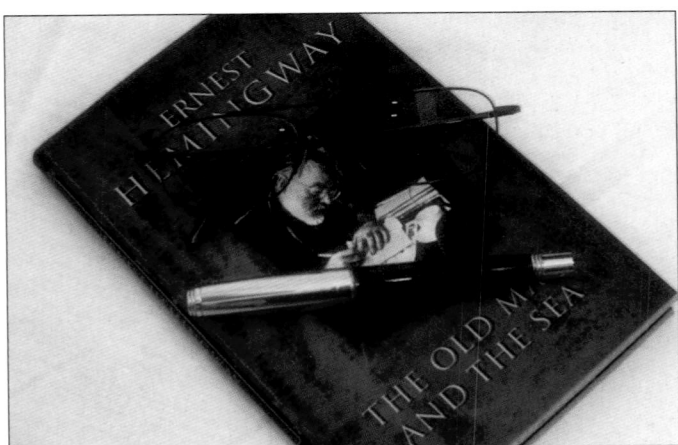

Figure 70-2: Create a unique lifestyle portrait that contains related objects.

Troubleshooting

✓ **The auto-focus lamp doesn't illuminate.** You're closer to your arrangement than the minimum focusing distance of the lens. Back up and press the shutter button halfway again. Keep backing up and pressing the shutter button halfway until the auto-focus button illuminates.

✓ **Some of the objects at the back of the composition are out of focus.** You achieved focus on the object in front of the arrangement. Focus on an object in the middle of the arrangement and take the picture again. If this doesn't cure the problem, switch to a smaller aperture (a larger f/stop number) that gives you an image with all of the objects in focus.

71 Outdoor Portrait

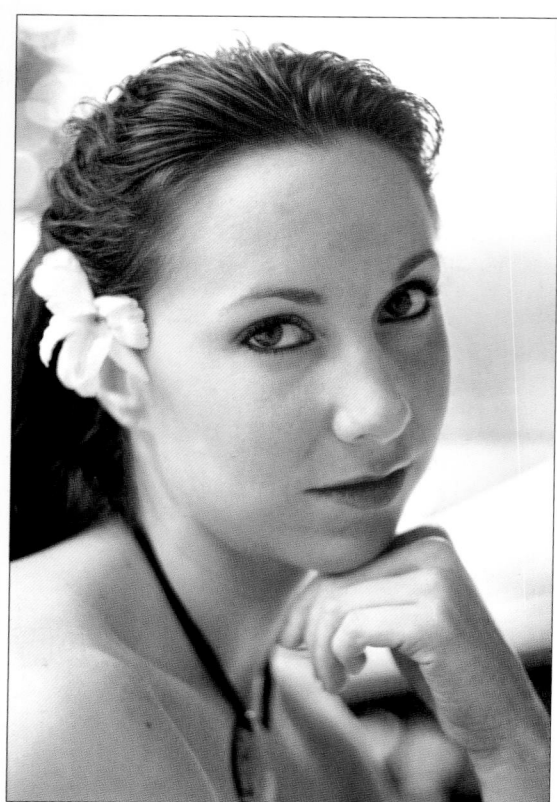

When you find a photogenic family member, friend, or neighbor, you can take a formal portrait (see Chapter 65) or a head-and-shoulders portrait (see Chapter 68). But you have another option: a portrait that you take outdoors. You just need to find an interesting area and photograph your subject when the light is good. For outdoor portrait photography, early in the morning or late in the afternoon is perfect on a sunny day because your subject is bathed in warm light with a golden hue; anytime during the day is great when it's overcast, due to soft almost shadowless light. You just need the settings in this chapter, and you're ready to roll.

Camera Settings

- **Metering Mode:** Evaluative
- **Drive Mode:** Single Shot
- **Shooting Mode:** Aperture Priority
- **Aperture:** f/3.5 or larger
- **ISO Setting:** 100
- **Focus Mode:** Single Shot
- **Auto-Focus Point:** Single auto-focus point
- **Focal Length:** 85mm to 105mm (35mm equivalent; see "Understanding focal lengths" in the appendix)
- **Image Stabilization:** On

Setting the Camera

Always have a shallow depth of field when you shoot portraits, even outdoor portraits, because this draws viewer attention to your subject. To get a shallow depth of field, use Aperture Priority mode and a large aperture. A shallow depth of field combined with a moderate telephoto lens gives you a wonderfully soft background, which draws your viewers to your subject. If you photograph portraits frequently, you might consider investing in a fast 85mm lens. (I use an 85mm f/1.8 for all my portrait work because I can use the largest aperture to create a wonderfully shallow depth of field.) The low ISO setting yields a noise-free image and is ideal for bright light. If you're photographing in overcast conditions, you may have to increase the ISO to 200. If your camera or lens has image stabilization, use it especially if you're photographing in dim lighting conditions, because the shutter speed selected by the camera will probably be too slow to ensure a blur-free image.

Taking the Picture

You need flattering lighting when you photograph a person. Schedule your portrait photo shoots for early in the morning or late in the afternoon, when the sun provides a golden color and casts soft shadows. Overcast conditions also provide great lighting for shooting portraits.

1. **Find a location for your photo shoot.**

   Scout out your location before the shoot. A park that has a lot of trees provides a location with an innocuous background that doesn't compete with your subject. The background is out of focus for the head-and-shoulders shots, but you may decide to take some full-length shots, in which the photos include more of the background. Avoid areas that have distracting manmade objects, such as utility poles and electrical wires.

2. **Enable the settings discussed previously in this chapter.**

3. **Tell your subject where you want her to stand or sit.**

   Unless you're moving from spot to spot, find a spot where your subject can sit and get comfortable.

4. **Find a suitable vantage point.**

   Position yourself at eye level with your subject. Alternatively, photograph your subject while you have the camera pointing up at him. If you photograph from above, you're sending a subliminal signal that your subject is a weak character.

5. **Tell your subject how you want her to pose.**

6. **Zoom in, position the auto-focus point over your subject's eye that's closest to the camera, and then press the shutter button halfway to achieve focus.**

7. **Compose the photograph.**

You get a more unique shot if you don't center your subject in the frame. If your subject has long hair, use it as a compositional element to draw your viewer into the picture (see Figure 71-1).

8. **Take the picture by fully pressing the shutter button.**

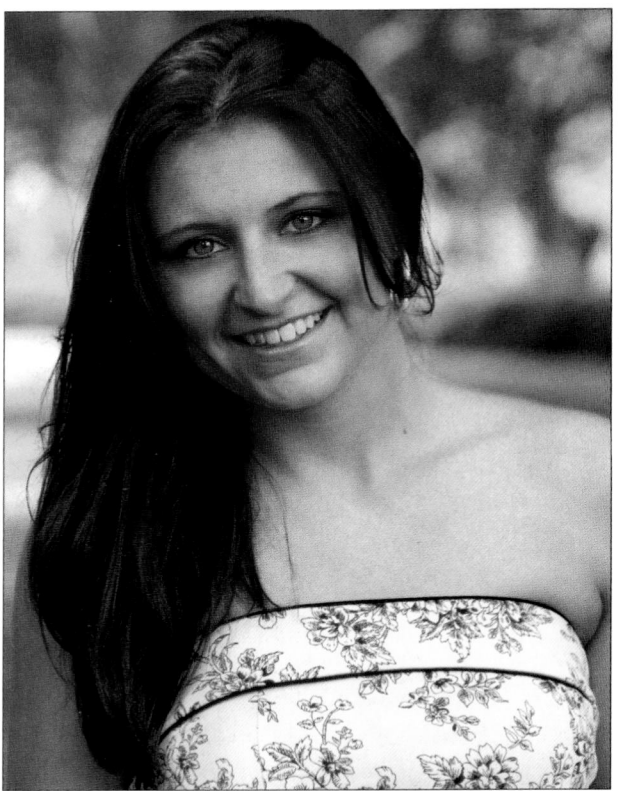

Figure 71-1: Create an interesting composition for your photograph.

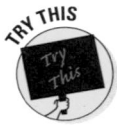

If the area in which you're taking photos includes interesting architectural elements, take a head-to-toe portrait of your subject. If you're photographing a short person, photograph him from a lower position. A photo taken from below makes the subject look taller than she actually is (see Figure 71-2). You can use a slightly smaller aperture (f/6.3 or f/7.1) to show more detail in the background, but still have a soft blur.

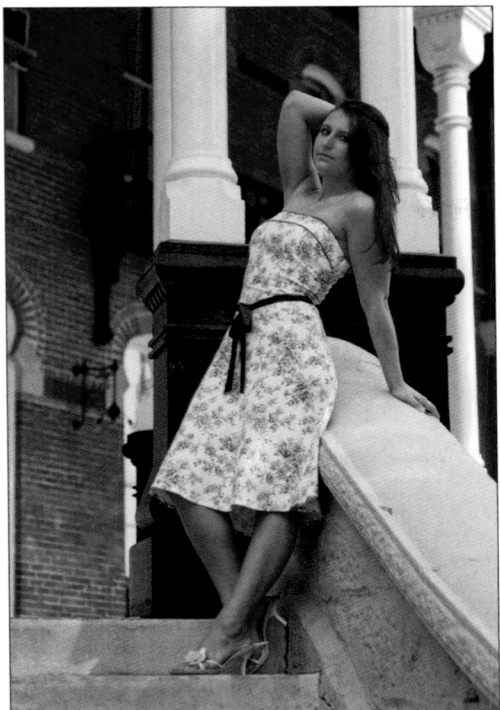

Figure 71-2: Shooting a portrait by using an extremely shallow depth of field.

Troubleshooting

- **My subject is dark in the photo.** This problem happens when strong light is coming from behind your subject. Use exposure compensation to increase the exposure by 1/3 to 2/3 of a stop, which overexposes the background, but properly exposes your subject. You can also bounce some light back into your subject's face by having a friend use a car sunshade or a large white T-shirt.

- **My subject doesn't seem relaxed.** You run into this problem when you photograph people who aren't professional models or don't spend a lot of time in front of the camera. Gain rapport with your subject. Talk about something he likes. When he starts smiling, you're ready to start shooting.

- **My subject isn't sharp.** You didn't position the auto-focus point over one of your subject's eyes when you achieved focus. Take another picture and make sure the auto-focus point is over one of your subject's eyes when you press the shutter button halfway to achieve focus. Make sure the auto-focus point illuminates before you compose the picture. If the eyes are in focus, the entire picture appears to be in focus.

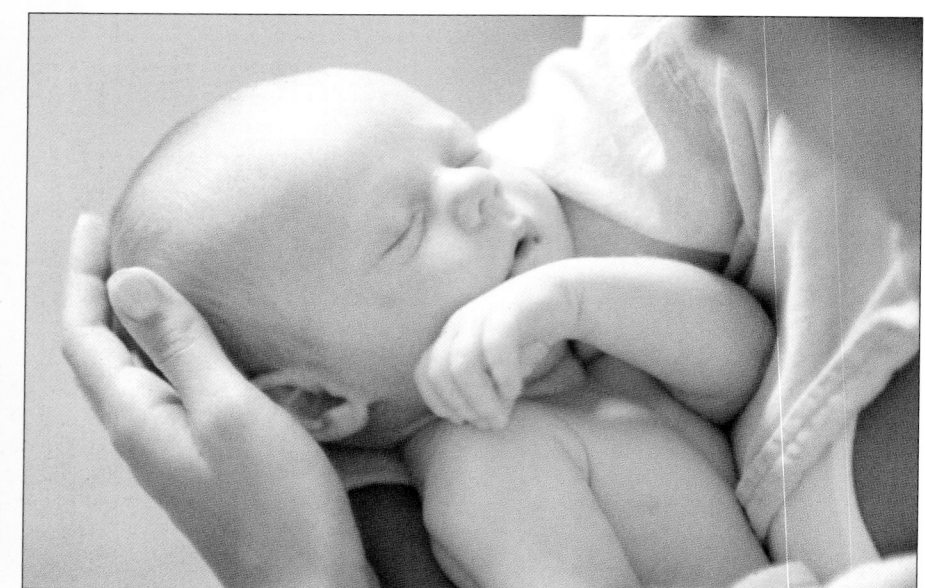

Purestock

72 Newborn Baby Portrait

When you become a proud parent, you can put your maternal or paternal instincts aside for a short while and put on your photographer's hat to capture some photos of your newborn child. Children grow very fast, so you need to document the first minutes of your baby's life and the next few months. If you put your camera aside and don't take pictures for a few months, you'll be surprised at the changes you miss. Soft window light is ideal for this type of portrait because it casts soft shadows.

Camera Settings

- **Metering Mode:** Evaluative
- **Drive Mode:** Single Shot
- **Shooting Mode:** Aperture Priority
- **Aperture:** f/3.5 or larger (smaller f/stop number)
- **ISO Setting:** 200 to 800
- **Focus Mode:** Single Shot
- **Auto-Focus Point:** Single auto-focus point
- **Focal Length:** 80mm to 100mm (35mm equivalent; see "Understanding focal lengths" in the appendix)
- **Image Stabilization:** On

Setting the Camera

When you photograph a newborn baby, you want soft light and a shallow depth of field. You get that depth of field by using Aperture Priority mode and a large aperture, which blurs the foreground and background, and keeps your baby in sharp focus. The ISO range is suitable for the first pictures of your baby in the hospital, as well as pictures illuminated with soft window light in your home. Use the highest ISO setting only if the light is very dim. The high ISO may add a bit of noise to the image, but you don't end up with many dark shadows, which is where the noise becomes most apparent. The focal length is ideal for intimate photos of the child with a parent or a close-up shot of the child all swaddled in soft blankets because it results in a photo with pleasing proportions. Use image stabilization if your camera or lens has it because any operator movement when you photograph an intimate portrait results in an image that's not as sharp as it could be. If you don't have image stabilization, steadying the camera with a tripod is always a good way to hedge your bets.

Taking the Picture

Photographing a baby is very rewarding for any parent or, for that matter, any photographer. If you or someone in your family has just become a parent, grab your camera and get ready to capture some great images. If you're not a parent, this type of photography will try your patience. If the baby starts crying, take a deep breath and relax while the parents soothe the infant.

1. **Place a table covered by a soft blanket near a window that's not getting direct sunlight.**

   Some photographers use several layers of blankets as padding for the child. Direct sunlight is hard on a newborn's eyes and is a bit harsh. Don't use camera flash because the light is harsh and, even if you diffuse it, the sudden flash can frighten the child.

2. **Ask one of the parents to place the child on the blanket.**

   The child may start crying. If he does, you need to wait for the parents to calm him.

3. **Zoom in to the desired focal length.**

4. **Position the auto-focus point over the baby's eye that's closest to the camera, and then press the shutter button halfway to achieve focus.**

5. **Compose the picture.**

   Look for an interesting angle. Compose the picture according to the Rule of Thirds, where the baby's eye intersects one of power points (see the appendix).

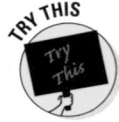

No baby pictures are complete unless you include a shot with one or both of the parents. Everyone will fondly remember a picture of the baby with her father when the child is grown. Choose a large aperture that has an f/stop of f/4.0 and focus on the baby. The child's parent is slightly out of focus but still recognizable (see Figure 72-1).

Troubleshooting

✔ **The baby's blankets look darker than they actually are.** When you have bright window light and bright blankets, the camera may underexpose the scene. Use exposure compensation to increase the exposure by 1/3 or 2/3 a stop.

✔ **When photographing the child with one of**

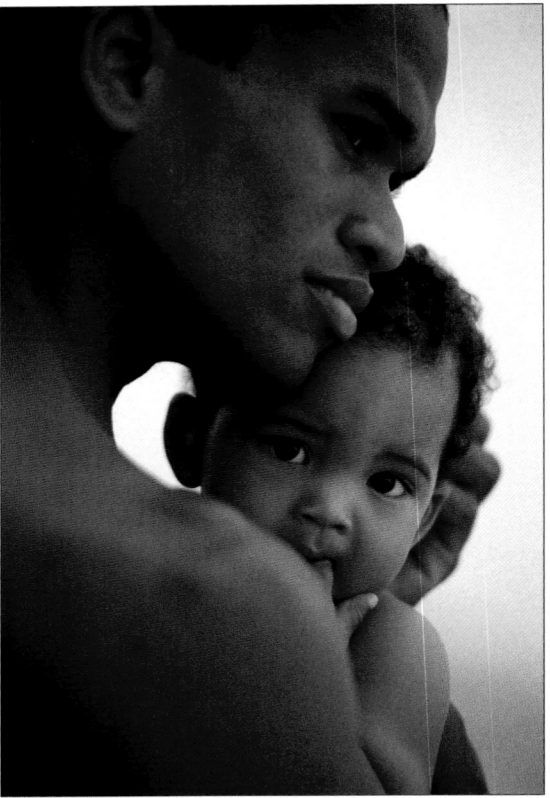

Purestock

Figure 72-1: Photographing the baby with his father.

his parents, one side of the image is too dark. This problem happens when the room is dark and the window light is bright. Don't turn on any room lights because those lights can throw the white balance out of whack. Ask a family member to use a white sheet to bounce light into the shadow side of your subjects. In lieu of a white sheet, you can use a car sunshade, if available.

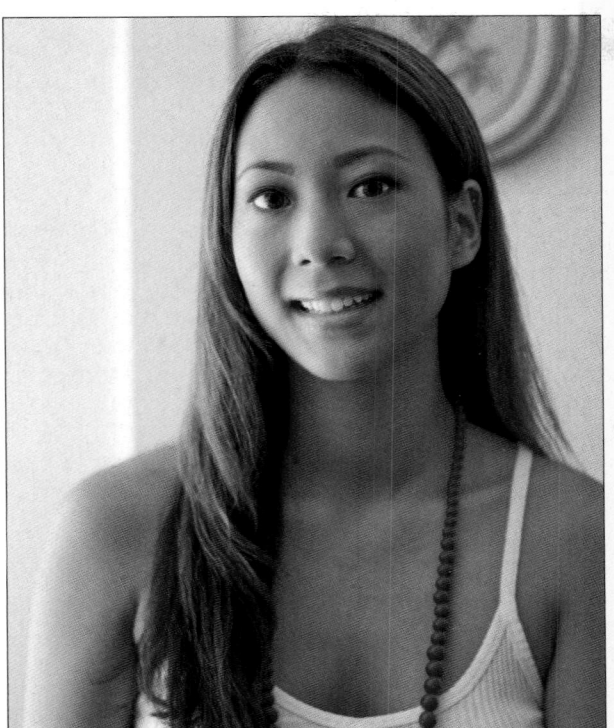

Camera Settings

- **Metering Mode:** Evaluative
- **Drive Mode:** Single Shot
- **Shooting Mode:** Aperture Priority
- **Aperture:** f/3.5 or larger (smaller f/stop number)
- **ISO Setting:** 100 to 400
- **Focus Mode:** Single Shot
- **Auto-Focus Point:** Single auto-focus point
- **Focal Length:** 80mm to 100mm (35mm equivalent; see "Understanding focal lengths" in the appendix)
- **Image Stabilization:** On

*Y*ou can create a very flattering portrait of a person by using the light that comes through a window (as shown in the image here). As long as the sun isn't shining directly through the window, the soft, diffuse window light casts very soft shadows, which is great for portrait photography. Of course, you have other issues, especially if you're photographing your subject in a dark room. You can turn on the room lights, but then you have to deal with harsh light sources, which defeats the purpose of creating a portrait by using window light.

Setting the Camera

When you photograph someone by using window light, you don't want any other details in the room detracting from your photo, so you shoot in Aperture Priority mode and use a large aperture to create a soft photo that draws your viewer's attention to your subject. The focal-length range gives you a pleasing rendition of your subject. The suggested ISO range works in most lighting conditions. If available, image stabilization is a plus because it can help ensure a blur-free photo.

Taking the Picture

Unless you photograph someone who has spent a lot of time in front of the camera, you may have a difficult time getting your subject to relax. Sometimes, you get lucky and get a great shot during the first exposure or two. But that's the exception. Be prepared to spend some time with the person you're photographing.

1. **Turn off all lights in the room.**

   Additional lighting can cause problems with white balance.

2. **Tell your subject where you want her to sit.**

   You can improvise with the seating. Some photographers like their subjects to sit on a backless chair, which is perfect a head-and-shoulders portrait, because all you see is your subject. Your subject can face the camera directly, or you can have her sit at a 45-degree angle to the camera.

3. **Tell your subject the pose you want her to take.**

   The subject of posing is above and beyond the scope of this book. As a general rule, avoid a symmetrical composition. For example, in the photo on the first page of this chapter, the girl's lovely hair is draped over one shoulder, which adds viewer interest to the picture. If your subject is sitting at a 45-degree angle to the camera, have him turn his head to the camera.

4. **Gain rapport with your subject.**

   If you know your subject well, talk about something she likes. If you don't know her well, ask her some questions to get the conversation flowing.

5. **Set up the camera by using the settings discussed earlier in this chapter.**

6. **Position the auto-focus point over the eye nearest to the camera, and then press the shutter button halfway to achieve focus.**

7. **Compose the picture.**

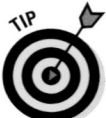

You can also capture wonderful candid photos by using window light. Figure 73-1 is a picture of a bride getting ready for an outdoor wedding. It started raining while her hair was being done. I took a picture and captured her expression seconds after the sky opened and rain started pouring.

8. **Press the shutter button fully to take the picture.**

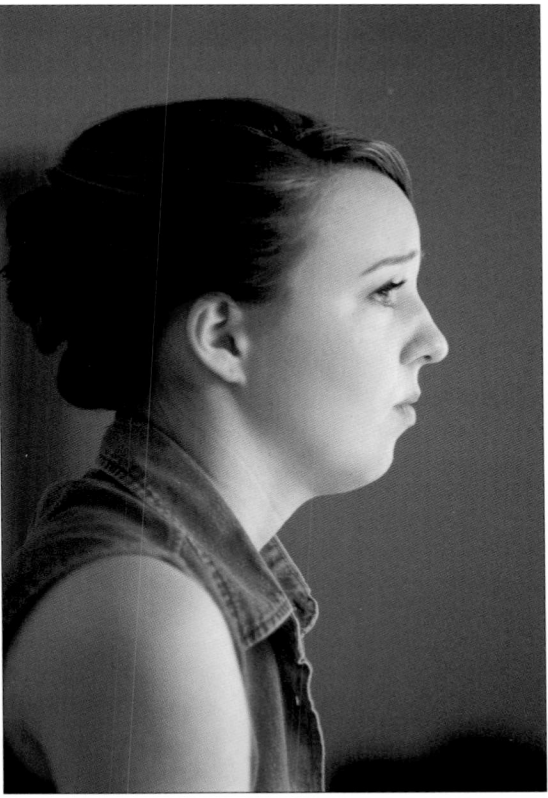

Figure 73-1: Be alert for any photographic opportunity.

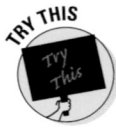

If your subject is wearing glasses, have him tilt his head down and then look over the glasses. You catch reflections of the light source (known as *catch lights* in photographer speak) in his glasses, as well as his eyes (as illustrated in Figure 73-2).

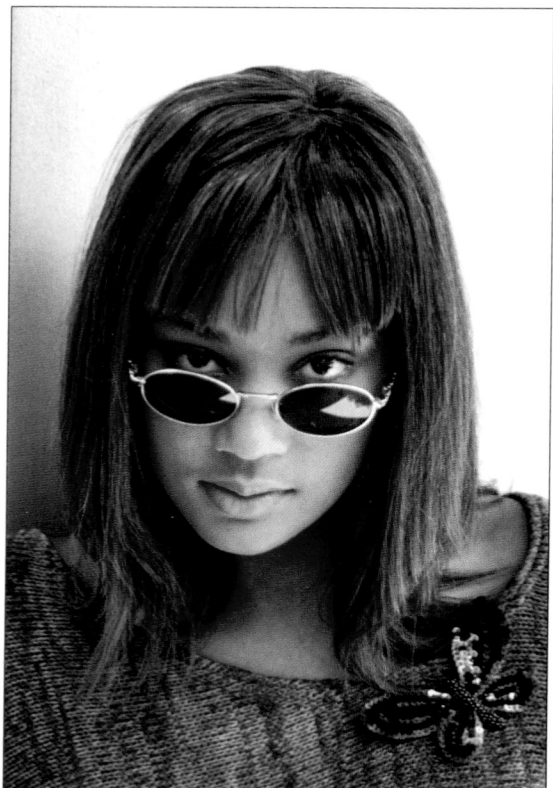

Figure 73-2: Photographing a subject who wears glasses by window light.

Troubleshooting

- **One side of my subject's face is dark in the photo.** You encounter this problem when you photograph someone in a dark room. The window light illuminates one side of your subject's face, but the other side is in dark shadow. Have someone hold a large white T-shirt or a blanket on the other side of your subject to reflect the window light into the shadow side of her face.

- **My subject's face has shiny spots.** The light can reflect off natural oil on your subject's skin or perspiration. If your subject is a man, ask him to wash his face. If your subject is a woman, ask her to wash her face and then apply a little makeup. A word of caution is in order here. Before you ask the subject to wash or apply makeup, show them the photo on the LCD monitor (they're likely to notice the problem) and tell them this is the cure.

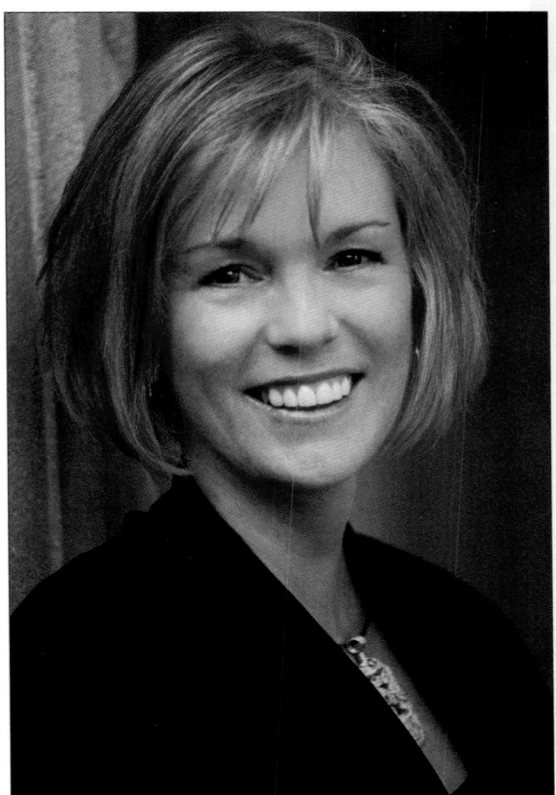

Camera Settings

- ✓ **Metering Mode:** Evaluative
- ✓ **Drive Mode:** Single Shot
- ✓ **Shooting Mode:** Aperture Priority
- ✓ **Aperture:** f/3.5 to f/7.1
- ✓ **ISO Setting:** 100
- ✓ **Focus Mode:** Single Shot
- ✓ **Auto-Focus Point:** Single auto-focus point
- ✓ **Focal Length:** 85mm to 150mm (35mm equivalent; see "Understanding focal lengths" in the appendix)
- ✓ **Image Stabilization:** On

People come in all shapes and sizes, and they change while they grow older. When you photograph someone who has had a lot of grains of sand sift through his hourglass, you can still get a wonderful portrait, but you have to keep some things in mind. You're not photographing a kid who has a peaches-and-cream complexion. Therefore, get creative with your posing and composition to capture a photo that you and your subject feel proud of.

Setting the Camera

Photographing a person who has stood the test of time is a challenge, yet at the same time, it's very rewarding when you get it right. The suggested aperture range gives you the option to create a soft, dreamy focus in which the person's hair is slightly out of focus (by using the smallest f/stop number) or create a portrait in which every detail is in apparent focus. The single auto-focus point lets you precisely focus on your subject's eyes. You definitely need to get the eyes in focus if you're shooting the picture by using a large aperture (a small f/stop number) because if the eyes aren't in focus, viewers will think the entire image is out of focus. The suggested focal-length range yields a nice portrait without distorting your subject's features. Use image stabilization, if your camera or lens has this feature, because the slightest operator movement results in an image that's not tack sharp.

Taking the Picture

When you're photographing an older person, lighting plays an important role. Soft window light (see Chapter 73) or an overcast day is flattering light for your subject with this type of photography. Alternatively, you can take the photographs in a shaded area. Using light from a diffused flash (see the appendix) is another option.

1. **Enable the camera settings discussed earlier in this chapter.**

2. **Find an interesting vantage point from which to photograph your subject.**

   Choose a place that has good light and a fairly bland background that doesn't distract your viewer's attention from your subject. Make sure no man-made elements, such as utility poles or wires, appear in the area. However, a window or a door can provide an interesting background, as long as your subject's not too close to it.

3. **If your subject is a woman, ask her to apply some light makeup.**

4. **Tell your subject the pose you want her to adopt.**

   If you're photographing your subject outdoors, as shown in Figure 74-1, ask her to do something.

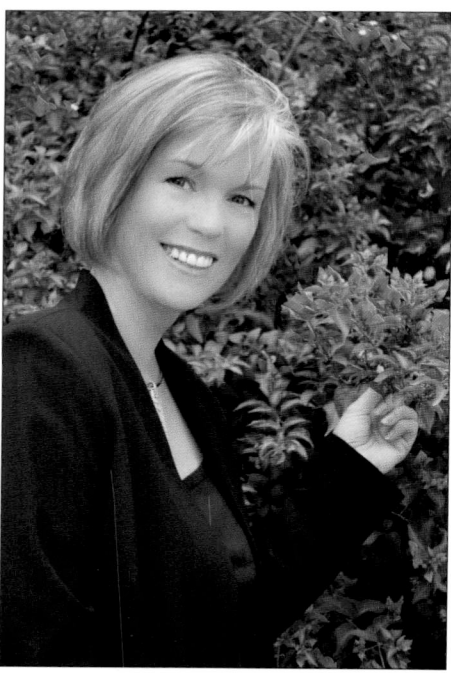

Figure 74-1: Ask your subject to do something.

5. **Zoom in, aim the auto-focus point over the eye closest to the camera, and then press the shutter button halfway to achieve focus.**

6. **Compose the picture.**

   Look through the viewfinder and make minute adjustments. You may have to zoom in or out, and move to a slightly different position.

7. **Fully press the shutter button to take the picture.**

   After you take the picture, review the image on your LCD monitor. You rarely get a good shot with the first few pictures you take. Use the image on your LCD monitor to make adjustments in your composition. You can review your exposure information and histogram as well to make sure the image is properly exposed.

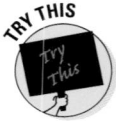

After you have some good images under your belt, relax and put your camera on the table or, if you wear a strap, leave it strapped around your neck. Start talking with your subject about something that interests her. When she strikes an interesting candid pose, raise the camera and take a picture (see Figure 74-2).

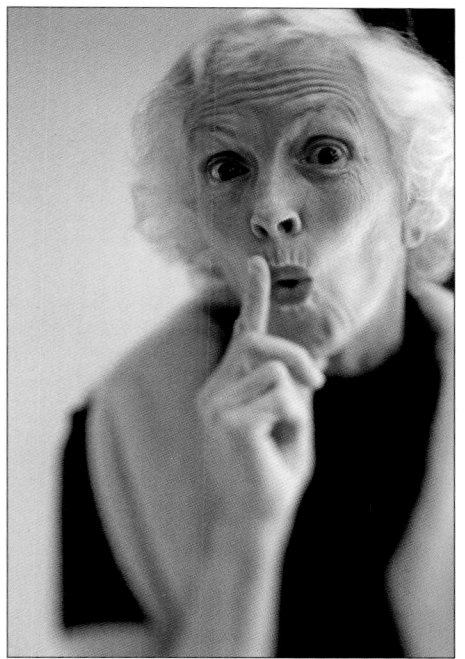

Purestock

Figure 74-2: Take a candid shot after you get some good ones on your memory card.

Troubleshooting

- ✔ **My subject has a lot of wrinkles, which show in the photograph.** Modern lenses are sharp and catch every subtle nuance, whether you want them in your photo or not. You can remove wrinkles in an image-editing application such as Photoshop Elements. You can also minimize character lines when you take the photograph by using a soft-focus filter, which adds a dreamy effect to the image. You can find soft-focus filters at your favorite camera retailer. They come in a variety of strengths. Get a fairly strong soft-focus filter when you're photographing an older person.

- ✔ **My subject doesn't want the lines in his neck to show in the photo.** You can minimize neck wrinkles when you take the photo. Have your subject lift his head slightly to minimize the wrinkles.

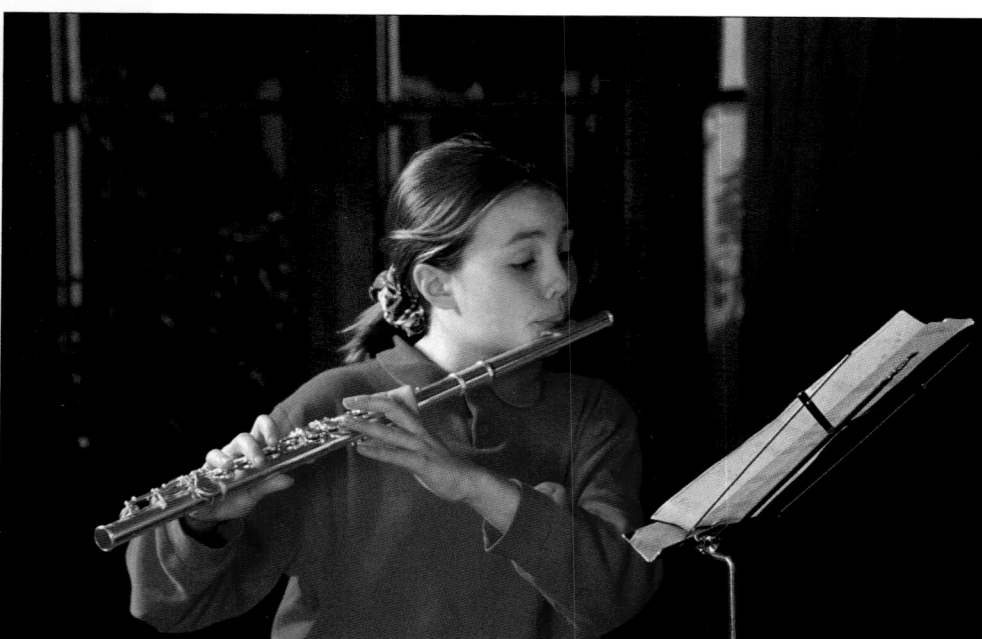

75 Musicians

The hills are alive with the sound of music . . . Music can be vibrant and exciting, or soothing and relaxing. Like photographers, musicians are artists. If you have a musician in the family or know a musician, take a lot of artistic photos of your musician friend. When you photograph a musician, you can use his instrument as a compositional element. When the musician picks up his instrument and starts to play, it's almost like photographing a couple in love.

Camera Settings

- **Metering Mode:** Evaluative
- **Drive Mode:** Single Shot
- **Shooting Mode:** Aperture Priority
- **Aperture:** f/4.0 or f/5.6
- **ISO Setting:** 100 to 400
- **Focus Mode:** Single Shot
- **Auto-Focus Point:** Single auto-focus point
- **Focal Length:** 50mm to 100mm (35mm equivalent; see "Understanding focal lengths" in the appendix)
- **Image Stabilization:** On

Setting the Camera

When you photograph a musician, she's the main subject of your photograph. Therefore, you take this type of photograph by using Aperture Priority mode and a small aperture. When you combine these settings with the suggested focal length, you get a wonderfully shallow depth of field that clearly makes the musician the center of interest. When you photograph one musician, you zoom in using the longest suggested focal length. When you photograph two or more musicians, zoom out. The suggested ISO range allows you to photograph musicians outdoors on bright sunny days (ISO 100), as well as indoors (ISO 400). Definitely use image stabilization, if your camera or lens comes with it, because even the slightest operator movement results in a blurry picture.

Taking the Picture

When you photograph one or more musicians, the main subjects of your image are the players and their instruments. The players, of course, are the center of interest in your photograph, but you can use the instruments to draw viewers into the image. The instruments serve as compositional elements and support players. Light is also important when you're photographing musicians. If you're photographing a musician outdoors, you want shade or overcast conditions, which is soft, diffuse light. If you do photograph a musician in sunlight, do so early in the morning or late in the afternoon to avoid harsh light and shadows. If you're photographing a musician indoors, soft window light is perfect for this type of photography because of the pleasing shadows and diffuse light.

1. **Ask your subject to start playing her instrument.**

    Try to have your subject lose herself in her playing.

2. **Enable the settings discussed previously in this chapter.**

    The time you take to prepare the camera gives your subject more time to get in the moment.

3. **Find an interesting vantage point.**

    When you photograph a musician at work, be creative. You can photograph the subject from above or at the subject's eye level. If you're photographing an orchestra that's performing on stage, consider using the vantage point of looking up from the pit.

4. **Zoom in.**

If your subject plays a fairly compact instrument, such as a flute, include all of it in the photo. If your subject plays a huge instrument, such as a bass cello for example, you can zoom in to include part of the body, the neck, and the player's arms and head.

5. **Position the auto-focus point over your center of interest, press the shutter button halfway to achieve focus, and then compose the picture.**

As a rule, you want to make your subject the center of interest. However, you can make an object — such as a flautist's fingers or a pianist's hands — your center of interest. The viewer can still recognize your subject, but that subject's fingers are the sharpest objects in the image. Position the auto-focus point over the players' fingers, and then press the shutter button to achieve focus.

Use the players' instruments to draw the viewer into the picture. In Figure 75-1, the keyboard draws the viewer's attention to the boy's hands, which are the sharpest objects in the picture. The girl is recognizable, but she doesn't appear in sharp focus. All the elements blend together to make the viewer spend some time looking at the image, instead of giving it a casual glance. In this case, fill flash is needed to augment the lighting due to the bright window light.

6. **Fully press the shutter button to take the picture.**

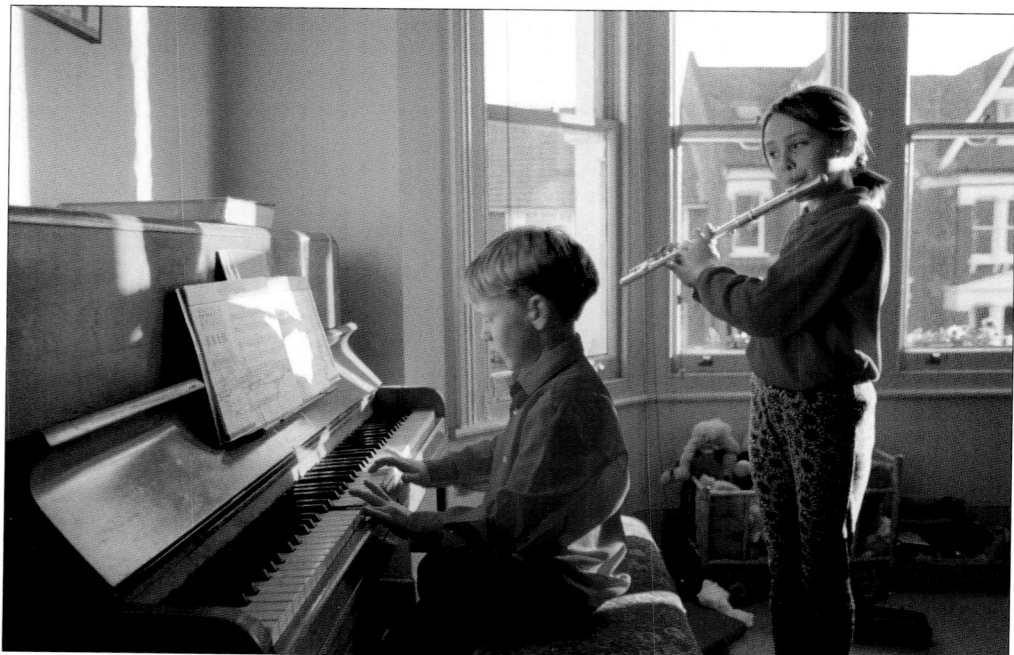

PhotoDisc, Inc./Getty Images

Figure 75-1: Use the instruments as compositional elements.

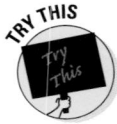

In many areas of the country, you can find musicians playing on the streets. As long as you're in a safe part of town, smile at the musician and raise your camera. If he smiles or nods back, he's given you permission to take the picture (see Figure 75-2).

Troubleshooting

↙ **Dark shadows appear on one side of my subject's face in the photo.** The light source is shining on one side of your subject, and the other side of your subject is considerably darker. You can use a large T-shirt or a white blanket to reflect light back into the shadow side of your subject.

↙ **The instrument is in sharp focus, but my subject isn't.** Take the picture again: Make sure the auto-focus point appears over your subject when you press the shutter button halfway to achieve focus and make sure the auto-focus point illuminates before you move the camera to compose the image.

PhotoDisc, Inc./Getty Images

Figure 75-2: Photograph street musicians.

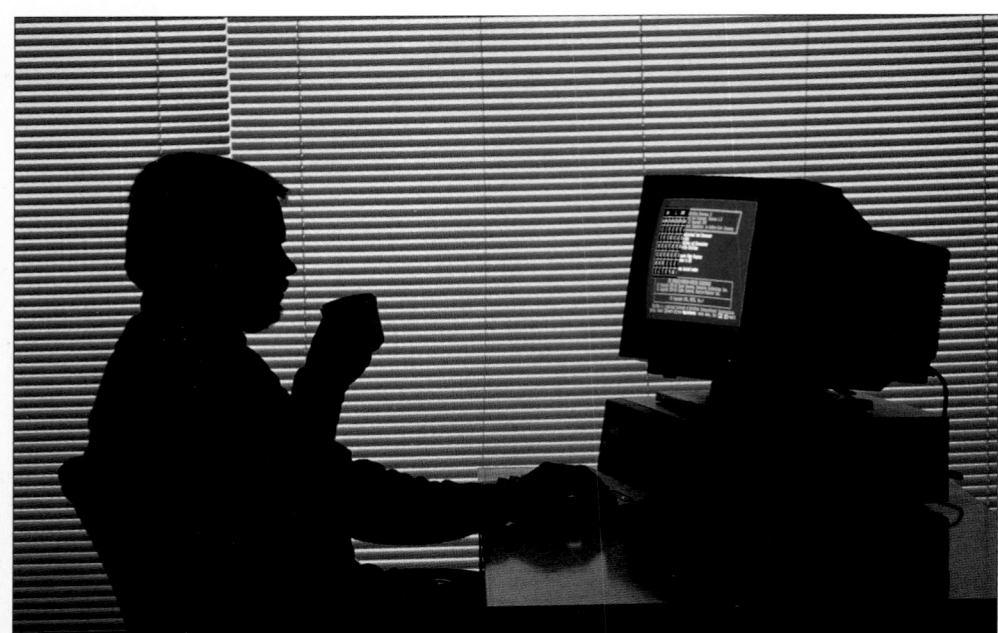

PhotoDisc, Inc./Getty Images

*P*hotographing a person as a *silhouette* — an artistic graphic representation of your subject — can often produce a moody, artistic photograph. You can also use this technique to tell a story or relate something about someone's lifestyle. A silhouette portrait of a man in his office (as shown here), for example, implies that the person is very motivated and task-driven. Creating a silhouette portrait can present you with some challenges, but this chapter gives you the information you need to overcome those.

Camera Settings

- **Metering Mode:** Evaluative
- **Drive Mode:** Single Shot
- **Shooting Mode:** Aperture Priority
- **Aperture:** f/8.0
- **ISO Setting:** 800 or higher
- **Focus Mode:** Single Shot
- **Auto-Focus Point:** Single auto-focus point
- **Focal Length:** 50mm to 80mm (35mm equivalent; see "Understanding focal lengths" in the appendix)
- **Image Stabilization:** On

Setting the Camera

When you create a silhouette portrait, you want to give viewers an indication of the surroundings, as well as the person. Therefore, shoot in Aperture Priority mode and use a medium aperture (f/8.0), which renders a sharp image with all details in apparent focus. You need the high ISO setting because you're photographing in dim light. Use a normal (50mm) to medium telephoto (80mm) focal length. This lets you capture the person and his surroundings or zoom in tight on the person.

Taking the Picture

When you create a silhouette portrait, the composition of the photo is important. You want the viewer's eye to move from one shape to the next and eventually to the person. You do this by looking at the scene through the viewfinder and positioning your subject off center, preferably on a power point according to the Rule of Thirds. You can use other elements to draw the viewer's attention to your subject. For example, the subject can extend his arm to pick up an object on the desk or use a computer mouse. The diagonal line of his arm leads viewers to your subject. Position the light source (which needs to be fairly bright) behind the person you're photographing.

1. **Enable the settings discussed previously in this chapter.**

2. **Tell your subject where you want her to stand.**

   She needs to be in front of a bright light source. If you're photographing your subject outdoors, photograph her in the morning shortly after the sun rises or in the afternoon anytime between sunset and an hour before sunset. If you're photographing your subject in a room, tell her to stand in front of a window.

3. **If you're photographing your subject in a room, turn off any interior lights.**

   Interior lights illuminate your subject, so he's not in silhouette.

4. **Zoom in, position the auto-focus point over your subject, and then press the shutter button halfway to achieve focus.**

5. **Compose the image.**

   You can get a more interesting picture if you don't center your subject. You can also use a prop to draw viewers into the image.

6. **Take the picture by fully pressing the shutter button.**

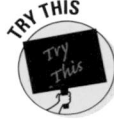

You can create a silhouette environmental portrait by photographing your subject by a product she uses in her work or one of her hobbies. For example, if your subject is a pilot, take a silhouette portrait of him beside his airplane (see Figure 76-1).

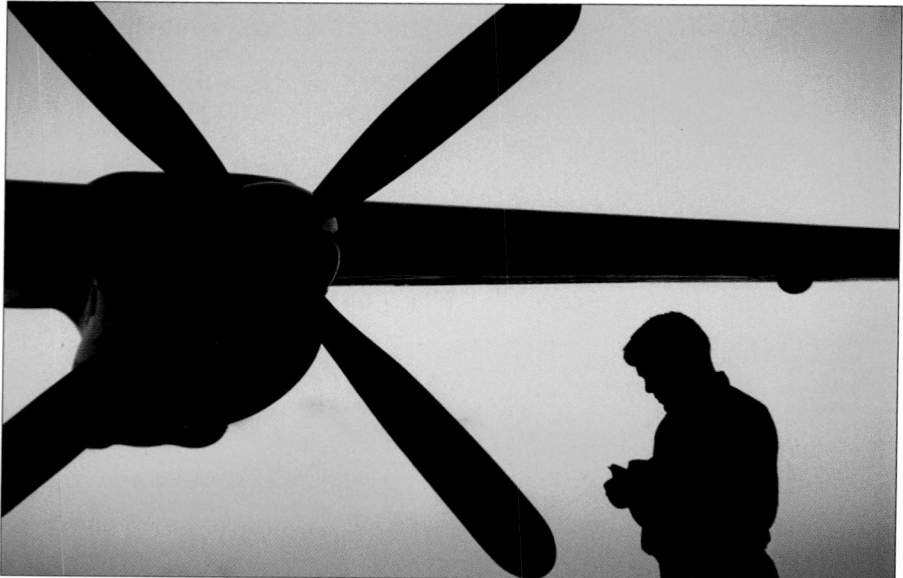

Corbis Digital Stock

Figure 76-1: Take an environmental silhouette portrait.

Troubleshooting

- **My subject is dark but not in silhouette.** You have this problem when the scene doesn't have a great difference in brightness between the light source behind your subject and the ambient lighting. You can take the photograph at a time when the light source is brighter — for example, when the sun is shining directly into the window. Alternatively, you can decrease the exposure by using exposure compensation to decrease the exposure until your subject is in total silhouette. Changing the exposure setting makes the entire photograph darker, so use this option only as a last resort.

- **The distant background is too sharp.** If you have details close to your subject that you don't want in focus, have your subject move away from the background (and toward you). You can also switch to a larger aperture (a smaller f/stop number).

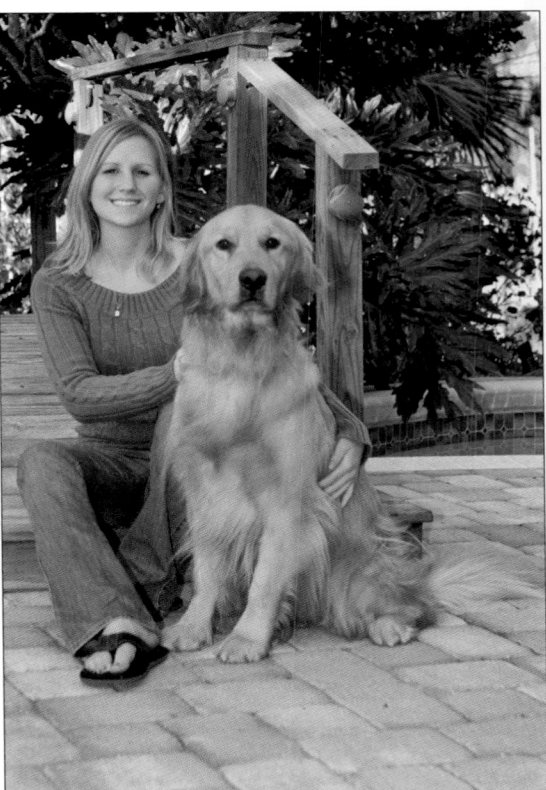

Camera Settings

- ✔ **Metering Mode:** Evaluative
- ✔ **Drive Mode:** Single Shot
- ✔ **Shooting Mode:** Aperture Priority
- ✔ **Aperture:** f/4.0 or larger
- ✔ **ISO Setting:** 100 to 400
- ✔ **Focus Mode:** Single Shot
- ✔ **Auto-Focus Point:** Single auto-focus point
- ✔ **Focal Length:** 50mm to 100mm (35mm equivalent; see "Understanding focal lengths" in the appendix)
- ✔ **Image Stabilization:** On

*1*n many families, a dog or cat has the same status as a child; in other words, a valued member of the family. Unfortunately, dogs and cats don't stay on the planet as long as their masters. As the family historian, you need to document family pets, along with other family members. You use similar techniques in this type of photography that you do when you take an outdoor portrait, but it has its own challenges. You want to take a picture of the pet and family member that has both subjects in a pleasing pose. In this chapter, I show you the settings to take a great picture, but you need to capture both of your subjects at their best.

Setting the Camera

When you photograph a pet and family member, make them the subjects of your photo. You want a shallow depth of field — which you get when you shoot in Aperture Priority mode and use a large aperture — because a shallow depth of field makes your subject stand out. The ISO range covers lighting conditions from bright sunlight to open shade. The suggested focal-length range is ideal for a portrait that has two subjects. The single auto-focus point lets you precisely control what part of the image is in focus. You even have the option to zoom in and capture a tight portrait. You may want to enable image stabilization if your camera or lens has it, especially if you're shooting in low light, because your camera may choose a shutter speed that is too slow to take a blur-free picture without image stabilization. If you don't have image stabilization, your alternative is to use a higher ISO setting or place the camera on a tripod.

Taking the Picture

When you photograph a pet and her owner, the owner is both the subject and handler. He can work with the pet while you get the camera ready. This type of photography looks best when you take the picture outdoors. Leave the portrait that uses a painted muslin background and studio lighting to the pros. Before you embark on the photo shoot, ask the owner to groom his pet.

1. **Find a suitable location.**

   You want a location that has an innocuous background. A busy background distracts the viewer's attention from your subjects. Also, photograph your subjects early in the morning or late in the afternoon, when the low angle of the sun creates a golden-colored light and removes any harsh shadows. Alternatively, you can photograph your subjects in open shade.

2. **Tell the owner how you want her to pose with the pet.**

   The owner can get the pet to cooperate. If the pet is small, tell the owner to hold the pet. It the pet is large, tell the owner you want the pet to sit and ask the owner to kneel beside the pet.

3. **Find a suitable vantage point.**

   Make sure you're at eye level with the pet and owner.

4. **Zoom to the desired focal length.**

You can capture the pet and owner from head-to-toe and -paw, or zoom in tight for a more intimate portrait (see Figure 77-1).

5. **Position the auto-focus point over the owner's eye nearest the camera, and then press the shutter button halfway to achieve focus.**

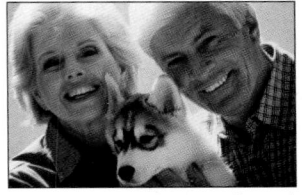

Purestock

Figure 77-1: Zoom in for an intimate portrait.

Always keep the eyes in sharp focus, especially when you're working with a shallow depth of field. If the eyes aren't in sharp focus, it appears that the entire image is out of focus because viewers are drawn to people's eyes when they look at a photo.

6. **Compose the picture.**

If possible, don't center the pet and owner in the frame. In Figure 77-1, the dog's tail caused the owner and pet to be repositioned so that the person and the animal's head are to one side of the image.

7. **Fully press the shutter button to take the picture.**

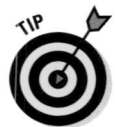

Be sure to get some candid photos after you take the formal ones. Keep the camera ready and take some pictures of the pet and family member interacting (see Figure 77-2).

Troubleshooting

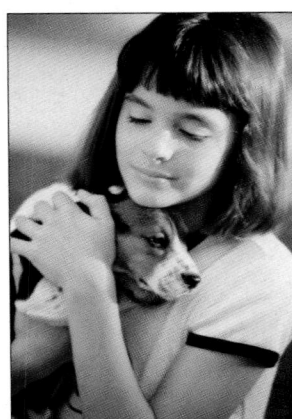

Purestock

Figure 77-2: A girl and her puppy.

✔ **The picture isn't in focus.** This problem happens if your camera doesn't achieve focus before you compose the image. Make sure the focus lamp in the viewfinder illuminates before you compose the picture and make sure you focus on the eyes of either the owner or the pet.

✔ **One subject isn't in focus.** You have this problem if the pet and her master's eyes aren't equidistant from the camera. If you notice that one subject is out of focus, get the out-of-focus subject to move the same distance from the camera as the other subject.

78 High Key Portrait

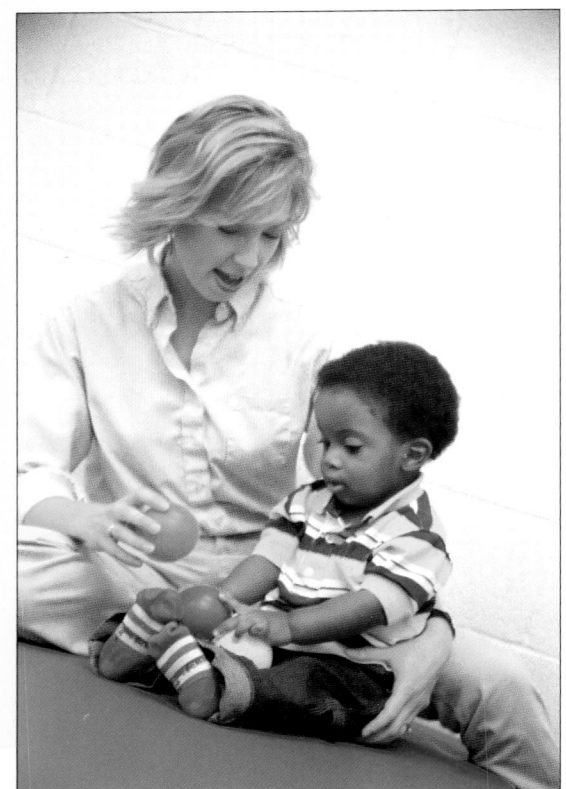

Corbis Images

*W*hen you photograph a light-haired person against a bright background, this kind of photo is known as a *high key portrait*. When you do these photos in a studio and use a lot of expensive lighting, the images look like the subject's hair is melting into the background. We mere mortals, with our digital SLRs and our camera flash units, don't have the luxury of expensive lights and pure white backgrounds. High key portraits are also shadowless, which professionals can do easily with studio lighting, but is not so easy when you're not using studio lights. Therefore, amateurs must improvise to achieve similar results. The image here shows a portrait of two people that was taken by using this technique.

Camera Settings

- ✔ **Metering Mode:** Evaluative
- ✔ **Drive Mode:** Single Shot
- ✔ **Shooting Mode:** Aperture Priority
- ✔ **Aperture:** f/4.0 or larger (smaller f/stop number)
- ✔ **ISO Setting:** 100 to 400
- ✔ **Focus Mode:** Single Shot
- ✔ **Auto-Focus Point:** Single auto-focus point
- ✔ **Focal Length:** 70mm to 85mm (35mm equivalent; see "Understanding focal lengths" in the appendix)
- ✔ **Image Stabilization:** On

Setting the Camera

High key portraits are feel-good pictures — pretty girls or kids against a plain, light-colored background. To draw attention to your subject, you need a shallow depth of field, so use Aperture Priority shooting mode and choose a large aperture (a small f/stop number). The ISO range is ideal for shooting in bright light (ISO 100) or indoors (ISO 400) as both settings yield relatively noise-free images The suggested focal-length range renders realistic images that have pleasing proportions, which makes it perfect for portraits. You shouldn't need image stabilization because you're photographing in good light, but it can help you get a sharper image.

Taking the Picture

Location and lighting is everything when you want to create a "faux" high key portrait. Because you don't have expensive studio lighting, you have to pick your location carefully. Even if your camera has an auxiliary flash triggered by the camera, that feature isn't powerful enough to blow out a background to pure white. Follow these steps for an alternative to traditional high key setups.

1. **Find a spot to take the portrait.**

   When you create a high key portrait, you need a light-colored background. A neutral-colored block wall or a wall covered with light-colored wallpaper that doesn't have a pattern provides the ideal background for this type of photography. If the background is brighter than the light falling on your subject, you have a scenario that is similar to a pro's studio setup. If you're taking the picture outdoors and the wall is in bright sunlight, find a shaded area for your subject. If you're indoors and the building has any bright overhead lights, place a plain white backdrop, such as a sheet, behind the lights, and place your subject in front of the lights.

2. **Enable the camera settings discussed previously in this chapter.**

3. **Tell your subject how you want her to pose.**

   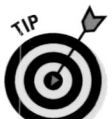

   Posing is beyond the scope of this book, but here are a couple of hints. Avoid a static face-forward look. You can get a more compelling photograph if your subject is slightly off center. He can also turn toward the camera and dip one shoulder.

4. **Position the auto-focus point over the subject's eye that's closest to the camera and press the shutter button halfway to achieve focus.**

5. **Compose the image and press the shutter button fully to take the picture.**

   You get a more interesting shot if your subject is not in the middle of the frame. Compose the image so that the subject's arms lead the viewer into the picture. Position one of her eyes on a power point according to the Rule of Thirds.

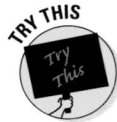

Create a makeshift outdoor studio by using sheer curtains that drape behind and over the top of your subject. You can use two ladders to support the curtains. The light source should be behind the curtains so that the curtains above your subject diffuse the light. Place your subject in front of the background curtain and directly below the overhead part of the curtain. Take several pictures. You may have to use exposure compensation or fill flash to properly expose your subjects (see Figure 78-1).

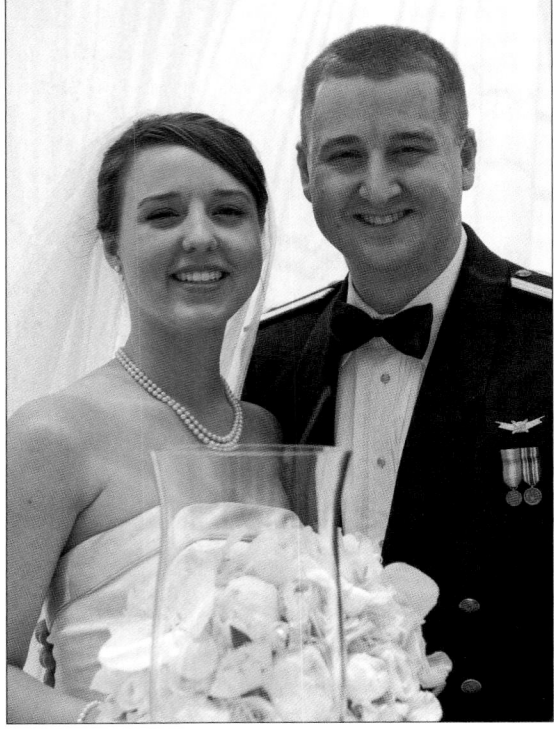

Figure 78-1: Create a makeshift studio by using sheer curtains.

Troubleshooting

⌐ **My subject is too dark in the photo.** You can turn this problem to your advantage. Increase exposure compensation until your subject is properly exposed, which also brightens the background — the goal of this kind of photography.

⌐ **I'm using interior lights and fill flash, and the color seems wrong.** This problem can happen when the interior lights have a different color temperature than your flash unit. Create a custom white balance. Refer to your camera manual for more instructions.

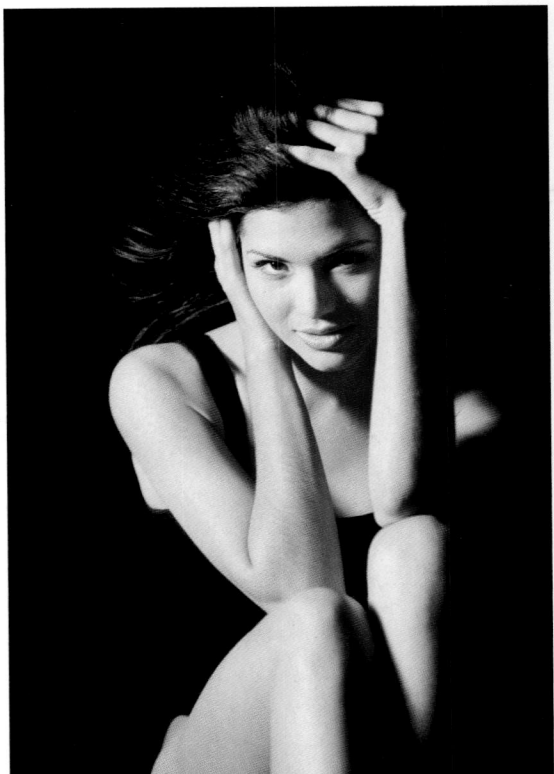

Purestock

Low key portraits are the yang to high key portraits' yin. Low key portraits are dark and moody. You photograph a person who has dark hair or dark skin against a dark background, or someone who has silver hair and a light complexion against a dark background. With this type of photography, you shed enough light on your subjects so that they're visible, but their clothing melts into the black background. Professional photographers go to great extremes when creating a low key portrait. You can't achieve the same results as a professional, but with a bit of work, we can get similar results.

Setting the Camera

Low key portraits are great for actors, athletes, and people with dark hair who look good against a dark background. In this type of photography, depth of field is important, so you shoot in Aperture Priority mode and use a large aperture (a small f/stop number). The ISO setting is ideal for a relatively dark lighting scenario. The focal-length range is perfect for portrait photography. Image stabilization is helpful.

Taking the Picture

Take one creative photographer, a willing model, and a dark background, and you have the key ingredients for this type of photograph. Mix in copious amounts of practice and the following steps to get some compelling portraits.

1. **Find a spot to take the portrait.**

   The ideal place for a low key portrait is in a dungeon. But seriously, you need to find a dark wall. In lieu of a dark wall, you can tack a dark sheet to the wall.

2. **Extinguish any lights in the room and enable the camera settings discussed previously in this chapter.**

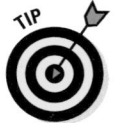

3. **Tell your subject how you want him to pose.**

   Posing is beyond the scope of this book. However, if you're photographing a macho kind of guy, the crossed-arm pose works well.

4. **Add auxiliary lighting.**

   If you can place the backdrop adjacent to a window, you can use window light to illuminate your subject. Alternatively, you can use diffused on-camera flash or an auxiliary flash unit that has a diffuser.

5. **Position the auto-focus point over the subject's eye that's closest to the camera, and then press the shutter button halfway to achieve focus.**

6. **Compose the image, and then fully press the shutter button to take the picture.**

   Compose the image so that your subject is to one side of the frame, as shown in Figure 79-1. In this figure, the basketball is perfectly aligned on a power point according to the Rule of Thirds.

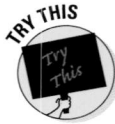

If you have seniors in your family, use them as subjects for this type of photography because their silver hair makes a good contrast with the dark background. Have them wear black clothing and photograph them against a black background. Window light shining on their faces completes the equation. Your subjects' hair and faces are readily visible, but their clothing blends into the background.

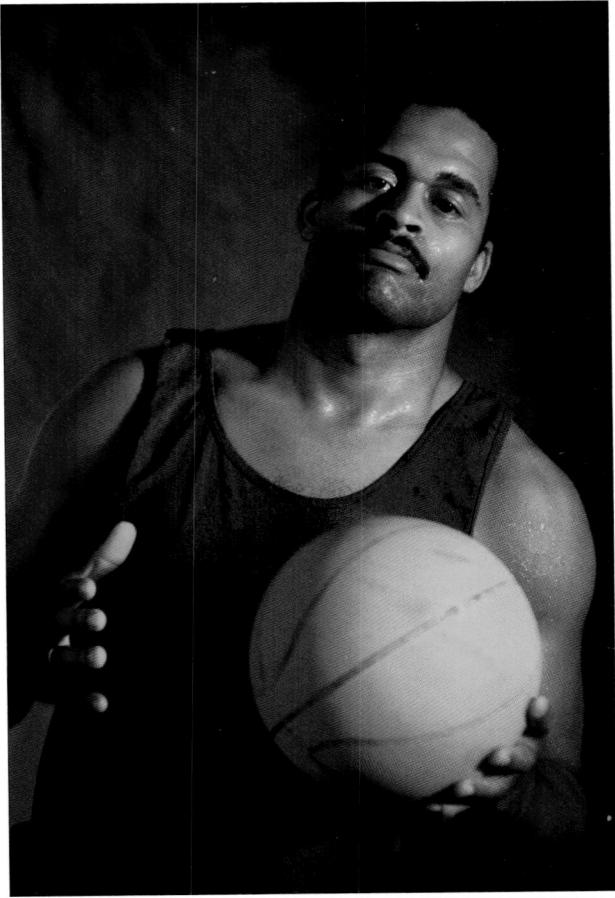

PhotoDisc, Inc./Getty Images

Figure 79-1: Compose the image to attract viewer attention.

Troubleshooting

- ✔ **My subject is too bright in the photo.** The camera may be fooled by the dark background and give you too much light. Use exposure compensation to decrease the exposure until the background is dark and your subject is properly lighted.

- ✔ **I'm using window light, and the shadow side of my subject's face is too dark.** Have someone use a white sheet or car sunshade to bounce light into the shadow side of your subject's face. Make sure your helper doesn't stand too close to your subject; otherwise, you get too much light, which defeats the purpose of this technique.

Part V
Places

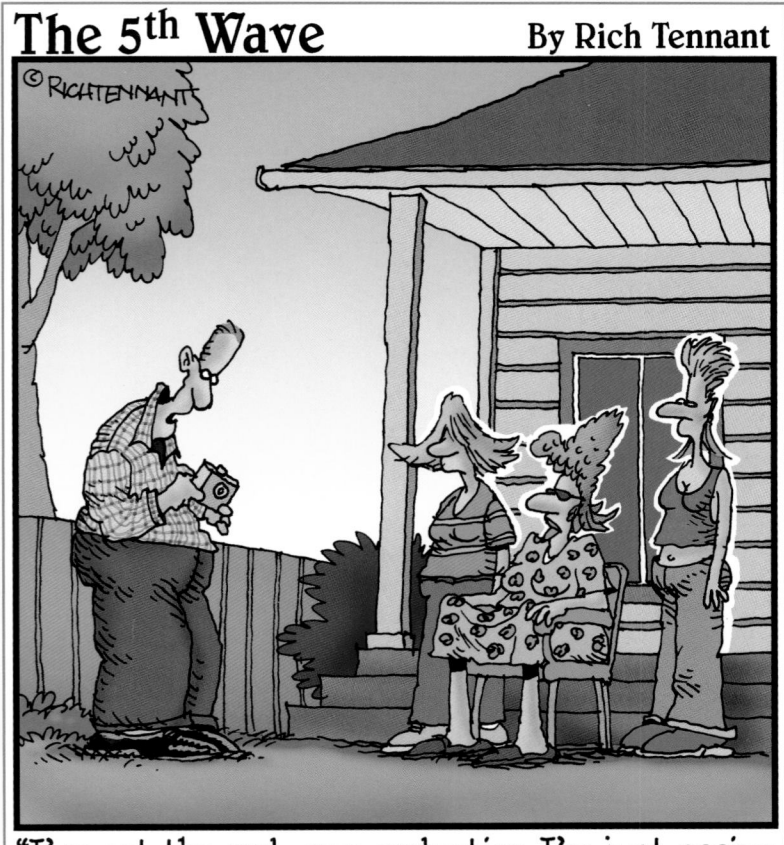

The 5th Wave · By Rich Tennant

"I've got the red-eye reduction, I'm just seeing if there's a button that'll fix your hair."

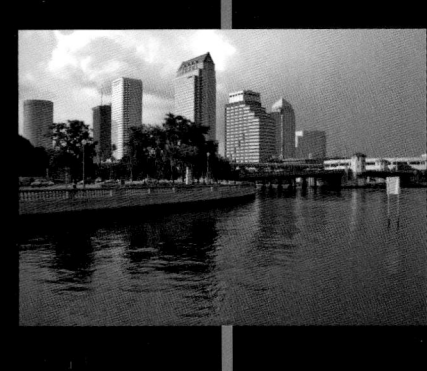

You live in a house, which is located in a town, which is located in a state. You may also live near places like marinas, historical landmarks, amusement parks, and so on. All of these places are interesting subjects for photographers, and you can get great pictures — as long as you know which settings to use. In this part of the book, I simplify the art of photographing places by providing the settings for photographing places.

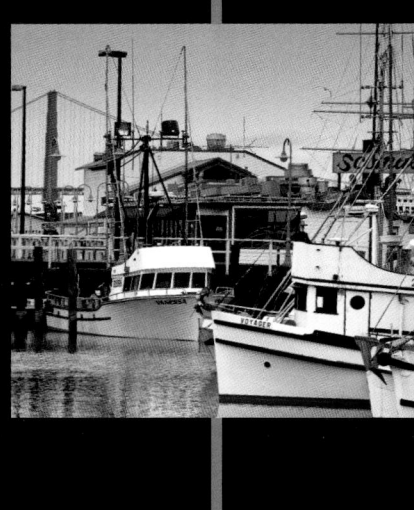

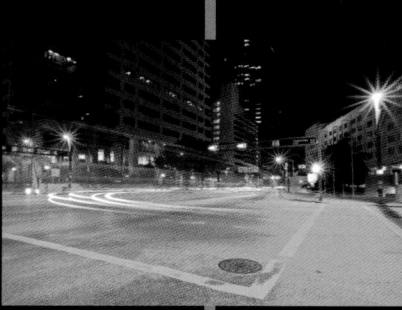

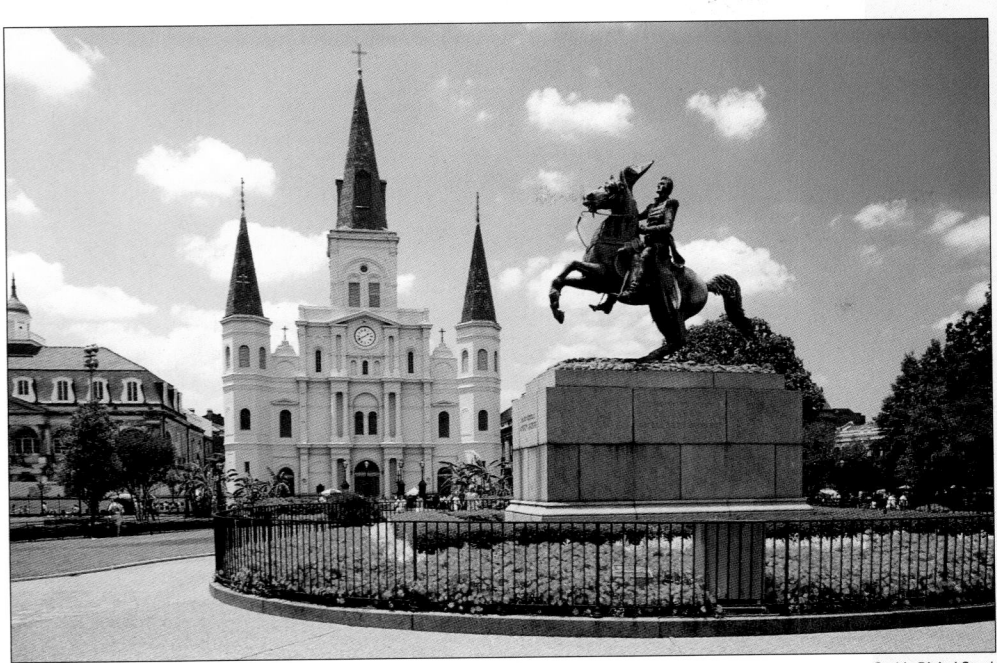

Corbis Digital Stock

Camera Settings

- ✓ **Metering Mode:** Evaluative
- ✓ **Drive Mode:** Single Shot
- ✓ **Shooting Mode:** Aperture Priority
- ✓ **Aperture:** f/11 to f/16
- ✓ **ISO Setting:** 100 to 400
- ✓ **Focus Mode:** Single Shot
- ✓ **Auto-Focus Point:** Single auto-focus point
- ✓ **Focal Length:** 28mm to 50mm (35mm equivalent; see "Understanding focal lengths" in the appendix)
- ✓ **Image Stabilization:** Optional

Churches are sacred places of worship for people of all nationalities, races, and religions. These locations are usually also unique buildings that can provide any photographer with interesting subjects. You can find intriguing churches in your hometown and the places you visit. The old churches in America and Europe (such as the one shown in this image) provide stunning examples of architecture and a window to our past. Armed with the settings in this chapter and your trusty digital SLR, you can photograph any church you come across in your travels. The same techniques apply when you're photographing temples and holy buildings other than churches.

Setting the Camera

When you photograph a church, you want the viewer to easily see all the details, so you need a wide view and a huge depth of field. The suggested focal-length range lets you photograph large churches from a fairly close range (28mm) and small churches from a distance (50mm). If you're photographing a church that's far away, you may need to call in the big guns and use a focal length of 100mm. The suggested f/stop yields an image that has a tremendous depth of field, especially when you use a wide-angle focal length. The ISO range covers bright conditions (ISO 100) or overcast conditions (ISO 400). Image stabilization (while always useful) is not needed unless the shutter speed drops below 1/50 of a second when you use a 50mm focal length or 1/30 of a second when you use the 28mm focal length.

Taking the Picture

When you photograph a church, choose a unique vantage point to create a compelling image that your viewer wants to examine in detail. Use the surrounding terrain and architectural elements to draw your viewer into and guide him through the image. Lighting is also very important when you photograph any building. Avoid photographing any building in the middle of a bright, sunny day because you end up with glaring light and harsh shadows in your photos. If you photograph the church early in the morning or late in the afternoon, you have wonderful golden light and shadows that help define the shape and details of the church.

1. **When you see a church that you want to photograph, enable the settings discussed previously in this chapter.**

2. **Find a unique vantage point from which to photograph the church.**

3. **Zoom in to crop out extraneous landscape.**

4. **Compose the image.**

   Move around until you see the image come to life in your viewfinder. Look for interesting architectural elements (for example, steeples) that you can use as focal points in your image. Try not to place the steeple smack dab in the middle of the image; instead, place it off-center, where it provides more visual interest in the photo, as shown in Figure 80-1. When I photograph buildings, I kneel to include some of the foreground in the picture. Also, make sure you don't have any unsightly objects (such as utility poles, garbage cans, or wires) in your picture, which can detract from your picture's subject.

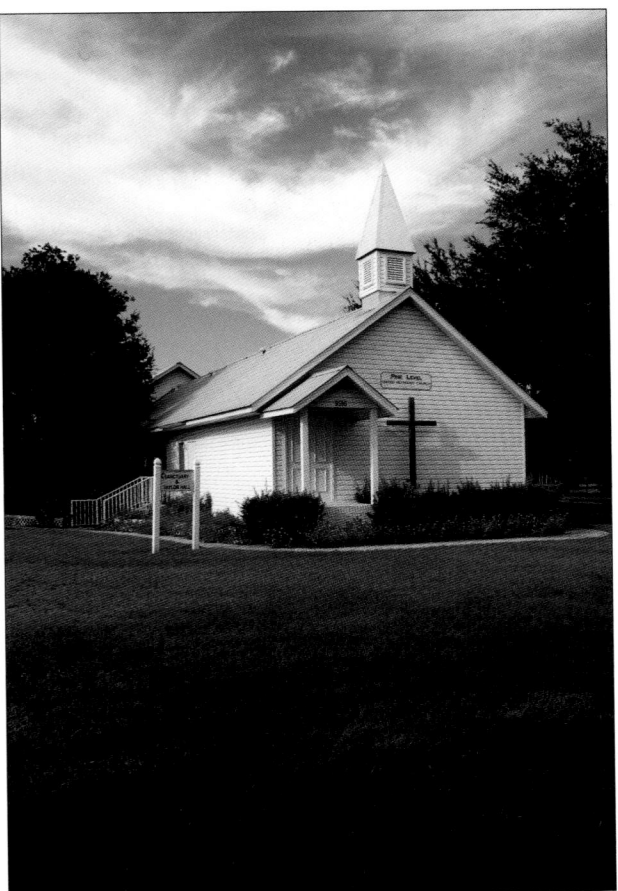

Figure 80-1: Place the steeple to one side to create a more compelling image.

5. **Press the shutter button halfway to achieve focus, and then press the button fully to take the picture.**

   After you take the picture, review it on the LCD monitor to check for any potential problems.

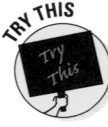

After you photograph the outside of the church, photograph the inside of it, which is often also beautiful (see Figure 80-2). You can use the same settings, but you need to use a slow shutter speed because you have less light inside the church. You can either switch to a slightly higher ISO rating (you get some noise, but you get the image), mount the camera on a tripod (if the church allows you to use a tripod), or place the camera on a solid surface (such as the top of a church pew or the floor).

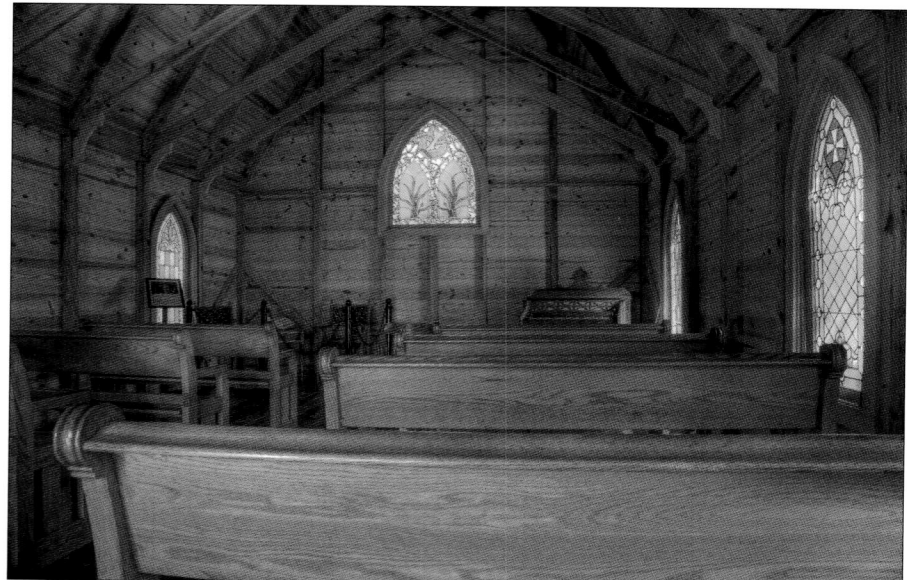

Figure 80-2: Photographing the inside of a church.

Troubleshooting

- **My photograph of the interior of a church is blurry.** Your tripod may not be sturdy enough for your camera. Or, if you have this problem when you take a picture with the camera resting on the floor or a church pew, when you press the shutter button, vibration is transmitted to the camera, which can result in a blurry image. Use your camera auto-timer set to its shortest duration. While the auto-timer counts down, any vibration that was transmitted when you pressed the shutter button dissipates, so you get a blur-free image.

- **The church appears to be leaning in my photo.** You're too close to the church and have to tilt the camera to get it all in the frame. Zoom out, if you can, or back up until you can fit the entire building in the frame without tilting the camera.

- **The doors of the church are recessed, and I can't see any detail in my photo.** This problem happens when the sun is behind the church or not low enough to shine into the doorway. Come back when the sun is low and shining directly at the door.

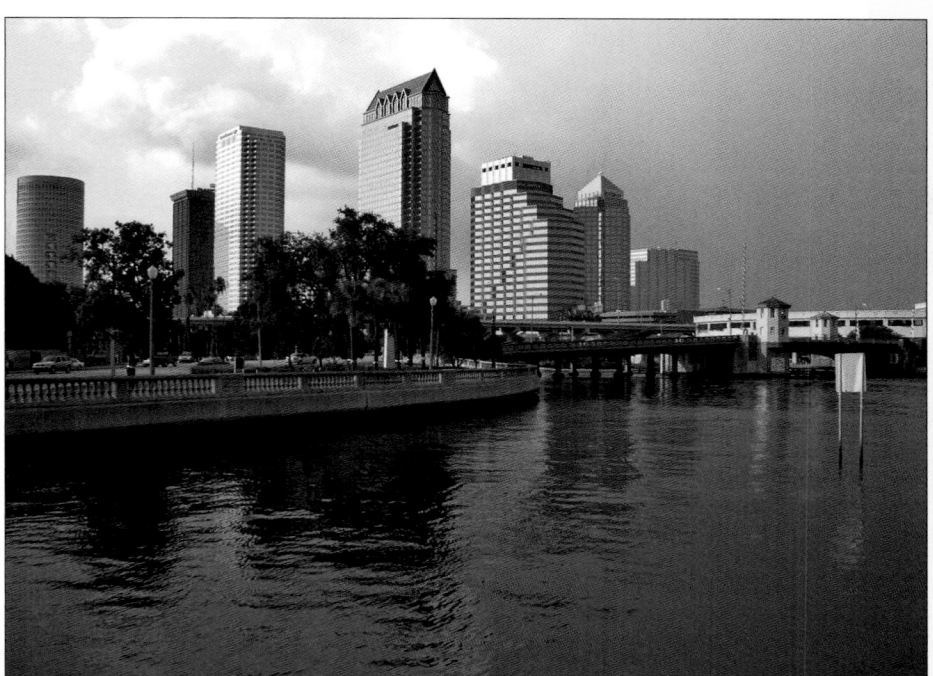

Camera Settings

- **Metering Mode:** Evaluative
- **Drive Mode:** Single Shot
- **Shooting Mode:** Aperture Priority
- **Aperture:** f/8.0 or smaller (larger f/stop number)
- **ISO Setting:** 100 to 400
- **Focus Mode:** Single Shot
- **Auto-Focus Point:** Single auto-focus point
- **Focal Length:** 28mm to 100mm (35mm equivalent; see "Understanding focal lengths" in the appendix)
- **Image Stabilization:** Optional

*E*very city has a unique skyline comprised of landmark buildings that form a shape anyone who has visited the city can readily identify. Big cities such as New York City have skylines that are indelibly etched into the memory even of people who have never been there. If you live in or visit a city that has an interesting skyline, you can capture some wonderful pictures by using the settings in this chapter. This image shows the skyline of Tampa, Florida.

Setting the Camera

When you photograph a skyline, you want to capture every subtle detail. Therefore, use Aperture Priority mode and a fairly small aperture because these settings give you a large depth of field, especially when you use a wide-angle focal length. The suggested focal-length range lets you either capture a wide expanse of the skyline or zoom in to photograph a single landmark building. The suggested ISO range lets you capture photos in bright sunlight or bright overcast conditions. If you photograph a skyline at dusk or during a dark day, you have to increase the ISO setting or use a tripod.

Taking the Picture

Some photographers get in too much of a hurry when they take a picture. When you want to photograph a city skyline, you may be tempted to take a photograph from the first vantage point that shows the entire skyline. But if everyone else photographs the skyline from the same vantage point, people viewing the photo may think it's nice, but they don't spend much time looking at the image. If you slow down and photograph the skyline from several different and perhaps unique vantage points, you end up with a few images that stand out as different from everybody else's.

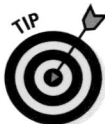

1. **Drive to the area from which you want to photograph the skyline.**

   You can see a lot more and locate interesting points from which to photograph the skyline if you're a passenger, rather than the driver.

2. **Enable the settings discussed previously in this chapter.**

3. **Find an interesting vantage point from which to photograph the skyline, and then press the shutter button halfway to achieve focus.**

4. **Compose the image and, if necessary, zoom in to crop out extraneous details.**

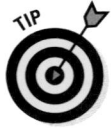

   If you're photographing a specific set of buildings, such as New York's Empire State Building and the surrounding area, rotate the camera 90 degrees so that you can match the format of the image to the shape of the building, like I've done here with the Bank of America building in Tampa, Florida (see Figure 81-1). Notice how the bridge and reflections lead your eye to the building.

5. **To take the picture, fully press the shutter button.**

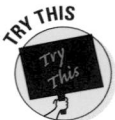

To create a unique photo of a landmark building in a city skyline, travel to a neighborhood that's readily identifiable to people who know the city and explore until you find a unique vantage point. Wait until one of the locals walks into the scene and take the picture (see Figure 81-2).

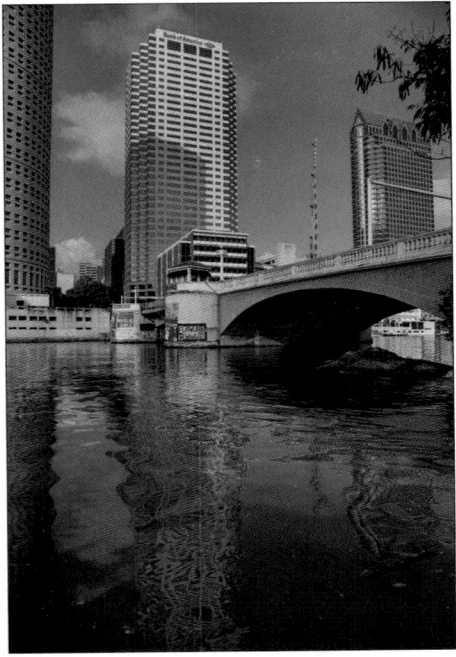

Figure 81-1: Rotate the camera 90 degrees to photograph tall buildings from the skyline.

Troubleshooting

- ✓ **The buildings aren't level in the photo.** When you photograph a city skyline, you may not have a horizon for reference and therefore end up with an image that's off kilter. Take the picture again and pay attention to the vertical lines in the center of the image: Make sure they go straight up and down, and aren't slanted.

- ✓ **The buildings appear distorted in the photograph.** You run into this problem if you photograph the scene with a wide-angle lens from up close. Back up a little bit and take the picture again.

- ✓ **The buildings appear to be falling over in the picture.** This problem happens when you're close to the buildings and tip the camera up to get everything in the frame. Back up until you can get everything in the frame without tilting the camera.

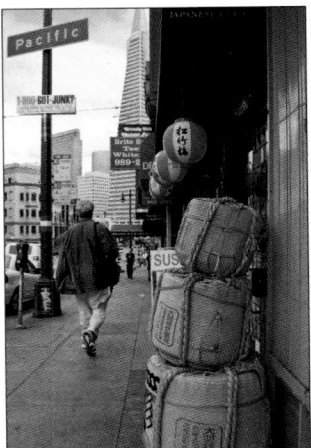

Figure 81-2: Photographing a landmark building from a unique vista.

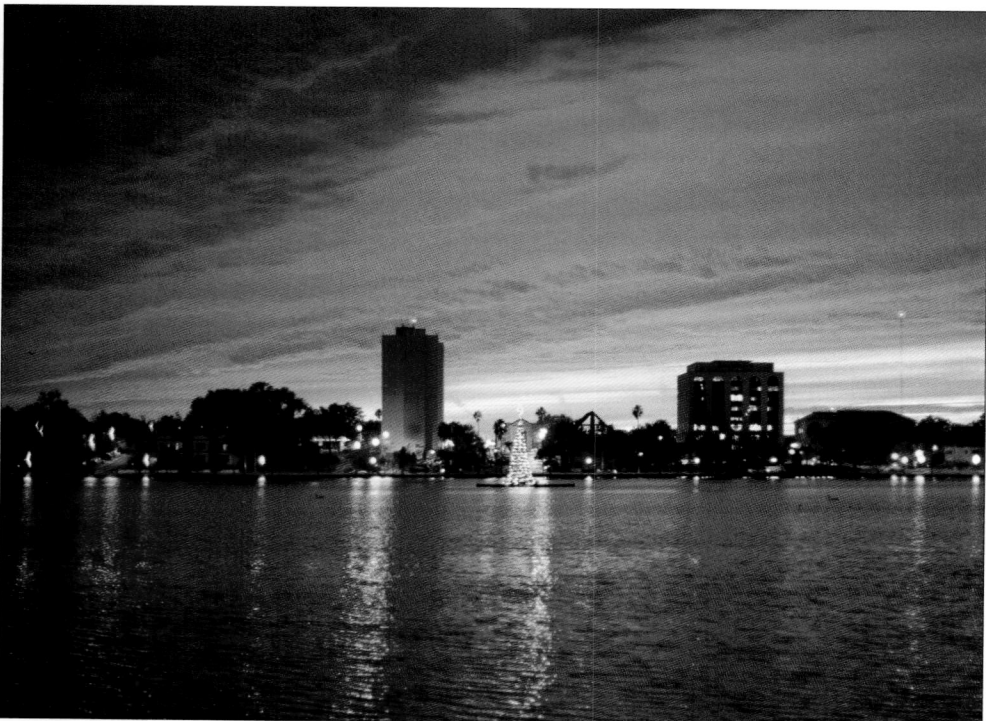

82 City at Dusk

After the sun goes down, you may want to put your camera away and enjoy the night life or spend a quiet, relaxing evening at home. But dusk can be a magical time of day. After the sun sinks below the horizon, building lights wink on one by one and the last hues of the sun dapple clouds with giddy hues of orange and purple. At dusk, you can use the settings in this chapter to get a very interesting picture of your city or a place you're visiting.

Camera Settings

- **Metering Mode:** Evaluative
- **Drive Mode:** Single Shot
- **Shooting Mode:** Aperture Priority
- **Aperture:** f/3.5 or larger (smaller f/stop number)
- **ISO Setting:** 800 to 1000
- **Focus Mode:** Single Shot
- **Auto-Focus Point:** Single auto-focus point
- **Focal Length:** 28mm to 50mm (35mm equivalent; see "Understanding focal lengths" in the appendix)
- **Image Stabilization:** On

Setting the Camera

When you photograph a city at dusk, you use Aperture Priority mode and the largest aperture (the smallest f/stop number) you have available. You get a very shallow depth of field, but it's sufficient when coupled with a focal length of 28mm to 50mm, as long as you focus on the center of interest in the scene. If you're photographing the city from a distance, like in Figure 82-1, this will be easy. If you're in the city, analyze the scene: Determine which object stands out and can draw your viewer into the picture. Use this object as your focal point. The recommended ISO speed is high, which can give you a noisy image, especially if you own an older camera. However, you need to use this high ISO speed to get the shot if you don't use a tripod. Image stabilization can really help if your camera or lens has this feature.

Taking the Picture

The obvious time to photograph a city at dusk is when you're photographing the sunset with some interesting clouds in the sky. Many photographers like to hang around after the sun goes down to see what happens. If you're photographing an interesting cityscape at sunset, you just have to wait until the lights start coming on, and then start snapping some pictures.

1. **Enable the camera settings discussed previously in this chapter.**

2. **When you see an interesting scene, find a suitable vantage point and zoom in, if necessary.**

   If you exceed the recommended focal-length range, the shutter speed may not be fast enough to ensure a blur-free image when you hand-hold the camera.

3. **Position the auto-focus point over the most important part of your scene and press the shutter button halfway to achieve focus.**

4. **Move the camera to create the desired composition.**

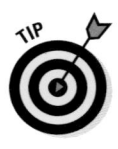

   If you're photographing tall buildings or the sky is interesting, place the horizon line in the lower third of the image. Rotate the camera 90 degrees if you need to get the effect you want.

5. **Take the picture by fully pressing the shutter button.**

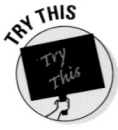

If your town has lakes, photograph the city at dusk with a still lake in the foreground. You get a mirror reflection of the city lights that adds interest to the photo (see Figure 82-1). This is the same town as shown in the image at the beginning of this chapter. Notice the difference in the photos. Figure 82-1 was shot with a smaller aperture and a lower ISO value. This resulted in a slow shutter speed so the camera was mounted on a tripod.

Figure 82-1: Photograph a city at dusk with a lake in the foreground.

Troubleshooting

- **The image is noisy.** The high ISO setting needed for this type of photography can cause this problem — especially if you have a large area of even color, such as dark sky or shadows. Photograph the scene from a different vantage point that doesn't include as many areas of even color.

- **Parts of the image are blurry.** This occurs because of the large aperture you're using. If you're bothered by the blurry parts of the image, move to a different vantage point that doesn't have many objects in the foreground or background.

- **The whole image is blurry.** This problem happens in very low-light conditions when the shutter speed isn't fast enough to get a blur-free image while you hold the camera in your hand. Use a tripod or bump the ISO setting to a higher level. Alternatively, place the camera on a solid surface, such as a park bench or brick wall, and switch the camera auto-timer to its shortest duration. When you press the shutter, the camera counts down and the picture is taken. Any vibration caused by pressing the shutter disappears by the time the picture is taken.

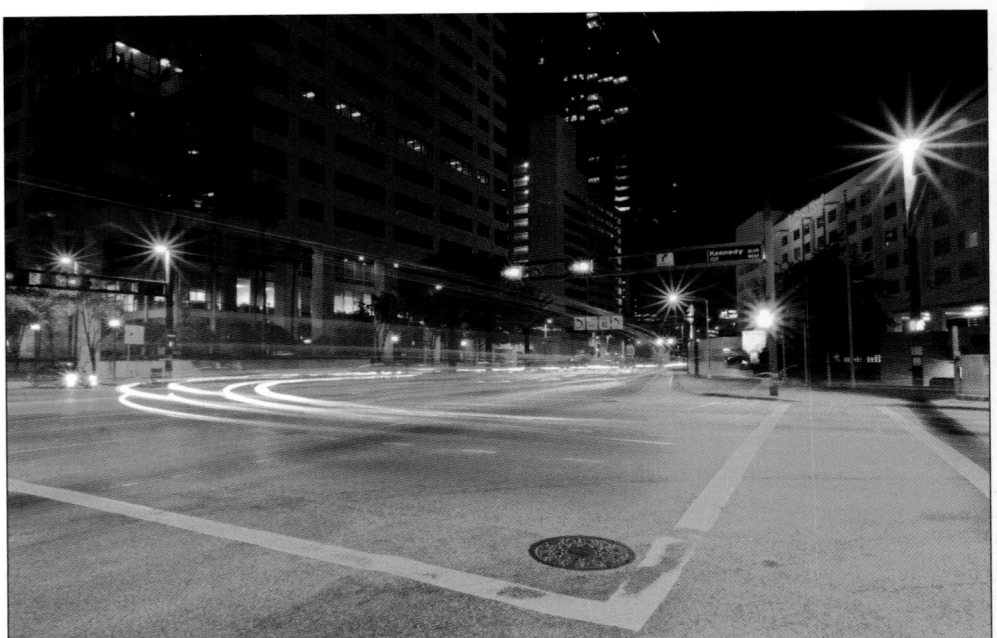

Camera Settings

- **Metering Mode:** Evaluative
- **Shooting Mode:** B (Bulb)
- **Aperture:** f/11 or smaller aperture (larger f/stop number)
- **Drive Mode:** Single Shot
- **ISO Setting:** 100
- **Focus Mode:** Single Shot
- **Auto-Focus Point:** Single auto-focus point
- **Focal Length:** 28mm to 50mm (35mm equivalent; see "Understanding focal lengths" in the appendix)
- **Image Stabilization:** No

If you live in a major city or visit one for a vacation, after the sun goes down you can capture some wonderfully abstract images of light patterns of cars traveling on city streets. With this type of photography, you create a time exposure, which keeps the shutter open as long as the shutter button is pressed. The resulting photo shows fine detail of stationary objects, but cars moving through the scene show up as streaks of light. If people are walking, they appear as ghostly apparitions. If you take a photo with this technique in a crowded city with lots of cars and lots of people milling about, you get a wonderfully abstract photo that captures the "Street Life" of the city. This technique requires two accessories: a tripod and a remote switch to trigger the shutter.

Setting the Camera

To take photographs of abstract headlight patterns, you choose the Bulb shooting mode, which keeps the camera lens open until you release the shutter button. You need a remote device to trigger the shutter. If you keep your finger on the shutter, you may transmit vibrations to the camera, which results in an image that is not tack sharp. You choose a small aperture to limit the amount of light entering the camera and choose your camera's lowest ISO setting, which gives you a properly exposed image in spite of the long exposure. The actual amount of time you leave the lens open depends on the amount of light in the scene. You use the camera histogram (see the appendix) plus a review of the image on the LCD monitor to determine whether the image is properly exposed. You use a wide angle to normal focal length to capture the scene. The actual focal length you use depends on the scene you're photographing. If you have lots of tall buildings in the foreground, choose a focal length that's wide enough to include the buildings on both sides of the street.

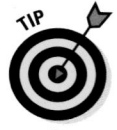

When you photograph a scene with bright lights, a star appears around each light. When you shoot with a smaller aperture (larger f/stop number), the star has more spikes.

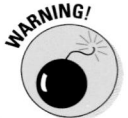

If you use image stabilization when photographing with your camera on a tripod, you may get undesirable results.

Taking the Picture

When you take a photograph of a busy city street at night, your goal is to create a photo that captures the essence of a city at night. The shutter will be open for a long time. Therefore, a tripod is essential.

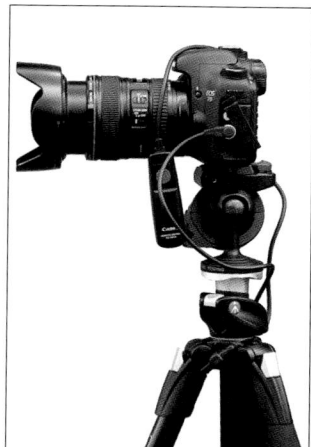

Figure 83-1: Mount the camera on a tripod and attach a remote switch.

1. **Enable the camera settings discussed previously in this chapter.**

2. **Mount your camera on a tripod and attach the remote switch.**

   Figure 83-1 shows a remote switch attached to a Canon digital SLR.

3. **Compose the picture and trigger the remote to engage the shutter button halfway to achieve focus.**

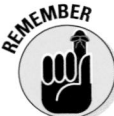

If the most important part of your scene is not under the auto-focus point, you can move the camera using tripod controls until the point is over the part the scene upon which you want to focus. Press the remote switch to trigger the shutter button halfway to achieve focus, and then use the tripod lever to move the camera to the desired position.

4. **When traffic starts moving, press the remote switch to fully open the shutter and hold the shutter open for 10–15 seconds.**

   Keep the shutter open for the maximum duration if there aren't many street or building lights illuminated.

   Use this technique on a winding road. The curved patterns of headlights will add interest to the picture.

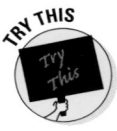

You can do a variation of this technique when you're a passenger in a car. Set the camera mode to B (Bulb) and while holding the camera in your hand, press the shutter button fully when the driver accelerates from a stoplight. Due to the movement of the car and the fact that you're holding the camera by hand, you'll end up with an image that has abstract patterns of car headlights and streetlights. (See Figure 83-2.)

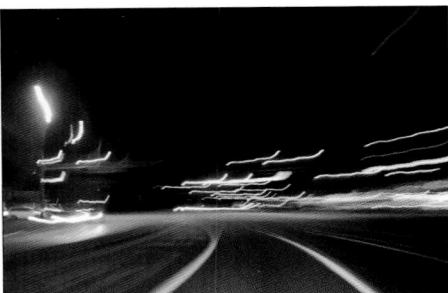

Figure 83-2: Create a picture with abstract patterns of light from the passenger seat.

Troubleshooting

- **There's no detail in the dark areas.** This means the image is underexposed. To properly expose the image, you can do one of the following: Hold the shutter open a few seconds longer, use a larger aperture (smaller f/stop number), or increase the ISO setting.

- **There are no details in the bright areas of the image.** This means the image is overexposed. Take another picture with the shutter open for a shorter duration of time.

- **The image is not level.** Make sure your tripod is perfectly level. Many tripods have a spirit level you can use. If your tripod doesn't have a level, you can purchase an inexpensive dual-axis level that fits in the hot shoe of your camera.

"*I*f the rain comes, they run and hide their heads . . ." You may feel it's prudent to run and hide your head and your camera gear when the rain comes. But if you do, you're missing some wonderful opportunities for great photographs. Rain has a way of making everything fresh, plus you get some wonderful reflections of city lights in wet pavement. As long as you protect yourself and your camera gear, you'll be able to capture some wonderful images when it's raining. Just don't venture outside during an electrical storm; that's just plain foolish. But if you're in your house, listening to the rhythm of the falling rain, pull the window curtains and take a look outside. As long as it's not a deluge, make an impromptu rain cover for your camera out of a shower cap (or plastic baggie) and duct tape. Then grab your raincoat, your protected camera, and use the settings in this chapter to get some great images in stormy weather.

Camera Settings

- **Metering Mode:** Evaluative
- **Drive Mode:** Single Shot
- **Shooting Mode:** Aperture Priority
- **Aperture:** f/8 to f/11
- **ISO Setting:** 400 to 800
- **Focus Mode:** Single shot
- **Auto-Focus Point:** Single auto-focus point
- **Focal Length:** 28mm to 50mm (35mm equivalent; see "Understanding focal lengths" in the appendix)
- **Image Stabilization:** On

Setting the Camera

When you photograph a city, or for that matter, a landscape in the rain (see Chapters 35 and 40), you want the viewer to see all the details, including the distant clouds. Therefore you take this type of photograph using Aperture Priority mode with a medium aperture with an f/stop of 8.0 to 11.0. This gives you an adequate depth of field, which shows detail, especially when you're using a wide-angle focal length (28mm). You get a slightly shallower depth of field when you use the longest recommended focal length of 50mm. The suggested ISO range gives you the latitude you need to take pictures in the low light that accompanies an overcast stormy day. Image stabilization will be a big help as you may end up with a fairly slow shutter speed, even with the higher ISO setting. Image stabilization (if available) is useful because you'll be shooting lots of images with a slow shutter speed.

Taking the Picture

When you take pictures in stormy weather, look for things that appear different than they do on a bright sunny day. If it hasn't rained in a while, the water will bead up at the stoplights due to the oil dropped by the stationary cars. The beads of water and wet pavement combine to create some wonderful reflections of the stoplights and lights from nearby buildings.

1. **Start walking in the rain.**

   When you walk in the rain, it's advisable to stay on the sidewalk as far away from the street as possible. If you're not careful, a rapidly moving taxicab plus a deep puddle can equal one thoroughly drenched photographer.

2. **Enable the settings listed previously in this chapter.**

3. **When you see something that you think would make a great photograph, stop and figure out what vantage point to photograph from.**

   If you've scouted out an area ahead of time, see whether you can find a parking garage that overlooks the scene you want to photograph. You can stay dry and protect your gear if you take your pictures from the second story of a three-story parking garage.

4. **Zoom to the desired focal length.**

   Review what you see in the viewfinder. Don't include anything more than absolutely necessary to create a good image. Also make sure you don't have any distracting elements like garbage cans or dumpsters. That is of course unless they contribute to the story you're telling with the picture.

5. **Compose the picture.**

When you photograph street life in the rain, you have lots of elements you can use to compose your picture. Compose the picture so the street line dividers are diagonal and lead your viewer into the picture. (See Figure 84-1.)

6. **Press the shutter button halfway to achieve focus and take the picture.**

After you take the picture, review the image to make sure the camera properly exposed the image and there are no obvious issues.

7. **Take pictures after the weather clears.**

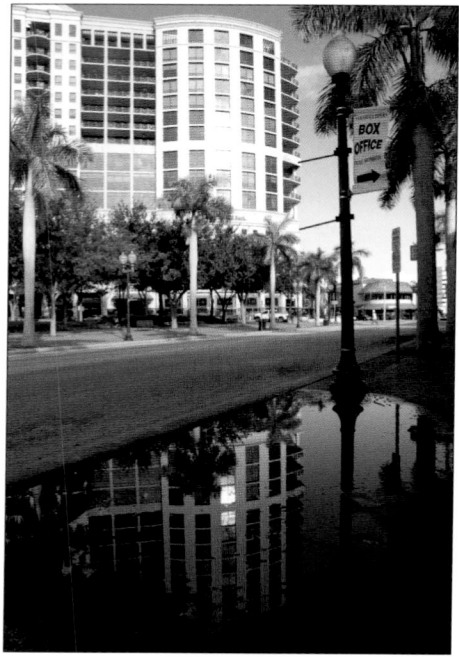

Figure 84-1: Take pictures after the storm clears.

If you live in a place where there are frequent rainstorms in the summer, take lots of pictures in the rain (unless it's an electrical storm). After the storm abates, wait a while and then take pictures of buildings reflected in puddles. (See Figure 84-1.)

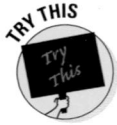

When you're riding in a car with a friend or family member at night during a rainstorm, switch to an ISO setting of 100 and then switch to an aperture of f/8. This gives you a slow shutter speed. Wait until your friend stops at a light, and ask him to switch off the windshield wipers. Wait a few seconds and then take a picture through the rain-streaked windshield to end up with a wonderfully colorful and abstract image. (See Figure 84-2.)

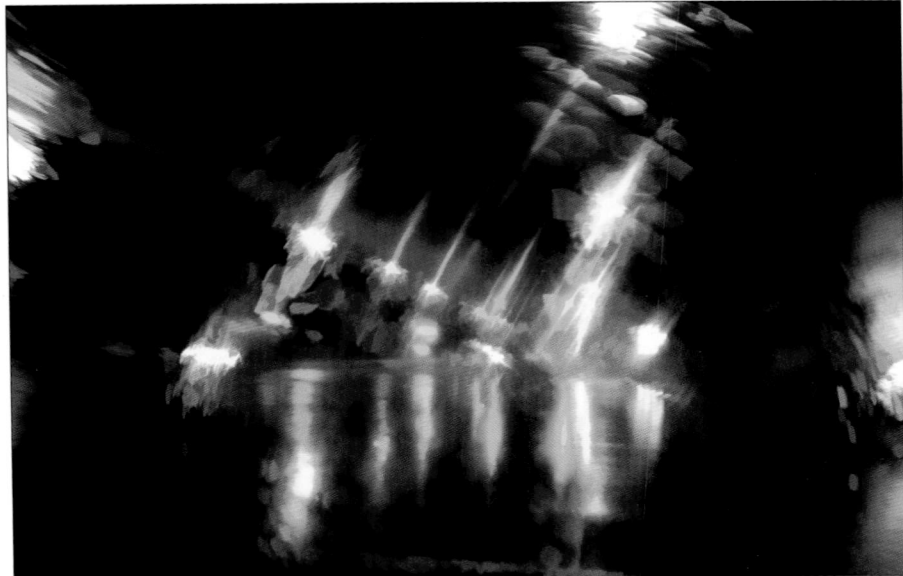

Photo courtesy of Roxanne Evans, www.dougplusrox.com

Figure 84-2: Photograph stormy weather through a rain-streaked windshield.

Troubleshooting

⮑ **My lens fogs over as soon as I go outside.** This happens when you walk from a conditioned space to an extremely humid place. If you're in an air-conditioned car, turn the air conditioner off and crack the windows open a few blocks before you get to the location. This gives the camera time to acclimate to the conditions. If you're leaving an air-conditioned building, place the camera in a baggie and then seal it up. When you walk outside, the condensation happens on the outside of the baggie and not on your expensive camera. After several minutes, poke a hole in the front of the baggie. This is for the camera lens to see the outside world. Use a rubber band to snug the baggie to the lens and keep rain-drops away from the camera.

⮑ **The moving objects in the scene are blurry.** This happens when the ISO setting and aperture combined with low light yield a shutter speed that's too slow to stop moving traffic. This is actually not a detriment. As long as the rest of the image is sharp, the blurred vehicles add drama to an otherwise static image.

⮑ **The image is too bright.** This often happens in dreary conditions. The camera thinks it should be bright outside and errs on the side of caution. If the image you review on your camera LCD monitor doesn't look like the scene in front of you, use exposure compensation to reduce the exposure until what you see on the monitor matches the scene before you.

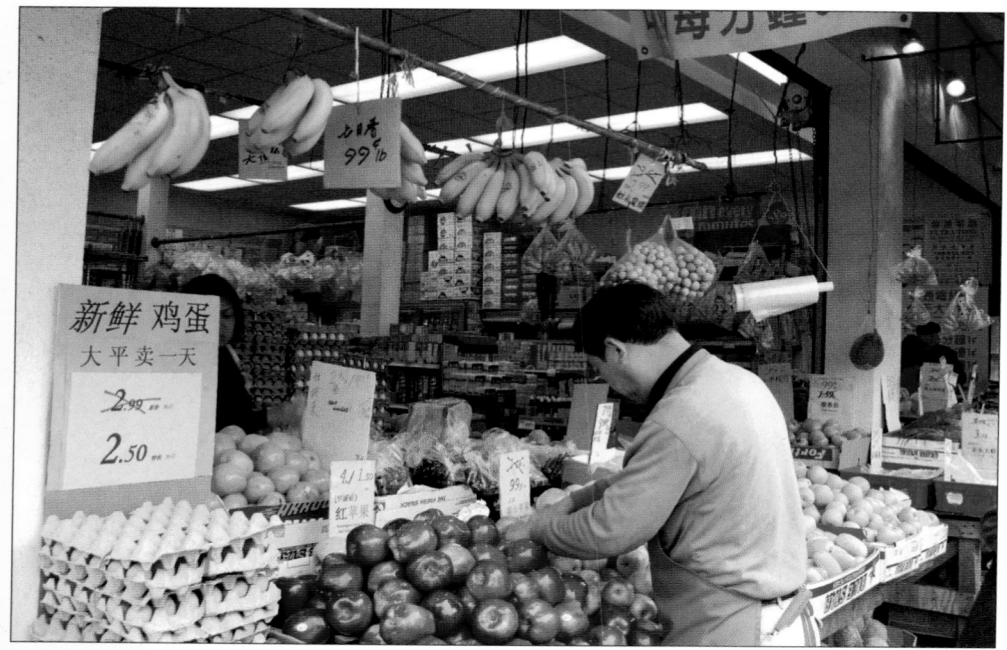

85 Street Life

Whether you live in a sleepy little town or a metropolis that overflows with humanity, what happens on the street tells a lot about the place where you live. Photographers have photographed street life for decades. Some street photographers who shot photos in the journalistic style were revered as photography legends. Henri Cartier-Bresson falls into that category. Some street photographers are clandestine, raising the camera and grabbing a quick shot of something that interests them. This can be risky, as many people don't like to have their photos taken. However, if you photograph from a distance, or just get a shot of streets bustling with humanity without being sneaky, you'll get some great photos.

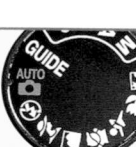

Camera Settings

- **Metering Mode:** Evaluative
- **Drive Mode:** Continuous
- **Shooting Mode:** Aperture Priority
- **Aperture:** f/4.0 to f/8.0
- **ISO Setting:** 100 to 800
- **Focus Mode:** Single Shot
- **Auto-Focus Point:** Single auto-focus point
- **Focal Length:** 100mm or longer (35mm equivalent; see "Understanding focal lengths" in the appendix)
- **Image Stabilization:** On

Setting the Camera

Photographing life on the streets is exciting. If you're on your toes, you can get some great shots. For this type of photography, I suggest using Continuous Drive mode. If you see something exciting happening, such as an impromptu street dance or a clandestine kiss, you can capture a sequence of images. The suggested ISO range lets you take photographs in bright light, or during dusk. You can even take photos on brightly lit streets with the highest suggested ISO setting. When you photograph a street scene, the people are the stars of the photograph; therefore you want to control depth of field, which means you use Aperture Priority mode for this type of photography. The suggested range lets you take a picture of one person (with his permission of course) or a group of people and the surroundings. You use a long focal length to zoom in on the scene without getting too close. It's my experience that people stop what they're doing as soon as they know they're being photographed. Respecting other people's rights while at the same time being a bit clandestine is the best way to take great shots in the street. Image stabilization is useful when you're photographing in dim conditions.

Taking the Picture

Okay. So although it isn't illegal to photograph a street scene, you have to have the right settings and be a bit clandestine. However, if you point a camera at people and take a picture, they may consider it a violation of their rights. If you see an interesting person you want to photograph, ask for permission before you take the photo. Or simply hold your camera in the air and smile. If he smiles back, you have permission to take the picture. Note that you won't be able to use these photographs commercially without getting a model release. But hey, you're not in it for the money; you're in it to have a good time and get some great photos.

1. **Enable the settings discussed previously in this chapter.**

   In addition to getting the camera set up, remove the lens cap and lens hood to be ready for action without fumbling. When you remove the lens hood, you look less like a professional photographer and more like a tourist. Leave your camera bag at home or at the hotel and walk the streets with one lens to look even more like a tourist. A shopping bag completes the façade and also gives you a place to store a baggie or shower cap that you can use to protect your camera if it starts to rain.

2. **Start strolling the streets.**

   As you stroll the streets, be alert to what's happening around you. You never know when a photo opportunity will present itself. In addition to photographing people, sometimes you can get great photos of store windows. You can see the people inside the store and the items they have for sale, plus you get a reflection of the surrounding area in the window. (See Figure 85-1.) When you do photograph a window, photograph it from an oblique angle; otherwise, you'll get your reflection in the window.

3. **When you see something interesting, compose the scene and then press the shutter button halfway to achieve focus.**

Many photographers put the camera up to their eye and move the camera toward the subject they want to photograph. This makes it look less like you're taking someone's picture.

4. **Press the shutter button halfway to achieve focus.**

5. **Take the picture.**

If you use the technique discussed in Step 3, keep moving the camera after you take the photo.

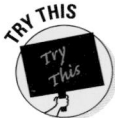

When you're photographing in the streets, watch the people who go by you and then turn around to see what they do or where they go. I was walking in the streets of Sarasota, Florida, and a man passed me with what looked like a waiter's uniform draped over his arm. He smiled and said, "Hi." After he passed, I turned around and grabbed this shot as he walked into a restaurant. (See Figure 85-2.)

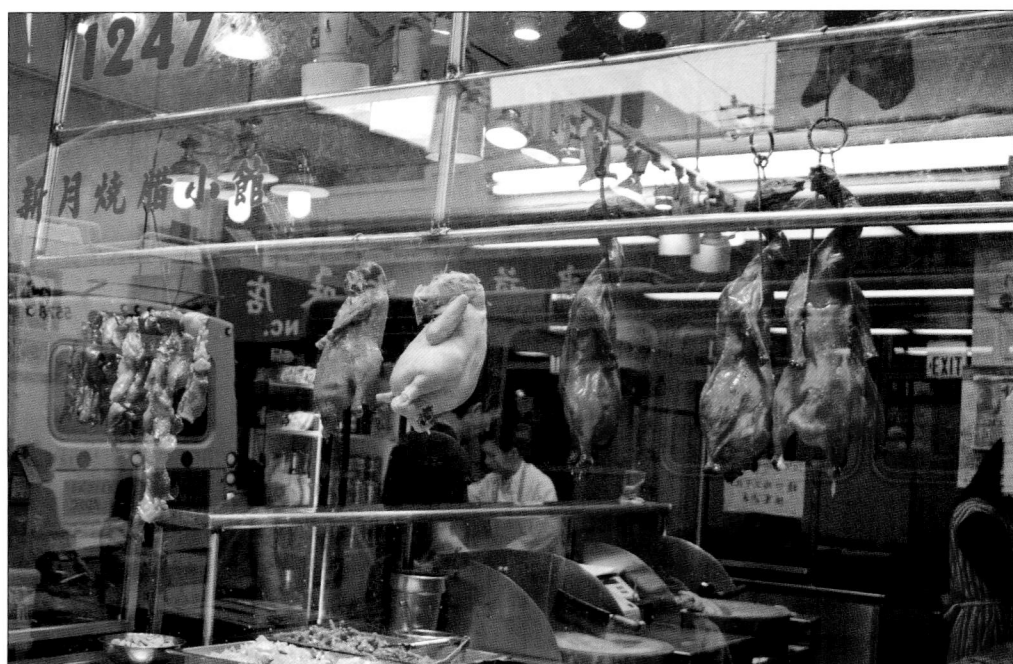

Figure 85-1: Photograph store windows to get a flavor of the area.

Troubleshooting

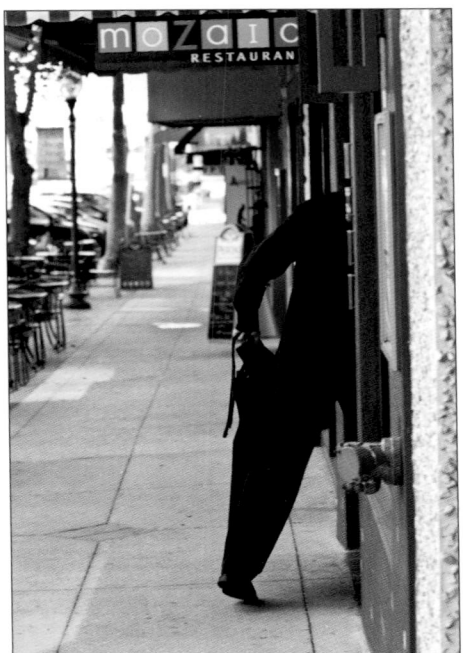

Figure 85-2: Be prepared for any eventuality.

- **The background is in focus, but my subject is not.** This happens when you shoot too quickly. Make sure the auto-focus point is over your subject when you press the shutter button halfway to achieve focus. Most street shots are a once-in-a-lifetime thing. You can't tap the person on the shoulder and ask him to do what he was doing when you weren't taking his photograph.

- **The person saw me photo-graphing him.** Street photography is not for everyone. If you feel uncomfortable photographing people in the street, don't do it. But if you're comfortable doing street photography and someone notices you, just smile and shrug your shoulders. If the person gives you a hard time, say you're sorry and delete the photograph in front of him.

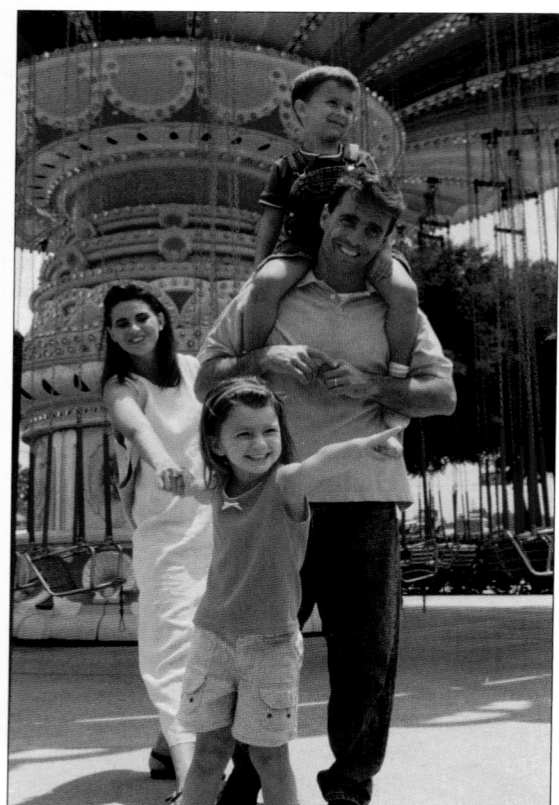

Purestock

A trip to the amusement park is fun for young and old and is an ideal opportunity to take some different pictures of your family than you normally shoot. A trip to the amusement park is all about a good time, and your pictures should reflect that. If you're brave, you may even take your camera on a ride or two. When you photograph the family at an amusement park, you're telling a story. If you want to get a picture of the family with you in it, you have to enable the settings in this chapter and show a friendly volunteer how to operate your camera.

Camera Settings

- **Metering Mode:** Evaluative
- **Drive Mode:** Single Shot
- **Shooting Mode:** Aperture Priority
- **Aperture:** f/5.6 to f/7.1
- **ISO Setting:** 100 to 200
- **Focus Mode:** Single Shot
- **Auto-Focus Point:** Single auto-focus point
- **Focal Length:** 50mm to 100mm (35mm equivalent; see "Understanding focal lengths" in the appendix)
- **Image Stabilization:** On

Setting the Camera

When you photograph the family at an amusement park, you want to show detail of the rides and other objects, but the objects shouldn't be in tack-sharp focus. Your family is the main subject of the photograph; therefore, you shoot in Aperture Priority mode. The suggested aperture range shows some detail in the background, but the detail isn't sharp enough to detract from the overall image. The suggested ISO range is suitable for bright daylight. The focal-length range gives you the option of capturing a lot of the surroundings or zooming in to capture a tight photograph of the family without much of the surroundings. (When you zoom in, it also compresses the distance between your subject and anything in the background.) Image stabilization can definitely be useful because, by the end of the day, you may be tired, so your hands aren't completely steady.

Taking the Picture

When you photograph your family in an amusement park, begin at the beginning and take a picture while you all enter the park. (You have to enlist a volunteer if you want to include yourself in the picture.) Then, capture the day while it unfolds.

1. **Enable the settings discussed previously in this chapter.**

2. **When you find an object, such as a ride, that you want to include in a picture with your family, ask them to move in front of it.**

   Alternatively, let your family go on the ride while you watch from the sidelines. Take a picture of your family when the ride comes past you. Getting a picture of your entire family, plus you, on a ride is tricky. In this instance, I suggest giving your camera to a friend who is at the park with you and have them stand by the sideline. You can show them how to take the picture before you get on the ride with your family to get a photo similar to the one in Figure 86-1.

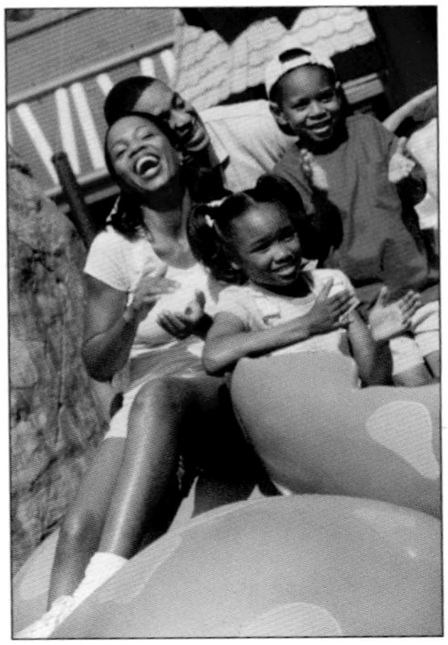

3. **Zoom in.**

   You can capture more of the surrounding area if you back up a bit and zoom out to about 50mm. If you choose a wide focal length, your family is no longer the star of the picture, unless you move close to them. You also introduce distortion when you photograph people at close range by using a wide-angle focal length.

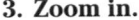

Purestock

Figure 86-1: Photograph your family when they've finished the ride.

4. **Compose the picture.**

   Don't take a police-line-up picture of your family. Get them to do something interesting. You can create an interesting shot if you photograph your family from a low vantage point, which makes them look taller, and any ride behind them looks very tall.

5. **Take the picture by fully pressing the shutter button.**

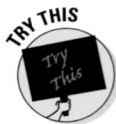

After your family gets off the ride, find a strategic spot near the ride that shows the ride but not much else. You may have to kneel and shoot up at your family to avoid including other people in the shot. Or you can lie down on the ground and shoot up. This is known as a snail's eye view. Have your significant other pick up your children and smile to show that they've conquered the ride successfully.

Troubleshooting

- ✔ **The photo of my family on the ride is blurry.** This problem can happen when you photograph your family from the sidelines, especially if they're on a fast ride. You may want to keep one blurry photo for reference that shows viewers how fast the ride is. To get a blur-free picture, switch to Shutter Priority mode and choose a shutter speed of 1/500 of a second or faster. This setting freezes the ride and your family members' priceless expressions in the photo for posterity.

- ✔ **The background is in focus, but my family isn't.** You have this problem when you don't position the auto-focus point over a family member when you're achieving focus. Take the picture again, but this time, make sure that the auto-focus point is over a family member when you press the shutter button halfway and that the auto-focus point illuminates before you move the camera to compose the shot.

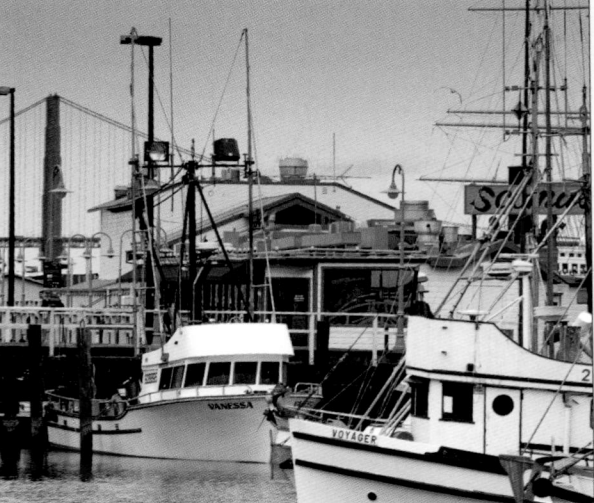

Camera Settings

- **Metering Mode:** Evaluative
- **Drive Mode:** Single Shot
- **Shooting Mode:** Aperture Priority
- **Aperture:** f/4.0 to f/16
- **ISO Setting:** 100 to 800
- **Focus Mode:** Single Shot
- **Auto-Focus Point:** Single auto-focus point
- **Focal Length:** 28mm to 150mm (35mm equivalent; see "Understanding focal lengths" in the appendix)
- **Image Stabilization:** On

Marinas are like trailer camps for boats. Boatniks keep their prized crafts in marinas to protect them from storms. Also, marinas provide a convenient place from which to launch a boat for a day's journey. And photographers can use marinas to photograph boats. But instead of photographing individual boats, you use the elements in the marina to create artistic compositions that include several boats and other elements, such as marine equipment and buildings.

You can capture a wide view of the marina by using a wide-angle focal length or zoom in to a focal length of 100mm or greater to compress the elements, making them look like they're closer to each other than they actually are. This image was photographed with a focal length that's the 35mm equivalent of 225mm at Fisherman's Wharf in San Francisco. The red spire from the Golden Gate Bridge looks much closer than it actually is.

Setting the Camera

When you photograph a marina, you can take many types of pictures. You shoot a marina by using Aperture Priority mode using a wide range of apertures. When you zoom in to photograph details, you want a limited depth of field, so use a large aperture that has an f/stop value of f/4.0. When you zoom out to photograph the entire marina, use a small aperture that has an f/stop value of f/8.0 to f/16, which creates an incredibly large depth of field. The focal-length range lets you both zoom in to photograph details or compress the scene (see the image on the preceding page), or photograph several boats and buildings in the marina. Figure 87-1 shows a marina along the banks of the Anclote River in Tarpon Springs, Florida. The wide-angle focal length and small aperture used for this photo captured detail from the anchor in the foreground to the buildings in the distance, and it's all in focus.

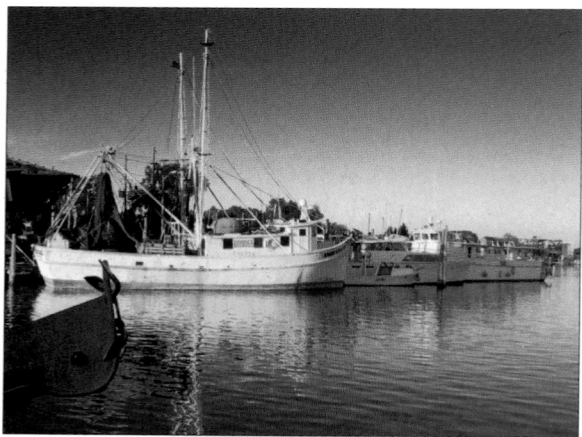

Figure 87-1: Use a wide-angle focal length and small aperture to capture a big view of the marina.

Taking the Picture

When you photograph a marina, photograph it during the early morning or late afternoon, when the sun bathes the boats in golden hues. Overcast skies also provide good light for photographing marinas.

1. **Go to the marina that you want to photograph.**

2. **Enable the settings discussed previously in this chapter.**

3. **Walk around until you find an interesting vantage point.**

   You can find many things in a marina worthy of photographing and many interesting spots from which to photograph the boats. Look for elements that lead your viewer's eye into the picture, such as docks, boardwalks, mooring lines, equipment such as boatlifts, and so on.

4. **After you find a great vantage point, compose the image.**

   Use items such as sailboat masts and structures as compositional elements. The mast of the leftmost tugboat in Figure 87-1 is perfectly aligned on a power point according to the Rule of Thirds. When you find the perfect vantage point, move around a bit until you see the elements come together. Placement of the horizon line is also important. In Figure 87-1 the horizon line is in the lower third of the image to include the mast of the closest boat in the image.

5. **Press the shutter button halfway to achieve focus, and then press the button fully to take the picture.**

   After you take the picture, review it on your camera LCD monitor to make sure it's properly exposed and doesn't have any other problems.

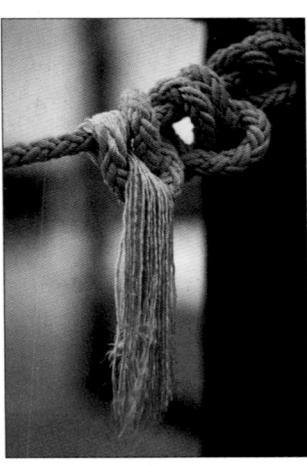

Figure 87-2: Photograph details in the marina.

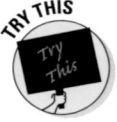

Photograph details in the marina. Elements such as mooring lines become interesting subjects when you zoom in tight. Make sure you have an element to attract your viewer's attention, such as the frayed rope in Figure 87-2, which is perfectly aligned on a power point according to the Rule of Thirds. Photograph details by using a large aperture so that you have a shallow depth of field in your photos.

Troubleshooting

- ✓ **The picture doesn't look interesting.** When an image you take doesn't look interesting, you probably didn't composed the image well. Move around slightly until the elements are arranged in a more interesting manner in the viewfinder. Sometimes, you may simply need to wait for something to enter the frame. A flying seagull reflected in the water can be the difference between a ho-hum image and one that you want to frame and hang on the wall.

- ✓ **I'm photographing a scene that has a lot of elements by using a small aperture, but the foreground elements aren't as clear as I want.** You can have this problem even if you use a short, wide-angle focal length and a small aperture. Try backing up just a bit. Alternatively, place the auto-focus point over an object in the middle of the scene, and then press the shutter button halfway to achieve focus. Focusing on an object in the middle of the scene brings the range of focus closer to the camera.

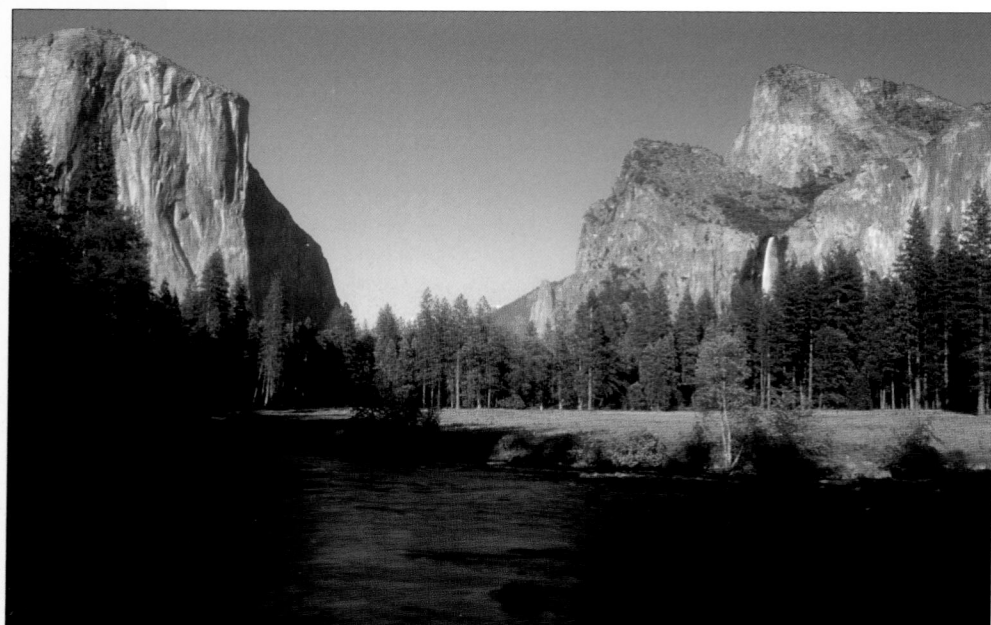

Robert Pierce

*Y*ou can discover a lot of lovely land-scapes, but you probably already know about many others. The iconic Golden Gate Bridge in San Francisco may be one of the most photographed famous places in the world. Yosemite National Park is another place that has been captured by photographers who have widely diverse skill levels. Ansel Adams created some wonderful photographs of Yosemite. Yet year after year, thousands of people visit Yosemite and return home with dull, medio-cre photographs because they don't take the time to slow down and see the beauty in front of them. They rush to take a picture, and then move on. Make it a rule to stay in the moment and drink in the landscape in front of you before you take one or more photographs so that you can get some great shots. Of course, study the work of the masters who have photographed the place you're going to visit. Combine that research with the set-tings in this chapter to get some great photos of famous places like Yosemite (as shown here).

Camera Settings

- ↙ **Metering Mode:** Evaluative
- ↙ **Drive Mode:** Single Shot
- ↙ **Shooting Mode:** Aperture Priority
- ↙ **Aperture:** f/11 to f/16
- ↙ **ISO Setting:** 100 to 400
- ↙ **Focus Mode:** Single Shot
- ↙ **Auto-Focus Point:** Multiple auto-focus points
- ↙ **Focal length:** 28mm to 50mm (35mm equiva-lent; see "Understanding focal lengths" in the appendix)
- ↙ **Image Stabilization:** On

Setting the Camera

When you photograph a famous place, the majority of the people who view your photograph recognize that place. When you photograph a wonderful vista like Yosemite, you want the viewers to see the vast beauty in detail, which means you need a large depth of field, so you shoot this type of photograph by using Aperture Priority mode and a small aperture (a large f/stop number). Multiple auto-focus points enable the camera to find areas of contrast on which it can focus. Just make sure the camera doesn't lock on an object that's in the foreground because even with a small aperture, that will throw your background out of focus. You use the widest focal length (28mm) to capture a grand scene such as Yosemite Valley. You also have the option to zoom to 50mm for a tighter view. Use the lowest ISO setting when you're photographing in bright conditions. The highest ISO setting is suitable for overcast days. You may have to increase the ISO setting to 800 if the light is very dim. When you increase the ISO setting, switch to the smaller aperture to increase the amount of light reaching the sensor and to give you a shutter speed that enables you to hand-hold the camera.

Taking the Picture

If you get a chance to look at pictures of the place you're going to photograph, you can use those pictures as reference material. Find the work of other photographers who have photographed the famous place by Googling that place. Study the images that catch your eye: Observe the vantage point from which the image was taken and note how the photographer composed the image. Keep these images in your mind's eye; add a pinch of your own creativity and the settings in this chapter to get some great pictures.

1. **Visit the famous place you want to photograph.**

2. **Enable the settings listed previously in this chapter.**

3. **Find an interesting vantage point.**

   Walk around the area. While you walk, look at the place you want to photograph. You can discover vantage points you recognize from the work of other photographers, which give you a great place to start. Then, try to find a totally unique vantage point. If you're photographing a place such as San Francisco's Golden Gate Bridge, you have a wide range of possibilities from which to choose (see Figure 88-1).

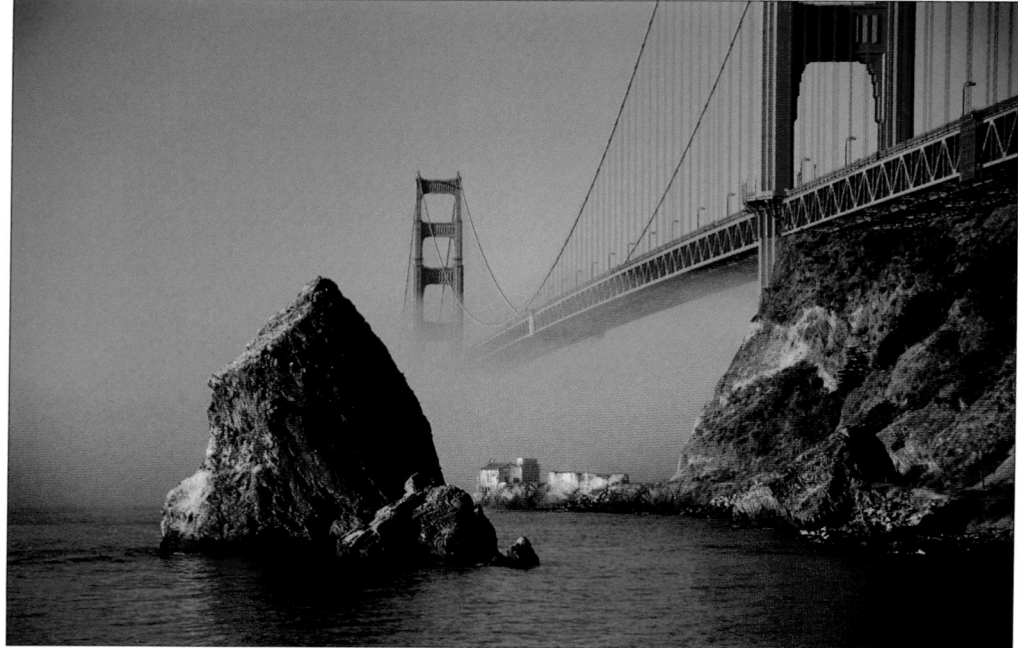

Figure 88-1: Walk around until you find a vantage point you like.

4. **Zoom to the desired focal length.**

   Capture more of the place than you really need to so that when you print your images, you can crop to different sizes in your image-editing program without losing important details. (The standard aspect ratio of a digital SLR is wider than the popular 8-x-10-inch print format.) If you don't leave a little extra room, you lose details when you crop to the desired size.

5. **Compose the picture.**

   You can get a more interesting picture if you don't use a symmetrical composition. For example, if you're photographing Yosemite's Half Dome, place the famous granite monolith on the right side of the image. Your viewers are drawn to Half Dome, and then follow the precipitous drop into the valley, eventually ending up at "Cloud's Rest."

6. **Press the shutter button halfway to achieve focus, and then press the button fully to take the picture.**

   After you take the picture, review the image to make sure that the camera properly exposed the image and the photo has no obvious issues.

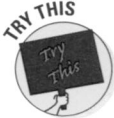

If you see something such as a small animal or tree, move to a position from which you can see the animal or tree, as well as the famous place, in the viewfinder. Zoom in on the animal or tree, and then choose an aperture that has an f/stop of 5.6 or 6.3, which blurs the background slightly but leaves the famous place still recognizable (see Figure 88-2).

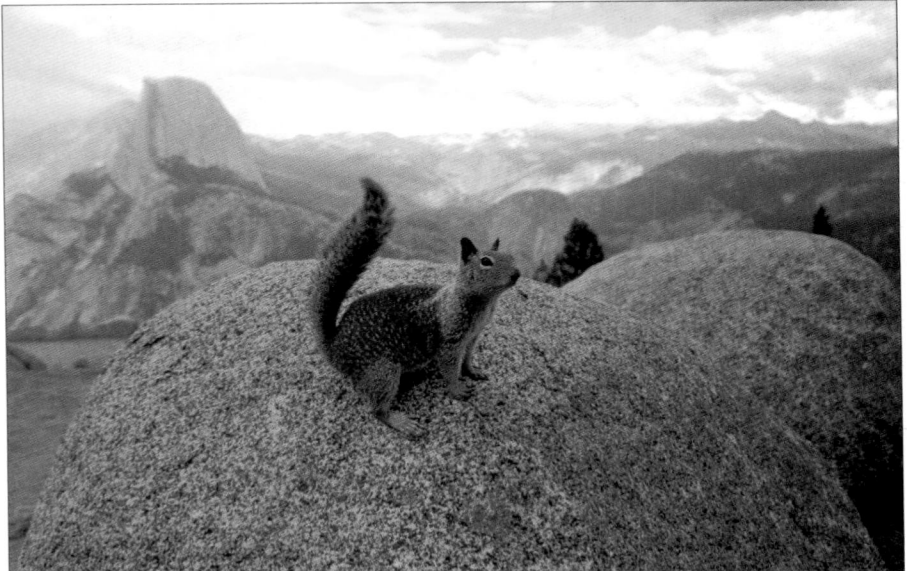

Image State

Figure 88-2: Find details to tell a story about the landmark.

Troubleshooting

- **The image is hazy.** This problem happens when you photograph distant objects in the summer or whenever the air has a lot of humidity. Use a UV filter to remove some of the haze.

- **The image is blurry.** The ISO setting and aperture, combined with a low-light environment, yield a shutter speed that's too slow for you to hand-hold the camera. If your camera or lens has the image stabilization feature, enable it and retake the picture, making sure the shutter speed is at least 1/15 of a second when you use a focal length of 28mm or 1/30 of a second when you use a focal length of 50mm. If you don't have image stabilization, use a slightly larger aperture that, with the suggested ISO, gives you a shutter speed of 1/30 of a second with a 28mm focal length or 1/50 of a second with a 50mm focal length. Alternatively, you can stay with the low ISO setting and mount your camera on a tripod.

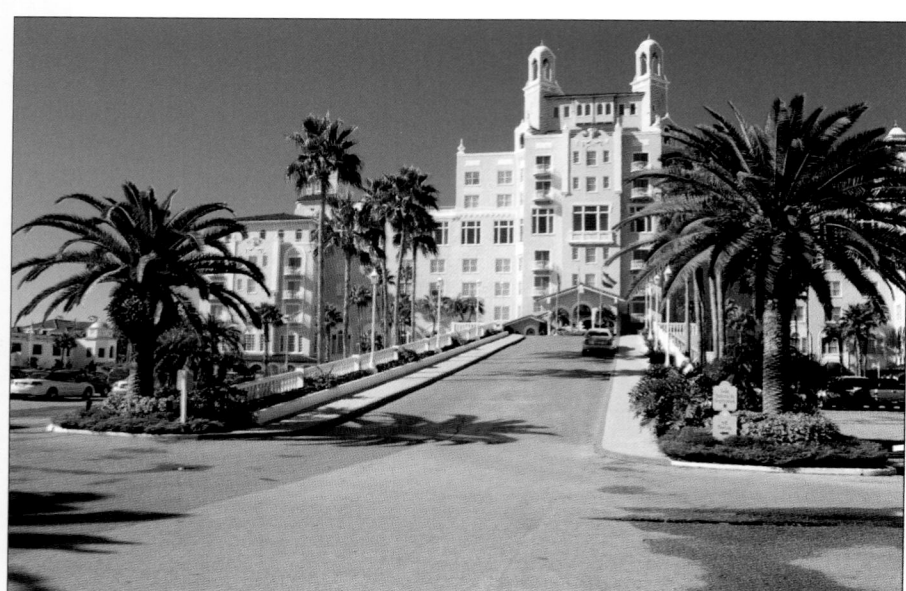

89 Historical Landmarks

Certain places in the world have stood the test of time and qualify as historical landmarks. The definition of an historical landmark can differ, depending on the source. You might think of an old building in your hometown as an historical landmark, but it doesn't appear in the National Register of Historic Places. When you decide to photograph an historical landmark, do your homework. Do an Internet search for the building that you want to photograph. You can find a lot of images captured by photographers, from amateurs to professionals. The research you do can give you an idea about what's already been done. Use the settings in this chapter and your creative juices to capture a unique image of an historical landmark, such as the Don CeSar hotel in St. Petersburg Beach, Florida (shown here).

Camera Settings

- **Metering Mode:** Evaluative
- **Drive Mode:** Single Shot
- **Shooting Mode:** Aperture Priority
- **Aperture:** f/11 to f/16
- **ISO Setting:** 100 to 400 (1000 if you're photographing the building at night)
- **Focus Mode:** Single Shot
- **Auto-Focus Point:** Single auto-focus point
- **Focal Length:** 28mm to 85mm (35mm equivalent; see "Understanding focal lengths" in the appendix)
- **Image Stabilization:** On

Setting the Camera

Photographs of historical landmarks are wonderful images to add to your portfolio. When you photograph a building such as the Don CeSar, you want the viewer to see every subtle detail, so you shoot in Aperture Priority mode and use a small aperture, which gives you a huge depth of field. Use the lowest ISO setting when you photograph the landmark in bright sun and use the highest suggested ISO when you photograph during overcast conditions. If you decide to photograph the building at dusk or at night, bump the ISO to 1000. In spite of the high ISO, you may still need to use a tripod. If you do use a tripod, remember to disable image stabilization, if your camera or lens has this feature. The suggested focal-length range lets you photograph fairly large buildings either at close range or from a distance.

Taking the Picture

With Internet research about the historical landmark fresh in your mind, you're ready to photograph that historical landmark. You can get your best pictures on days when clouds appear on the horizon.

1. **Go to the historical landmark that you want to photograph.**

2. **Enable the settings listed previously in this chapter.**

3. **Walk around the building until you find an interesting vantage point.**

   Your Internet research can help you here as well. While you walk around the building, you probably recognize vantage points from which photographs you've seen of the building have been taken. By all means, take photos from these vantage points. The back of some historical landmarks can also be excellent vantage points (see Figure 89-1).

   Note that this is the same building as in the image at the beginning of this chapter, and it was photographed at the same time. This is the west side of the building. The morning sun reflected off the sand into the building, but there are some nice shadows that do a good job of defining the different sides of the building.

4. **Zoom in to crop to the landmark you're photographing.**

   Leave a bit of breathing space around the building to give viewers an idea of what the surrounding area looks like.

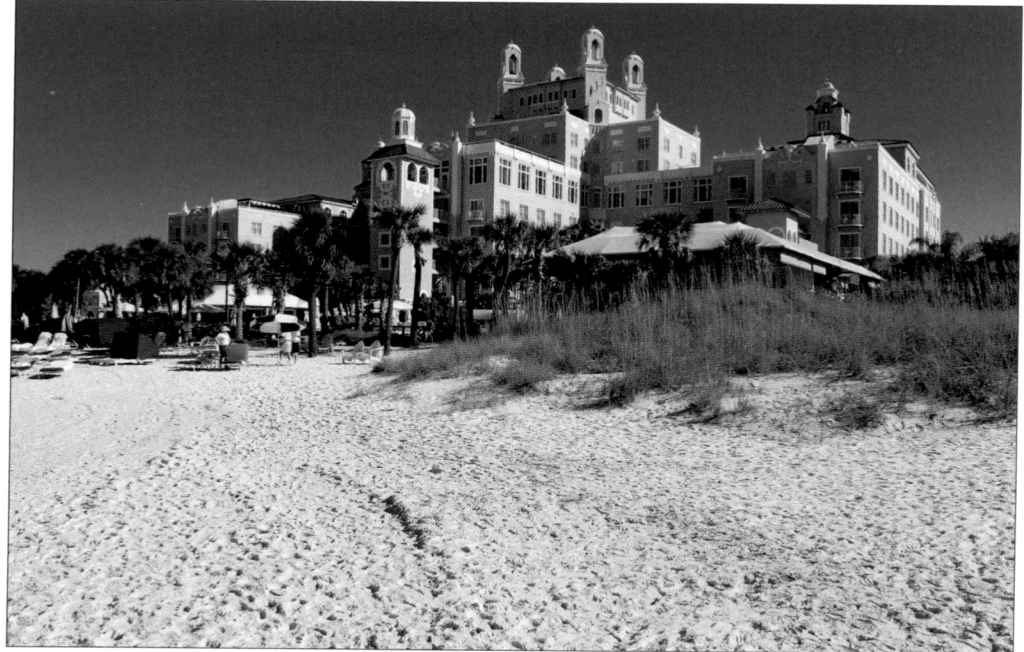

Figure 89-1: Photograph all sides of the building.

5. **Compose the picture.**

   After you find your ideal vantage point, decide whether you want to photograph the landmark from a snail's-eye view or straight on. You may also find some steps across the street from the landmark that you can climb to photograph the building. Or perhaps you can find a higher vantage point, such as a hill or the second or third story of a nearby parking garage, to photograph the building from a bird's-eye view. If you can find a parking garage nearby, spend a couple of dollars to park your car for an hour and photograph the landmark and surrounding area from the top level of the garage.

6. **Press the shutter button halfway to achieve focus, and then press the shutter button fully to take the picture.**

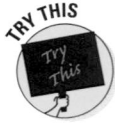

Look for details that you can include to tell a story. For example, if you're photographing the Vietnam War Memorial, look for flowers that friends or relatives have placed on the wall (as shown in Figure 89-2).

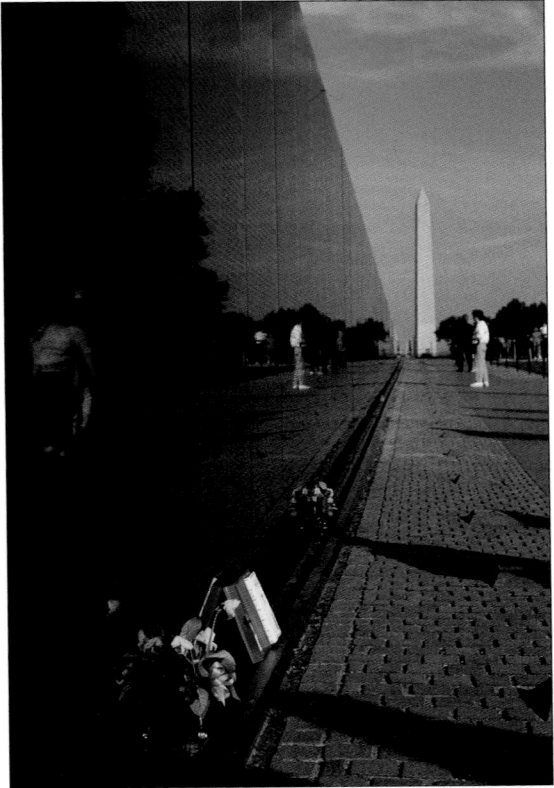

PhotoDisc, Inc./Getty Images

Figure 89-2: Find details to tell a story about the landmark.

Troubleshooting

✔ **The shadows are too harsh in my photo.** This problem happens when you photograph the landmark during the middle of the day. You can get your best photos early in the morning or late in the afternoon. Visit the landmark the following morning before breakfast and take the pictures again.

✔ **The sky is boring (#1).** If you have a pale blue sky that contains no clouds, you can put a polarizing filter on your camera and rotate that filter until the sky becomes a deep shade of blue. The first two images in this chapter were photographed by using a polarizing filter. Despite the fact that the sky is a monotone blue, the photographs are interesting because the sky provides contrast to the pale pink building.

✔ **The sky is boring (#2).** If you photograph the building on an overcast day, you have wonderful light but a monotone sky. If you're on vacation, you have to take what the weather gods have given you, unless you have some flexibility in your schedule and can return on another day. If you live where the landmark is, you can return another day. Professional photographers get great pictures of iconic landmarks by visiting the scene over and over until the lighting and atmospheric conditions are perfect for great photographs.

Part VI
Things

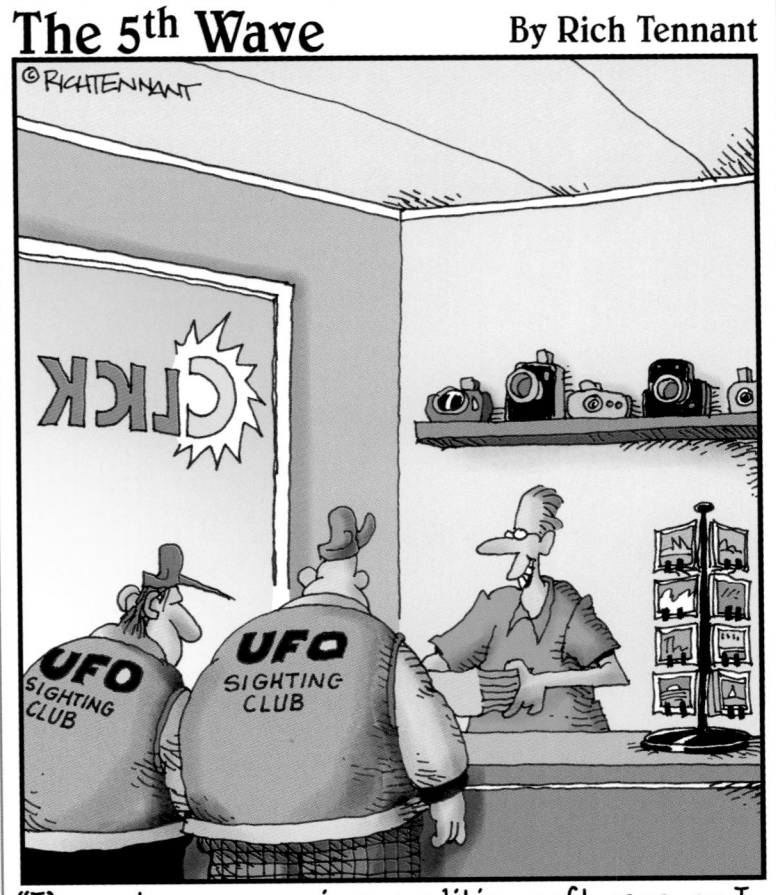

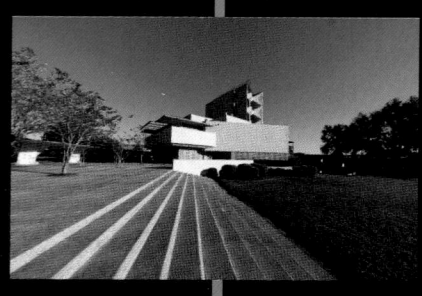

*Y*our camera is a thing that you use to photograph other things. If you enjoy looking at
things like architecturally striking buildings, lighthouses, cars, boats, and flowers, you'll enjoy photographing them as well. With the settings in these
chapter, you can create compelling photographs
of the things around you.

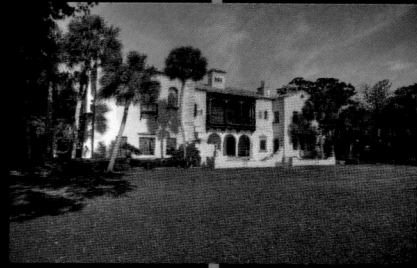

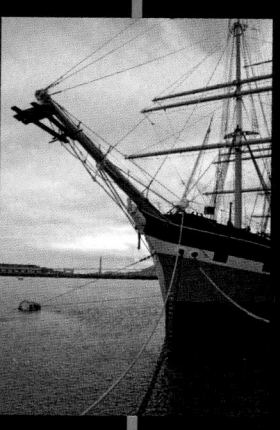

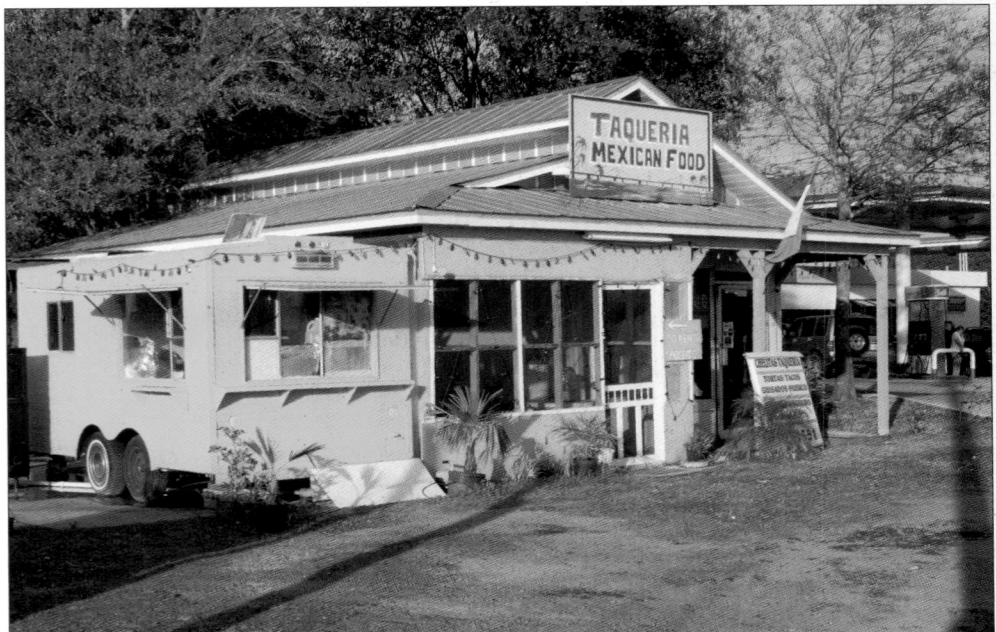

Camera Settings

- **Metering Mode:** Evaluative
- **Drive Mode:** Single Shot
- **Shooting Mode:** Aperture Priority
- **Aperture:** f/11 to f/16
- **ISO Setting:** 100 to 400
- **Focus Mode:** Single Shot
- **Auto-Focus Point:** Single auto-focus point
- **Focal Length:** 28mm to 85mm (35mm equivalent; see "Understanding focal lengths" in the appendix)
- **Image Stabilization:** On

Interesting buildings are everywhere. The town in which you live may have modern buildings that are prime subjects for photography. Old buildings and buildings in ghost towns are also great subjects for photographers. When you photograph an interesting building, you're photographing something that's probably been photographed hundreds or maybe thousands of times before. To create an image that gets someone's attention, you have to put a different spin on the photograph, so take your picture from an unusual vantage point or get creative when you compose the photograph. Sometimes, you can even find unique buildings, such as a small restaurant, that make wonderful additions to your portfolio.

Setting the Camera

Unique buildings are wonderful subjects for photographers. When you photograph a building, you want a large depth of field to show every detail, so use Aperture Priority mode and a small aperture. The ISO setting enables you to take pictures of buildings in either bright sunlight (ISO 100) or overcast conditions (ISO 400). If you're photographing buildings at night, you need to use an ISO setting of at least 800 and the largest suggested aperture of f/11. In a pinch, you can stop down to f/9.0 and still get good results at night. You may also have to mount your camera on a tripod. If you do mount your camera on a tripod, and if the camera or lens you're using is equipped with image stabilization, disable it. The suggested focal-length range lets you photograph large buildings at fairly close range or small buildings from a distance. The long focal length also gives you the option to zoom in tight and photograph details of buildings, such as entryways (see Figure 90-1).

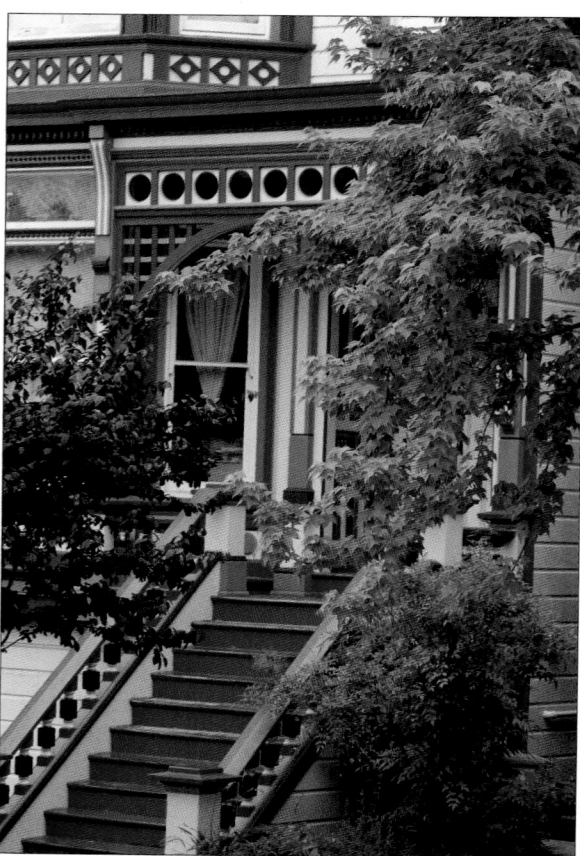

Figure 90-1: Zoom in to photograph entryways.

Taking the Picture

If you're photographing a building in your town that's been photographed before, visualize any images you've seen in your mind's eye before you photograph the scene. While you visualize the photograph and then look at the building, ask yourself what you can do to create a different type of image. Then pick up your camera and start shooting.

1. **Find a building that you want to photograph.**

2. **Enable the settings listed previously in this chapter.**

3. **Find a unique vantage point from which to photograph the building.**

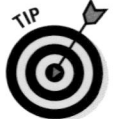

   If the building has been photographed many times by many photographers, choose a vantage point that's different. Viewers recognize the building but look at your image longer because of the unique perspective. For example, if you're photographing a museum that has steps leading up to the first floor, use a wide-angle focal length and photograph the scene with the camera lying flat on the sidewalk that leads up to the stairs, letting the stairs fill the bottom of the frame. You may not be able to photograph the entire building from this viewpoint, but unless the building is extremely tall, your viewers can readily identify the building in the photo, but the photo looks different than those taken by other photographers.

4. **Zoom in to crop to the building you're photographing.**

   Leave a bit of room around the building to give viewers a sense of location. For example, if you're photographing the Washington Monument, you want to include the reflecting pool that leads up to the famous structure.

5. **Compose the picture.**

   After you choose your vantage point, move to slightly different locations and look at the building through your viewfinder. Many photographers choose a symmetrical composition for a building. However, some buildings are not symmetrical and have objects such as chimneys on one side of the building. Align these objects on power points according to the Rule of Thirds (see the appendix).

6. **Press the shutter button halfway to achieve focus, and then fully press the button to take the picture.**

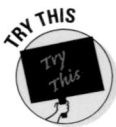

Photograph a well-known building from a unique vantage point by using a super wide-angle lens. Use elements such as sidewalks to draw your viewers into the image. Figure 90-2 was photographed with a 20mm lens. The sidewalk fills the bottom of the frame and draws the viewer's attention to the marquee of the old theater.

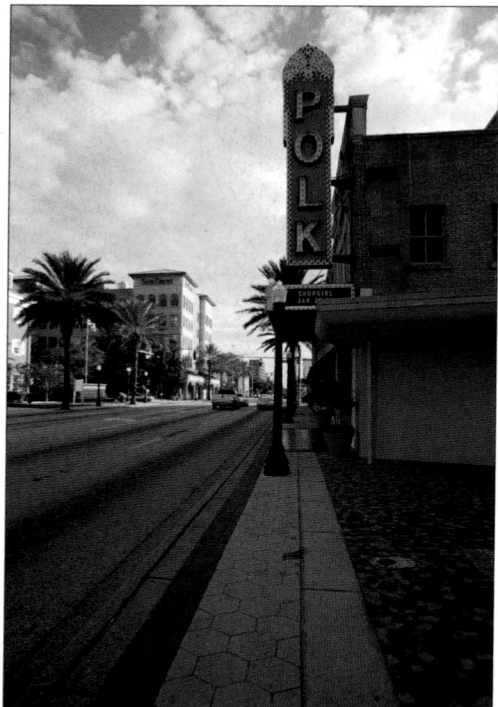

Figure 90-2: Use elements to compose your image.

Troubleshooting

- **The building looks like it's falling over.** This problem happens when you photograph a structure and have to tilt the camera to fit the entire building in the viewfinder. Back up until you see the entire building in the viewfinder without having to tilt the camera.

- **The corners of the image are darker than the rest of the image.** Some lenses experience light falloff (known as *vignetting*) in the corners of images when you use the smallest or largest aperture at either end of the lens's focal-length range. Choose an aperture that's one or two steps less than the smallest aperture available for the lens.

- **The light is harsh.** The best time to photograph anything outdoors is early in the morning or late in the afternoon. If you photograph a building when the sun is shining directly overhead, you get lots of harsh shadows. In fact, due to the huge dynamic range, you may not be able to see any details in setback entryways. If you photograph the building when the sun is shining on it (in the late afternoon or early morning depending on the building's location), the building receives even lighting that fills in the shadow areas. A bonus is that the light has a wonderful golden hue.

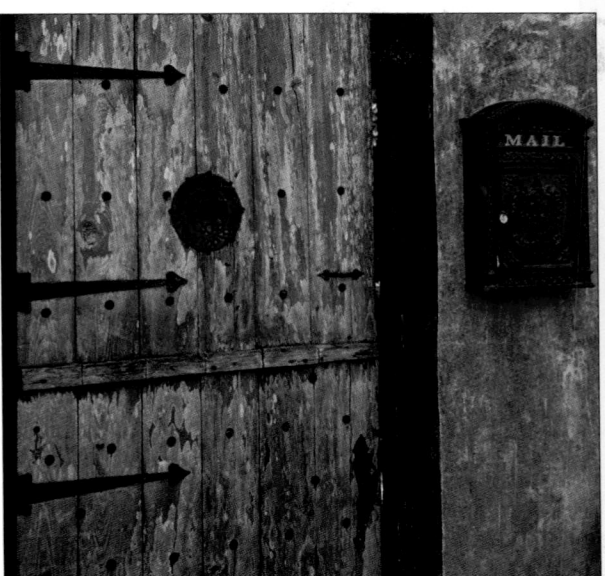

Camera Settings

- **Metering Mode:** Evaluative
- **Drive Mode:** Single Shot
- **Shooting Mode:** Aperture Priority
- **Aperture:** f/4.0 to f/5.6
- **ISO Setting:** The lowest ISO setting that will enable you to hand-hold the camera using a focal length of 85mm to 100mm
- **Focus Mode:** Single Shot
- **Auto-Focus Point:** Single auto-focus point
- **Focal Length:** 50mm (35mm equivalent; see "Understanding focal lengths" in the appendix)
- **Image Stabilization:** Recommended, unless you're using a tripod

Art takes many forms, and form follows function; at least it should when it comes to useful items like tools and the buildings in which we live and work. When you take lots of pictures, you develop an eye for beautiful and unusual things. When you're out and about with your camera and your goal is to photograph the world around you, you can create some wonderful photos of architectural details of items like doors, ornate mailboxes, and so on.

When your goal is to photograph details, you have to cut to the chase and notice the smallest details. Like the lens on your camera, you have to train your eye to zoom in on small parts of the scene and notice interesting details. Then it's a matter of composing the scene to create a compelling picture of an interesting architectural object. When you compose the image, look at everything in the frame: You don't want extraneous objects in the frame that will detract from the subject you're photographing. If you see anything that will divert your viewer's attention, move to a slightly different vantage point or zoom in. You can also use elements in the image to compose your image. The photo shown here, for example, uses the diagonal hinges to draw your eye into the image. The vertical lines of the door keep the viewer in the picture longer.

Setting the Camera

This type of photography stretches your creative envelope. You're looking for interesting details that you'll photograph with a telephoto or macro lens. You use Aperture Priority shooting mode with a large aperture (small f/stop number) for a shallow depth of field. This draws your viewer's attention to your subject.

The medium telephoto focal length results in an image that faithfully depicts the subject you photographed without distortion. Use image stabilization if your camera or lens has this feature. (If your camera doesn't have image stabilization and you don't want to use a high ISO setting, you can stabilize the camera with a tripod.) When you photograph details, especially small ones, the slightest bit of operator movement will cause the image to look blurry.

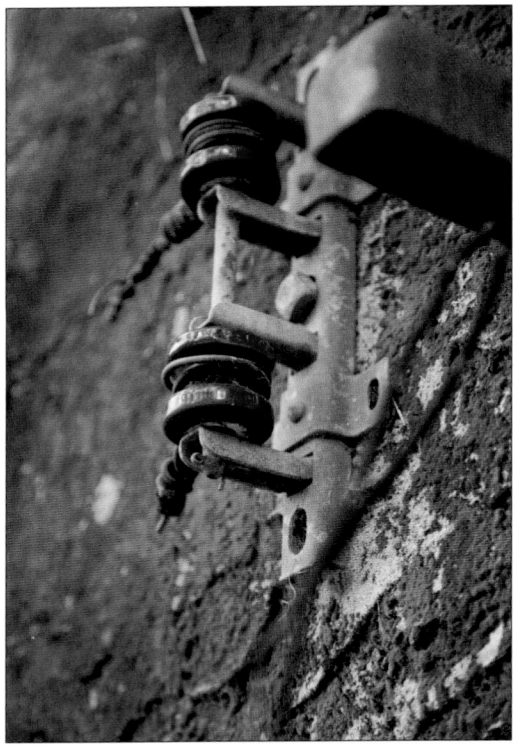
Figure 91-1: Photographing history.

 If lighting conditions force you to use an ISO setting higher than 800 (or lower if you have an older camera), the resulting image may have unacceptable amounts of digital noise in the darker areas of the photo.

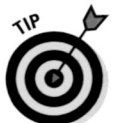 If you're visiting a ghost town or some historical place, look for details like old electric components (see Figure 91-1), locks, or doorknobs. Objects from bygone eras are interesting subjects for photography.

Taking the Picture

When you want to create fine-art photographs of architectural details, you need to have an open mind, a bit of the creative muse, and an eagle eye. If you're good at multitasking, you can incorporate this type of photography with other types of photography. However, until you get the knack of photographing details, it's a good idea to devote some time to mastering this technique.

1. **Enable the camera settings previously discussed in this chapter.**

2. **Zoom in on the object you want to photograph.**

3. **Position the auto-focus point over the object and then press the shutter button halfway to achieve focus.**

4. **Compose the scene in the viewfinder and then press the shutter button fully to take the picture.**

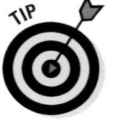

The manner in which you compose the image depends on the object you're photographing. It's a good idea *not* to put the object, which of course is the center of interest, in the middle of the photograph. Frame the photograph so that the subject appears to the left or right of center.

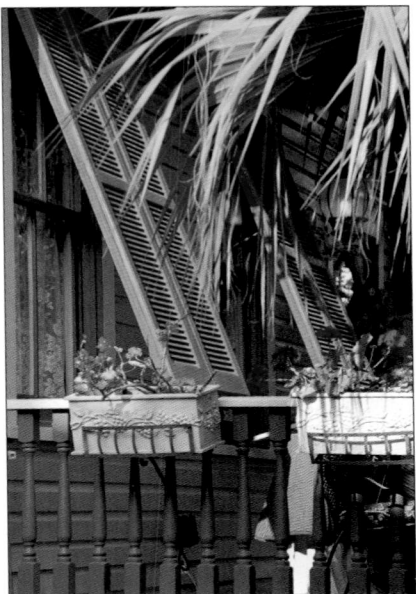

Figure 91-2: Use elements to compose your image.

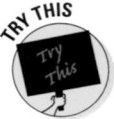

Look for a scene with strong elements that you can use to compose your image. For example, the shutters in Figure 91-2 are strong diagonal elements that draw the viewer's attention to the horizontal slats.

Troubleshooting

- ✔ **The image is too busy.** You're trying to include too much in the image. Zoom in a little tighter on your subject.

- ✔ **There's too much detail in the image.** This problem occurs when there are too many objects in the background. Choose the largest aperture (smallest f/stop number) to achieve an even smaller depth of field. Then make sure your camera achieves focus on your center of interest and retake the picture. The alternative is to move to a slightly different position and photograph the subject again.

- ✔ **The object is blurry.** Take the picture again and make sure you place the auto-focus point over the center of interest in your scene when you press the shutter button halfway to achieve focus. Don't compose the scene until the focus light in your viewfinder appears.

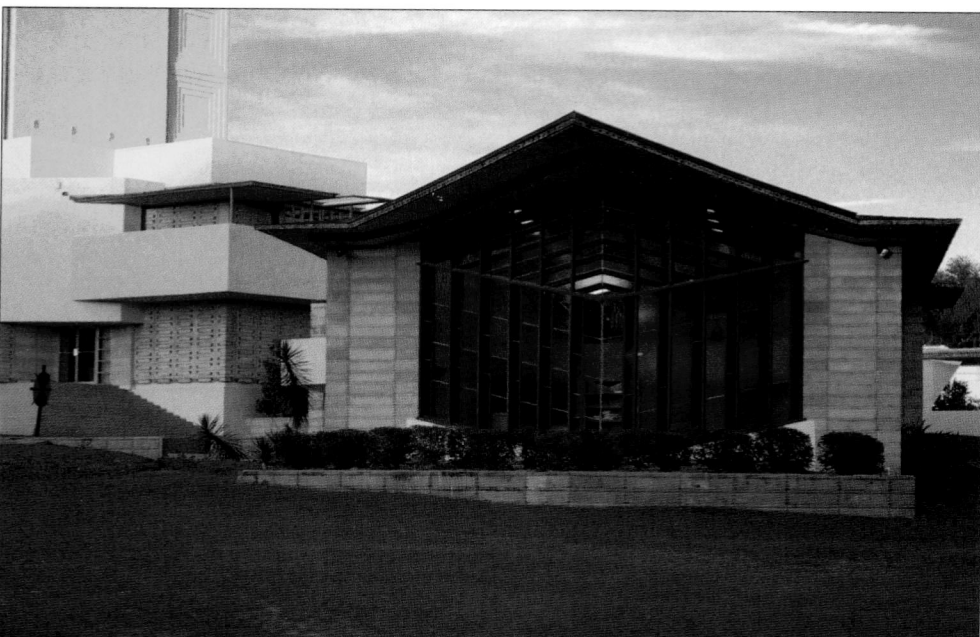

1f you live in or visit a town with famous buildings, you have a great subject for one or more photographs. Buildings like the William Danforth Chapel designed by Frank Lloyd Wright (shown here) are scattered all over the country.

When you find one you'd like to photograph, use the settings in this chapter and apply your own creative touch to create an interesting photograph.

Camera Settings

- **Metering Mode:** Evaluative
- **Drive Mode:** Single Shot
- **Shooting Mode:** Aperture Priority
- **Aperture:** f/7.1 to f/11
- **ISO Setting:** 100 to 400
- **Focus Mode:** Single Shot
- **Auto-Focus Point:** Single auto-focus point
- **Focal Length:** 28mm to 100mm (35mm equivalent; see "Understanding focal lengths" in the appendix)
- **Image Stabilization:** Optional

Setting the Camera

When you photograph a famous building, the settings are similar to those you'd use to photograph any architecture. Buildings don't move, so you use Aperture Priority mode to control depth of field. The suggested aperture range gives you a decent depth of field for the building you're photographing. The focal-length range gives you the option of photographing a large building from nearby, or zooming in on a distant building.

Taking the Picture

When you photograph a famous building, you're photographing a building that has been photographed a thousand times or more. You've probably seen many photos of the building you're about to photograph, and you obviously have some favorite ones. Keep your favorite photos of what you're about to photograph in the back of your mind, but be prepared to add your own touch to create a photo that's unique:

1. **Travel to the building you want to photograph and enable the settings discussed in this chapter.**

2. **Examine the building from different angles and find an interesting vantage point from which to photograph the building.**

3. **Press the shutter button halfway and compose the image.**

   If necessary, zoom in to crop out surrounding details.

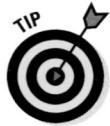

   If you're photographing a building that's taller than it is long, flip the camera 90 degrees (Portrait mode) and take the picture. (See Figure 92-1.) Don't place the building smack dab in the middle of the picture. Move it to a power point according to the Rule of Thirds.

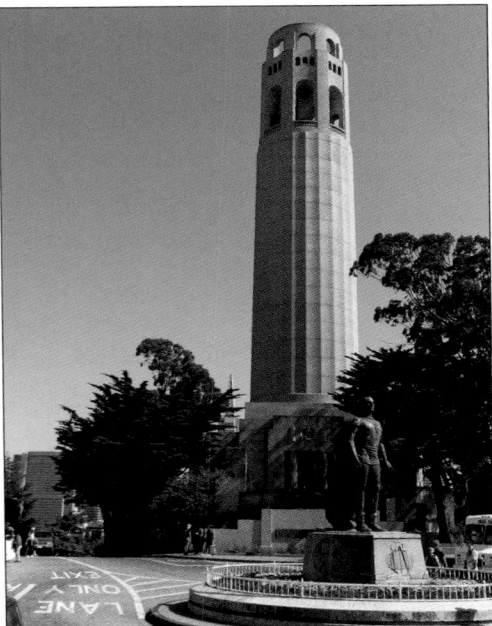

Figure 92-1: Use an element to draw your viewers into the image.

Take a good look through the viewfinder before you take the picture. If you see anything in the background like power lines, move to a slightly different vantage point so they're not visible in the image. If you see anything like leaves or debris that detracts from the image, do a little housekeeping before taking the picture.

4. **Take the picture.**

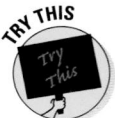

Find an architectural element that you can use to lead your viewer into the picture. Figure 92-2 shows Frank Lloyd Wright's Annie Pfieffer Chapel photographed with a wide-angle lens. The nearby steps lead the viewer into the picture.

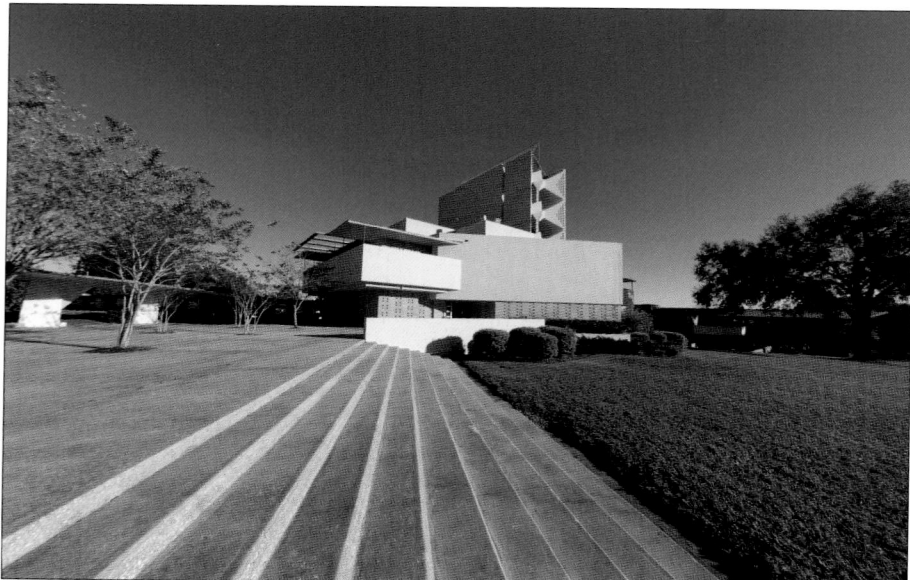

Figure 92-2: Photograph a tall building in portrait mode.

Troubleshooting

✔ **The building looks like it's falling over.** This happens when you're too close to the building and you tilt the camera up to get everything in the frame. The solution is to back up until you can hold the camera level to the ground and see the whole building in the viewfinder.

✔ **The resulting picture isn't interesting.** This happens when you photograph the building from the same vantage point as everybody else. You've seen those images before, and they look clichéd. Take a minute or two and walk around the building until you find an interesting vantage point.

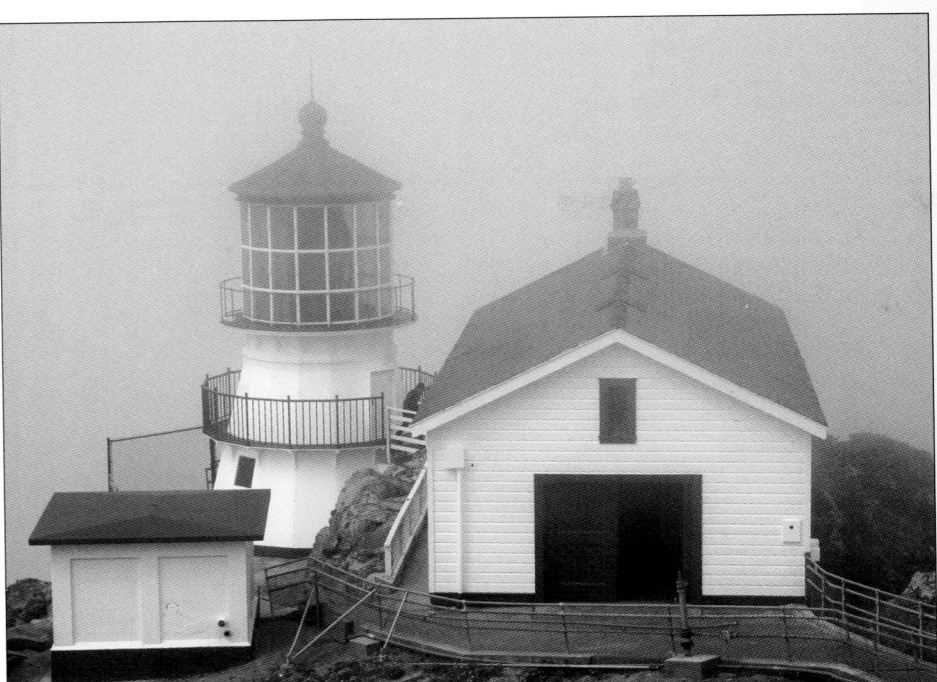

Camera Settings

- **Metering Mode:** Evaluative
- **Drive Mode:** Single Shot
- **Shooting Mode:** Aperture Priority
- **Aperture:** f/11 to f/22
- **ISO Setting:** 100 to 800
- **Focus Mode:** Single Shot
- **Auto-Focus Point:** Single auto-focus point
- **Focal Length:** 24mm to 35mm (35mm equivalent; see "Understanding focal lengths" in the appendix)
- **Image Stabilization:** On

*L*ighthouses are lonely sentinels that keep ships out of harm's way. They are also beacons used by savvy captains as points of reference when sailing the coastline. Today, lighthouses are a dying breed because they're no longer practical due to the maintenance costs and modern navigation.

You find lighthouses on craggy outcroppings such as Pt. Reyes (shown here) on the coast of California. Lighthouses also dot the coast of Florida where you find them on sandy beaches. The best time to photograph a lighthouse is early in the morning, or late in the afternoon when the lighthouse will be bathed in warm golden light. Another great time to photograph a lighthouse is when it's shrouded in fog.

Setting the Camera

When you photograph a lighthouse, you want a huge depth of field, which means you should take the photograph in Aperture Priority mode using a small aperture with an f/stop in the range from f/16 to f/22. The suggested ISO range is suitable for photographing lighthouses in bright sunlight (ISO 100 or 200), early morning or late afternoon light (ISO 400), or foggy conditions (ISO 800). The focal-length range lets you capture the lighthouse and the surrounding area. Image stabilization is always useful, especially if you're photographing in dim conditions where you may end up with a slow shutter speed.

Taking the Picture

If the lighthouse you photograph is a reasonable driving distance from your home, you can take potluck and show up when you think conditions will be right. If you're traveling a long distance to photograph the lighthouse, do your homework ahead of time. Find out the direction from which the sun will be shining and look at photos of the lighthouse taken by other photographers. In fact, studying photos of the lighthouse that were taken by other photographers is a good idea no matter how far the structure is located from you. Google the name of the lighthouse, and you'll find lots of photos.

1. **Travel to the lighthouse you want to photograph.**

   As you're traveling, keep an eye on conditions. Lighthouses are tall structures. If you don't have any clouds, the resulting shot will be kind of boring. If the lighthouse you want to photograph is near your home and the clouds are dispersing as you drive toward it, find another subject to photograph.

2. **Enable the settings discussed previously in this chapter.**

3. **Find a suitable vantage point from which to photograph the lighthouse.**

   This is where your research comes in handy. As you explore the area near the lighthouse, you'll notice the vantage points used by other photographers. By all means use the popular vantage points, but try to find a unique vantage point as well.

4. **When you find a great vantage point, compose the image.**

   Don't place the lighthouse smack dab in the middle of the frame. Position it on the right or left side of the image. The placement of the horizon line is important as well. If you have a wide expanse of ocean leading up to the lighthouse, shoot from a snail's eye view to get as much of the water in the picture as possible as well as the entire lighthouse.

You can also photograph the lighthouse from a cliff (refer to the image at the beginning of this chapter) or from a vantage point that includes a beautiful sky with lots of clouds (as shown in Figure 93-1). In Figure 93-1, the lighthouse is perfectly aligned on a power point according to the Rule of Thirds, and the horizon line is in the lower third of the photograph to emphasize the beautiful clouds in the sky.

5. **Press the shutter button halfway to achieve focus and then take the picture.**

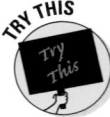

Rules are made to be broken. When you photograph a tall lighthouse you can get close to, tilt the camera up and take a picture. The structure of the lighthouse guides the viewer to the top of the picture. Sure it looks like it's falling over, but you have a unique shot from a unique perspective (see Figure 93-2). Note that this is the same lighthouse as in Figure 93-1. When you find a great subject, milk it for all it's worth.

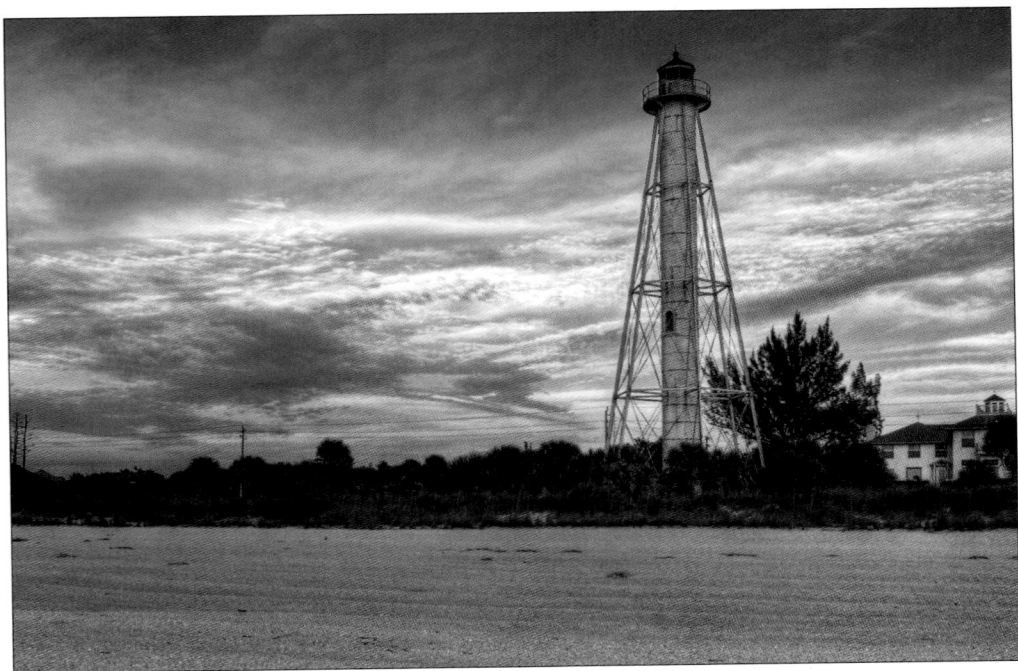

Figure 93-1: One lighthouse plus a sky full of clouds equals a compelling photograph.

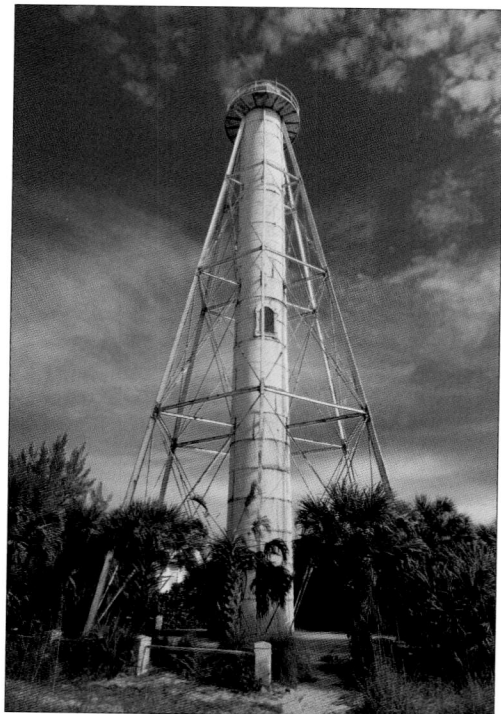

Figure 93-2: Find a unique vantage point.

Troubleshooting

- ✔ **The edges of the photo are soft.** Many wide-angle zoom lenses show this characteristic when you're using the shortest focal length and the smallest or largest aperture. In this case, you're probably using the smallest aperture. Select an aperture that's 2 or 3 f/stops wider to solve the problem.

- ✔ **The scene is too bright.** This often happens when you photograph early in the morning or late in the day. The camera thinks the scene should be brighter and ends up overexposing the scene. Use exposure compensation to reduce the exposure until what you see on the camera LCD monitor matches the scene before you.

- ✔ **The image is darker than the scene:** Fog can fool a camera into thinking the scene is too bright. The cure is to use exposure compensation to increase the exposure. You may also have to focus manually in foggy conditions.

- ✔ **The entire image is soft.** This happens when you photograph a lighthouse in heavy fog. It's a rather charming look, but if the image is too soft, some cameras give you the option to create a custom setting and increase the contrast. Refer to your camera manual for details. If your camera doesn't have this option, you can increase the contrast in your image-editing program.

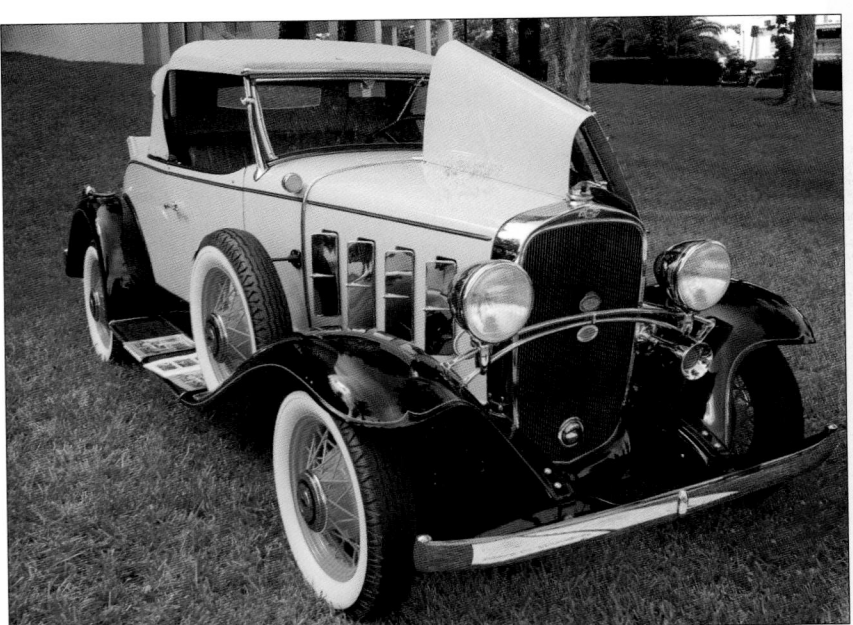

Camera Settings

- **Metering Mode:** Evaluative
- **Shooting Mode:** Aperture Priority
- **Aperture:** Choose a large aperture like f/4.0 or larger (smaller f/stop number) if you're photographing the car from the side. Choose a larger f/stop like 8.0 if you're photographing a long vehicle from front to back.
- **ISO Setting:** 100 or 200 or the lowest ISO setting that enables you to achieve a shutter speed of 1/30 of a second (using image stabilization) or 1/50 of a second without image stabilization
- **Focus Mode:** Single Shot
- **Auto-Focus Point:** Single auto-focus point
- **Focal Length:** 50mm (35mm equivalent; see "Understanding focal lengths" in the appendix)
- **Image Stabilization:** If your camera or lens is equipped with this feature, use it if the ISO you choose drops the shutter speed below 1/50 of a second.

Cars and motorcycles serve a very mundane purpose: They get you from point A to point B. Vehicles, however, are very much a part of the American culture and lifestyle. Some cars and motorcycles can be classified as rolling sculptures, a fact to which anyone who's admired a Ferrari or tricked out motorcycle can attest.

Photography and vehicles go hand in hand. When a photographer sees a photogenic car or motorcycle, he can't help but stop and take a picture of it. You'll find photogenic vehicles in your travels or at events like car shows and auctions. When you find one that piques your curiosity and begs to be photographed, the following settings will serve you well.

Setting the Camera

A shiny hot rod and your digital SLR were meant for each other. They're both high-tech, and they look good. Shooting pictures of vehicles in Aperture Priority mode using a large aperture (small f/stop number) gives you a shallow depth of field that draws your viewer's attention to your subject. Using a single auto-focus point gives you the option of choosing the point on the car upon which the camera will focus. This is important when you're dealing with a limited depth of field. If the camera focuses using the default method of multiple points, it may inadvertently focus on something other than the car, or a place on the car that you don't want to be the center of interest. Using a 50 mm focal length gives you a realistic depiction of the car with no distortion.

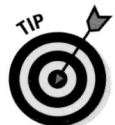

Most cameras have a depth of field preview button that stops down the lens before the shutter is opened. You can preview the depth of field at any aperture by pressing this button. Consult your camera manual to see whether your camera has this option, and if so, where the button is located.

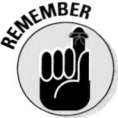

If you're photographing in overcast conditions, you may have to increase the ISO setting to get a shutter speed that's fast enough to take photographs hand-holding the camera. The alternative is to use a tripod.

Taking the Picture

Unless you're attending a car show, opportunities for photographing cars or motorcycles occur when you least expect them. You go out with your camera with the goal of photographing flowers, and you see a drop-dead vintage Porsche on your way to your intended photo shoot. If you're like me, you pull over and take a picture of the car.

1. **Enable the camera settings discussed previously in this chapter.**

2. **When you see a car or motorcycle you want to photograph, find a good vantage point and zoom in to compose the image.**

   You don't have to take a picture of the entire vehicle. You can zoom in to highlight a specific part of the vehicle. (See Figure 94-1.)

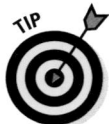

If you're serious about photographing vehicles, study the pictures in car magazines. Another good source for inspiration is the photographs in car and motorcycle ads. Look at a photo you like and try to determine the vantage point from which the picture was taken.

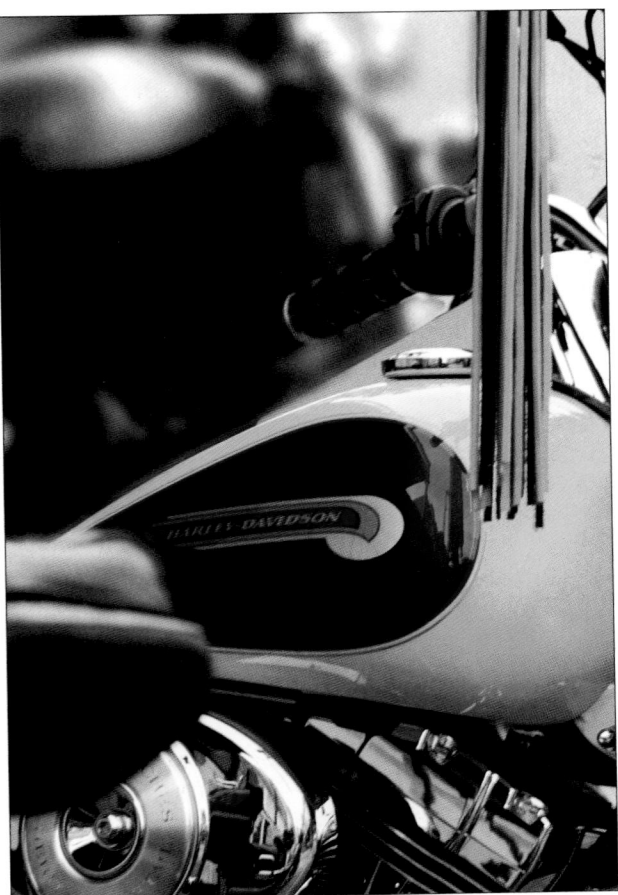

Figure 94-1: Zoom in to create an interesting picture of part of the vehicle.

3. **Position the auto-focus point over the part of the car upon which you want the camera to focus and then press the shutter button halfway to achieve focus.**

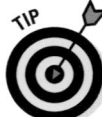

If you're photographing a long car from a 3/4 view using an aperture of f/8.0 or smaller (larger f/stop value), focus in the middle of the car to make the entire car appear to be in focus.

4. **Move the camera to recompose the picture and then take the picture.**

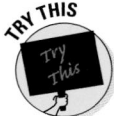

If you have a fast prime lens (a single focal-length lens) with a minimum f/stop of f/2.8 or smaller (a large aperture), walk close to the vehicle you're photographing, position the auto-focus point over the part of the vehicle that you want to be your center of interest, and then press the shutter button halfway to achieve focus. Recompose the picture and then press the shutter button fully to take the picture. This technique is known as *selective focus.* (See Figure 94-2.)

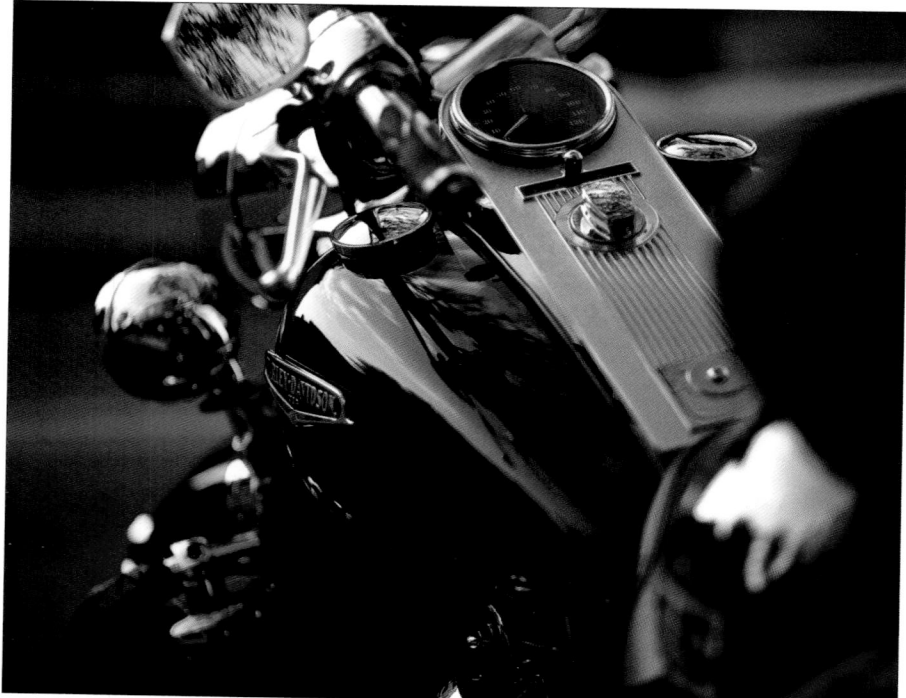

Figure 94-2: Selectively focusing on part of the vehicle.

Troubleshooting

✏ **There's no detail on the chrome.** This happens when bright points of light, such as the sun, shine on chrome trim. When this happens, use exposure compensation to reduce the exposure by 1/3 or 2/3 a stop.

✏ **There are bright pinpoints of light on shiny parts of the vehicle.** You can turn this problem into an artistic highlight by shooting the picture again with an f/stop of f/8. When you photograph an object with a bright point of light at a smaller aperture, it almost looks like a small star.

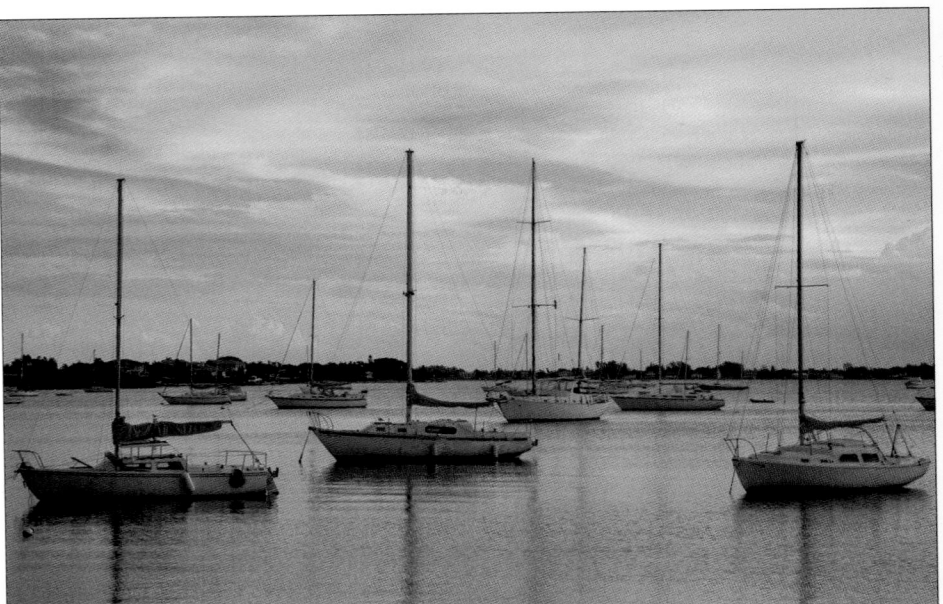

Camera Settings

- **Metering Mode:** Evaluative
- **Drive Mode:** Single Shot
- **Shooting Mode:** Aperture Priority
- **Aperture:** f/11 to f/22
- **ISO Setting:** 100 to 800
- **Focus Mode:** Single Shot
- **Auto-Focus Point:** Single auto-focus point
- **Focal Length:** 24mm to 70mm (35mm equivalent; see "Understanding focal lengths" in the appendix)
- **Image Stabilization:** On

1 f you live near the ocean or a lake, you have a wonderful subject for photography: boats. Boats come in all shapes and sizes. Sailboats with the tall masts are things of beauty when standing still, or skimming along the water in a stiff breeze. Powerboats are also photogenic, especially the old, wooden boats from the 1800s. You can also take pictures of commercial boats or historic tall ships. You can even take a picture of several boats moored in a placid bay at sunset.

To photograph boats, all you need to do is go to a body of water. You'll find boats in motion and boats at rest. Then all you need to do is add a bit of creativity, find a good vantage point, and use the settings in this chapter to photograph one boat, or a hundred.

Setting the Camera

Boats allude to man's love of the sea. A well-done photograph of a boat is a work of art. To capture a picture of a boat, you want the viewers to see all the details. Therefore you take pictures of boats using a small aperture in Aperture Priority mode. This gives you a huge depth of field. The ISO setting range is suitable for photographing boats in bright sunlight (ISO 100) or overcast conditions (ISO 800). The suggested focal-length range lets you capture several boats or zoom in on a single boat. Image stabilization is not necessary but will help you get a sharper picture when photographing in dim conditions that sometimes yield a slow shutter speed. However, image stabilization won't help you if the boat is rocking due to wave action.

Taking the Picture

This is another photograph that needs clouds for interest, especially when you're photographing lots of boats. Still water is also a great help. You get reflections of the boats and clouds in the still water — all the ingredients you need for a compelling photo. Travel to your favorite lake, bay, or harbor.

1. **Enable the settings discussed previously in this chapter.**

2. **Walk around until you find an interesting vantage point.**

   Walk around and bring the camera to your eye when you see elements that interest you. Bringing the camera to your eye is a great way to frame a scene when you begin. After a while, you'll recognize good vantage points without having to bring the camera to your eye.

3. **After you find a great vantage point, compose the image.**

   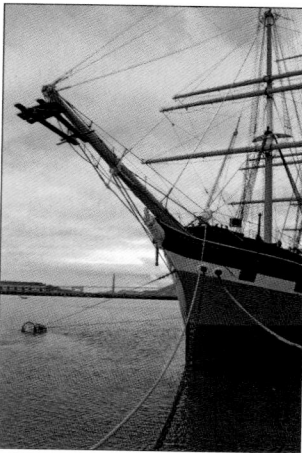

   As you do with any photograph, look for elements to draw your viewers into the picture. You can use anchor and mooring lines as strong diagonals to lead your viewers into the picture. For example, the leftmost sailboat in the figure at the beginning of this chapter captures your attention, and then your eye follows the diagonal line of boats. Your eye stops at the right side of the image and is then drawn to the sailboat in the lower-right corner of the picture, which draws your eye to the leftmost sailboat, and you've gone full circle.

   The placement of the horizon line is also important. If you're photographing a tall ship, such as the Balclutha in San Francisco Bay (see Figure 95-1), rotate your camera

Figure 95-1: Rotate the camera 90 degrees to photograph tall ships.

90 degrees. Notice how the mooring lines lead you into the picture. Your eye follows the mast to the top of the image, and then the lines lead you to the bowsprit, which takes you full circle. Viewers will also recognize the Golden Gate Bridge in the background.

4. **Press the shutter button halfway to achieve focus and then take the picture.**

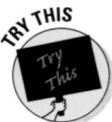

Boats out of the water are also good subjects for photographers. While exploring a fishing village in Placida, Florida, I spotted the boat in Figure 95-2. I walked around until the composition came together.

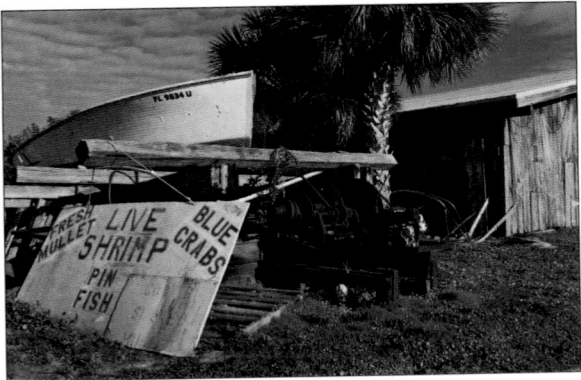

Figure 95-2: Photograph boats on dry land.

Troubleshooting

✔ **I'm photographing boats at sunset; the boats are dark, and the sky is bright.** This happens when you photograph directly into the sun. You can either change your vantage point slightly so you're not shooting directly into the sun, or hide the sun behind something like a palm tree.

Another alternative is to use a graduated neutral density filter if the sun is still fairly high in the sky, or a reverse neutral density filter if the sun is ready to set. These filters reduce the amount of light reaching the sensor. For more information about graduated neutral density filters, visit www.singh-ray.com/grndgrads.html. For more information about reverse neutral density graduated filters, visit www.singh-ray.com/reversegrads.html.

✔ **The sailboats don't appear to be level.** This can occur when you're photographing several sailboats in a moderate chop. They're bobbing about, and the masts are going in all different directions. When this happens, use the horizon line as your guide for a level picture.

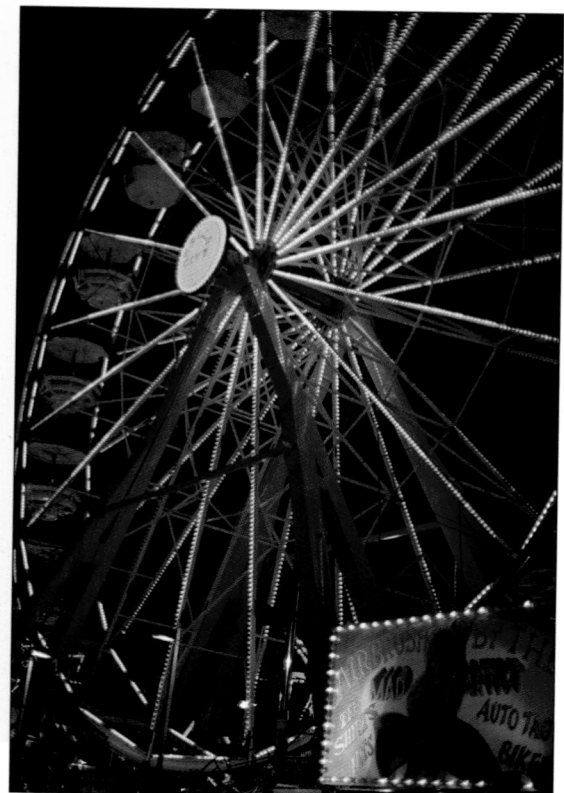

"What goes up must come down, spinnin' wheel got to go 'round . . ." Ferris wheels are great subjects for songs, fun to ride, and great subjects for pictures. County fairs and carnivals are great places to have a good time and also to capture unique photographs of people and rides, so when you go to a carnival or fair, take your camera with you. You'll have the opportunity to photograph people at the fair, sideshows, and food such as fluffy swirls of cotton candy. You can also have fun on the rides, capture lasting memories of the event, and get some cool pictures of Ferris wheels.

Camera Settings

- **Metering Mode:** Evaluative
- **Drive Mode:** Single Shot
- **Shooting Mode:** Aperture Priority
- **Aperture:** f/4.0 to f/8.0
- **ISO Setting:** 100 to 800
- **Focus Mode:** Single Shot
- **Auto-Focus Point:** Single auto-focus point
- **Focal Length:** 28mm to 50mm (35mm equivalent; see "Understanding focal lengths" in the appendix)
- **Image Stabilization:** On

Setting the Camera

Ferris wheels are gaily decorated mechanical devices that are designed to scare the living daylights out of the people who ride them. If you're a sensible kind of photographer, you'll take pictures of the thrill rides rather than actually go on them.

To take a picture of a stationary Ferris wheel, you shoot in Aperture Priority mode, which enables you to control depth of field and control the amount of light that enters the camera. If you photograph a Ferris wheel during the day, use the lowest suggested ISO setting and a fairly small aperture, which yields a properly exposed image with a large depth of field. If you photograph the Ferris wheel at dusk or at night, you'll have to bump up the ISO setting and use a larger aperture (smaller f/stop number). Even though you're using a large aperture, you'll still get a decent depth of field using a focal length from the suggested range. With this focal-length range, you have the option of capturing the Ferris wheel and surroundings from a nearby vantage point, zooming in on part of the Ferris wheel, or taking a picture of the Ferris wheel from a distance. Image stabilization is useful, especially if the lighting conditions and ISO setting yield a shutter speed slower than 1/30 of a second.

Taking the Picture

After you've had your fill of cotton candy and good, old-fashioned carnival food, you're ready for some exercise. Grab your camera, walk to the nearest Ferris wheel, and follow these steps:

1. **Find the ideal vantage point from which to photograph the Ferris wheel.**

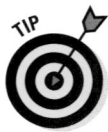

   If you're really adventurous, take your camera on another ride that's near the Ferris wheel, preferably a ride that stops at a place from which you can photograph the Ferris wheel. If the ride you're on stops at an altitude higher than the ride you want to photograph, you'll capture an image with a unique bird's-eye view.

2. **Press the shutter button halfway to achieve focus, zoom to the desired focal length, and then compose the photograph.**

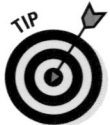

   You don't have to photograph the entire Ferris wheel. You can zoom in to photograph interesting pieces of the structure and any lights. (See Figure 96-1.)

3. **Take the picture.**

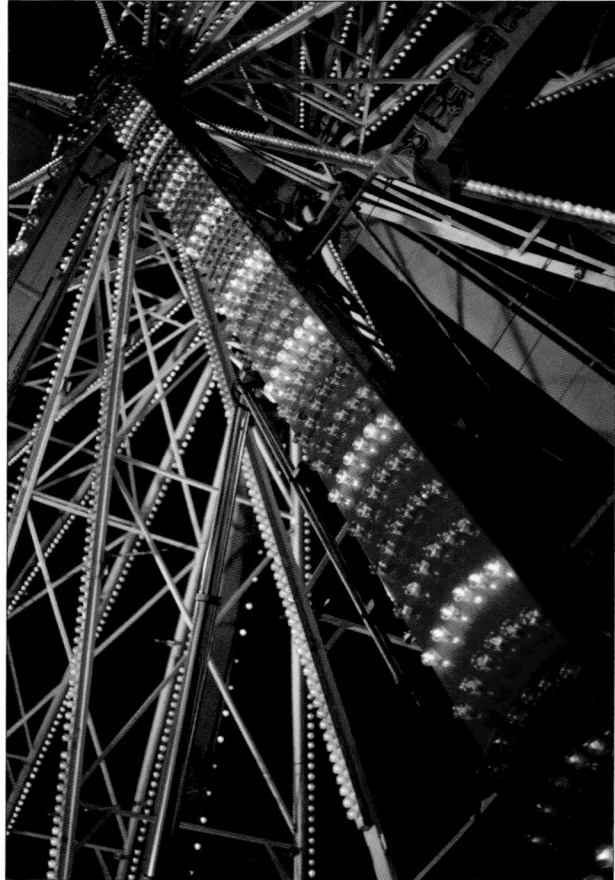

Figure 96-1: Zoom in to capture details of the Ferris wheel.

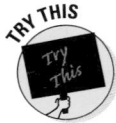

If you're photographing the Ferris wheel at night, switch to the smallest aperture (largest f/stop number) and take a picture. The small aperture and dim lighting conditions give you a long shutter speed. Move the camera while the shutter is open to create an abstract photograph. (See Figure 96-2.)

Troubleshooting

✔ **The bright lights are blown out.** This often occurs when you're photographing a Ferris wheel at night. The camera overcompensates for the darkness and bumps the exposure, which blows out the bright lights to pure white. If this occurs, use exposure compensation to reduce the exposure by 1/3 to 2/3 of a stop.

✔ **The image is blurry.** This can occur when you photograph a Ferris wheel at night, even when you use the highest ISO, smallest aperture, and enable image stabilization. When this occurs, you can use a tripod to stabilize the camera or set the camera on a solid surface such as a bench. It's also helpful to use your camera auto-timer set to its shortest duration. This gives the camera a couple of seconds to stabilize from any vibration that may occur when you press the shutter button.

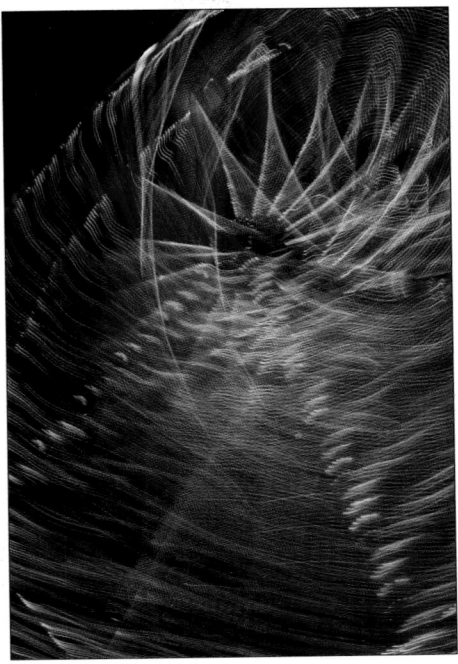

Figure 96-2: Capturing an abstract photo of a Ferris wheel.

✔ **The Ferris wheel looks like it's tipping over.** This happens if you tip the camera up to include the entire structure in your picture. (Note that this also happens when you tip the camera up to photograph a tall building or lighthouse.) You can use this anomaly to create an abstract or comical rendering of the Ferris wheel. If you don't like the distortion, back up until you can see the entire Ferris wheel in your viewfinder without tipping the camera.

97 Fireworks

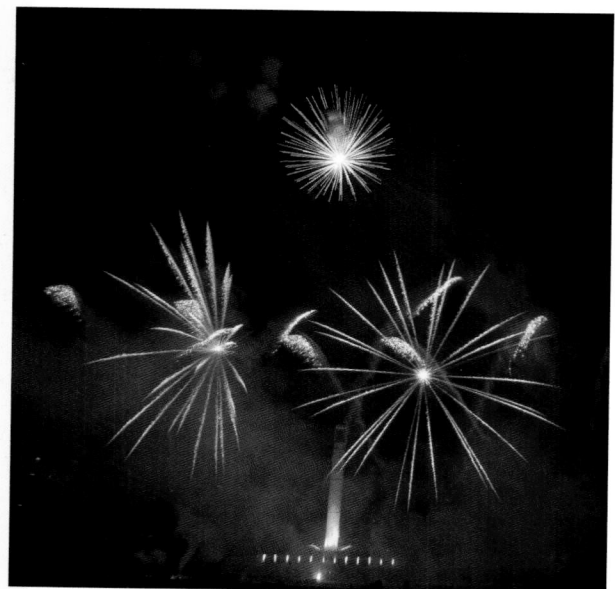

Jakubaszek/Getty Images

O n the 4th of July, Americans remember our forefathers' struggle for freedom and celebrate the holiday with fireworks displays, to signify "the bombs bursting in air" verse in our national anthem. But the 4th of July isn't the only time you'll see fireworks. Many state fairs and automobile races feature fireworks at the start of the event. Various local fairs and gatherings in your area might also feature fireworks displays. As long as the event takes place at night, you'll be able to get some wonderful fireworks shots by using the settings in this chapter.

Camera Settings

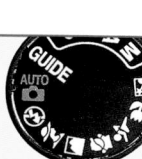

- ⮑ **Metering Mode:** Evaluative
- ⮑ **Drive Mode:** Single Shot
- ⮑ **Shooting Mode:** Manual
- ⮑ **Aperture:** f/11
- ⮑ **Shutter Speed:** 4 to 6 seconds
- ⮑ **ISO Setting:** 100 or 200
- ⮑ **Focus Mode:** Single Shot
- ⮑ **Auto-Focus Point:** Single auto-focus point
- ⮑ **Focal Length:** 28mm to 50mm (35mm equivalent; see "Understanding focal lengths" in the appendix)
- ⮑ **Image Stabilization:** Off

Setting the Camera

When you photograph a fireworks display, you want the image to be sharp with a huge depth of field. That's why you use an aperture with an f/stop of f/11. You shoot this type of image in M (Manual) shooting mode, with your shutter speed set to 4 or 6 seconds. This leaves the shutter open long enough to capture a couple of bursts of fireworks. The suggested ISO setting gives you a noise-free image. Shoot at your lowest ISO setting, which on most Canon cameras is ISO 100 and on most Nikon cameras is ISO 200. The focal length you choose depends on how close you can get to the display. If the fireworks are being shot from a barge and you're photographing from the beach, a wide-angle focal length is perfect. If you're farther away, you can zoom in. You need a tripod to steady the camera; therefore, image stabilization should be turned off.

Taking the Picture

Photographing fireworks is fun. But if you get close enough to use the widest aperture, it will get very loud, so remember your earplugs.

1. **Find a convenient location from which to photograph the display.**

   Get there early and claim your spot.

2. **Before the display starts, mount your camera on a tripod and enable the settings discussed previously in this chapter.**

3. **Set the lens to manual focus.**

   Your camera won't be able to focus properly when it's dark.

4. **Set the lens focus to Infinity.**

   This setting combined with the small aperture gives you a huge depth of field.

5. **Attach the hood to your lens.**

   This prevents any ambient sidelight from washing out parts of the image.

6. **Wait for the fireworks display to start, compose your image, and then zoom in.**

   When the fireworks start, you'll know which way to point the camera and which focal length to use. As the event progresses, you can experiment with different focal lengths. Zoom in, and you may get lucky and capture one burst followed by another device ascending.

7. **Set the auto-timer for its shortest duration.**

   The auto-timer counts down before opening the shutter. This gives the camera a chance to stabilize from any vibration that occurs when you press the shutter button.

8. **Press the shutter button fully.**

The auto-timer counts down, and the shutter is opened. After the shutter closes, review the image on your camera's LCD monitor. Fine-tune your settings quickly. Fireworks displays are fairly short, usually 30 minutes in duration. And remember to take lots of pictures. You have no way of predicting which burst will look great and whether you'll capture that burst.

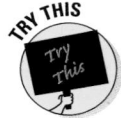

Photograph a fireworks display from a vantage point that includes a famous landmark with the fireworks exploding above the landmark. (See Figure 97-1.) This isn't something you can plan on the spur of the moment. Unless you know exactly where the fireworks are exploding, you'll have no idea where to set up. You may be able to get this information from the event organizers. If you decide to try this, make sure you get there early. You'll have lots of competition from other photographers.

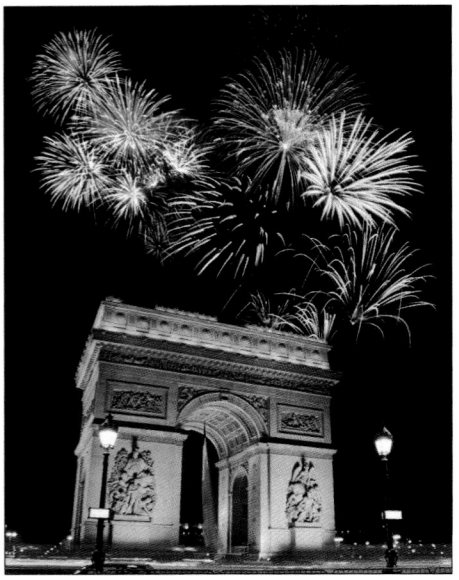

Digital Vision

Figure 97-1: Photograph fireworks above a landmark.

Troubleshooting

🖙 **The sky isn't dark enough.** This generally means the image is over-exposed. It's important to keep the shutter open for a few seconds to capture more than one burst. The shutter should be open for at least 4 seconds or up to 6 seconds. If you opted for the longer exposure, reduce the shutter speed to 4 seconds. If the sky is still not dark enough, use a smaller aperture, which lets less light into the camera.

🖙 **The sky color is off.** The camera white balance can get fooled by all of the different colors. Try switching your white balance to tungsten. This gives you a deep blue sky.

🖙 **The fireworks are out of focus.** This can happen if you're close to the fireworks display. The solution is to switch to automatic focus and move the auto-focus point to a spot where the fireworks are exploding. Press the shutter button halfway. When the camera locks focus, switch to Manual to prevent the camera from searching for focus when the next barrage of fireworks explodes. Try locking focus and then switching to manual in your home with the lights on to make sure you can easily find the AF/M switch on your camera when it's dark.

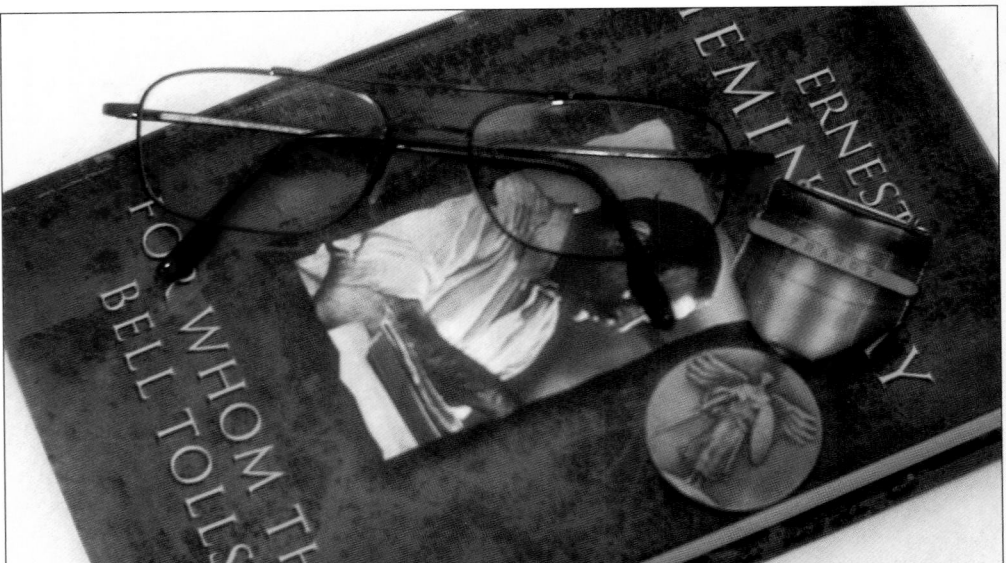

Camera Settings

- ✔ **Metering Mode:** Evaluative
- ✔ **Drive Mode:** Single Shot
- ✔ **Shooting Mode:** Aperture Priority
- ✔ **Aperture:** f/5.6 to 7.1
- ✔ **ISO Setting:** 200 to 400
- ✔ **Focus Mode:** Single Shot
- ✔ **Auto-Focus Point:** Single auto-focus point
- ✔ **Focal Length:** 100mm or longer (35mm equivalent; see "Understanding focal lengths" in the appendix)
- ✔ **Image Stabilization:** On

*1*t's the dead of winter, a weekend, and it's snowing so hard that you can't see your hand in front of your face. Or perhaps you live in Florida, and it's raining so hard that frogs are seeking higher ground. Yet you have a perfectly good digital SLR with a battery that's fully charged in your closet. It's like being all dressed up with nowhere to go. If you find yourself in this dilemma, rummage through the house 'til you find some interesting items, have some fun arranging them, and then photograph them. This is known as a *still life*. You can capture some wonderful photos when the weather's lousy by using a bit of creativity, stuff you find in your house, and the settings in this chapter.

Setting the Camera

Photographing stuff is fun. You can make your own artistic arrangements of your stuff and create unique photos that your family members will instantly recognize. When you get really good at it, you'll have pictures suitable for framing. This is another type of photography where lighting is important. Window light is soft and diffuse — excellent light for this type of photography. To control depth of field, photograph this type of image using Aperture Priority mode. The suggested aperture gives you enough depth of field to show details of a few small objects. The suggested ISO range lets you photograph indoors without using flash. The suggested focal length lets you zoom without distorting the objects. Small object image stabilization is a plus because even the slightest operator movement can cause an image to be less than tack sharp.

Taking the Picture

You'll get some nice shots if you can set up an impromptu studio on a table facing a window. Then it's a matter of going on a scavenger hunt for stuff to photograph. Do you have any antiques in your house? Antique cameras, coins, fishing lures, and the like are great objects for still life photography.

1. **Set up an impromptu studio on a table facing a window.**

   Place a white sheet on the table and raise it at the end of the table. If you don't have a wall to tack the sheet to, ask a friend to hold it while you take the pictures. The sheet serves as the backdrop and the fabric upon which you place your objects.

2. **Arrange the objects on the table.**

   Still lifes look better when you photograph an odd number of small objects. Photograph no more than five objects when you create a still life. Using three objects is better yet.

3. **Enable the settings discussed previously in this chapter.**

   If you have it, a macro lens is ideal for this type of photography.

4. **Zoom in on your subject.**

   If you're going to print your still life, leave a bit of white space. This will leave room when you crop the image to aspect ratios other than that of your camera's image. For example, most digital cameras have a 4-to-6 aspect ratio. An 8 x 10 print has a 4-to-5 aspect ratio. If you zoom in tight, and you try to crop the resulting image for an 8 x 10 picture, you'll crop out some of your subject.

5. **Position the auto-focus point over an object in the middle of your arrangement and then compose the picture.**

When you create still life images, use the objects to pique your viewers' curiosity and draw them into the image. The edges of the book in the figure at the beginning of this chapter are diagonal lines, which are more compelling than straight lines. The antique pin from World War I is placed on a power point according to the Rule of Thirds. (See the appendix.)

6. **Press the shutter button half-way to achieve focus and take the picture.**

   After you take the picture, review the image to make certain the camera properly exposed the image and there are no obvious issues.

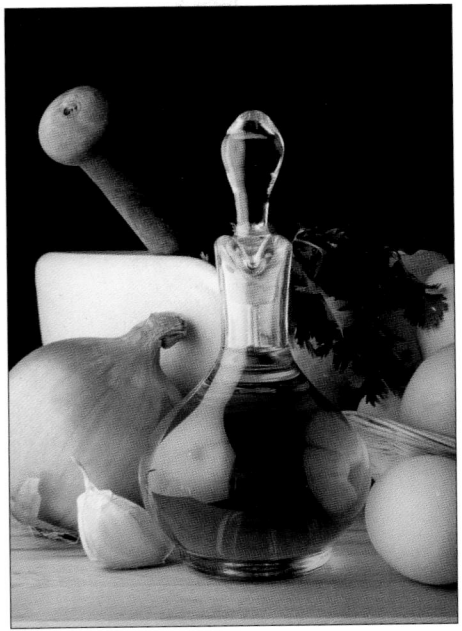

Figure 98-1: Photograph kitchen items.

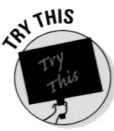

Kitchen items are also great subjects for still life images. Arrange some food items and kitchen utensils on a cutting board. Instead of photographing them on a white background, photograph them on a black background using the settings in this chapter. (See Figure 98-1.)

Troubleshooting

✓ **The camera can't achieve focus.** This happens when you're closer to the objects than the minimum focusing distance of the lens you're using. Back up until the auto-focus point illuminates when you press the shutter button halfway. If you find you like still life and other close-up photography, consider purchasing a lens with macro capabilities.

✓ **The shadows of the front objects obscure the objects at the back of my arrangement.** The solution to this problem is to change your vantage point, or change the way in which the objects are arranged until the shadows are no longer problematic. Another solution is to place the objects closer to the window, which in essence gives you a larger light source. This produces softer shadows.

99 Flower Arrangement

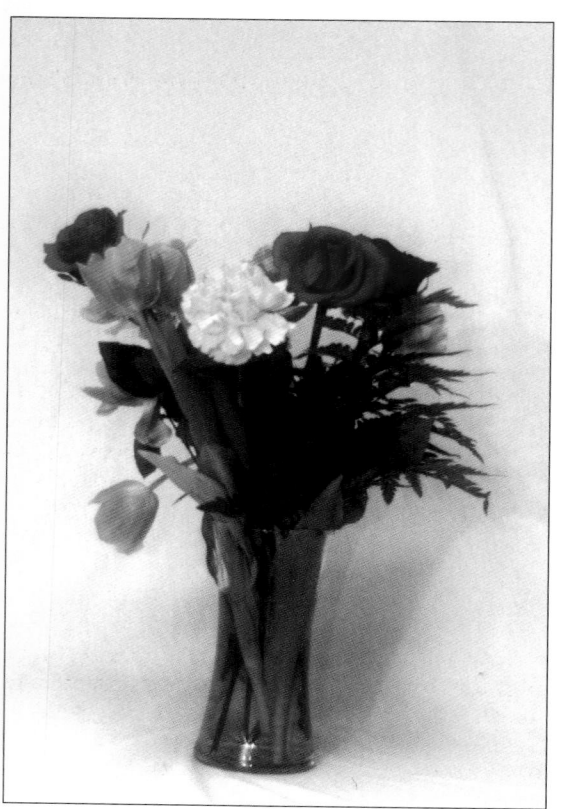

*W*hen you or a loved one receives a flower arrangement, you marvel at the beauty and fragrance of the lovely flowers, but you know that in a few days the flowers will wilt, and the beauty will soon be a memory. If the flower arrangement signifies a memorable event, you can save the beauty of the arrangement forever by photographing the arrangement. You photograph a flower arrangement against a plain backdrop to draw the viewer's attention to the flowers. You can photograph this type of image using soft window light or using soft window light with diffuse fill flash. You can also have an assistant direct light toward the flowers by using white cardboard or a white t-shirt to bounce light back onto the flowers.

Camera Settings

- **Metering Mode:** Evaluative
- **Drive Mode:** Single Shot
- **Shooting Mode:** Aperture Priority
- **Aperture:** f/4.0 to 7.1
- **ISO Setting:** 200 to 400
- **Focus Mode:** Single Shot
- **Auto Focus Point:** Single auto-focus point
- **Focal Length:** 85mm to 150mm (35mm equivalent; see "Understanding focal lengths" in the appendix)
- **Image Stabilization:** On

Setting the Camera

When you photograph a flower arrangement, you want a shallow depth of field to draw your viewer's attention to the flowers. Therefore, you photograph the arrangement using Aperture Priority mode. If you're photographing a small flower arrangement with two or three flowers in a small vase, use a large aperture with an f/stop of 4.0. If you're photographing a large arrangement with lots of flowers in a big vase, use an f/stop of 7.1. The suggested ISO range lets you photograph flowers in a brightly lit room or by the soft light of a window, which is actually the best light for this type of photography unless you have a flash unit with a diffuser (see the appendix). The focal length lets you photograph a large arrangement from a comfortable distance (85mm) or zoom in tight on a small flower arrangement.

Taking the Picture

Before the lovely flower arrangement starts to wilt (preferably when the arrangement is first received), follow these steps to create a beautiful picture of the flower arrangement.

1. **Place a table near a window with some soft light streaming in.**

   Find a window that's getting a fair amount of light. Early morning or late afternoon light shining directly in the window casts a warm golden hue on the flowers.

2. **Place a white sheet on the table and elevate it at the end of the table.**

   You can tack the sheet into a wall behind the table or ask a friend to hold the sheet upright. Position the table so that it receives the direct light from the windows. When you place the table close to the window, you're dealing with a large light source. However, you will have to leave enough room for you to photograph the flowers from a comfortable distance.

3. **Place the flower arrangement on the table.**

   Look at the arrangement through the viewfinder and move the vase until you get an interesting composition. At this time, you can do some house-cleaning on the arrangement. Cut away any dead foliage and rearrange the flowers if necessary.

4. **Enable the settings discussed previously in this chapter.**

5. **Zoom in on the flowers.**

   Leave a bit of space around the flowers if you're going to crop to different image sizes in an image-editing application.

6. **Position the auto-focus point over a flower in the middle of the arrangement and then press the shutter button halfway to achieve focus.**

   The auto-focus button illuminates when the camera locks focus on the arrangement.

7. Take the picture.

After you take the picture, review the image to make sure the camera properly exposed the image and there are no obvious issues.

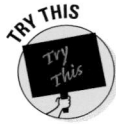

If you have a macro lens, zoom in on one or two flowers in the arrangement. (See Figure 99-1.)

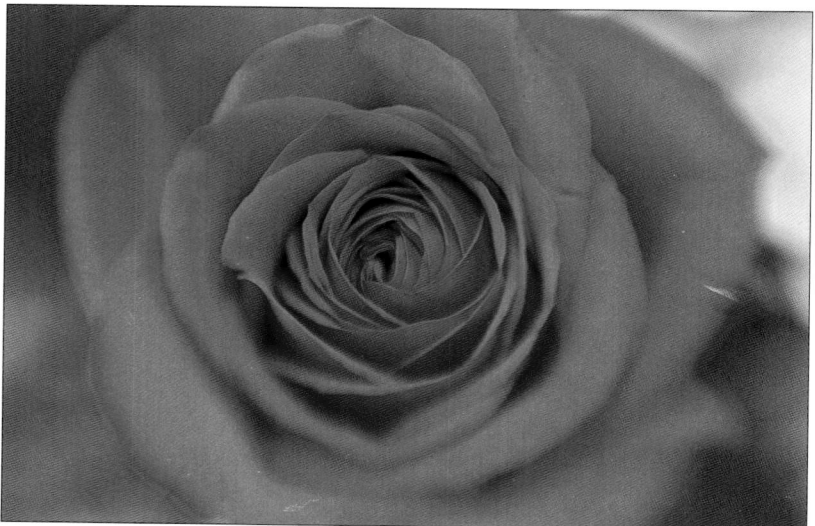

Figure 99-1: Zoom in tight on one or two flowers.

Troubleshooting

✔ **There are deep shadows behind the flowers.** This happens when the backdrop is close to the flowers. Your solution is to move the flowers away from the backdrop, which isn't possible unless you're photographing on a long table. Your other alternative is to add some diffuse fill flash to lighten the shadows.

✔ **The flowers at the rear of the arrangement are blurry (#1).** This happens when you photograph a very large flower arrangement. To solve this problem, you can use a smaller aperture, which gives you a slower shutter speed. If the shutter speed is too slow to get a blur-free picture holding the camera by hand, you'll have to increase the ISO or mount the camera on a tripod.

✔ **The flowers at the rear of the arrangement are blurry (#2).** Another solution is to focus on a flower that's near the front of the arrangement using an aperture of about f/8.0. When you review the resulting image, the flower upon which you focused are sharp, and the rest of the flowers are relatively sharp.

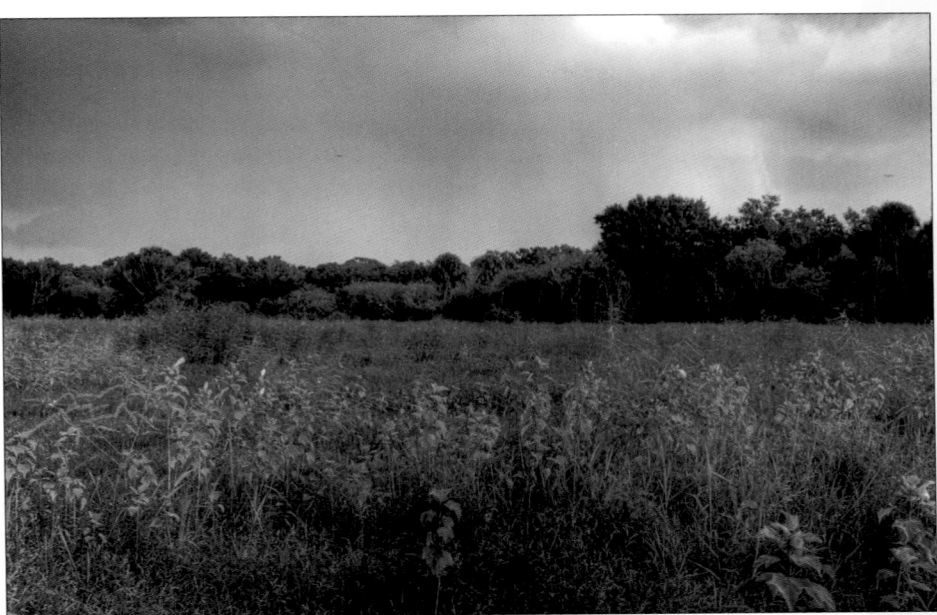

Camera Settings

- **Metering Mode:** Evaluative.
- **Drive Mode:** Two-second auto-timer
- **Shooting Mode:** Aperture Priority
- **Aperture:** f/11 or f/16
- **ISO Setting:** 100 or 200
- **Focus Mode:** Single Shot
- **Auto-Focus Point:** Single auto-focus point
- **Focal Length:** 28mm to 35 mm (35mm equivalent; see "Understanding focal lengths" in the appendix)
- **Image Stabilization:** Off

*P*hotographers use HDR (high dynamic range) photography to capture an image that closely resembles the dynamic range that humans can see with the naked eye. Your digital camera can capture only about 6 stops of dynamic range, and humans can see about 11 stops of dynamic range. What does this mean? It means you can see more detail in dark areas, and more detail in light areas. Your camera exposure is a compromise. To capture the full beauty of a landscape, you take three exposures that are bracketed. One image is two stops overexposed to capture the details in the dark areas, and the other image is two stops underexposed to capture the details in the bright areas. Then you can merge the three images using software like Photoshop or Photomatix (as I did with the photo shown here).

If this technique interests you, download a trial version of Photomatix at www.hdrsoft.com/download.html and then try the technique in this chapter. As of this writing, Nik Multimedia announced software called HDR Efex Pro, which should be available when you read this book. For more information, visit www.niksoftware.com/hdrefexpro/usa/entry.php.

Setting the Camera

When you decide to photograph a scene that you'll process using HDR software, you use the same basic landscape photography techniques. The shots must be *pin registered,* which means they need to be identical with the exception of the exposure. Therefore, the camera needs to be mounted on a tripod to ensure that the details will match up when you blend the images into an HDR shot in Photomatix or Photoshop. You also want the shots to be blur-free, which is why you use the two-second auto-timer, which counts down after you press the shutter button and gives the camera a chance to stabilize from any vibration that occurred when you pressed the shutter button. You use Aperture Priority mode with a small aperture to ensure a large depth of field. You also use your camera's lowest ISO setting, which on most Canon cameras is 100 and on most Nikon cameras is 200. You want to capture the wide view; therefore, you shoot the scene with a wide-angle focal length. Because the camera is mounted on a tripod, image stabilization is disabled.

Taking the Picture

When you find a scene you want to photograph and turn into an HDR photograph, follow these steps:

1. **Mount your camera on a tripod.**

   You can shoot directly into the sun when taking an HDR photo.

2. **Enable the settings discussed previously in this chapter.**

3. **Find the auto-exposure bracketing option in your camera menu.**

   Set the exposures for –2 EV, 0 EV, and +2 EV.

4. **Find the ideal vantage point and then compose your picture.**

   You can move the tripod and camera to get in the ballpark, but you'll have to do the final fine-tuning with the tripod controls.

5. **Press the shutter button halfway to achieve focus.**

6. **Press the shutter button fully.**

   The camera counts down and takes three pictures. Figure 100-1 shows the three images used to create the image at the beginning of this chapter.

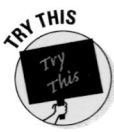

Photograph a historic building using this technique. You'll open up the shadow areas and reveal some wonderful detail in the skies. (See Figure 100-2.)

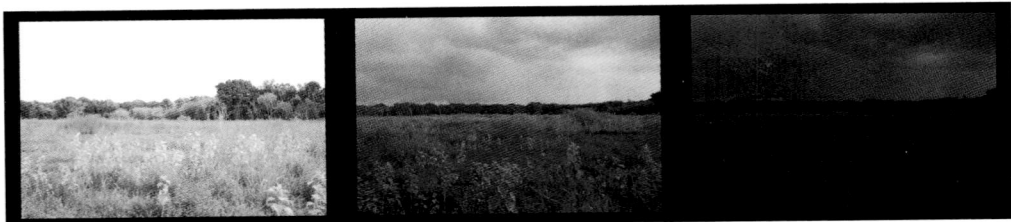

Figure 100-1: Three images prior to merging them in an HDR application.

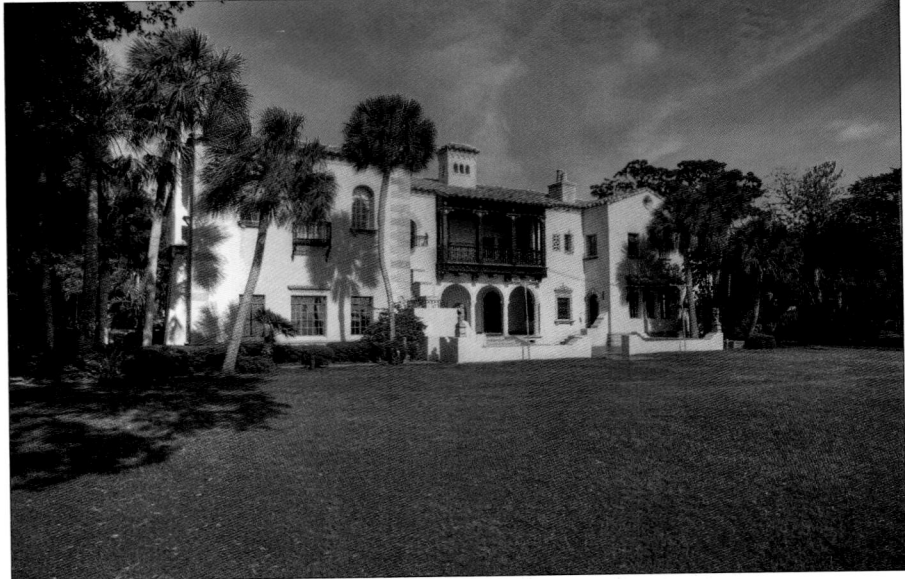

Figure 100-2: Photograph a historic building using HDR to capture all the details.

Troubleshooting

- ✔ **Most of the first and third image are blown out.** This means that the dynamic range is large enough to warrant a range of 4 EV. Change the bracketing to –1 1/2 EV and + 1 1/2 EV.

- ✔ **You're having a hard time figuring out which images go together.** This can be a problem when you're taking several different variations of the same scene. Before you take a sequence of pictures, disable the auto-exposure bracketing and take one picture with your hand over the lens. The black shot signifies the start of sequence. Just remember to enable your auto-exposure bracketing after you take the picture of your hand.

Appendix

Beyond Point and Shoot Photography

You have a great digital SLR and want to capture some wonderful pictures of the times of your life such as family gatherings, your children playing, and things of beauty near your home. However, deciphering most camera manuals is an exercise in masochism; in fact, I'm convinced that sadists write most camera manuals. You read a camera manual trying to figure out how to take a certain picture. Then you put the book down, scratch your head, and still don't have a clue what settings you need to use to capture a specific type of picture. Sure you have these neat little scene settings that work sometimes. But the camera manual doesn't give you a specific recipe to capture a picture of your son hitting a ball with the ball frozen in mid-air just beyond the tip of his bat.

That's what this book is all about: providing recipes for specific picture-taking situations. But like any cookbook, you use tools to mix the ingredients, which in this case are your camera, lens, and settings. You also need a basic understanding of the ingredients before you can successfully prepare or follow a recipe. In this appendix, I show you how to become familiar with your camera and introduce you to some basic information to help you understand how photographs are made.

Mastering Your Camera Controls

If you've just graduated from a point-and-shoot camera to your first digital SLR, you may be wondering what each bell and whistle on the camera is used for. This information may also be useful if you've had your digital SLR for a while but have used only the automatic settings. To master your camera, you have to know it like the back of your hand. You must know what each control does and know where each control is in order to master a specific picture-taking situation. I explain which control to use for a picture-taking scenario, but the position of these controls varies from camera to camera. The following is a list of important camera controls and what they do:

- **Mode dial:** On most cameras this is a round dial on top of the camera. This is the shooting mode dial. On Canon cameras, the dial is on the left side when you hold the viewfinder to your eye and take pictures. On Nikon cameras, it's on the right side. You use the dial to choose the desired shooting mode. I show you which shooting mode to use for each picture-taking scenario in this book.

- **Shutter button:** You press this button to prefocus the camera and take a picture.

- **ISO setting:** You use this feature to change the ISO setting of the camera. The ISO determines how sensitive the sensor is to light. You use higher ISO settings to take pictures in low light conditions. On many cameras, a dial is used to change the ISO. Some cameras use a menu command to change the ISO setting.

- **Aperture setting:** The aperture determines how much light enters the camera. When you choose Aperture Priority as the shooting mode, you use a dial to change the aperture, and the camera automatically selects the shutter speed to properly expose the image.

- **Shutter speed setting:** The shutter speed setting comes into play when you shoot in Shutter Priority mode. After choosing Shutter Priority for the shooting mode, you use a dial to change the shutter speed, and the camera automatically selects the correct f/stop to properly expose the image.

- **Exposure Compensation setting:** This is used to increase or decrease the exposure. You increase or decrease the exposure when the camera gets it wrong. When you review an image on your LCD monitor and it looks too dark or too bright, you use this option to correct the problem by increasing or decreasing the exposure.

- **Histogram display:** This option displays a graph that shows you the distribution of pixels from the lightest parts of the image to the darkest parts of the image. If you notice a spike on the right side of the histogram, your image is overexposed. In other words, some of the highlights are blown out to pure white and no details are visible. If you see a spike on the shadow side of the histogram, part of the shadows are pure black, and no details are visible. For more information, check out the "Using the Histogram" section of this appendix.

✔ **White balance:** You use this setting to set the white balance. The human eye can compensate for different lighting scenarios to see white as white. In most cases, your camera's default white balance setting, Auto White Balance (AWB), can get the job done. If the camera gets confused due to multiple light sources, the whites have a color cast to them and may have an green, orange, or blue tint. You can rectify this problem by choosing a preset white balance (such as Fluorescent, Tungsten, or Shade) or by manually setting the white balance. Refer to your camera manual for detailed information on how to set the white balance for your specific camera.

✔ **Metering mode:** This feature is a button on Canon cameras, and a menu control on Nikon cameras. The metering mode determines which area of the viewfinder is used to meter the image. In most instances, your camera's default metering mode does an excellent job. However, in some picture-taking scenarios, you may need to change the metering mode.

✔ **Flash control:** If your camera has a built-in flash unit, you push this button to pop the flash unit up and enable it. You can use flash to light the scene or add additional light to a scene by filling in the shadows. The latter is known as *fill flash*.

✔ **Hot shoe:** You slide a flash unit that's compatible with your camera into this slot. The contacts in the hot shoe communicate between the camera and flash unit. Canon flash units are called Speedlites; Nikon calls its flash units Speedlights.

✔ **LCD panel:** This panel shows you all the current settings. When you change a setting such as the shutter speed or ISO setting, the panel updates to show you the new settings. If your camera doesn't have an LCD panel, these settings are visible in most camera viewfinders.

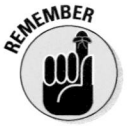

I show you which settings to use for specific picture-taking scenarios. However, each digital SLR is different. The location of the controls you use to change these settings depends on the camera model you have. Refer to your camera manual for detailed instructions regarding the location of camera controls.

Getting to know your camera

When you know a little bit about the controls on your camera, it's time to memorize where they are. You should know where all the controls on your camera are and be able to find them without taking your eye from the viewfinder. The easiest way to get to know your camera is to use it. Take pictures several times a week.

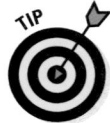

You can also get to know your camera when you're doing something important like communing with your cat or dog. While your pet is contentedly purring or sleeping at your feet, take the camera out of the camera case and put it around your neck. Using your pet as the subject, look though the viewfinder and then touch the buttons and dials to make changes. After you do this several times, you'll be able to identify where the buttons are by feel.

I know that the ISO setting for my camera is the second button on the right side of the camera. If I notice that the shutter speed is too slow when I press the shutter button halfway, I just press the second button and rotate a dial to increase the ISO setting without taking my eye from the viewfinder.

Previewing images

Digital photography is all about instant gratification. You get to see your images on the camera LCD monitor almost immediately after you take them. Some photographers take digital cameras for granted and take pictures in wholesale fashion, only to delete the bad ones after downloading them to a computer. If you slow down a bit and review images after you take them, you'll know whether or not the shot is properly exposed. You also know whether the shot is properly composed, whether your subject is smiling, and the like. Reviewing your images helps you get more keepers and fewer duds.

You have several different options for displaying images on your camera LCD monitor. You can display the image; the image and shooting information; or the image, shooting information, and a histogram. On most digital SLRs, you press a button on the back of the camera to change the information that's displayed with the image. On some cameras, you can also view thumbnails of multiple images.

Understanding How a Picture Is Made

Each *pixel* (picture element) in an image represents a single dot of color. When viewed at 100 percent magnification, the pixels all blend to produce a recognizable image. Each individual pixel is a mixture of red, green, and blue. Most digital cameras capture images with 24-bit color depth, which means 16.8 million shades of color are available. That's equivalent to what the human eye can see.

The camera's job is to accurately measure the scene and produce a distribution of colors from shadows to highlights. If the shadow areas are pure black, detail is lost. If the highlight areas are pure white, detail is lost. Imagine a picture of a bride in bright sunlight. If the lace on the bride's gown is blown out to pure white, no details are visible, and the bride is not going to be very happy with the resulting image.

Your job as a photographer is to analyze the scene, analyze what the camera gives you, and modify the exposure if necessary.

Understanding how exposure works in the camera

Digital cameras expose images the same way as film cameras did. When the camera exposes an image, the duration of the exposure and the amount of light entering the camera determine whether the resulting image is too dark, too bright, or properly exposed.

The duration of the exposure is known as the *shutter speed*. Digital cameras have a shutter speed range from several seconds in duration to as fast as 1/8000 of a second. A fast shutter speed stops action, and a slow shutter speed leaves the shutter open for a long time to record images in low light situations.

The *aperture* is the opening that determines how much light enters the camera, which corresponds to an f/stop, which is a number. A low f/stop number (large aperture) lets a lot of light into the camera, and a high f/stop number (small aperture) lets a small amount of light into the camera. Depending on the lens you're using, the f/stop range can be from f/1.4, which sends huge gobs of light into the camera, to f/32, which lets in a miniscule splash of light into the camera. The f/stop also determines the depth of field, a concept I explain in the next section.

As you can see, the camera has a number of different ways to create a perfectly exposed image. The camera's metering device examines the scene and determines which shutter speed and f/stop combination will yield a properly exposed image. The camera can choose a fast shutter speed and large aperture, or a slow shutter speed and small aperture.

If you've been shooting in automatic mode, the camera makes both decisions for you. But you're much smarter than the processor inside your camera. If you take control of the reins and supply one piece of the puzzle, the camera will supply the rest. When you're taking certain types of pictures, it makes sense to determine which f/stop will be best for what you're photographing. In other scenarios, it makes more sense to choose the shutter speed and let the camera determine the f/stop. I show you which combination to use for each picture scenario.

Controlling depth of field

Depth of field determines how much of your image looks sharp and is in focus. When you're taking pictures of landscapes on a bright sunny day, you want a depth of field that produces an image where you can see the details of everything from the blades of grass in the foreground to the distant mountains that disappear into the haze. Then there are other times when you want to have a very limited depth of field, such as when you're shooting a portrait or taking a picture of a flower or bird.

You control the depth of field in an image by selecting the f/stop and letting the camera do the math to determine what shutter speed will yield a properly exposed image. You get a limited depth of field when using a small f/stop (large aperture), which lets a lot of light into the camera.

A fast lens has an f/stop of 2.8 or smaller that gives you the capability to shoot in low light conditions and have a wonderfully shallow depth of field. When shooting at a lens's smallest f/stop, you're letting the most amount of light into the camera. This is known as shooting *wide open*. Figure A-1 shows two pictures of the same subject. The first image was shot at f/1.8, and the second image was shot at f/10. In both cases, I focused on the subject. Notice how much more of the image shot at f/10 is in focus. The detail of the flowers in the second shot distracts the viewer's attention from the subject.

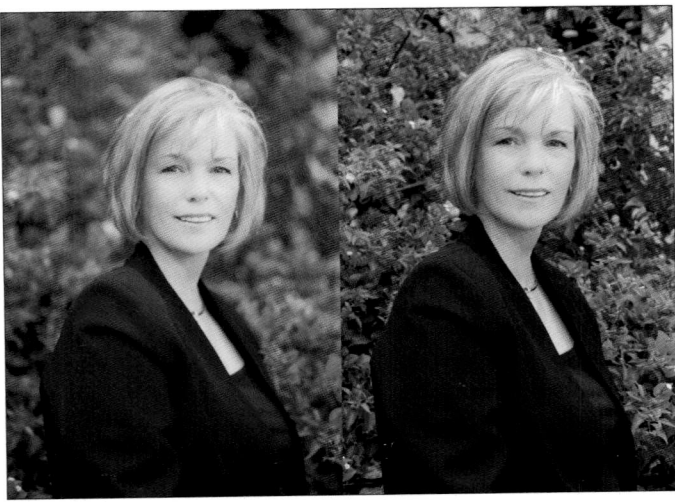

Figure A-1: Control depth of field by choosing the proper aperture.

Understanding shooting modes

You've graduated to the major leagues now. You won't see a single reference to Portrait, Sports, or any other automated shooting mode in this book. The shooting modes you will use for the picture-taking scenarios in this book require that you make a choice from the setting suggestions I supply. The camera fills in the rest of the equation to render a properly exposed image. Here are the camera modes that give you complete control over any picture-taking scenario:

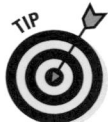

- **Aperture Priority:** When you take a picture using Aperture Priority mode, you have complete control over depth of field. In this mode, you choose the aperture (f/stop number), and the camera chooses the shutter speed needed to properly expose the image. Use a large aperture (small f/stop number) for a shallow depth of field, or a small aperture (large f/stop number) for a large depth of field.

  It might help to remember it this way: A small f/stop number equals a shallow depth of field, and a large f/stop number equals a large depth of field.

- **Shutter Priority:** When you take a picture using Shutter Priority mode, your goal is to freeze or accentuate motion. You use a fast shutter speed to stop subjects in their tracks, or a slow shutter speed to create an artistic rendition of motion. You can also use a technique known as panning to capture the essence of motion. When you shoot in Shutter Priority mode, you choose the shutter speed, and the camera calculates the aperture needed to properly expose the image.

- **Bulb:** In Bulb mode, the shutter stays open as long as the shutter button is fully depressed. This is also known as a *time exposure*. You use Bulb shooting mode to create images with artistic patterns of car headlights and capture nighttime images of starry skies and star trails.

- **Manual:** When you shoot in Manual mode, you supply both the shutter speed and aperture for the effect you're after. Most digital SLR meters show you guides in the viewfinder that let you know when you've picked a combination that results in a properly exposed image.

Understanding focal lengths

The focal length of the lens you use determines how the camera records the scene in front of you. A short focal length includes a wide view of the scene, which is why a lens with a short focal length is referred to as a wide-angle lens. Wide-angle lenses cover focal lengths from 12mm (very wide field of view) to 35mm. A long focal length magnifies the scene, essentially capturing a small part of the scene (also known as *field of view*) and magnifying it to fill the frame. Lenses with long focal lengths are called *telephoto lenses*. Telephoto lenses begin with a focal length of 80mm and exceed 500mm. A lens with a focal length that is 50mm encompasses the same field of view as the human eye.

When you have a lens that encompasses a range of focal lengths, you have a zoom lens. You can zoom in on your subject to focus on a small area, or zoom out for the big picture. You may see zoom lenses referred to as Wide-Angle to Telephoto Zoom, or Normal to Telephoto Zoom.

Why is it important to know the 35mm equivalent of a focal length?

There's one very important thing to remember about focal lengths: They don't act the same as they did on 35mm film cameras if you have a sensor that is smaller than a 35mm frame of film. If you do have a camera with a smaller sensor, your camera doesn't capture as much of the scene in front of you as a 35mm film camera. In essence, the focal length crops to a smaller area of the scene, which is the same as zooming in.

This is great when you're a wildlife photographer. You can get closer to your subject without having to break the bank on an expensive telephoto lens with a long focal length. However, when you shoot landscapes, you're at a disadvantage if you own a camera with a sensor that is smaller than a frame of 35mm film. A full-frame sensor has dimensions of 36mm x 24mm. If your sensor is smaller than that, you need to calculate your focal-length multiplier and apply it to the focal length of the lens you're using to get the 35mm equivalent focal length.

You may also see the focal-length multiplier referred to as the *crop factor*. Figure A-2 shows two images of the same scene taken with two different cameras. The image on the left was taken with a camera that has a full-frame sensor. The image on the right was taken with the same focal length on a camera with a sensor that is smaller than a 35mm frame of film. Notice that you see more of the scene with the picture taken by the camera with the full-frame sensor.

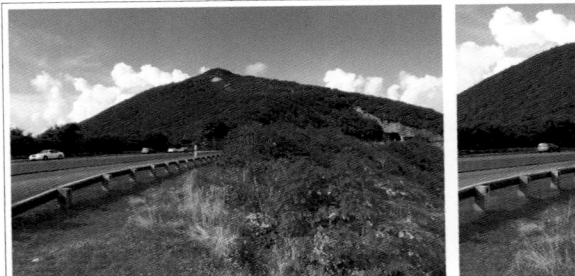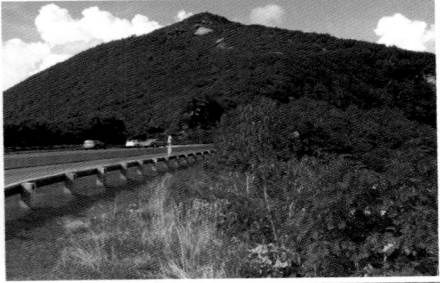

Figure A-2: Consider the crop factor when choosing a focal length.

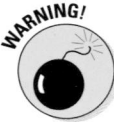

Throughout the course of this book, I suggest a range of focal lengths or a single focal length for each picture-taking scenario. All focal lengths mentioned in this book are 35mm equivalents. If your camera has a sensor with dimensions smaller than a frame of 35mm film, you have to factor in the camera's focal-length multiplier to get the 35mm equivalent for that lens on your camera.

What's my focal-length multiplier?

If you own a camera with a sensor smaller than a frame of 35mm film (36 x 24 millimeters), the sensor records only part of what the lens captures. The net result is that the lens acts like a longer focal length would on a full-frame sensor. The focal-length multiplier depends on the size of your camera's sensor in relation to a full-frame sensor. The focal-length multiplier generally falls in a range from 1.3 to 2.0. If you slap a lens with a 50mm focal length on a camera with a focal-length multiplier of 1.6, the resulting 35mm equivalent is 80mm (50 × 1.6). If you put the same lens on a camera with a focal-length multiplier of 1.5, you end up with a 35mm equivalent of 75mm (50 × 1.5). It's important to know your camera's focal-length multiplier when choosing accessory lenses for your camera. Most Canon cameras that don't have full frame sensors have a focal-length multiplier of 1.6 (with the exception of the Canon EOS 1D MK IV, which has a focal-length multiplier of 1.3). Nikon cameras without full-frame sensors have a focal-length multiplier of 1.5.

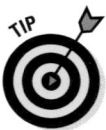

If you can't find the focal-length multiplier for your camera, you can easily calculate it. For example, the sensor on a Canon EOS 7D is 22.3mm x 14.9mm. To find the focal-length multiplier for the camera, divide the width or height of a 35mm frame of film by the width or height of your camera sensor. In the case of the EOS 7D, 36 divided by 22.3 equals 1.614, which rounds off to 1.6. Therefore, the focal-length multiplier for that camera is 1.6.

Using the Histogram

Most digital SLRs have great metering systems, but even a great metering system can get it wrong when you're shooting under difficult lighting conditions. That's why your camera gives you the option to display a histogram alongside the image on your camera LCD monitor. A *histogram* is a wonderful thing; it's a graph — well actually it looks more like a mountain — that shows the distribution of pixels from shadows to highlights. You study the histogram to decide whether the camera — or *you,* if you manually exposed the image — properly exposed the image. The histogram can tell you whether the image was under-exposed or overexposed. A sharp spike on the right side of the histogram indicates that all detail has been lost in some of the highlights. Your camera can display a single histogram or display one histogram each for the red, green, and blue channels (as shown in Figure A-3).

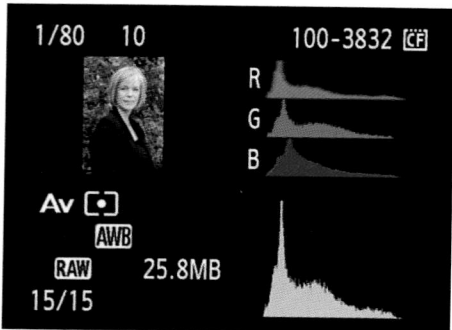

Figure A-3: Examine the exposure with the camera histogram.

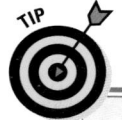

Taking blur-free photos

Many new photographers have a problem getting blur-free photos. The guideline for taking blur-free photos when holding the camera by hand is to never shoot with a shutter speed that is lower than the reciprocal of the focal length you're using. If you're taking a picture with a lens with a focal length of 150mm, the slowest shutter speed you can use while hand-holding the camera is 1/150 of a second. If your camera or lens has image stabilization, the shutter speed drops to about 1/100 of a second or slower depending on the manufacturer and how steady you are while holding the camera. If your camera or lens doesn't have image stabilization and the shutter speed is slower than the reciprocal of the focal length, you have to put the camera on a tripod. If your camera or lens does have image stabilization and you're in a situation where you need to put the camera on a tripod, disable image stabilization because the camera may deliver unpredictable results due to the fact that it's trying to compensate for operator movement when there is none.

There's also a technique to taking a blur-free photo. Cradle the camera lens with your left hand and rest your elbows by your side. Spread your feet slightly before taking the picture. This creates the human equivalent of a tripod. Inhale slowly before taking the picture, and then exhale slowly while gently pressing the shutter button.

You see a peak in the histogram where there are a lot of pixels for a brightness level. A valley indicates there are fewer pixels at that brightness range. Where the graph hits the floor of the histogram, you have no data for that range of brightness.

When analyzing a histogram, you look for sharp peaks at either end of the scale. If you have a sharp peak on the shadow (left) side of the histogram, the image is underexposed. An image can also be underexposed if the graph is on the floor of the histogram in the highlight (right) side of histogram. If there's a large spike that's right up against the highlight side of the histogram, the image is overexposed, and a lot of the detail in the image highlights has been blown out to pure white. You can correct for overexposure and underexposure to a degree in your image-editing program, but it's always best to get it right in the camera. If you analyze a histogram and notice that the image is overexposed or underexposed, you can use your camera's exposure compensation feature to rectify the problem.

The histogram is a tool. Use it wisely. When you're analyzing a scene that doesn't have any bright highlights, you may end up with a histogram that is relatively flat on the right side anyway. That's when you'll have to judge whether the image on the camera LCD monitor looks like the actual scene.

Understanding ISO

Your digital camera has an option to determine how sensitive the camera sensor is to light. If you used film, you may remember that film's sensitivity to light was determined by its ISO rating. Digital cameras are the same. With a film camera, you needed to change to a different film when shooting in lighting conditions that required a different ISO rating. With a digital camera, you can change ISO ratings on the fly.

When you increase the ISO rating, you increase the camera's sensitivity to light, which means you can shoot with faster shutter speeds in low light situations. Increasing the ISO setting also increases digital noise, which is prevalent in shadow areas of your image or in large areas of similar color, such as the sky in a landscape picture. Many people think digital noise is like film grain. It's not. It's digital hodge-podge that doesn't look good and degrades the quality of your image. If you own a high megapixel camera with a sensor that is smaller than a 35mm frame of film, the images are more susceptible to digital noise when you increase the ISO setting. You also end up with more digital noise when you take a picture with a shutter speed slower than 1 or 2 seconds.

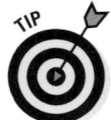

If you own an image-editing application like Photoshop Elements or Photoshop, you can purchase a plug-in to clean noisy images.

When you increase ISO, you run the risk of creating an unusable image. How far can you crank up the ISO and get an acceptable image? That depends on the camera you own and the age of your camera. The sensors on the newer cameras are more efficient and produce less noise than older ones.

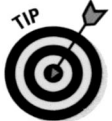

The only way to be sure is to take test shots of the same subject in the same lighting at every ISO setting on your camera. Make sure you have some shadow areas in the scene you're photographing. Download your test shots to your computer, open them in your image-editing application, and zoom in to 100 percent. *Digital color noise* shows up as tiny specks of color in the shadow areas, and *luminance noise* shows up as gray clumps in the shadow areas. When the amount of visible noise in an image is unacceptable to you, note the ISO setting with which the image was taken and never exceed the next lowest ISO setting on your camera.

Throughout the book, I suggest an ISO setting for each shooting scenario. Always use the lowest possible ISO that gives you a blur-free image while hand-holding the camera.

Using Fill Flash

Sometimes the available light just isn't enough. If you review an image on your camera's LCD monitor and you notice that your subject is in shadow or there are lots of shadows, you can augment the ambient lighting using fill flash. To use fill flash while shooting with Aperture or Shutter Priority mode, or in Manual mode, enable the flash. If you have an on-camera flash, there's a button with a lightning icon on it. Click the button to pop up the flash. If you have an auxiliary flash unit, attach it to the hot shoe of your camera and turn it on.

When you have the flash unit enabled, it sends out a small flash of light when you press the shutter button halfway. The flash unit communicates with the camera to determine the amount of light needed to properly expose the image. When you use fill flash, it's a good idea to diffuse the light with an attachment that you can purchase from camera retailers. The attachment spreads out the light, making it appear as though it came from a much larger light source. The end result is a more pleasing light that also eliminates the phenomenon known as *red eye.*

Composing Your Images

Many beginning photographers point the camera at a scene or a person and press the shutter button. This "method" generally results in a photo that, quite frankly, leaves a lot to be desired. When you photograph a person, place, or thing, put some thought into how you arrange the elements within the frame. Consider what you see through the viewfinder and then determine what the most important element is. This is the center of interest, the focal point of the image. Just because the word *center* is involved, that doesn't mean you should place the center of interest in the middle of the image. Use rules of composition to draw the viewer's attention to the center of interest. Compose the photograph in a way that makes your viewer spend time looking at the image, instead of just giving it a casual glance. In the following list, I briefly describe certain elements that can help you create more pleasing compositions in your photos:

✔ **Rule of Thirds:** When you use this rule of composition to compose a photo, imagine that the viewfinder is divided like a tic-tac-toe grid, with nine equally sized squares. The points where the lines that define the borders of the square meet are known as *power points*. Place your center of interest on a power point. Figure A-4 shows the Rule of Thirds grid superimposed on a photo. Notice that the girl's eye is positioned on a power point.

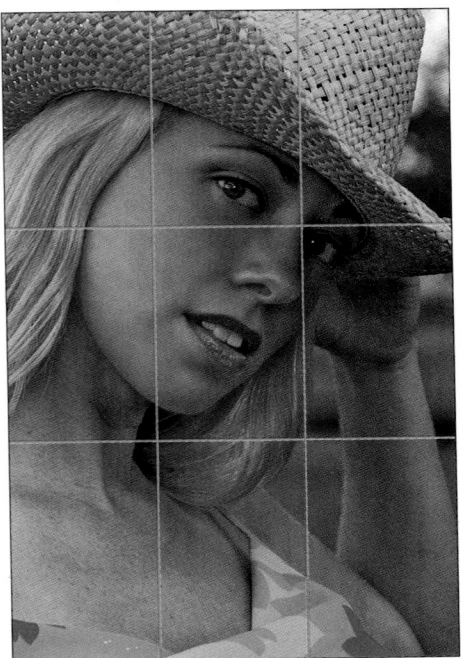

Figure A-4: Composing an image according to the Rule of Thirds.

✔ **Horizon line:** If you place the horizon line in the center of the image, you end up with a lackluster photo that doesn't look very interesting. This is another area where you have to make a decision about what is important to you in the photograph. If you're photographing a sunset with billowing clouds, placing the horizon line in the lower third of the image draws attention to the top of the image where your focal point is (the billowing clouds). If you're photographing trees reflection on a still stream, placing the horizon line in the upper third of the image puts more importance on the reflection.

✔ **Straight lines:** If all the lines in your image are vertical or horizontal, you don't have much to draw the viewer into the picture. However, if you have some diagonal lines, the viewer latches onto the diagonals and follows them into the image. Consider the sun shining behind a forest of tall aspen trees. If the trees and shadows are vertical, there's little or no visual interest for the viewer. However, if you move to a different location so that the shadows are now diagonal lines, the shadows act like magnets to draw the viewer to the trees.

✔ **Color:** People are attracted to bright lights instead of dark shadows. People are attracted to warm colors (yellows and reds) instead of cool colors (greens and blues). When you look at a scene through the viewfinder, move around until the parts of your image with warm colors align on a power point according to the Rule of Thirds or are at the end of a diagonal line. You can also add a splash of color to an otherwise monotonous image by introducing color. For example, if you're photographing a girl with brown hair and brown eyes wearing a brown blouse, grab a red flower and ask your subject to place it behind her ear.

- **Sharpness:** People are attracted to objects that are in focus. You control what's in focus by the focal length and aperture you use. When you want to attract attention to a specific spot in the image, such as the eyes of a person you're photographing, put a medium telephoto lens (a focal length that is the 35mm equivalent of 80mm) on your camera, choose a large aperture (small f/stop number), and focus on the eye nearest the camera. I show you how to use selective focus in many of the picture-taking scenarios in this book, such as when creating portraits or taking pictures of flowers.

Visualizing Your Photograph

Anybody can point a camera at something or somebody, press the shutter button, and create a photograph. The resulting photograph may or may not be good. But that's not really photography. True photography involves more than just random chance. True photography requires you to study your subject and then visualize the resulting photograph in your mind's eye. When you visualize the photograph, you know the focal length needed to capture your vision, the camera settings to use, and the vantage point from which to shoot your image. Only when all these decisions are made do you point the camera and press the shutter button.

Establishing a Post Shoot Ritual

You've returned from a great photo shoot with a couple of memory cards filled with images. Now it's time to get your images into the computer and think about your next photo shoot. If that's all you do, you're heading down the highway to disaster. After a photo shoot, there are several things you should do before the next time you use your camera. Here's what I suggest you do after every shoot:

1. **Download the images to your computer.**

   After you download the images to your computer, you should give them a meaningful name and add keywords. This does take a bit of time, but makes it much easier to find your images after you download a few hundred — or a few thousand — to your computer. Refer to your image-editing application for more information on renaming images and creating keywords. If you don't have an image-editing program, consider getting Adobe Photoshop Elements 9 (www.adobe.com/products/photoshopel), which is an excellent program for organizing and editing images.

2. Back up your images to an external hard drive.

This is extra work, but it prevents the loss of your valuable images if the hard drive on your computer ever decides to go belly-up on you. External hard drives are quite inexpensive these days. If you religiously back up your work and your system hard drive crashes in the future, your images are safe and sound on your external hard drive. If you don't have an external hard drive, back up your images to CDs or DVDs. Most CDs and DVDs last only about 5 years. To safeguard your backed up images, purchase archival CDs or DVDs. These cost more but have a life expectancy of about 35 years. Another alternative is to investigate backing up images online. Google *online backup.*

3. Clean your camera.

Follow the manufacturer's instructions for cleaning the camera body. Clean your lenses with a soft brush and a lens-cleaning cloth. You can find these accessories at your local camera store.

4. Return your camera settings to their default states.

Check all settings. For example, if you changed your white balance setting to cope with tungsten light and forget to set it back, you'll end up with blue pictures the next time you shoot in bright sunlight. Make sure to change your ISO setting back to its lowest value as well.

5. Format your memory cards.

If you start shooting with a partially full card, you'll end up mixing images from two photo shoots. If you're dealing with a minimal number of memory cards, you can run out of room before you expect to. And this always happens at the worst possible time. Always format your cards in the camera.

6. If necessary, recharge your camera battery.

Look at the battery life in your LCD monitor. If it's close to being exhausted, recharge it. Some people recharge their battery after every shoot. It's great to start a shoot with a full battery, but your camera battery has a limited number of charges. I advise purchasing at least one extra battery and keeping the spare fully charged and with you when you're shooting.

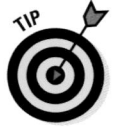

Swap batteries at regular intervals to make sure your batteries have equal recharging performance. Many newer cameras have intelligent batteries that tell you how many shutter actuations have occurred since the last recharge and also show you the recharging performance of the battery.

Camera Accessories

When you purchased your digital SLR, you purchased a camera body and a lens. However, as you gain experience, you'll most likely develop a tendency to experiment with different types of photography; photography that requires additional equipment. You should also have some minimal accessories such as a camera bag and some cleaning equipment. The following is a list of accessories to consider.

Choosing a camera bag

When you get your first digital SLR, you won't need a big camera bag, but it's always good to think ahead. A camera bag is a place for your stuff. It protects the gear and is a place to store your equipment when you're not using it. It should also be practical. Here are some tips for finding the perfect bag for your digital gear:

- **Get a bag that's big enough for the gear you now own and also any additional equipment you anticipate buying in the near future.**

- **Purchase a bag that's comfortable.** Make sure you try the bag on for size in the camera store. Place your camera and any accessories you currently own in the bag and put it over your shoulder. If it's not comfortable, ask the salesperson to show you a different bag. There's nothing worse than a chafed neck after a day-long photography adventure.

- **Make sure the bag has enough pockets for your stuff.** The bag should have a place where you can park extra memory cards, spare batteries, and other accessories. It should also have removable inserts, which enables you to customize the bag to fit your camera and lenses.

- **Make sure the bag is sturdy enough to protect your gear.**

- **Make sure the bag is made so that you can get to your gear quickly.** Fumbling for a piece of equipment as your digital Kodak Moment disappears is frustrating. If you have an accessible bag and your gear is neatly arranged, you'll be able to quickly find the right piece of gear whenever you need it.

- **Divide your equipment into manageable portions.** If you have a lot of gear, consider purchasing a hard-shell case that's big enough for all your equipment and also a soft bag for day trips.

- **Prepare for the elements.** If it rains a lot where you live and you shoot portraits on location, purchase a water-resistant camera bag or one with a built-in rain cover.

Using filters

If you were really into 35mm film photography, you had a camera bag full of goodies, including filters. *Filters* are used to create special effects and manipulate the light coming into your camera. When you want to use a filter, you screw it into the accessory threads on the end of your lens. Here's a list of filters that are useful for photography:

- **Skylight filter:** A skylight filter slightly warms the colors in your image. Many photographers permanently affix a skylight filter to every lens they own for protection.

- **Polarizing filter:** This filter deepens the blue hues in the sky and makes clouds look more prominent. It also reduces or eliminates glare, a useful option if light is reflecting off your subject's glasses. You rotate the outer ring of the polarizing filter until you get the effect you're after.

- **Neutral density filters:** Neutral density filters come in different strengths and reduce the amount of light entering the camera, which enables you to shoot at lower f/stops in bright lighting conditions. A lower f/stop gives you a smaller depth of field, which is ideal for portrait photography.

- **Graduated neutral density filters:** A graduated neutral density filter is useful when one part of your scene is brighter than the other. If you're photographing a scene with a sky full of puffy white clouds, the camera does its best to produce an acceptable image. However, the clouds probably won't have a lot of detail and will look brighter than they actually are. A graduated neutral density filter is dark at the top, which means less light reaches the top part of the sensor and gradually becomes clear in the middle of the filter. This gives you a realistic looking scene with nice detail in the clouds. There's also a reverse-graduated filter, which is clear at the top and dark in the middle. This is useful for photographing sunsets, where the camera almost always renders the sun as an orange blob with absolutely no detail. For more information on graduated neutral density filters, visit www. singh-ray.com/grndgrads.html. For more information on reverse graduated filters, visit www.singh-ray.com/reversegrads.html.

- **Soft-focus filters:** A soft-focus filter is a great accessory when you're creating head and shoulders portraits. A soft-focus filter maintains image sharpness but lowers contrast. The filter also diffuses details like skin texture and wrinkles to give your portrait a more pleasing appearance. Soft-focus filters come in varying strengths. Use a filter with low diffusion for younger subjects and a filter with high diffusion for older subjects. Don't use a soft-focus filter when shooting someone with character lines like Clint Eastwood. As a rule, I use a soft-focus filter only when photographing a woman.

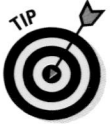

Lenses come with different accessory thread sizes. Purchase filters for the lens with the largest accessory thread size and then purchase *step-up rings* that enable you to use the large filters on all your lenses. A step-up ring has a small inner ring with male threads to attach to the lens and a larger outer ring with female threads into which you insert the filter.

Steadying the camera with a tripod

Holding the camera steady and not shooting below a shutter speed that's the reciprocal of the focal length you're using results in a sharp image. If you shoot with a digital SLR lens or camera that has image stabilization, you can shoot a couple of f/stops lower. But when you're shooting in very low light conditions or shooting portraits with diffuse window light, your only solution is to crank up the ISO or put the camera on a tripod. A tripod is always a better solution, especially when you're shooting images with a sensor that is smaller than a frame of 35mm film. If you increase the ISO on a camera with a small sensor, you add digital noise to the image.

Here are some things to consider when purchasing a tripod:

- **How much weight can the tripod support?** The tripod needs to support the weight of your camera body and your heaviest lens. To be on the safe side, include a fudge factor of 20 percent. You never know when a manufacturer is being optimistic with data. The fudge factor will also accommodate a heavier camera if you upgrade or if you add a heavier lens to your digital photography arsenal.

- **How heavy is the tripod?** If you use the tripod at home only, weight isn't a factor. However, if you're going to be lugging it around on vacation or shooting portraits on location, consider one of the low-weight tripods or consider a tripod like the Joby GorillaPod, which is versatile and lightweight. Its unique design lets you use it like a regular tripod or bend the legs to wrap the tripod around an object such as a tree limb or a pipe. (See Figure A-5.) GorillaPods are also easy to fit in luggage when you go on vacation.

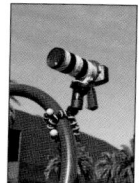

Figure A-5: The Joby GorillaPod.

- **Are you using the tripod outdoors?** If so, look for a tripod that has retractable rubber feet that reveal a sharp, stainless steel spike. Twist the rubber feet to reveal the spikes and then push the tripod legs into the ground. The spikes anchor the tripod.

- **Does the tripod have a spirit level?** This device makes it possible for you to level the tripod, which means you'll get level horizon lines in your photos.

- **Does the tripod have a quick-release platform on top of the head?** This option is handy when you're attaching a camera to a tripod. Instead of attaching the camera to the head and the tripod, you're attaching the tripod to the platform, which is much easier to do.

- **What is the maximum extended length of the tripod?** Make sure it's tall enough for any scenario you're likely to encounter.

- **What is the folded length of the tripod?** This factor is important if you intend to travel with your tripod. If this is the case, make sure it can fit in your luggage.

- **Is it easy to lock and unlock the legs?** The better tripods have a twist lock or a lever.

Purchase a carrying case for your tripod. Sling the carrying case with the tripod over your shoulder when you're shooting on location and will be moving around. It's much easier than lugging the tripod around without a case.

There are lots of tripod manufacturers. In fact, many tripod manufacturers are creating high-tech tripods made of lightweight materials (an ideal, albeit expensive, alternative if you embrace a technique such as night photography that requires you to frequently carry a tripod with you). It's a good idea to look at a tripod and try the controls before you buy it. Many superstores have camera departments with tripods at reasonable prices.

Choosing other accessories

When you buy your digital SLR, you get a camera, a battery, and a lens. That's enough to get you by when you're shooting close to home, but what happens when you take a daylong journey in search of cool places, people, and things to photograph? Or maybe you're going on vacation. Well, the battery charge dwindles as you photograph, and you fill up the memory card pretty quickly. You also have to maintain your equipment. Here are some additional accessories you should consider:

- ✓ **An extra battery:** I always keep one fully charged spare in my camera bag for each camera. If you decide to buy a third-party battery, make sure you're not voiding your camera warranty by using it.

- ✓ **Extra memory cards:** Memory cards come in different capacities and different data transfer rates. High-speed memory cards decrease the amount of time it takes the memory card to accept the data from your camera, which means your camera's memory buffer won't fill up as quickly when you hold the shutter button to capture a sequence of images. High-speed memory cards are expensive, but well worth the money if you like to photograph sports or other genres of photography where you use Continuous Drive mode. Some manufacturers include data recovery software with their high-speed cards. Data recovery software is handy if a card should ever become corrupt, which means you won't be able to download the images to the computer. The data recovery software may make it possible for you to recover the corrupt data.

- ✓ **A lens-cleaning brush:** A lens-cleaning brush has soft hairs that you use to whisk dust off the leans.

- ✓ **A lens-cleaning cloth:** A good microfiber lens-cleaning cloth is used to clean any smudges off the camera lens. Use the cloth after you use the brush.

- ✓ **A memory card holder:** When you have lots of memory cards, a memory card holder is a great way to keep everything organized. The holder I use has two sides. I put my empty cards on one side, which has a gray background. When I fill a card, I place it in the other side of the memory card holder, which has an orange background.

- ✓ **A comfortable camera strap:** The strap that comes with most cameras has the camera manufacturer's name on it in big bold letters, but is very thin. This becomes a problem if you have a camera around your neck for several hours during the day. Consider purchasing a wide, padded camera strap that will be comfortable when you carry your camera and a long telephoto lens.

A company named Black Rapid has invented a unique camera strap (see Figure A-6) that attaches to the tripod screw on the bottom of your camera. The strap slings around your shoulder, which positions the camera by your side, ready for action. The strap takes the pressure off your neck and is more comfortable than conventional camera straps. The company even has models that have pockets for memory cards and other small accessories. For more information, visit www. blackrapid.com.

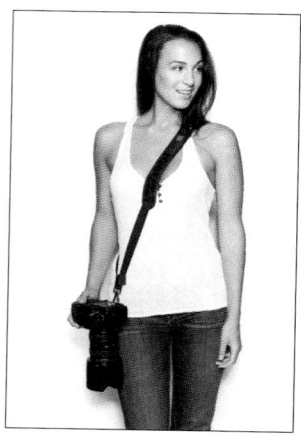

Figure A-6: Purchase a comfortable camera strap.

Working with RAW Files

When the RAW format was first introduced, photographers didn't embrace it because the images needed to be processed before they could do anything else with them. The first applications that were available to process RAW images were hard to work with and required the user to process one image at a time. Is it any wonder that photographers would rather endure a root canal instead of processing a couple hundred RAW images?

The current batch of RAW processors are much better than their predecessors. They're easier to work with, and they enable you to process lots of images quickly. Photoshop Elements 9 uses a watered-down version of the Camera Raw editor that ships with the full version of Photoshop. But you can still do a lot with it. Adobe Photoshop Lightroom 3 is another great application that enables you to process and catalog thousands of images.

You may wonder what's so great about the RAW format. First and foremost, when you use the camera's native RAW format, the camera does minimal processing to the image. If you shoot in JPEG format, the camera processes and compresses the file. There's not much you can do to rescue a JPEG image if the camera gets it all wrong. A RAW file, however, is like a digital negative. When you open the file in a RAW editor, you can change the exposure, white balance, brightness, and much more. After you process the image, you save it in a format such as TIFF or JPEG that can be read by other image-editing applications. After you save the file, your original RAW file is unaltered. You can process the file again and use different settings to get different results. When you're serious about your photography, RAW is the way to go.

Index

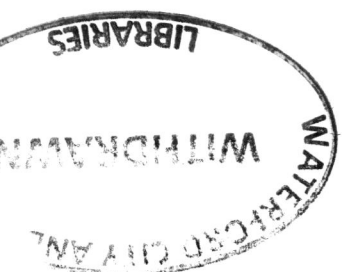